M. N. Pokrovskii
and the Origins of Soviet Historiography

Historical Materialism Book Series

The Historical Materialism Book Series is a major publishing initiative of the radical left. The capitalist crisis of the twenty-first century has been met by a resurgence of interest in critical Marxist theory. At the same time, the publishing institutions committed to Marxism have contracted markedly since the high point of the 1970s. The Historical Materialism Book Series is dedicated to addressing this situation by making available important works of Marxist theory. The aim of the series is to publish important theoretical contributions as the basis for vigorous intellectual debate and exchange on the left.

The peer-reviewed series publishes original monographs, translated texts, and reprints of classics across the bounds of academic disciplinary agendas and across the divisions of the left. The series is particularly concerned to encourage the internationalization of Marxist debate and aims to translate significant studies from beyond the English-speaking world.

For a full list of titles in the Historical Materialism Book Series available in paperback from Haymarket Books, visit: www.haymarketbooks.org/series_collections/1-historical-materialism.

M. N. Pokrovskii
and the Origins of
Soviet Historiography

James D. White

Haymarket Books
Chicago, IL

First published in 2024 by Brill Academic Publishers, The Netherlands
© 2024 Koninklijke Brill NV, Leiden, The Netherlands

Published in paperback in 2025 by
Haymarket Books
P.O. Box 180165
Chicago, IL 60618
773-583-7884
www.haymarketbooks.org

ISBN: 979-8-88890-510-4

Distributed to the trade in the US through Consortium Book Sales and
Distribution (www.cbsd.com) and internationally through Ingram
Publisher Services International (www.ingramcontent.com).

This book was published with the generous support of Lannan
Foundation, Wallace Action Fund, and the Marguerite Casey Foundation.

Special discounts are available for bulk purchases by organizations and
institutions. Please call 773-583-7884 or email info@haymarketbooks.org
for more information.

Cover art and design by David Mabb. Cover art is a detail from *Leftover
(Cross XIII,) Elegy to the Third International*. Paint on paper mounted on
canvas (2017).

Printed in the United States.

Library of Congress Cataloging-in-Publication data is available.

Contents

Preface

This book grew out of my PhD dissertation, which I submitted at Glasgow University in 1971. I didn't publish it then, because I began to research other things, some of which were aspects of my work on Pokrovskii. More recently, at Sébastien Budgen's prompting, I took up the study of Pokrovskii again, this time with the benefit of knowledge gained over the years of research into different aspects of Russian and Soviet history.

For my PhD thesis I was lucky enough to have as my supervisor Dr Rudolf Schlesinger, who was at that time a lecturer in the Institute of Soviet and East European Studies (ISEES), and an editor of the journal *Soviet Studies*. Rudolf had been a member of the Austrian and German Communist Parties and had lived in the Soviet Union in the 1920s and 1930s, where he worked at the International Agrarian Institute in Moscow. At the Institute, Rudolf had as his secretary and librarian Stalin's wife Nadezhda Allilueva and in that way came into contact with her husband. Rudolf had been in Moscow during the purges, and had himself been expelled from the party. After fleeing from the Nazis in 1939, he had sought refuge in Britain, where he found academic employment at Glasgow University. I first met him at ISEES in the early 1960s. Rudolf was a very large man, with spiky grey hair and a booming voice. He spoke English with a strong German accent and German syntax. He had the knack of typing illegibly.

Rudolf was not like a supervisor of today, someone who would hold regular sessions, read draft chapters, and correct typos. It would never have occurred to him to do these things, nor did I expect them of him. We would meet up every now and again and go for lunch at a Chinese restaurant. We would talk in the restaurant, on the way there, and on the way back. Sometimes it was about Pokrovskii, but more often it was about Rudolf's revolutionary past and the people he had known. I would get him to elaborate on aspects of his book *Marx His Time and Ours*, which I greatly admired, and he would gladly do so.

What I got from Rudolf was much more valuable than technical supervision. It was contact with a real Central-European Marxist intellectual, and through him, a connection with the Soviet world between the wars that I knew only from books. He would have been a valuable source for me if only I had known better what to ask. I saw less of Rudolf when he retired in 1966, and he never saw my finished dissertation, as he died at his home in Argyll in 1969. I hope he would have approved of it.

What has changed between the dissertation, and the present book? The Soviet Union has collapsed; archives have opened; new research has appeared. It is true that I have more factual information on Pokrovskii now than I had in 1971, but not greatly. In any case the main sources for the subject were, and remain, the published writings of Pokrovskii and other historians.

The main thing that has changed in the intervening period is that I have followed up some of the avenues for research that I discovered while working on my dissertation. The study of Pokrovskii is a gateway to many aspects of the intellectual life of late nineteenth-century Russia and the early Soviet years. The present work provides the opportunity to bring together these offshoot investigations and present Pokrovskii's life and ideas in a broader context than was possible when the dissertation was written.

Until 1918 Russia used a different calendar from Western Europe. The dates of the Russian (Julian) calendar were twelve days behind the Western (Gregorian) in the nineteenth century, and thirteen days in the twentieth. Rather than give both versions of every date, I have used the Russian calendar in those cases where the events take place in Russia, and the Western calendar where the events take place in Western Europe.

I have used a modified version of the Library of Congress system of transliteration from Russian, exceptions being where there exist generally accepted forms of proper names. I have used these rather than the forms that a strict adherence to the Library of Congress system would have dictated (e.g. Trotsky instead of Trotskii).

My thanks are due to Sébastien Budgen at Brill for his encouragement and advice, and to Danny Hayward and Jamila Squire for their careful copy-editing. This project would not have been possible without the resources of the Soviet Studies section and the Trotsky Collection of Glasgow University Library. I am also grateful to the Inter-Library Loan staff at GUL for their tireless efforts in obtaining for me the more obscure items.

Among the friends and colleagues who gave me help and encouragement in my Pokrovskii project over the years, and to whom I give my sincere thanks are: Alec Nove, Bill Wallace, Ian Thatcher, John Gonzáles, John Lowrie, Jon Smele, John Biggart and Paul Zarembka. Special thanks go to my wife Nijole for her critical reading of the text and the many valuable suggestions she has made. To her I dedicate this book.

JDW
2023

Abbreviations

Agitprop	Agitation and propaganda. A department of the Central Committee of the Communist Party.
Bund	*Algemeyner yidisher arbeter-bund in lite, poyln un rusland* The General Jewish Labour Union in Lithuania, Poland and Russia.
Comintern	*Kommunisticheskii internatsional* Communist International.
FON	*Fakul'tet obshchestvennykh nauk* Faculty of Social Sciences.
GUS	*Gosudarstvennyi uchenyi sovet* State Academic Council of Narkompros.
IKP	*Institut krasnoi professury* Institute of Red Professors.
Istpart	Commission for the collection and study of materials on the history of the October revolution and the Russian Communist Party.
Kadets	Constitutional Democratic Party.
Narkompros	*Narodnyi Komissariat Prosveshcheniia* People's Commissariat of Education (Enlightenment).
NEP	*Novaia ekonomicheskaia politika* New Economic Policy.
OGPU	*Ob''edinennoe gosudarstvennoe politicheskoe upravlenie* United Main Political Administration (political police, successor to the ChEKA and GPU, predecessor of the NKVD).
Proletkul't	Proletarian cultural-educational organisations.
Rabfak	*Rabochii fakul'tet* Workers' faculty (of higher education institution).
RANION	*Rossiiskaia assotsiatsiia nauchno-issledovatel'skikh institutov obshchestvennykh nauk* Russian Association of Social Science Institutes.
RKP(b)	*Rossiiskaia kommunisticheskaia partiia (bol'shevikov)* Russian Communist Party (Bolsheviks).
RSDRP	*Rossiiskaia sotsial-demokraticheskaia rabochaia partiia* Russian Social-Democratic Workers' Party.
RSFSR	*Rossiiskaia Sovetskaia Federativnaia Sotsialisticheskaia Respublika* Russian Soviet Federative Socialist Republic.
Sovnarkom	*Sovet narodnykh komissarov* Council of People's Commissars.
SR	*Sotsialist-Revoliutsioner* Socialist-Revolutionary.

Introduction

M.N. Pokrovskii (1868–1932) is a rewarding subject for study in many respects. He was the first historian to attempt to present the whole of Russian history from a Marxist point of view. He was a key figure in the Russian revolutionary movement, and one of the main organisers of the 1917 Bolshevik revolution in Moscow. On the accession of the Bolsheviks to power in Russia Pokrovskii was among those who established the intellectual and educational institutions of the young Soviet regime. It was around Pokrovskii too that the Soviet academic world revolved in the 1920s. The study of Pokrovskii and the intellectual environment in which he operated helps explain the origins of perceptions of modern Russian history which persist to the present day. It can for that reason be regarded as a preliminary to the study of the Russian revolutionary era, and a means of critically evaluating the historical sources for the period.

The present work is an exploration of Pokrovskii's life and writings in the context of pre-revolutionary Russian historiography, and of evolving Soviet attitudes to the history of Russia. The time-span is from the 1890s, when Pokrovskii was a student at Moscow University, to the anti-Pokrovskii campaign of the 1930s. The subject is treated as intellectual biography, with the evolution of Pokrovskii's scheme of Russian history approached as the history of ideas. As a whole, the book is structured chronologically, but within this overall framework there are some thematic sections. The sequence of the chapters is as follows:

The first chapter deals with Pokrovskii's family and upbringing, and his career as a student of History at Moscow University. Much of the chapter is devoted to examining the historical views of Pokrovskii's two teachers at the university, Vasilii Kliuchevskii and Paul Vinogradov. This gives an insight not only into the influences that Pokrovskii encountered as a student, but also into the directions being taken by Russian historiography in the 1890s, as represented by the works of Kliuchevskii and Vinogradov. In later years Pokrovskii would pay tribute to the intellectual legacy of pre-revolutionary historiography, which, he believed, had prepared the ground for his own, materialist, approach to history. It was in the series of *Readers in Medieval History* edited by Vinogradov that Pokrovskii had his first scholarly publications. It was through Vinogradov's influence that Pokrovskii contributed to collections of essays devoted to advancing the cause of liberalism in Russia.

The second chapter covers Pokrovskii's life in and around the revolution of 1905. It was at this time that Pokrovskii ceased to frequent liberal circles and joined the group of Moscow radicals who contributed to the recently founded monthly journal *Pravda*. It was as a member of this group that Pokrovskii participated in the 1905 revolution, and joined the Bolshevik fraction when the group became attached to the Moscow Committee of the RSDRP. The Marxist ideas espoused by the Moscow Bolsheviks came not from Lenin, but from Alexander Bogdanov, who was at that time a major influence on Russian social democrats through his theoretical writings. It was natural that the article on Heinrich Rickert's philosophy of history which Pokrovskii published in *Pravda* in 1904 should reflect Bogdanov's ideas.

The third chapter takes up the story of Pokrovskii's life following the 1905 revolution and ends with a survey of the myriad of functions which he performed in the early Soviet years. Most of this period was spent in emigration in France, during which time Pokrovskii twice changed his political affiliation. Initially an adherent of Bogdanov's 'Vpered' group, he broke with Bogdanov in 1911, after which he allied himself with Trotsky and contributed to Trotsky's publications. Following the outbreak of war in 1914, however, Pokrovskii gravitated towards the Leninist camp. He returned to Russia in 1917 in time to participate in the October revolution in Moscow, becoming Chairman of the Moscow Soviet. He accompanied Trotsky to Brest-Litovsk to take part in the peace negotiations with the Central Powers. On his return to Moscow, he took up the post of Lunacharskii's deputy in the Commissariat of Education (Narkompros), and was involved in the establishment of a number of key academic and teaching institutions.

The fourth chapter examines the chief historical works that Pokrovskii produced before the Soviet period of his life. It was during this time that he was most productive and made his most important methodological discoveries. While in exile Pokrovskii worked on three major historical projects: the chapters in *History of Russia in the XIX Century*, the five-volume *Russian History from the Earliest Times*, co-authored with N.M. Nikol'skii, and *Study in the History of Russian Culture*. It was in this latter work that Pokrovskii introduced the concept of 'merchant capitalism'.

A salient feature of Pokrovskii's contributions to *History of Russia in the XIX Century* is the large amount of attention given to Russian foreign policy. This was an area in which Pokrovskii took a special interest, and, as a result, was one of the few Bolsheviks to have expertise in the field of foreign relations. This was no doubt why Trotsky insisted that he be part of the team sent to Brest-Litovsk to negotiate the treaty. That his expertise was not called upon soured his relations with Trotsky, whom he considered to have wasted the opportunity to engage in serious diplomacy by grand-standing on the international stage in the hope of inciting a revolution in Germany.

The fifth chapter is centred on Istpart, the organisation established in 1920 to collect and publish materials on the history of the Russian Communist Party and the October revolution. The practice of promoting a particular interpretation of the October revolution had been begun in 1918 with Trotsky's pamphlet *From October to Brest-Litovsk*, which was an attempt to justify the Bolshevik revolution to an international audience. By the time the Second Congress of the Communist International was held in 1920, a new interpretation had emerged. It was that the October revolution had been organised and led by the Bolshevik party, and it was this doctrine that Istpart was set up to promote. The short work which incorporated this doctrine, *The Historical Significance of October*, was written by Ia.A. Iakovlev and edited by Trotsky in 1922.

In that year Pokrovskii's conception of Russian history collided with that embodied in Trotsky's book *1905*. Whereas Pokrovskii held that the Russian autocracy expressed the interests of merchant capital, Trotsky argued that in Russia the economy was poorly developed, and that the State stood above society. In the debate with Trotsky, Pokrovskii was held to have emerged victorious, and his scheme of Russian history, which stressed indigenous economic development, was taken to give ideological support to the doctrine of 'socialism in one country'.

The sixth chapter describes the two institutions on which Pokrovskii's academic activities were centred: the Institute of Red Professors (*Institut krasnoi prefessury* – IKP) and the Society of Marxist Historians. IKP, founded in 1921, was an elite graduate school for Soviet academics, initially specialising in history, economics and philosophy. It was this Institute which produced the first cohorts of Soviet historians, including people who would become prominent in later years.

Teaching at IKP was by seminar, the students being expected to produce independent historical works. It was these seminars which gave rise to two substantial collections of essays, one on the history of the Russian revolution, and the other on Russian historiography. Pokrovskii's own lectures at IKP on Russian historiography are an integral part of his scheme of Russian history. In Pokrovskii's view, it was not only the events of Russian history that were conditioned by material interests; so too were the historians' accounts of those events.

The Society of Marxist Historians was established in 1925 as a means of forming a community of historians who were either Marxists or were sympathetic to Marxism. One of the objectives of the Society was the elaboration of a Marxist approach to history. This proved to be more difficult than expected, because the available works of Marx and Engels provided very few indications of how this should be done. Moreover, the unpublished writings of Marx and Engels were still in the process of being assembled. The collected works of Lenin, however, had already been published, and, prompted by Bukharin, it was to these that Soviet scholars looked for guidance on what a Marxist approach to history should be. From 1924 onwards Lenin's pronouncements increasingly became the ultimate criterion of truth for any historical interpretation.

The seventh chapter is on the historical works that Pokrovskii wrote in the Soviet period. The first of these was *Tsarism and Revolution*, published in 1918. In this short work, Pokrovskii takes up the concept he had introduced in *Study in Russian Culture* – the struggle between merchant and industrial capital, arguing that the tsarist autocracy in Russia was the incarnation of merchant capital. As he expressed it, 'merchant capital ruled in the cap of Monomakh'.

In 1920 Pokrovskii published his *Brief History of Russia*, the book for which he would be best known. Like *Tsarism and Revolution*, it interprets events in the light of the struggle between merchant and industrial capital, the original version of the book having two sections, corresponding to the eras of merchant capitalism and industrial capitalism. Later, Pokrovskii added a third section, devoted to the revolution of 1905. Lenin thought highly of the *Brief History*, but recommended that Pokrovskii add a chronological table to make clear the sequence of events.

In 1924 Pokrovskii published his most controversial book, *Studies in the History of the Russian Revolutionary Movement in the XIX and XX Centuries*. In it he carried the struggle between merchant and industrial capitalism into the modern era, interpreting the economic policies of Sergei Witte and Petr Stolypin in these terms. Pokrovskii also attempted to explain Russia's territorial expansion in the modern era as the outcome of the imperialist policies of tsarism, which he considered dated from the 1880s.

Throughout the Soviet period, Pokrovskii wrote about the reasons for Russia's participation in the Great War. In these works there is continuity with the articles on foreign policy which he published in *Russian History in the XIX Century*. For Pokrovskii, the theme which ran through Russian foreign policy in the XIX century, and which motivated Russia's involvement in the War, was the desire to acquire Constantinople and the Straits to serve as an outlet for Russian trade with Western Europe.

The eighth chapter analyses the various criticisms and objections that Pokrovskii encountered to his interpretation of Russian history, most often by his former students at IKP. The most serious challenge to Pokrovskii's conception of the part played in modern Russian history by merchant capitalism came from the research of N.N. Vanag published in 1925. Vanag's findings were that foreign capital controlled three quarters of the whole Russian banking system. The implication of this result was that, since Russia had not managed to create its own indigenous system of finance capitalism and imperialism, it was unlikely that it would be able to build a socialist economy with its own resources. Vanag's research could be taken to signify that Trotsky had been right in his analysis of Russian economic development, and this was the conclusion drawn by the Left Opposition at this time.

The ninth chapter looks at the challenges to Pokrovskii's interpretation of Russian history that he faced at the end of the 1920s and beginning of the 1930s from critics who were sceptical about the major role in Russian history he attributed to merchant capital. The period coincides with Stalin's 'Great Turn'– the collectivisation of agriculture and the launch of the five-year plans. It also saw the first show trials, as Stalin blamed the failures of his economic policies on 'wrecking' by 'bourgeois specialists'. In a move that mirrored Stalin's campaign against 'bourgeois specialists', Pokrovskii set in train a purge of scholars from the Academy of Sciences, many of whom were banished to remote regions of the country. Their appeals to Pokrovskii for help were forwarded by him to the secret police.

Had he not been seriously ill at the time, it might have fallen to Pokrovskii to review the first volume of Trotsky's *History of the Russian Revolution*, published in 1931, and to refute the accusations of anti-Leninism against Stalin that it made. In the event, Stalin himself responded to Trotsky's book by a letter to the editorial board of the journal *Proletarskaia revoliutsiia*. In it he complained that an article they had published contained 'Trotskyist contraband' and asserted that there were some matters that were axioms and were not open to question or historical investigation. Stalin's letter effectively brought an end to history as an independent discipline in the Soviet Union.

The tenth chapter is concerned with events that took place after Pokrovskii's death, principally the process by which he and his school were discredited. This began in 1934 with Stalin's orders to a team of historians headed by Vanag to produce a history textbook for schools that would present events chronologically, and in a lively way. Stalin implied – quite unjustly – that the reason why no such textbooks existed was because Pokrovskii and his followers wrote in a dull and schematic way. Henceforth Pokrovskii would be castigated for turning Russian history into sociological schemes, and for denying the possibility of objective historical writing, by declaring that history was 'politics projected into the past'. This, despite the fact that history in the Stalin era was anything but objective and was to a large extent determined by political considerations.

The sources for this book are first and foremost the writings of Pokrovskii himself. These include his major historical works mentioned above, his journal and newspaper articles, his correspondence and his reminiscences. I have also used the memoirs of Pokrovskii's contemporaries and former students, such as those of Kizevetter, Sidorov, Gukovskii, Ostroukhova and Piontkovskii. Much information about the developments in Russian and Soviet historical writing comes from the newspapers and journals of the time, including *Pravda, Istorik-marksist, Proletarskaia revoliutsiia* and *Bor'ba klassov*. Of secondary sources, I have drawn upon the biographies of Pokrovskii by Sokolov, Chernobaev, Artizov and Enteen. As a principle, I have tried, as far as possible, to use only first-hand material, and form my interpretation of it independently.

Pokrovskii and his Teachers

1 Family Background

Mikhail Nikolaevich Pokrovskii was born in Moscow on 17 August 1868 into the family of a civil servant. In past generations the Pokrovskiis had been priests, but in 1828 Mikhail's grandfather, Mikhail Iakovlevich, had broken with this tradition and entered the civil service. After a distinguished career he was awarded the Order of St Vladimir, which brought with it the privilege of hereditary nobility. His son (Pokrovskii's father) Nikolai Mikhailovich followed in his father's footsteps to become an official in the customs service, rising to be deputy director of the bonded warehouse at the Nikolaev railway station. He was involved in organising the Russian presence at international exhibitions in Vienna and in Paris, and for this service he was awarded a decoration. Pokrovskii's father died suddenly in 1899. His mother, Lidiia Petrovna Pokrovskaia (née Bogoliubova), for the rest of her life was concerned with her only son, often helping him materially. Pokrovskii reciprocated his mother's affection and maintained a close relationship with her in later life.[1]

Pokrovskii's relatively privileged family background enabled him to gain an insight into the life of the upper echelons of Muscovite society. His father's proximity to power did not engender in him any great respect for it, and much of this attitude rubbed off on the young Pokrovskii. Later he would recall:

> My father's attitude to the authorities ... and to the church was very realistic to say the least. From childhood I listened to all kinds of stories about the abuses of the administration, the unedifying life of the higher nobility, the tsar's entourage etc. Thanks to this I was never a monarchist for a single moment of my life.[2]

Whatever the Pokrovskiis may have felt about the regime under which they lived, they recognised the futility of any public demonstration of discontent. They kept up appearances. Pokrovskii's father was an atheist, but he considered it the obligation of a respectable person to attend church services. His mother

---

1 Sokolov 1970, p. 45; Chernobaev 1992, p. 7.
2 Sokolov 1970, p. 45.

was a devout Christian who observed all the fasts and went on pilgrimages, but whose attitude towards priests and the official church hierarchy was deeply sceptical. Pokrovskii himself denied ever being religious in the sense demanded by the church; he regarded the fasting that all pupils at his school were expected to do merely as a ritual. Nevertheless, during his schooldays Pokrovskii was never an oppositionist. He was repelled by the hypocrisy of the Russian liberals. He recalls:

> It simply seemed strange to me that a person in private conversation should criticise the autocracy, but when making a speech in public he should not only fail to criticise the autocracy but should all the time mouth various complimentary phrases – wise, good, eternal: and then when a holiday came along, he would appear in uniform with a ribbon and star. And how he would protest if he were not given this star when his turn came round.[3]

Pokrovskii does not say explicitly what his own position was, but he hints at something with almost religious overtones. Judging by the extent of his knowledge of religious matters in his earliest historical articles, this is not unlikely, despite his professed atheism. He explained in 1928:

> On the one hand, the might of the petty bourgeoisie tearing each other's eyes out for the sake of material goods, and, on the other, my disgust at bourgeois liberalism, were the reasons why I fell into historical idealism. This is a paradox, but it is nevertheless the case. The bourgeois liberalism of those days flirted with materialism ... What the bourgeois liberals flirted with repelled me. Of course, this was an infantile disorder of ultra-leftism, nothing more ... .[4]

During his school days Pokrovskii was an avid if unsystematic reader. Even in those years he showed a marked interest in historical subjects, the first serious books he read being ones on history. By the time he left school he was already something of an authority in this field, though the area which interested him most was military history and battles, especially the Napoleonic campaigns.[5]

At school Pokrovskii was an exemplary student and on his graduation from the 2nd Moscow *gimnaziia* at the age of 19 he was awarded a gold medal, having

---

3 Pokrovskii 1933c, pp. 297–8.
4 Pokrovskii 1933c, p. 298.
5 Sokolov 1970, p. 47.

distinguished himself in all of the twelve subjects, including Russian language and literature, mathematics, physics, Latin, Greek, French and German. His behaviour, it was noted, had been beyond reproach. In 1887 he was accepted by the Historico-Philological Faculty of Moscow University to continue his historical studies.

Alexander Kizevetter, who knew Pokrovskii in his student days, writing in his Prague exile in 1928, describes him thus:

> Of slight build with a whining voice, he devoted himself to wide reading, to glib literary speech and the ability to embellish it with snide, sarcastic remarks against his opponents. Outwardly quiet and meek, he concealed beneath the surface an exaggerated self-esteem.[6]

At university Pokrovskii was extremely fortunate in having as his teachers two of the most outstanding historians of their day, Vasilii Kliuchevskii and Paul Vinogradov. Kliuchevskii taught Russian history, and Vinogradov the history of ancient and medieval Europe. Both scholars had a profound and lasting influence on Pokrovskii. It is worth examining in turn the respective careers of Kliuchevskii and Vinogradov, because this not only explains much in Pokrovskii's approach to history, but it also provides an insight into the wider academic environment at the end of the nineteenth century in which Pokrovskii received his training as a historian.

2   Kliuchevskii

Vasilii Osipovich Kliuchevskii (1841–1911) was born in the province of Penza in the family of a village priest, so that his early youth was spent close to peasant life. He was educated at an ecclesiastical seminary before entering Moscow University in 1861, enrolling in the Historico-Philological Faculty, where he studied under S.M. Soloviev, the author of the 29-volume *History of Russia from the Earliest Times*. In recognition of his outstanding scholarship Kliuchevskii was chosen to succeed Soloviev to the chair of Russian History at Moscow University in 1879. In addition to lecturing at the University, he also taught in the Higher Women's Courses and at the Ecclesiastical College.

Kliuchevskii's success as a scholar came from his ability to discover themes for research in Russian history that were well defined, but capable of illuminat-

---

6   Kizevetter 1974, pp. 284–5.

ing key aspects of Russia's social and economic evolution. The first such theme was the subject of the candidate's dissertation he wrote in his final year as an undergraduate and published in 1866. This was *Travellers' Tales of the Muscovite State* which viewed Russian society between the fifteenth and seventeenth centuries through the eyes of foreigners who had visited the country. The study gave an insight into the functioning of the Russian institutions which the foreign travellers encountered, as well as into the role of trade in the Muscovite economic system, for, as Kliuchevskii pointed out:

> The arrival of a foreign ambassador ... had often an important commercial significance: for often accompanying the embassy would be a whole caravan of merchants with foreign goods.[7]

The study also highlighted the cultural gulf that separated Russia from Western Europe as evidenced in the attitudes of foreign observers to a society that was less advanced than their own.

The theme of Kliuchevskii's master's dissertation on the lives of Russian saints as a historical source was suggested by Soloviev's contention that Russia was a country which colonised, extending its territory to the north and east as Russian settlement advanced. This was a process, Soloviev believed, that would be accompanied by the foundation of new monasteries as colonisation by Orthodox Russians progressed. Soloviev reasoned that this phenomenon would be documented in the lives of the canonised founders of the monasteries in question.

Kliuchevskii's research consisted in the painstaking analysis of hundreds of saints' lives to determine their value as historical sources. His dissertation, *Old-Russian Lives of Saints as a Historical Source* was published in 1871. His conclusions were that the lives of the saints were not as useful in documenting the expansion of monasteries in the north-east as he had hoped, and that because the biographies conformed to certain hagiographical stereotypes, their meagre factual content had to be seen in this particular context.[8] However, the biographies that Kliuchevskii examined did supply him with information on the economic activities of the monasteries that gave rise to the monograph *The Economic Activities of the Solovetsk Monastery in the Belomor Region*, published in 1867.[9]

---

7   Kliuchevskii 1866, p. 37.
8   Kliuchevskii 1871, p. 1.
9   Kliuchevskii 1867, p. 2.

For his doctoral dissertation Kliuchevskii took up the study of the Boiar Duma. This was an institution that was central to Russian history, for, as Kliuchevskii explained: from the x to the xviii century the Boiar Duma stood at the head of the old Russian administration. It was the 'flywheel' which set in motion the entire mechanism of government, a mechanism which to a great extent the Boiar Duma had created. Moreover, the Boiar Duma was a legislative organ, but whether the laws it passed were obligatory or merely advisory was unclear, since these distinctions were not observed by contemporaries. For Kliuchevskii the Boiar Duma was a constitutional institution with wide political influence, but without a constitutional charter, a constitutional space with a wide range of issues within its purview. It had no chancery and no archive.[10]

Although the Boiar Duma had retained its title throughout its existence, the character of the Boiars had changed considerably over time. The study of the Boiar Duma consequently involved the investigation of the formation of the Boiars as a social class in Russia. In Kliuchevskii's view, the conditions that had seen the emergence of social classes in Russia were similar to those that had given rise to social classes in other European countries. But in Russia these conditions were in different combinations and operated under different external circumstances, so that the society that they produced had a particular stamp and took on novel forms.

Kliuchevskii considered that social classes were formed through the action of both economic and political factors. Economic forces brought about the division of labour in society, identifying people with the type of capital with which they worked. The dominant form of capital became the source of political power, its owners forming the government, so that the economic class was transformed into a political estate.

In this order of things, political facts arose from economic ones. But Kliuchevskii could envisage a situation where politics could determine economics. This was when a country that had achieved an appreciable level of economic development was invaded by a hostile power and its wealth plundered by the invader.[11]

One type of capital that Kliuchevskii thought the Boiar class worked with was merchant capital, and the political significance of the elite connected with it is mentioned in several places in *Boiar Duma*. Pokrovskii would later claim that he had been the one who had discovered the role of merchant capital in Russian history,[12] but what in fact he did was to give greater prominence to

---

10   Kliuchevskii 1902, p. 3.
11   Kliuchevskii 1902, p. 7.
12   Pokrovskii 1924c, p. 6.

a phenomenon that Kliuchevskii had already noted. That the 'Marxist' historian Pokrovskii should follow in the footsteps of his teacher is understandable,
given the importance that Kliuchevskii attributed to economic factors in the
evolution of society. Peter Struve, indeed, believed Kliuchevskii's economic
interpretation of history was not dissimilar to Marx's. As he observed:

> About my own generation I can honestly say that we learnt the economic
> interpretation of history not only from Marx's *Das Kapital*, but also from
> Kliuchevskii's *Boiar Duma*, where the influence of economic forces and
> stimuli on the social evolution of Russia are depicted in the kind of clas-
> sical relief that Marx was never able to master.[13]

If Kliuchevskii was not exactly a Marxist, what was he? In fact, there was no
necessity for him to adhere to any particular doctrine, since he had the ability to present any given topic in the way that was most appropriate to it. The
question of doctrines, however, did arise when Kliuchevskii was delivering his
lectures on historical methodology, which formed a section of the first volume
of his *Course of Russian History* published in 1904. In his review of the volume,
Pokrovskii stated that over the years, Kliuchevskii had been subject to various influences, including Hegel, Comte and Petr Lavrov; that Kliuchevskii's
approach to historical theory could best be described as 'eclectic'.

The subject of *Boiar Duma* was not without its political implications. What
Kliuchevskii described was a representative legislative assembly and therefore
a kind of parliament. The existence of such an institution in the past gave
encouragement to those who wished to see the emergence of a Western-style
parliamentary system in Russia. Kliuchevskii's work demonstrated that in Russia there were historical roots for such a constitutional order. His was an interpretation of Russian history that contradicted the 'legalist' school of thought
represented by B.N. Chicherin, who saw political initiative emanating exclusively from the State. It was from among the adherents of this school that *Boiar
Duma* found its most severe critics.[14]

The work that brought Kliuchevskii most renown was his *Course of Russian
History*. This consisted of the lectures he delivered at Moscow University and
was published from an edited version of students' notes. Reading the *Course*,
one can observe that woven into it are the results of the research which had
gone into his dissertations. The *Boiar Duma* was especially useful in this respect

---

13   Struve 1952, p. 332.
14   Nechkina 1974, pp. 199–203.

because of its extensive timescale. But while Kliuchevskii's original research formed the skeleton of the course, investing it with immediacy and authority, the fact that the course consisted of spoken lectures rather than of a text designed to be read imbued it with a character quite different from his other scholarly publications.

Kliuchevskii cultivated the art of lecturing to a high degree, so that his lectures were performances which enthralled and entertained his audiences. They were enlivened with aphorisms, anecdotes, and witticisms, all delivered with appropriate intonations and gestures. This would have been impossible with the mere recital of economic and social analyses, so that in order to give his lectures the wide appeal that they enjoyed, he introduced personal elements, the characterisations of historical figures, their individual traits and eccentricities. In Kliuchevskii's *Course of Russian History* the content was to some extent determined by its intended audience.

3   Pokrovskii's Relations with Kliuchevskii

In 1891 Pokrovskii graduated from the University with a first-class diploma. He gladly accepted Kliuchevskii's proposal that he should undertake further study with a view to becoming a lecturer at the University. In order to qualify for his master's degree, he embarked upon a course of study with an examination at the end of three years. In the first year Pokrovskii studied *Russkaia pravda* and the Primary Chronicle, paying special attention to the history of Novgorod, its social structure, and its external trade. During the second year he investigated the reforms of the central administration under Peter the Great and studied the history of medieval Europe under the supervision of Vinogradov. In 1894 he passed his master's examination, becoming a *magistrant*, though, as he later remarked: 'The cramming ... gave me a solid academic foundation, but it probably held back my social development by three years'.[15]

After passing the master's examination, the next stage on the way to qualifying as a *magister* would have been to submit a dissertation on a particular historical topic, probably involving archival research, but Pokrovskii did not do this. His contemporary Kizevetter suggests that it might have been to do with some conflict with Kliuchevskii, though what the conflict was he was unable to say. This conjecture seems highly probable, because after 1894 Pokrovskii took nothing further to do with Kliuchevskii, and left Moscow University.[16]

---

15   Sokolov 1970, pp. 49–51.
16   Kizevetter 1974, pp. 280–1.

The break with Kliuchevskii had serious consequences for Pokrovskii. He never produced the kind of major original scholarly works that his teachers Kliuchevskii and Vinogradov had, and that his contemporaries N.A. Rozhkov, A.A. Kizevetter, P.N. Miliukov and M.K. Liubavskii would in the form of their master's and doctoral dissertations. The break also prevented Pokrovskii from admitting any intellectual debt to Kliuchevskii and made him invariably seek to distance himself from his former teacher.

As well as for Pokrovskii, 1894 was a fateful year for Kliuchevskii. It was the year in which Alexander III died and the Moscow University authorities required Kliuchevskii to make a speech in commemoration of the deceased Emperor. Kliuchevskii, who was well known for his liberal views, found himself in an awkward situation. He could either win the plaudits of liberal opinion but risk his career with a speech critical of Alexander, or he could make a diplomatic speech, and risk being accused of hypocrisy. Kliuchevskii chose the latter course, and on 28 October at a meeting of the Russian Historical and Antiquity Society delivered an oration full of praise for Alexander III.

Kliuchevskii had assumed that, as his speech had been made within the confines of a Historical and Antiquity Society meeting, it would go no further. However, it was printed in pamphlet form as well as being published in the *Proceedings* of the Society. In this way it became widely known among the students at the university, who were dismayed that Kliuchevskii could speak as he had done about thirteen years of reaction.

A young Moscow school teacher, Ivan Skvortsov-Stepanov, devised a method of demonstrating the disapproval of the student body for Kliuchevskii's hypocrisy. The students bought up some two hundred copies of the pamphlet version of Kliuchevskii's speech, and to each copy attached a duplicated sheet on which was printed Fonvizin's fable of the fox who praised the dead lion for its 'love of cattle'. On the title page of the pamphlet was inscribed 'Second edition, enlarged and emended'. The students then distributed the new edition of Kliuchevskii's speech through the post. It was decided to arrange a protest demonstration at Kliuchevskii's regular lecture on 30 November.[17]

On the appointed day students from various faculties crowded into Kliuchevskii's lecture, and when the historian mounted the dais, he was greeted with a cacophony of whistles from his opponents and applause from his supporters. The tumult continued for several minutes, the applause eventually triumphing over the whistles, when most of the crowd departed, and Kliuchevskii was left to deliver his lecture to his history students. The incident was reported

---

17   Byvshii student 1896, p. 494; Nechkina 1974, p. 350.

to the rector, though without any mention of the counter-demonstration by Kliuchevskii's supporters, and the university authorities began enquiries to discover who the instigators of the disturbance had been. Skvortsov-Stepanov was not discovered, but several students noticed at the lecture were held responsible and were disciplined accordingly. Three of them were expelled from the university.[18]

The Moscow police authorities took advantage of the situation to carry out the arrest of all the students who for some reason or another they suspected of subversion. No specific charges were brought against them, but from the night of 4 December batches of students were sent to the provinces, sentenced to a period of banishment of three years. Among them were people who, a decade later, would be Pokrovskii's associates: Alexander Bogdanov and Vladimir Bazarov. Another future associate of Pokrovskii's would be Skvortsov-Stepanov, the real instigator of the anti-Kliuchevskii demonstration.

Could it have been this episode involving Kliuchevskii that caused Pokrovskii's alienation from Kliuchevskii? It was, after all, a situation in which Kliuchevskii acted in a way that Pokrovskii declared he detested: a liberal criticising the autocracy in private, but in public speeches praising it to the skies. How Pokrovskii reacted to the anti-Kliuchevskii demonstration was a question that intrigued M.V. Nechkina, Kliuchevskii's biographer and pupil of Pokrovskii. She first discovered the episode in the 1920s when she began her research on Kliuchevskii and brought the matter up at a seminar. Pokrovskii was taken aback, and in an interval told Nechkina with some irritation that she should not be delving into this episode, that she was being disrespectful to Kliuchevskii.[19]

The implication is that at the time Pokrovskii had been sympathetic to Kliuchevskii's predicament. But Nechkina also draws attention to the fact that when Pokrovskii reviewed the first volume of *Course of Russian History* in 1904, he had made particular mention of the year 1894, as it were, reminding Kliuchevskii of the events surrounding the Alexander III speech.[20] It is more likely that in 1894 Pokrovskii was appalled by Kliuchevskii's behaviour, and this was the cause of the rupture in personal relations. Pokrovskii's deference to Kliuchevskii that Nechkina witnessed was not in evidence at a seminar at the Institute of History on 2 March 1930, when S.A. Piontkovskii records Pokrovskii as saying:

18   Nechkina 1974, p. 351.
19   Nechkina 1974, p. 37.
20   Nechkina 1974, p. 452.

... as a good actor, in his lectures, Kliuchevskii gave his audience the impression that he was more left-wing than he really was. His real character emerged at a lecture on Alexander III after that tsar's death. Here Kliuchevskii showed his true face, and diverged from his audience. The audience subjected him to catcalls, and this produced a terrible impression on Kliuchevskii.[21]

Neither Pokrovskii's break with Kliuchevskii in 1894 nor his failure to complete a master's dissertation damaged his relations with Vinogradov, who regarded him highly enough to choose him to play a major role in producing a series of *Readings in Medieval History*, a project very near to Vinogradov's heart. Pokrovskii's contributions to the *Readings* established him as a scholar of some standing, perhaps even more surely than the publication of a specialised master's dissertation would have done. One might even suspect that the prospect of participating in Vinogradov's project made researching for a master's dissertation under Kliuchevskii's supervision seem less attractive.

4   Vinogradov

Paul Vinogradov was a scholar whose distinguished career spanned Russia and England. Born in 1854 in Kostroma, Vinogradov was thirteen years younger than Kliuchevskii. He was also from a more comfortable background. From being a history teacher in Kostroma, his father progressed to the position of headmaster at a boys' school in Moscow. From 1866 he held the post of director of a group of Moscow schools for girls. Vinogradov's mother was the daughter of a general who had fought in the 1812 war against Napoleon. Vinogradov's early education was at home with tutors, and by the time he entered *gimnaziia* at the age of thirteen he already knew French and German and was well on the way to mastering English.

In 1871, at the age of seventeen, Vinogradov entered Moscow University, where he studied Universal History under Professor V.I. Ger'e (Guerrier). His candidate dissertation, written in 1875, was on 'Landed Property among the Merovingians', an examination of the emergence of feudal relations in medieval France. Upon graduation Vinogradov was awarded a scholarship which enabled him to spend a year studying at Berlin and Bonn Universities. In Berlin he attended the seminars of Mommsen and Brunner in the field of Historical Jurisprudence, a field in which Vinogradov would later specialise.

---

21   Piontkovskii, Litvin, Brandenberger, and Dubrovskii 2009, p. 300.

On his return to Russia Vinogradov gave lectures in the Higher Education Courses for Women that had been established by Ger'e, and in 1877 he was invited to lecture on Medieval History at the university itself. In the following year Vinogradov travelled to Italy to collect materials for his Master's degree. For the purpose, Vinogradov researched in archives in Florence, Rome, Sienna, Arezzo and Monte Cassino. His dissertation, *The Origin of Feudal Relations in Longbard Italy*, was published in St Petersburg in 1880.[22]

In this same year there appeared the monograph by Maxim Kovalevsky on *The Social Structure of England at the End of the Middle Ages*, and, Kovalevsky believed, it was this work which inspired Vinogradov to take up the study of medieval England, a study that made his reputation. After a brief spell of teaching at Moscow University, in 1883–84 Vinogradov made his first trip to England, where he worked intensively in the Public Record Office, the library of the British Museum and the libraries of Oxford and Cambridge Universities. He quickly made his mark on English medieval scholarship by identifying a manuscript he had found in the British Museum as a notebook belonging to the 13th century jurist Henry Bracton. Vinogradov's friend F.W. Maitland brought out a scholarly edition of the document as *Bracton's Note Book* in 1887.[23]

On his return to Moscow Vinogradov was appointed assistant Professor at the University, and in 1887 was promoted to full Professor of History on the publication of his doctoral dissertation *Studies in the Social History of England in the Middle Ages*.[24] With the help of Maitland, Vinogradov produced a re-worked English version of his dissertation which was published in 1892 as *Villainage in England*.

Besides delivering lectures, Vinogradov set out to train up a school of historians in the methods of Western scholarship, to teach them how to find, evaluate and extract the kernel of significant truth from the sources. He did this by means of seminars, which he conducted on the German model. Pokrovskii was one of the beneficiaries of this innovation. In 1926, when Pokrovskii compared Kliuchevskii and Vinogradov as teachers, it was much in Vinogradov's favour. He recalled:

> A purely spontaneous and unselfconscious person, Kliuchevskii came to an understanding of the past by instinct; he could unravel it very convincingly, but how he arrived at this understanding it was not clear even to himself. Vinogradov in this respect was a genuine European with clear

---

22   Vinogradov 1880.
23   Vinogradoff 19 July 1884; Vinogradoff 1888, pp. 436–41.
24   Vinogradov 1887.

well-defined and well-considered methods and modes of working. It was possible to learn things from him and he taught, in essence, not only general historians but historians of Russia as well. Vinogradov's seminars were the focus of all historical work that went on in the University between 1880 to 1890.[25]

In this connection Pokrovskii evokes the enthusiasm that was generated in Vinogradov's seminars:

We young people felt on the threshold of a genuine science which could establish certain rules (in those days we were very much concerned with the intriguing debate on whether there were 'laws of history') ....[26]

It is very likely that the answer that Vinogradov would give to the question of whether there were laws of history would be in the affirmative. Vinogradov's drive to raise the level of education in Russia did not stop at the University. He wrote a textbook on general history for secondary school pupils. He entered the Moscow City Duma and became chairman of its education committee, his objective being to provide a school place for every child in Moscow. In 1897 he founded a Pedagogical Society to enable teachers of all levels to meet and discuss educational problems. The Society had a Historical section to which Kliuchevskii and other historians at Moscow University belonged. Pokrovskii was a regular speaker at its meetings, and a contributor to its projects. He wrote reviews of historical textbooks, campaigned for equal rights of female *gimnaziia* teachers with their male counterparts, and advised on the preparation of history lessons.[27] To improve standards of history teaching in schools Vinogradov acted as general editor of a series of *Readers in Medieval History*, about which more will be said below.

Vinogradov believed that the function of schools should be to disseminate education as widely as possible throughout the community. His idea was that in the lower classes of the secondary schools the instruction should cover all the main subjects of human interest, that it should deal with mankind, with nature, and with art. At the more advanced stage a certain element of specialization should be permitted. For the younger children he favoured the teaching of nature through excursions, so that the children might have explained to them what they were actually seeing, no matter how many different sciences were

---

25   Pokrovskii 1926c.
26   Ibid.
27   Chernobaev 1992, p. 16.

invoked for the purpose.[28] As Deputy Commissar for Education Pokrovskii would later introduce this educational method in Soviet Russia, calling it the 'complex method'.

In the course of a student disturbance at Moscow University in the autumn of 1901 Vinogradov established a commission to look into the student grievances. Representatives were elected from within the student body to meet with the professors on the 'Vinogradov Commission'. Vinogradov proposed that a standing professorial committee should be established, free from government interference, to keep in touch with the student bodies, and to deal with student grievances. When, however, the scheme was put to General Vannovskii, the Minister of Education, he rejected it completely. The incident convinced Vinogradov that the obstacles placed by the Russian government to progress were insurmountable. He resigned his chair at the University and made preparations to leave Russia for England.[29]

Two years later Vinogradov was appointed to the Corpus Christi Chair of Jurisprudence at Oxford University through the resignation of Sir Frederick Pollock. He returned to Russia for a short visit in 1905, when there was hope that the situation there might improve. Apart from some short visits to Russia in later years he was to remain in England for the rest of his life.

5   Vinogradov's Historical Views

As Vinogradov makes plain in the introduction to the work, his *Studies in the Social History of England in the Middle Ages* was a contribution to a particular current in historical scholarship that had as its focus the village community. The initiator of this current was the German historian Georg Ludwig von Maurer with his series of studies of the communal Mark organisation in Germany, beginning with his general introduction to the subject published in 1853.

In Maurer's view, the original inhabitants of Germany had been free people living in communities which held the land they cultivated in common. He found support for this view in passages from Julius Caesar's *De bello gallico* and Tacitus's *Germania*. Periodically, the families would re-divide the land amongst themselves to eradicate any inequalities that had arisen since the last distribution. The leaders of the Mark were elected and functioned as representatives of

28   Fisher 1927, p. 25.
29   Kheraskov 1952, pp. 226–8; Fisher 1927, pp. 28–9.

the community. According to Maurer, it was with the disintegration of the Mark community that private property in land emerged, and along with it, social inequalities.[30]

Maurer's work was given an international dimension by Henry Sumner Maine. Maine's first book, *Ancient Law* (1861) was a comparative study of legal practices, mainly in ancient Rome and Greece, but also those in India, Anglo-Saxon England, and Russia. This was followed by Maine's *Village Communities in the East and West* (1871), which drew upon Maurer's study of the German Mark organisation, Haxthausen's account of the Russian *mir*, and his own experience of agrarian communities as a civil servant in India. In this way, Maine was able to present a comparative study of village communities in the Indo-European world. In the gradual disintegration of these communities Maine found the emergence of feudal relations and the consolidation of private property in land.

Maine was the first occupant of the Corpus Christi Chair of Jurisprudence at Oxford that Vinogradov was elected to in 1903. In view of this, Vinogradov chose for the theme of his inaugural lecture delivered in March 1904 'The Teaching of Sir Henry Maine'. The lecture reveals how he saw his own relationship to Maine, and what he believed the political significance of Maine's ideas to be. For Vinogradov, the attraction of Maine's comparative approach to jurisprudence was the implication that Russia, whose peasants lived in village communities very like the ones Maine described, would evolve in a way that more advanced societies like England had done, and produce the same kind of democratic institutions. In his lecture Vinogradov told his audience that he had first been attracted to the study of English law by 'those features of English life which had always strongly appealed to the interest of the foreign observer, notably the rule of law and the ... spirit of freedom'.[31] According to Fisher, Vinogradov 'never doubted for a moment that where the Western nations had led, Russia would in due time follow'.[32]

6   *Readings in Medieval History*

While teaching at Moscow University, Vinogradov set out to improve the quality of history teaching in secondary schools and *gimnazii*, which he thought was being done badly. The knowledge was imparted to the pupils in a disjointed and

---

30   Maurer 1854, 6, 72, 139–41.
31   Vinogradoff 1904, p. 1.
32   Fisher 1927, p. 10.

fragmentary manner. They had to learn by heart various names and dates, but without any kind of coherent connection between them. This, in Vinogradov's view, was a serious shortcoming, since a knowledge of history was necessary, not only to those who would study it at university, but also to those who in the future would take up a great variety of occupations. He believed that if one did not succeed in imparting into the minds of pupils a consciousness of the close causal connection between historical phenomena, the organic growth of the State, the mutual relations between people's aspirations and the conditions under which these aspirations are realised, then one could say that the teaching of history had been to no avail.[33] It was for these considerations that Vinogradov compiled a textbook on Universal History for use in secondary schools. He planned to produce two parallel series of works: one series would consist of textbooks, which would establish the essential basis of historical knowledge; the other series would be produced with teachers in mind and would be compilations of readings designed to illustrate the most characteristic episodes and actors of history with a wide choice of articles arranged in an exemplary way. Vinogradov resisted the idea that books on history intended for school pupils had to be pitched at a low intellectual level. The second series of books for secondary schools edited by Vinogradov appeared under the title of *Readings in Medieval History*, and it was in this series that Pokrovskii had his first academic publications.[34]

As contributors to the *Readings*, Vinogradov was able to enlist a number of his colleagues and students, making the project a showpiece of Moscow University's talent in the field of Medieval History. Besides Pokrovskii and Vinogradov himself, the contributors included Ger'e, Miliukov, Kizevetter, R. Vipper, M.K. Liubavskii and D.M. Petrushevskii, whose article on the Watt Tyler uprising would appear in book form in 1901. The *Readings* went through several editions and won the Peter the Great prize. Pokrovskii made a considerable contribution to the series, at least one of his articles appearing in each of the three volumes. There were eight articles in all covering a range of subjects in the field of European medieval history. They conformed to the specifications set out by Vinogradov, being concise, informative and not overly simplified.

The subjects of Pokrovskii's articles were: 'The Restoration of the Western Roman Empire' (1896), 'Symeon the Bulgarian tsar', 'Medieval Heresies and the Inquisition', 'The Fourth Crusade and the Latin Empire' (1897), 'The Rule of the

---

33   Vinogradov 1914, p. 6.
34   Vinogradov 1914, pp. 5–8; Vinogradov 1896, pp. 4–5.

Medicis in Florence', 'The Greeks in Italy and the Revival of Platonic Philosophy', 'The Turks in Europe and the Fall of Byzantium' and 'The Economic Life of Western Europe at the End of the Middle Ages' (1899). Each article begins with a list of textbooks for further reading, but almost all quotations in the articles are from primary sources, indicating that the author has engaged in original research. Although the articles are disparate in their subjects, there are themes which tie some of them together. One such theme is the fate of Byzantium and its implications for Western Europe. Thus, the article on Symeon the tenth-century Bulgarian tsar examines Symeon's unsuccessful attempt to become the ruler of Byzantium. The article on the Fourth Crusade recounts the sacking of Byzantium by the crusaders in 1204. The final capture of Byzantium by the Ottomans in 1452 is dealt with in the article on 'The Turks in Europe and the Fall of Byzantium'. Byzantine scholars who brought knowledge of Greek culture and philosophy to Western Europe are the subject of the article on 'The Greeks in Italy and the Revival of Platonic Philosophy'. It is connected with the article on 'The Rule of the Medicis in Florence', since Cosimo de' Medici admired the Byzantine scholar Gemistus Pletho and sponsored the foundation of the Platonic Academy in Florence.

Apart from the short essay 'The Restoration of the Western Roman Empire' on the emergence of the Holy Roman Empire under Charlemagne, all of Pokrovskii's articles deal with their subjects in some depth. Pokrovskii shows his versatility by the ability to adopt different approaches to suit the demands of the given subject. On the origins of the wealth of the Medicis, for instance, his approach is economic. For the article on the revival of Platonic philosophy in Italy he expounds Pletho's teaching in the intellectual context of the times. On the capture of Byzantium by the Turks Pokrovskii reconstructs the military tactics employed by the opposing sides. It is notable too that in the latter article he abandons Europocentrism and recounts the episode as one in the history of the Ottoman Empire.

Pokrovskii's clarity of exposition goes with an exemplary objectivity of approach. This is most evident in the article on 'Medieval Heresies and the Inquisition', which is centred on the Cathar movement in thirteenth century Languedoc. The doctrines of the Bogomils, the Manichaeans and the Cathars are expounded in such a way that the reader can appreciate how these differed from orthodox Catholicism, and from each other. Pokrovskii's description of the ascetic ideals of the Cathar spiritual leaders, the *perfecti*, and their preparedness to give their lives for their faith, allows one to understand how these evoked the admiration of contemporaries. Although it would appear that the Catholic Church indulged in wanton cruelty by having heretics burnt alive, with the help of a passage from the writings of St Thomas Aquinas,

Pokrovskii provides the reasoning that impelled otherwise humane and compassionate priests to visit such a terrible death on errant members of their
flock.

The final article, 'The Economic Life of Western Europe at the End of the
Middle Ages', written in 1899, is rather different from the rest. It is much longer,
extending over eighty pages, and acts as a kind of summing up of the entire
series of readings on Medieval history. It does not deal with religious or philosophical subjects, but is mainly an essay on European economic history. Among
the sources listed are Maxim Kovalevsky's *The Economic Growth of Europe*,
Vinogradov's *Villainage in England* and Rogers's *Six Centuries of Work and
Wages*. The article's starting point is the disintegration of the medieval manor,
with its serf labour and self-sufficient production. It traces the emergence of
exchange and money relations to the growth of towns, and the emergence of
guilds and a merchant class. In the article Pokrovskii makes occasional references to phenomena in Russia, with the clear indication that, although it may
come later, Russian economic development does not differ in any essential
respect from that in Western Europe. In this connection Pokrovskii makes the
observation:

> Industrial capital was the offspring of merchant and usurer capital: every
> where in the world of capitalist production capitalist-merchants were the
> forerunners of capitalist-entrepreneurs, factory owners and mill owners.
> Russia stands closer to this first stage of large-scale economy than West
> ern Europe; until the present time, the class of capitalists bears the name
> 'merchantry' and we number, for example, the Moscow factory owners
> among the 'merchants', although we are well aware that their function
> does not consist in exchange.[35]

The idea that all countries underwent the same stages of economic development was entirely in accord with the light in which Vinogradov saw the relationship of Russia's economic, and especially its political development with
regard to the West.

However, according to Pokrovskii, writing in 1927, there was a feature of his
article of which Vinogradov did not approve. Seemingly, Pokrovskii had ended
the article by giving an account of primary capitalist accumulation according
to Marx, and when Vinogradov had read these concluding pages, he objected
that they were quite out of place and demanded that they be removed. Hence,

---

35   Pokrovskii 1899, p. 468.

Pokrovskii stated, a reader could not fail to notice that the article had been cut, since the concluding part was missing.

In Soviet times Pokrovskii was understandably at pains to establish his revolutionary credentials, and to have fallen foul of Vinogradov over his Marxist approach to history could only have been to the good. But contrary to what Pokrovskii says, it is unlikely that anyone would notice that the article had been cut. In fact it is rounded off neatly with a conclusion comparing the manor to an industrial enterprise. It is quite possible, however, that Vinogradov could have objected to the inclusion of an account of primary capitalist accumulation according to Marx, but the objection is more likely to have been because of the article's inordinate length, and because the subject of primitive capitalist accumulation was inappropriate in a work on Medieval History.

7   Conflict with Struve

If the article on 'The Economic Life of Western Europe' brought Pokrovskii into conflict with Vinogradov, it also contains a clue to what caused Pokrovskii's clash with Peter Struve in 1898. In speaking of the causes which brought about the liberation of the serfs in medieval France, Pokrovskii observes that unfree labour is unprofitable, because the serf has no incentive to work. That the free man works harder was an observation made both by the Russian landowners of the XIX century and the French seigneurs of the Middle Ages. Here, in essence, was Pokrovskii's explanation for the liberation of the Russian peasantry in 1861: that serfdom had become unprofitable, and it had become advantageous to the landowners to employ free labour.

Struve however, had come to the conclusion that this explanation was not borne out by the evidence. He found that, far from being in decline, serf labour was on the increase on the eve of the 1861 emancipation. Serfdom, he asserted, had not been abolished for economic reasons. In December 1898 Struve announced his findings at two public lectures at the Moscow Juridical Society.[36] The lecture hall was filled to capacity with the speaker's ardent young admirers, aspiring social democrats. According to Alexander Kizevetter, who was present at the occasion, at the end of Struve's lecture:

A small insignificant looking individual asked for the floor and began in a whining voice to raise objections to what had been said. He did not

---

36   Pipes 1970, pp. 197–200.

agree with the speaker's new-fangled ideas and defended the generally accepted tenets of the older liberal historiography. And this person who opposed the standard-bearer of Marxism was none other than Mikhail Pokrovskii ...[37]

Of the episode, Pokrovskii himself recalled:

> Due to my complete awkwardness and lack of skill I was defeated, and it was difficult at that time to go against the authority of Struve. Several hundred students of both sexes applauded Struve furiously for about five minutes. But Struve's lecture, and especially the concluding part, showed me how meagre the scholarly credentials of this 'leader' were. It was all the more galling to leave the dispute defeated; but, as they say, defeated armies learn well.[38]

When Struve's lecture was published in a collection of articles in 1914, Pokrovskii took the opportunity to make his arguments against it in writing. The main point of contention was:

> Derived by Struve from the Russian Hegelians – through the mediacy of Miliukov – the idea that in Russian history the State has primacy over society leads the author to the conclusion that 'Serfdom as such had not ripened economically in 1861' and 'Serfdom was abolished against the interests of the landowning class. I consider any opposing view to be without merit and at variance with the facts'.[39]

In his debate with Struve Pokrovskii was defending the approach to historical events which saw the initiative as coming from below, rather than from the State. Kizevetter classed this approach as 'liberal', and he was right; that was indeed its origin, because it was promoted by people who saw Russia's future as a constitutional democracy. But Pokrovskii would deploy the same approach in the service of Marxism, as an approach, as he saw it, that would explain historical phenomena in terms of an economic base, rather than of a political superstructure.

Because Pokrovskii did not complete his master's degree with a dissertation, he was unable to make a contribution of new knowledge to the historical field,

---

37   Kizevetter 1974, p. 220.
38   Chernobaev 1992, p. 14.
39   Pokrovskii 1933c, p. 84.

as his contemporaries Miliukov and Rozhkov did. Nevertheless, his eight articles for *Readings in Medieval History* represent a substantial scholarly achievement. Writing them allowed him to study in considerable depth a variety of subjects, rather than specialising in one. The articles are knowledgeable, cogent and fair-minded. They show Pokrovskii as a serious and versatile scholar with a talent for literary expression. There are echoes of these early articles in his later writings right into Soviet times.

8   Teaching

After leaving the University, Pokrovskii taught history at teachers' training courses and at the Higher Courses for Women, which had been founded by Vinogradov's predecessor Ger'e. This experience, he claimed, had a considerable influence both on his approach to history and his political standpoint, since he was coming into contact with people who already had some knowledge of Marxism. He explained:

> I came to them and proceeded to expatiate on my idealist nonsense of Plato's philosophy, idealism and so forth. Unfortunately, they heard me out, but I was quite aware that I was talking about things which were quite useless, that I was leaving them quite discontented, and for the next course I began to speak in a more business-like fashion, that is, I tried to convey to my audience those historical facts which that audience required. And so I inevitably came to historical materialism. I arrived at this by practical means, from the facts. Every time a person seriously gets to grips with a historical subject, he becomes a historical materialist ... And that is how the first masses with whom I came in contact, the mass of girl students, made me, for the first time, a historical materialist, not a Marxist in the true sense of the word, rather an economic materialist. It made me a democrat at the same time.[40]

It was while teaching on the Higher Courses for Women that Pokrovskii met Liubov' Nikolaevna Zaraiskaia, a girl from a wealthy Muscovite family. After leaving school, she had gone to work as a governess, giving private lessons in English, French and German. From 1899 she lived in the house of her relative S.I. Shchukin, described by a historian of the Moscow merchant dynasties as

---

40   Pokrovskii 1933c, pp. 298–9.

'one of the most dynamic businessmen of his generation as well as a collector of French impressionist paintings and financial angel of the Psychological Institute of Moscow University'.[41] To further her education, Liubov' enrolled in the Higher Courses for Women, where Pokrovskii taught Russian history. She and Pokrovskii fell in love and were married in 1901, much to the delight of Pokrovskii's mother, but to the horror of Liubov's parents, who disowned their daughter for marrying so much beneath her.[42]

For their honeymoon the couple made a tour of Italy, a country that had featured so prominently in the articles Pokrovskii had submitted to the *Readings in Medieval History*. Later Liubov' spent some time studying medicine at the University of Lausanne, but never completed the course due to ill health. In 1907 Liubov' gave birth to a son, Iurii, who was their only child.

That Pokrovskii had made an advantageous match by marrying Liubov' goes without saying. But it also had, one might say, a sociological significance. The Shchukins, to whom Liubov' was related, were a Moscow merchant dynasty, like the Guchkovs, Konovalovs, Tretiakovs and Morozovs, families who had risen from peasant origins through trade and had acquired their wealth as entrepreneurs in the manufacture of textiles.[43] Pokrovskii was not just a historian of merchant capitalism; he was someone who had married into it.

It was about this time too that Pokrovskii became connected with the University Extension movement in Russia. It had been founded in 1893–4 by E.N. Orlova, who had been impressed by the University Extension movement in the USA, and on her return to Russia had enlisted the support of Miliukov in an attempt to set up a similar institution in Russia. The main difficulty which they faced was to find some means by which the organisation could function without falling foul of the tsarist authorities.[44]

It was decided that the University Extension should take the form of a commission attached to the Educational Section of the Society for the Dissemination of Technical Knowledge. This move had the dual advantage that it was immediately put above suspicion by the word 'technical' in the Society's title, which implied that it would proliferate little in the way of political subversion. It also meant that the institution of University Extension was easily established, since new commissions of the Educational Section were set up simply by their announcement in the press. It then came into being as the Commission for

41   Ruckman 1984, p. 85.
42   Chernobaev 1992, p. 16.
43   Buryshkin 1954, p. 111.
44   Miliukov 1955, p. 156.

the Organisation of Home Reading attached to the Educational Section of the Society for the Dissemination of Technical Knowledge.[45] The project had an immediate and widespread success since the ideas of self-education and self-improvement were fashionable at that time. Nor was there the slightest difficulty in financing the scheme, as the Moscow publisher I.D. Sytin was willing to undertake the printing and distribution of the Commission's programmes and textbooks, a special series of which was projected under the general title of Library of Self-Education.[46] It was a volume in this series, edited by V.N. Storozhev, *History of Russia to the Time of Troubles*, published in 1898, which contained Pokrovskii's earliest published article on Russian history, 'The Reflection of Economic Conditions in *Russkaia Pravda*'.

Russkaia pravda (Russian truth), an ancient Russian law code, was among the works that Pokrovskii had studied for his master's degree, and in his article he demonstrates his familiarity with the text, and the commentaries upon it made by other authors. His article is divided into two sections, one on property in land, and the other on movable property. According to Pokrovskii, academic opinion was divided on the subject of land ownership at the time of *Russkaia pravda*. Some scholars thought that only clan agriculture existed, land being owned collectively. Others maintained that besides collective property, there was individual ownership of lands by persons who had acquired them through clearing wild fields and forests. Pokrovskii himself does not come down in favour of either opinion but makes the observation that the practice of removing fencing from around arable fields after the harvest, mentioned in *Russkaia pravda*, was also followed in parts of Germany. Here Pokrovskii refers to Maurer's book, thereby indicating the similarities between Russia and the West, and also his adherence to the village community school of thought.

On movable property in *Russkaia pravda* Pokrovskii could be more informative. The most highly valued items of private property were slaves, whose ownership was strongly protected by the law. Anyone found helping a slave to flee was subject to a massive fine. Beavers were also protected, as fur was traded with Byzantium and the East.

The University Extension movement was a fruitful source for Pokrovskii's earliest teaching experience in the field of popular education, and a valuable model for later Soviet practice in the 1920s. Certainly, in its day it was a movement which attracted the enthusiastic support of the cream of the young Russian academics, since it provided excellent teaching practice, a proving ground

---

45   Kizevetter 1974, p. 289.
46   Kizevetter 1974, p. 291.

for new educational methods, and experience in organising courses on a university level. It was, moreover, an institution which brought young academics into contact with people of all ages and social backgrounds from all parts of the Russian Empire who were eager to further their education. It was a school through which not only Pokrovskii passed, but a whole generation of Russian scholars in various fields.

Pokrovskii records that it was while he was engaged in teaching work that he began to study Marxism. 'It was only when I was already giving lectures', he writes, 'that I began to study Marxism seriously, in the first years, no doubt, deviating towards revisionism'.[47] He recalled: 'In the second half of the nineties I was considered by the Legal Marxists to be one of them, and I received an invitation to contribute to *Novoe slovo*, *Nachalo* and *Zhizn*".[48] Considering that *Novoe slovo* and *Nachalo* were edited by Struve, and were published between 1896 and 1899, it emerges that Pokrovskii's dispute with Struve in 1898 did not prevent his being invited to contribute to the journals. That Pokrovskii did not do so is probably to be explained by the fact that in the period in question he was fully occupied with writing his chapters for *Readings in Medieval History*.

Pokrovskii's teaching activities eventually aroused the suspicions of the education authorities, and in 1902 he was barred from further lecturing on the grounds of 'unreliability' (*neblagonadezhnost'*).[49] For not only did Pokrovskii utilize the Commission for Home Reading for the propagation of Marxism, but the history classes in the Order of St Catherine School as well. This is clear from his reminiscences of the period, given in a speech to Soviet teachers, delivered on 28 May 1924. He stated:

> I taught in the old school, on the subject system [Pokrovskii was addressing an audience of schoolteachers who used the 'complex' system, which ignored subject boundaries. тw] but I must say that I used to convey to the pupils a Marxist understanding of history ... and they were extremely receptive. I happened to do this within the walls of this very teaching institution ... whence I was expelled exactly 25 years ago for unreliability. I introduced an older age group consisting of adolescent girls to historical materialism, and I can assure you that they understood it. I did not simply lecture to the class, but I gave them plenty of practical exercises. I made them write essays, so I have proof that the better part of the class took in the basic concepts of historical materialism. In a word, I have had

---

47   Lutskii 1965, p. 341.
48   Tikhomirov 1966, p. 6.
49   Pokrovskii 1924a, p. 6.

experience, and it is all the more convincing, since it took place in very unfavourable circumstances, where various people of authority did not assist me, but stood in my way. There would visit my class the worthy trustees in cavalry uniforms, and all kinds of society ladies, to listen to my lessons; and I had to manoeuvre very carefully in order to be able to go on explaining history in a materialist fashion even in the presence of such visitors. I remember how hussar Olsuf'ev, the head of this educational institution, once came into my class. He listened to my lesson and when I explained that the rise of serfdom had economic roots, he snorted expressively: 'a fine story!'[50]

Pokrovskii may well have been a theoretical Marxist in 1902, but he did not belong to any avowedly Marxist organisation. At that time his political affiliations were with liberal zemstvo groups, to whose publications he contributed, and with the Liberation group, which was formed in exile by Peter Struve. As Pokrovskii recalled: 'Iskra never reached me at that time, it may well be through my own fault; whereas I received Osvobozhdenie (Liberation) regularly'.[51]

9   Liberal Politics

Pokrovskii's alliance with the zemstvo liberals reflected developments in Russia following the death of Alexander III in 1894. It was hoped that his successor, Nicholas II, would introduce reforms to liberalise the autocratic regime. The need for change was especially felt in the light of the devastating famine in the countryside that had occurred in 1891–92. The new tsar was encouraged in the direction of reform by the zemstvo organisations up and down the country, who presented him with 'addresses' requesting that he establish a consultative assembly. Nicholas's curt reply that what the zemstvos proposed were 'senseless dreams' provoked the zemstvos into collaborating at a national level to discuss possible future action. The organisation that emerged was the Beseda (Colloquium) Circle, which never itself adopted any political programme in order to maintain unity of different strands of liberal opinion. Beseda's significance, according to its historian Terence Emmons, was to act as an intermediate stage between the zemstvos and the formation of political parties.[52]

---

50   Pokrovskii 1924a, p. 10.
51   Sokolov 1970, p. 52.
52   Emmons 1973, p. 462.

In order to appeal to a wider public than zemstvo activists, *Beseda* published a journal and a series of books on political and social issues, subjects such as popular education, the peasant question, and the expansion of local self-government. As Emmons notes, *Beseda's* publishing activities provided the opportunity for contacts to be made between zemstvo political leaders and the 'intelligentsia', academics like Pokrovskii.[53] The book to which Pokrovskii contributed the chapter 'Local Government in Ancient Rus' (1903), *The Small Zemstvo Unit*, put the case for creating a sub-district level zemstvo organ and provided descriptions of self-government institutions in Western Europe and the USA.

In 'Local Government in Ancient Rus' Pokrovskii for the first time uses history in a political cause. His article appears alongside that of his teacher Vinogradov's on parish and district councils in England, and Kovalevsky's on how settlers from England carried these institutions to the New World.

The argument of Pokrovskii's article is that, despite its autocratic government, Russia has a long tradition of local self-government and initiative from below. In modern parlance, he demonstrates the existence in Russia from ancient times of a 'civil society', one that is capable of being developed and of supporting modern democratic institutions of local self-government.

The article is an erudite piece of writing, made possible by the intimate knowledge Pokrovskii had of the Primary Chronicle, *Russkaia pravda*, and other contemporary sources that he had studied as part of his master's degree programme. He surveys the succession of the territorial divisions that had existed in Russia since the time of Kievan Rus', and the kind of local institutions that existed within them to carry out police, judiciary, fiscal and other functions for the population. Pokrovskii finds that these functions were carried on independently, without the intervention of the State.

In arguing in favour of an autonomous local influence in Russian history there are echoes in Pokrovskii's work of Kliuchevskii's approach in *The Boiar Duma*, and in fact he refers to this work in support of his contention that by the XVII century a money economy existed in Russia. In this regard, Pokrovskii contests the opinion of 'Statist' writers such as Boris Chicherin, who maintained that in ancient Rus' a natural economy prevailed. In rebuttal of this conception Pokrovskii cited not only Kliuchevskii, but the more recent findings of M.I. Tugan-Baranovskii and Rozhkov, the latter being one of Kliuchevskii's pupils.

---

53   Emmons 1973, p. 486.

'Local Government in Ancient Rus' is an important landmark in Pokrovskii's intellectual development. It brings together the historical approaches of his two teachers – Kliuchevskii and Vinogradov. From Vinogradov comes the conception of the importance of local government in the political life of a country, the foundation of constitutional government. From Kliuchevskii comes the idea that the driving force of Russian history is not from above, from the State, but from the classes in society, from below.

Pokrovskii himself locates his article in the context of the historical doctrines of the times. He notes a shift of interest that has taken place in the past decade in historical literature: whereas in the first half of the XIX century historians studied constitutional history, in the second half they focus on village communities. In his famous collection of documents on English constitutional history, for example, Stubbs gives extracts from Tacitus depicting the village commune of the ancient Germans. In his history of the political institutions of ancient France Fustel de Coulanges begins by tackling the problem of this German commune, devoting a whole volume to the Merovingian period. Pokrovskii himself endorses this 'microscopic' approach to history, observing that the history of the English village helps us understand better how the rule of law came about rather than volumes of parliamentary speeches.[54] These opening passages of his article show Pokrovskii as an adherent of the school of thought to which Maurer and Maine belonged. They also show how compatible this school was with the approach of Kliuchevskii, who viewed the evolution of political institutions in social and economic terms.

10   *Zemskii sobor* and Parliament

Pokrovskii's article 'Zemskii sobor and Parliament' published in the *Beseda* collection entitled *Constitutional Government* was a product of the 1905 revolution. Its publication was prompted by the rescript of 18 February announcing the tsar's intention to summon elected representatives of the people to participate in the business of government. This unprecedented step encouraged the belief that Russia's autocratic structure was on the point of being dissolved, and that the time had come for the creation of a new constitutional order on the Western-European model. The aim of the *Constitutional Government* collection was to acquaint its readers with the workings of a constitutional order.

---

54   Pokrovskii 1903, p. 224.

A companion volume entitled *The Political Order of Contemporary States* had a chapter by Vinogradov on England, one by Kovalevsky on the USA, and one by Miliukov on Bulgaria. M.A. Reisner's introduction to the volume is significant because it sets out the Positivist historical presuppositions that underlay the aspiration to give Russia a constitution on the Western-European model.

Reisner begins by posing the question: can Russia use the experience of other countries? The Slavophiles in their day denied that it could, but, as Reisner pointed out, sociology had made great strides since that time. Nowadays, scarcely anyone would dispute that sociology had succeeded in establishing the main stages of human social development. The initial stage was the clan, which was followed by feudalism (in the broad sense of the term). Out of feudalism there emerged the third stage, that of the military-national state, and from this there would develop the industrial-legal state. According to Reisner, Russia conformed to this scheme of development, in that its present political order was unstable, and that a constitutional regime was likely to emerge.[55]

Pokrovskii's article 'Zemskii sobor and parliament' in *Constitutional Government* provided a historical perspective on the question of representative assemblies in Russia. In this respect, it is comparable to his essay on local government in Russia. While the earlier work argued that there was a long tradition of local initiative in the country, the later one contended that blind obedience was not a characteristic of the Russian people, and that this people was as capable of political self-determination as any other. Also, as in the article on local government, in 'Zemskii sobor and parliament' Pokrovskii deploys his extensive knowledge of first-hand sources of the period to provide convincing evidence for his case.

The Russian institution which bears the closest resemblance to the representative assemblies of Western Europe is the *zemskii sobor* (assembly of the land) first convened by Ivan the Terrible in 1566. In a lengthy article serialised in the journal *Russkaia mysl'* between 1890 and 1892 Kliuchevskii had presented his findings on 'The Composition of Representation of the *zemskii sobors* of Ancient Rus'. According to Kliuchevskii, the *zemskii sobor* of the XVI century differed essentially from an institution of popular representation, being neither for legislation nor consultation. In convoking it, the government wanted to have, not representatives of the people, but an assembly of its own agents, people who would carry out its bidding. It sought from them neither authorisation nor advice, but an expression of readiness to carry out the government's decisions.[56]

---

55   Dolgorukov and Petrunkevich 1905, pp. 5–7.
56   Kliuchevskii 1990, p. 372.

Pokrovskii contests Kliuchevskii's opinion by drawing upon contemporary accounts of the *zemskii sobor* which suggest that the body was by no means subservient to the will of the ruler but had an autonomous role in the politics of the day. In Pokrovskii's opinion, Kliuchevskii's misapprehension comes from his over-estimation of the power of the Russian autocracy. He points out that under Ivan the Terrible the Russian state was still in the process of formation: it still lacked a standing army, a steady income from taxation and a strong bureaucratic organisation, the attributes of a contemporary state structure.

Ivan knew only too well that despite all the tortures and executions, his medieval government was not strong enough to compel the obedience of his subjects: he needed to enlist their support if he wanted to finance his war against Poland and Sweden. The *zemskii sobor* provided the platform for Ivan to make a plea for more money to continue hostilities.[57]

Pokrovskii's article 'Zemskii Sobor and Parliament' is significant for its being a polemic against Kliuchevskii. Two years previously, in 'Local Government in Ancient Rus' Pokrovskii had cited *Boiar Duma* with approval, but in 'Zemskii sobor and Parliament' he was highly critical of Kliuchevskii's article on the composition of the *zemskii sobor*. Here Pokrovskii is reacting to the difference in approach between Kliuchevskii's two works: whereas the *Boiar Duma* stresses initiative from below, the article on the *zemskii sobor* adopts an explicitly Statist approach. Kliuchevskii dedicated his article to Boris Chicherin, the leading exponent of the Statist school. Since Kliuchevskii was propounding a doctrine that contradicted the interpretation of Russian history which favoured the development of parliamentary democracy in Russia, it is natural that Pokrovskii should dispute Kliuchevskii's conclusions.

The way in which Pokrovskii conducted his polemic with Kliuchevskii is also significant. It was done on two levels. The first one was the normal scholarly interchange, in which Pokrovskii presented documentary evidence which he believed undermined Kliuchevskii's interpretation of events. The other level was to show that Kliuchevskii's views were ideologically motivated. As Pokrovskii himself indicated, he had already employed this method with regard to Chicherin in 'Local Government in Ancient Rus'. There he had argued that what gave rise to the Statist school was the situation in Russia on the eve of the peasant liberation in 1861. The reform had been virulently opposed by the landowning class, and it was only through the determination of the government that it had been carried through. It was a situation in which liberal opinion in the

---

57   Pokrovskii 1905b, p. 453.

country was on the side of the State. Chicherin's Hegelianism, which saw the State as the prime mover of historical progress was the intellectual expression of the liberalism of Russia's era of reforms.[58]

In the case of Kliuchevskii, Pokrovskii remarked that his interpretation of the *zemskii sobor* proved the famous maxim that 'whatever a historian writes about, he always writes about his own times'. In this respect, Kliuchevskii's account of the *zemskii sobor* was modernised. He had depicted the *zemskii sobor* as though it was the predecessor of the numberless bureaucratic commissions that had been established under Alexander III.[59]

Pokrovskii of course knew that Kliuchevskii had served on such a commission under Alexander III, and may have suspected that his retreat from the radicalism of the *Boiar Duma* to the Statism of the article on the *zemskii sobor* reflected an increasing subservience to the government. In that case, one should perhaps interpret the term 'eclecticism' in Pokrovskii's 1904 review of Kliuchevskii's book as a euphemism for 'opportunism' or 'lack of principle'. When Pokrovskii reviewed the fifth volume of Kliuchevskii's *Course of Russian History*, which appeared posthumously in 1923, he left his readers in no doubt that he considered Kliuchevskii an opportunist.[60]

Besides contributing to liberal publications, Pokrovskii kept abreast of developments in the liberal camp. A major step towards the formation of a liberal political party was the foundation in Stuttgart in 1902 of the journal *Osvobozhdenie* edited by the former Marxist Peter Struve. It gained wide popularity in oppositionist circles, and Pokrovskii was one of its regular subscribers.[61] The *Beseda* organisation considered adopting *Osvobozhdenie* as its official organ but rejected the idea to avoid being identified too closely with constitutionalism, a current to which not all *Beseda* members subscribed.[62]

The other publication inspired by Struve to appear in 1902 was the collection of essays *Problems of Idealism*. Ostensibly a work on philosophical idealism, its political purpose was to convince the zemstvo liberals that they had nothing to fear from former Marxists like himself, Berdyaev, Bulgakov and Frank, who had joined the liberal camp. These were people who had abandoned Marxism and Positivism for idealism and were prepared to provide a powerful philosophical defence of liberal values.[63] To keep the more radical elements on board

---

58   Pokrovskii 1905b, pp. 226–7.
59   Pokrovskii 1905b, p. 437.
60   Tikhomirov 1966, pp. 272–6.
61   Sokolov 1970, p. 52.
62   Emmons 1973, p. 475.
63   Poole 2003, pp. 11–2.

in *Osvobozhdenie*, Struve expressed his support for the revolutionary groups, though in such a way as not to alienate the liberals.

In August 1903 Struve and his associates founded the political organisation The Union of Liberation, which aimed to unite all the forces which opposed the Russian autocratic regime, from the zemstvo liberals to the revolutionary groups, including the Socialist Revolutionaries and the Social Democrats. The Union had its headquarters in Moscow, and there it formed several sections with specialised functions, such as agitation among women and peasants. It also had a Historians' Section, of which Pokrovskii was a member.[64]

In 1904 the main platform for Pokrovskii's political activities was the Moscow Pedagogical Society. Confrontation took place in the organisation between the democratically inclined membership and the liberal management. The conflict had arisen because one of the teachers had complained to the authorities about the 'subversive historical-materialist spirit which dominated the Historical Section of the Society'. The incensed teachers demanded that the informant be expelled from the Society. The management demurred but had to call a general meeting to discuss the matter. The meeting took the side of the Historical Section, and the management as a whole resigned. In the elections that followed Rozhkov became the new Chairman of the Pedagogical Society and Pokrovskii his Deputy.

The new management of the Pedagogical Society put forward the demands for 'A free school in a free society', and for far-reaching governmental reforms. Henceforth, both professional and political questions were discussed at the Society's meetings, where the influence of the Social Democrats was increasingly felt. In response to 'Bloody Sunday' on 9 January 1905 a general meeting of the Society expressed its sympathy with the victims of the massacre, and voiced the conviction that a repetition of such an atrocity could be avoided only by the establishment of a new political order based on democracy and the rule of law.[65]

---

64   Pipes 1970, p. 345.
65   Chernobaev 1992, pp. 24–5.

From Liberal to Bolshevik

1   *Pravda*

Speaking in 1928 on the occasion of his 6oth birthday, Pokrovskii recalled how he had joined the Bolshevik party:

> And then 1905 came along. My convictions, sincere and scientific, but deeply democratic, led me into the revolution. I entered the only revolutionary party that there was – the Bolshevik party. None of the others were really revolutionary parties.[1]

In fact, Pokrovskii's transition from liberal to Bolshevik was not so straightforward. It was effected through his association with a group of Moscow intellectuals whose leading light was Alexander Bogdanov (Malinovskii). Bogdanov had been a natural science student at Moscow University at the time Skvortsov-Stepanov organised the demonstration against Kliuchevskii and had been caught up in the arrests that took place in the aftermath. He was banished to Tula, where he began teaching in workers' circles, and it was on the basis of his lectures there that he wrote his influential textbook on Marxist economics. Arrested in 1899 for conducting propaganda among the workers, Bogdanov was exiled first to Kaluga, where he made the acquaintance of Anatolii Lunacharskii, and thence to Vologda.

In his exile in Vologda Bogdanov debated philosophical questions with Nicholas Berdyaev, who at that time was becoming disillusioned with the 'dialectical materialism' propounded by Plekhanov, which he found lacking in an ethical dimension. His search for this dimension led him increasingly to Kantian idealism. Berdyaev was not alone in this rejection of Marxism in favour of idealism; so too were Peter Struve and Sergei Bulgakov. These former Marxists joined with several established idealists to produce a volume of essays criticising Marxism and Positivism entitled *Problems of Idealism* published in 1902.

In reply to *Problems of Idealism* Bogdanov organised the publication of a volume of essays entitled *Studies in the Realist World View*, published in 1904, with contributions by himself, his friends and fellow exiles.[2] Even before Bog-

---

1 Pokrovskii 1933c, p. 299.
2 *Ocherki realisticheskogo mirovozzreniia. Sbornik statei po filosofii, obshchestvennoi nauke i*

danov returned from exile at the beginning of 1904, a new platform for the polemic with the *Problems of Idealism* group had appeared. This was *Pravda: A monthly journal of art, literature and social life.*

The moving spirit behind the journal was its patron V.A. Kozhevnikov, a wealthy railway engineer. Kozhevnikov was singularly successful in recruiting contributors for his journal. Among the writers, poets and dramatists were Ivan Bunin, N. Teleshov, Stanislaw Przebyszewski, V.M. Mikheev, E.N. Chirikov. It was also announced that among future contributors there would be Leonid Andreev, Maxim Gorky and Skitalets (S.G. Petrov).

Kozhevnikov's success in attracting popular figures from the literary world was matched by his ability to secure some talented people to comment on 'social life'. The nucleus of this group comprised Bogdanov and some of the authors who had contributed to *Studies in the Realist World View.* Augmented by Pokrovskii, Rozhkov and Skvortsov-Stepanov, it would form the editorial board of *Pravda*.

Pravda consisted of a literary component presided over by Ivan Bunin, a philosophical part managed by Bogdanov, and the 'survey' (*obozrenie*) – which was the province of Rumiantsev, Lunts and Finn-Enotaevskii. What was most striking about *Pravda* was its narrow elongated format and the wide variety of typography. Deploying such artistry and elegance, Kozhevnikov clearly had a discerning and cultured readership in mind.

It was natural that *Pravda* should continue the campaign against *Problems of Idealism*. Lunacharskii in a series of articles entitled 'The Evolution of a Thinker' gave a detailed analysis and refutation of Bulgakov's idealism and his strictures on Marx. Other articles, including those by Pokrovskii and Rozhkov, were directed against those philosophers on whom the *Problems of Idealism* group had based themselves: Stammler, Windelband and Rickert.

It was probably through Rozhkov that Pokrovskii came to know Bogdanov. Bogdanov's term of exile was due to end in 1904, but Rozhkov recalls that he first met him in 1903, when Bogdanov made surreptitious visits to Moscow, and on these occasions would stay in Rozhkov's flat. It would be at this time that Bogdanov started to gather contributors for *Pravda*, which began publication in January 1904.[3]

Pokrovskii's review of Heinrich Rickert's book *Die Grenzen der naturwissenschaftlichen Begriffsbildung* (translated as *The Limits of Concept Formation in Natural Science*) was a contribution to the campaign, since Rickert's ideas

---

zhizni (St. Petersburg, 1904). The contributors were: S. Suvorov, A. Lunacharskii, V. Bazarov, A. Bogdanov, A. Finn-Enotaevskii, P. Maslov, P. Rumiantsev, V. Shuliatikov, V. Friche.

3   Rozhkov and Sokolov 1925, p. 5; González 2017, p. 66.

were in keeping with those espoused by *Problems of Idealism*. As the editor P.I. Novogrodtsev explained in the foreword, *Problems of Idealism* was directed against 'Positivist philosophy'. Since both Comte and Marx are equally regarded as belonging to the Positivist school, the authors rely heavily for the refutation on the current opponents of positivism in German critical philosophy – Wilhelm Windelband and Heinrich Rickert. These two names consequently figure prominently on the pages of *Problems of Idealism*, a fact which was noted by Rozhkov in his reply to the collection in an article written in 1903.[4] The second part of Rickert's work, however, published in 1902, appeared too late to be used by the contributors to *Problems of Idealism*. Thus, Bulgakov regretted that:

> The present work had already been completed when Heinrich Rickert's definitive work ... appeared. The thesis on the impossibility of establishing historical laws and making predictions is there proved quite conclusively ... .[5]

2   Idealism and the Laws of History

Pokrovskii's review article 'Idealism and the Laws of History' is a unique source for the investigation of his philosophical development. It is written at a turning point in his intellectual life, during his transition from liberalism to social democracy. It is also Pokrovskii's most concentrated piece of purely philosophical writing, and it is worth examining in some detail, since it deals with themes which Pokrovskii constantly returned to throughout his life. In many respects Rickert may be seen not only as one of Pokrovskii's intellectual adversaries, but also as one of his influences.

Rickert's book took its inspiration from the inaugural lecture 'History and Natural Science' that his teacher Wilhelm Windelband had given on being elected dean of Strasbourg University in 1894. Belonging to the Kantian school of philosophy, Windelband accepted Kant's idea that the real world with all its infinity of forms was inaccessible to the human intellect directly. Concepts, with which the human understanding functioned, abstracted from actual objects and presented consciousness with a generalised account of what existed. Philosophers who succeeded Kant, such as Fichte, Schelling and Hegel, took Kant's conception of the part played by the Concept as a starting point

---

4 Rozhkov 1903, p. 322.
5 Poole 2003, p. 119.

for their respective systems. Windelband developed the contrast between the abstract generalisation of the Concept and the concrete particularity of the world of objects into a contrast between the universalising method of natural science and the attention shown by history to the particularity and individuality of an event in the past.

Windelband was eager to show that, although the natural sciences had made enormous strides in recent times, they were not all-encompassing, that history was an area of knowledge in which they had no application. His reasoning was that the natural sciences collected and analysed data in order to be able to form generalisations and universal laws of motion. For the natural scientist each particular datum of knowledge was of interest only in so far as it could provide an insight into some general rule. For the historian, on the other hand, the objective was not to abstract from reality, but to present the past in such a way that all of its concrete and distinctive features were reconstructed. Whereas the natural scientist produced abstract laws, the historian recreated the past in lively images.

For the natural scientist phenomena that were singular and unique could have no interest; these were exactly the material for historical study. It was events that were unique which the historian valued most. An event would lose interest for the historian if it proved to be merely one of many, a representative of a number of such events.

Of course, as Windelband pointed out, not every fact, albeit unique, could count as history. For example, there was reliable documentary evidence that in 1780 Goethe had had a doorbell installed, but this fact had no bearing on the history of German literature, or on Goethe's biography. Because not all facts formed part of history, an essential element in the work of a historian was the selection of data. For this there had to be some criterion for the choice, and this criterion, Windelband held, was a system of human values that were generally held to be valid. These universal human values were the standard against which the facts of history were evaluated.[6]

Rickert developed the ideas of Windelband in his book *The Limits of Concept Formation in Natural Science*, published in two parts in 1896 and 1902.[7] In the Foreword to the book, he explained his mode of exposition. This was that, taking the limits of concept formation in natural science, he would try to understand the nature of history as it was currently written; he was not going to draw up plans for sciences of the future. On the other hand, he had no intention of limiting himself to the analysis or description of what existed but saw his task

---

6   Windelband 1980, p. 362.
7   Rickert 1902.

as discovering the inner logical structure of the formation of all historical concepts. On how far he had succeeded in this enterprise Rickert requested his readers to suspend their judgement until they had read through his book's 743 pages.[8]

Following Windelband, what Rickert considered to be the limitations of natural scientific concepts was that, because they abstracted from all the properties that constituted the distinctive characteristics of objects, they could never picture reality as it actually existed. Reality in its concrete actuality and individuality, he maintained, could never be subsumed under the concepts of natural science. On the other hand, the science which did embrace the unique and the individual in events which had taken place in the past was the science of history.

Like Windelband, Rickert was aware of the problem of selection or simplification facing historians, since not all historical facts could or should be recorded. And, like Windelband, Rickert believed that the criteria of this selection were values. These values, in Rickert's view, were cultural values, those of civilised peoples, thus ensuring that the values were objective, and not simply the subjective judgements of particular historians. Examples of the different areas of culture included law, morals, ethics, religion and art.

Rickert devoted considerable attention to examining the characteristic features of the individual and unique historical event. Such an event was an integral whole, and not simply the aggregate of its constituent parts. It was held together by an inner spiritual nexus. Such an event, in Rickert's terminology, was an 'in-dividual', an internally coherent entity. Because of this inner nexus the historical event was a totality, in which both the event as a whole and the elements which composed it were individual and distinctive, so that, for example, the Italian Renaissance was as much a historical individual as Machiavelli, and the Romantic School just as much as its poet Novalis.[9]

In the light of his conception of history as the science of the unique and individual, Rickert pointed out the futility of those theories which sought to define the meaning of the entire history of humanity by means of a formula. In this respect he held that Comte's theory of three stages differed little from the schemes of Fichte and Hegel. Like Fichte, Comte had viewed the development of human progress as a progression from instinct to the science of reason. And both thinkers had been hostile to the religiosity of the Middle Ages.[10]

---

8   Rickert 1986, p. 4.
9   Rickert 1986, p. 108.
10   Rickert 1986, p. 182.

As might be expected, as a practising historian, Pokrovskii pointed out that Rickert had an antediluvian conception of what the historian's craft was, and what its methods were. Rickert seemed to think that the practice of history consisted in producing books which brought the past to life in lively imagery, that it was in essence a literary exercise. But, Pokrovskii observed, Rickert was apparently unaware what a colossal amount of work went into establishing historical facts, compared with which the writing up was a mere detail.[11]

The historian that Rickert had most in mind was Ranke, who claimed to present historical events 'as they really were', but, as Pokrovskii indicated, if one looked further afield it was plain that Guizot's *History of Civilisation in France*, and Alexis de Tocqueville's *Ancien régime* used the 'natural-scientific' method of observation and generalisation. In Pokrovskii's view: 'The historian will not derive anything useful from Rickert's book, and the non-historian will not be informed about the modes and methods of the real historical science. The methodological significance of this bulky treatise is nil'. But, Pokrovskii added, this was a pity, because Rickert's point of departure was completely correct and only lacked a consistent application. What Pokrovskii considered that Rickert had got right was the idea that concepts could never picture reality as it actually existed because of its extensive and intensive variety of forms.[12]

Pokrovskii thought that a weakness of Rickert's book was its lack of consistency. He was unconvinced by Rickert's claim that the Italian Renaissance and the Romantic School could count as individuals; in his view, they were undoubtedly general concepts. Nor could he see any great difference between the concepts of 'individual' and 'in-dividual'. To Pokrovskii, distinctions such as these were examples of the deliberate obscurity of German scholarship. As an example of the same kind he regarded Rickert's insistence that the book should be read all through before the overall argument could be understood.[13]

If one accepted Rickert's premiss that 'reality is irrational', it followed that one could not understand phenomena, i.e., subsume it under general concepts, without depriving it of its individual features. But, Pokrovskii pointed out, there was no way to express historical individuality other than by general concepts. If one took Luther, for example, a historian would be forced to describe both his activities and his psychological attributes in terms of general concepts: 'reform', 'love', 'hatred', 'fear' and so on.[14]

---

11   Pokrovskii 1933c, p. 10.
12   Pokrovskii 1933c, p. 11.
13   Pokrovskii 1933c, p. 15.
14   Pokrovskii 1933c, pp. 29–30.

In the case of Ranke, whom Rickert so admired, one found that his portrayal of Charlemagne was made up of general concepts. Charles was a genius; he had a natural talent as a strategist; he was sensible, consistent; he tried to be just in everything he did; he had a taste for the details of government; he had a natural talent for ruling and giving orders. What was this description, Pokrovskii asked, if not in terms of general concepts? Consequently, he concluded, all existing historical writing, even of Ranke's type, could not serve as examples of a method which was different from the natural sciences. Even if one agreed that history was made by great men – one of Rickert's main ideas – it was impossible to imagine these great men in their direct individuality. For, in order to make them accessible to our understanding, we have to subsume them under general concepts.[15]

As for Rickert's idea that the historians selected their material according to values, Pokrovskii posed the question: values for whom? Rickert had made it clear that the values he had in mind were not universal values. He states that:

> It is quite impossible to set up mankind as a whole as an ethical ideal ... On the contrary, the expressed national character must be recognised as having an important significance as an ethical value.

In other words, Rickert's values are to be understood as German values. The audience his historians are addressing is a German audience.

Besides their national character, Pokrovskii reveals that Rickert's values also have a social class dimension. According to another work of Rickert's, 'the historical essence of a peasant or a factory worker ... is that each one is like the other and therefore they can be described by natural concepts. Here, consequently, the purely individual plays a secondary part.' Pokrovskii observes with some sarcasm that it is a pity that Rickert did not lay down exactly from what rank a person was entitled to be classed as an 'individual'. Taking in conjunction, Rickert's national and social conception of values leads Pokrovskii to conclude that Rickert's political credo is German bourgeois nationalism.[16]

In Pokrovskii's opinion, Rickert did not succeed in demonstrating that history had a methodology that was different from natural science. Moreover, despite the fact that Rickert tried to distance himself from Positivism, his premiss of a chaotic reality requiring simplification to be comprehended, brought him very close to the variety of Positivism represented by Ernst Mach,[17] a philo-

---

15   Pokrovskii 1933c, p. 30.
16   Pokrovskii 1933c, p. 40.
17   Alexander Bogdanov considered Mach's philosophy to belong to the Positivist current. He

sophy to which Pokrovskii himself subscribed. In so far as Rickert's book popularised these ideas, Pokrovskii was prepared to recommend it to his readers.[18]

3 The Literary-Lecturing Group

Towards the end of 1904 *Pravda* was beset with internal difficulties. The section of the editorial board responsible for political and philosophical contributions voiced dissatisfaction with the policy of the literary section. Seemingly, Bunin was accepting articles of too 'pessimistic' a character, and a heated quarrel took place. Kozhevnikov sided with Bunin, and because the censor had recently been severely critical of the 'surveys', he insisted that Rumiantsev would have to leave. Bogdanov, Rozhkov, Pokrovskii and others thereupon announced that, as they had joined the journal as a group, they would leave as a group. After their departure Kozhevnikov invited the Mensheviks to take over the journal, Plekhanov replacing Bogdanov as head of the philosophical section. During 1905 and 1906, therefore, *Pravda* was in Menshevik hands, though between them and Kozhevnikov discord also arose. Kozhevnikov then attempted to bring back the original editorial board, but by that time they were engaged in other pursuits and had to refuse.[19]

With the onset of the revolution in 1905 the circle of intellectuals which had formed around *Pravda* widened to constitute a literary-propagandist group. 'Occasionally', Rozhkov records, 'the meetings would be attended by the Bolshevik V.L. Shantser (Marat). Until the autumn of 1905 at least, this group had no formal connections with the Bolshevik party, though ... there was present a certain party spirit which found its incarnation in the person of V.L. Shantser. Towards the end of 1905 the group became finally attached to the Bolshevik party'.[20] This then was presumably how and when Pokrovskii entered the party.

The party that Pokrovskii joined had been divided into two fractions at its second congress in 1902, but at the third congress in 1905 Bogdanov still hoped to re-unite the party. He thought that this could be done by making the party as democratic as possible, with its procedures as transparent as possible, even at

---

states: 'Empiriocriticism is a contemporary form of positivism that has developed on the basis of the modern methods of natural science, on the one hand, and of modern forms of philosophical criticism, on the other. This philosophical current found its most prominent exponents in Ernst Mach and Richard Avenarius ...' Bogdanov 2020, p. 6.

18   Pokrovskii 1933c, p. 42.
19   White 1974, pp. 198–9.
20   Rozhkov and Sokolov 1925, p. 15.

a time of revolution. Bogdanov rejected Lenin's conception of party organisation as authoritarian and implemented his own democratic model during his leadership of the Bolsheviks in 1905. The Bolshevik party that Pokrovskii joined in 1905 was not Lenin's party, but Bogdanov's. Pokrovskii recalls:

> I first attended the meetings of the literary group attached to the Moscow Committee on 9 April 1905 at P.G. Dauge's flat. Of the others present I can remember, besides I.I. Skvortsov-Stepanov, Rozhkov and Dauge himself, V.D. Bonch-Bruevich and, I think, I.G. Naumov. It was there that I met the now deceased V.L. Shantser (Marat).[21]

It is interesting that the member of this group with whom Pokrovskii formed the closest friendship was Skvortsov-Stepanov, the man who had organised the demonstration against Kliuchevskii in 1894.

According to Skvortsov-Stepanov, the composition of the group was ever changing, but the permanent core was made up of P. Dauge, M.G. Lunts, V.Ia. Kanel', D.I. Kurskii, N.L. Meshcheriakov, V.A. Obukh, K.N. Levin, S.I. Mitskevich, Pokrovskii, Rozhkov. S.Ia. Tseitlin, M.A. Sil'vin (Taganskii), Skvortsov-Stepanov, and, from the middle of 1906, V.M. Shuliatikov.[22]

Skvortsov-Stepanov adds that in 1906, in connection with the 'unification tendencies', there were times when the meetings of the group would be attended by Mensheviks V.G. Groman, and P. Nezhdanov-Cherevanin etc. Those occasions would invariably be marked by barren discussions since the views of the two fractions diverged so sharply as to preclude any possibility of effective cooperation between them. Despite the resolutions of the IV Congress of the Social-Democratic party, the literary-lecturing group remained purely Bolshevik until its demise in 1908.[23]

In the initial stages, the chief activity of the group was giving lectures on current political themes. This had become possible by the spring of 1905, when the confusion in government circles had brought about a *de facto* freedom of assembly, a freedom which was utilized by all social groups alike, without, apparently, any great regard being paid to class differences and antagonisms. Skvortsov-Stepanov relates that from the spring of 1905 the group was able to hold its meetings, not only in the flats of those prominent people with left-wing sympathies, such as Mikhailovskaia-Garina, Firsanov and I.I. Fidler, but even of V.A. Morozova, wife of the great Moscow industrialist. These meetings

---

21   Sokolov 1966, p. 8.
22   Skvortsov-Stepanov 1925, p. 10.
23   ibid.

would be attended by 100–200 people, sometimes as many as 400, and often a charge would be made for entrance, each ticket costing one rouble. The proceeds would be given to the Bolshevik Moscow Committee.[24]

The audience at such gatherings would be largely made up of professional people: teachers, civil servants, doctors, zemstvo workers and liberal writers. Workers, initially at least, would appear rather infrequently, and it was then that the meetings tended to be dispersed by the police.[25]

Prokrovskii recalls:

Late in the spring of 1905 we would already hold meetings quite openly. 'Subversive lectures' were delivered as early as May 1905. I myself had the honour to give one of them on 13 May in the Muisskii Institute ... There was an audience of 250–300 people at the lecture of mine, that being a usual attendance at a public lecture given by a speaker of average popularity. There were tickets being sold and I remember that those responsible for the sale were well satisfied and told me that the Moscow Committee had made a reasonable profit. The subject of my talk was entirely seditious – the history of the revolutionary movement in Russia and the perspectives of the coming revolution. I can well remember how I proved then that the revolution would lead not only to the overthrow of the autocracy – this was accepted by everyone without objection – but to the fall of tsarism in general, and that the awe before the supposed monarchist sentiments which were said to inspire the peasantry was without foundation. This was very sceptically received by the audience, judging from the notes which were passed to me.[26]

Bogdanov did not take part in the activities of the literary-lecturing group, because during the 1905 revolution he was in St Petersburg leading the party organisation in the capital city. Though, as Skvortsov-Stepanov states, the group dispersed in 1908, its core element at least continued to exist in other guises. It supplied the leading members of the anti-Lenin 'Vpered' group, and in February 1917 it was resurrected as the nucleus of the Moscow Soviet.

Having joined the Social-Democratic party, Pokrovskii found himself in disagreement with its leadership. This concerned the tactics of the Bolsheviks at

---

24   Skvortsov-Stepanov 1925, p. 17.
25   Pokrovskii 1925b.
26   ibid.

the conferences which were held in April–June 1905 in connection with the formation of professional unions. There was strong competition between the political parties for control of the emergent unions, and it fell to the lot of Pokrovskii and Rozhkov to represent the Bolsheviks at the two schoolteachers' congresses, one held in Moscow and the other in St Petersburg. In speaking of the congresses Pokrovskii relates:

> We played no 'leading' role there because we declined to enter it when it refused to accept the Social-Democratic programme. At that time this was the directive for all the professional-political unions: to demand that the congress should accept our programme, and if they refused, to shake the dust from our feet – leaving the congress to the mercy of the SRs and the Liberationists, who already at that time were falling into decline.[27]

The reason for such a tactic was to ensure that the workers understood that there was a radical difference between the Social Democrats and the 'bourgeois' parties. If the Social Democrats were to share a platform with the 'bourgeois' parties it might give the impression that they endorsed the bourgeois point of view. Pokrovskii conceded that in the case of some professional unions the tactic might be justified, but he considered it entirely inappropriate at schoolteachers' congresses, where there was a mass of village teachers who were a direct channel to the countryside and to the peasants. Nevertheless, Pokrovskii and Skvortsov-Stepanov succeeded in winning over the Moscow teachers for the Social Democrats, and later, in 1906, Pokrovskii won over the teachers in Vologda, and for a time managed to counteract the influence of the SRs. But at the union congresses, in spite of Pokrovskii and Skvortsov-Stepanov's efforts, the SRs emerged victorious, while the Liberationists ceased to attract support.[28]

Further, Pokrovskii makes some revealing remarks on his attitude to the complex matter of the Bolshevik-Menshevik relations. Apparently he found the tactical collaboration troublesome and would have preferred to see a permanent split between the two wings of the Social-Democratic party. He says:

> … the fractional disputes were of course the most powerful weapon against us in the hands of the SRs who would say to their naive listeners: 'What kind of party is this whose members tear each other to shreds in

---

27   ibid.
28   ibid.

every issue of their newspaper?' To answer the question why we inveighed against the Mensheviks would, I suppose, have been easy, but then to explain why, in spite of this, we remained in the same party with them was much more difficult.[29]

Those were the issues which Pokrovskii raised with Lenin when he travelled to Geneva in June to bring back a load of illegal party literature. Lenin, for his part, listened with great interest to Pokrovskii's account of his work among the Moscow intelligentsia, and invited him to set out his criticisms of party tactics at the professional unions' conference in an article in *Proletarii*. The article which he produced not only throws considerable light on Pokrovskii's political attitudes, but it also contains some indirectly autobiographical material, in that it explains quite clearly how a person could be a liberal one day and a Bolshevik the next. The answer lay in the nature of Russian liberalism itself. Pokrovskii explained:

> The Union of Liberation is not a party, and cannot be such. Among the disparate elements of this non-party there are of course bourgeois democrats, but they are by far the minority. On the other hand, there are all shades of opinions which are close to the Social Democrats and the Socialist Revolutionaries ... .[30]

It was because of this fluid nature of political attitudes among the intelligentsia that Pokrovskii considered the Bolsheviks' hard line to be quite inappropriate. In his opinion:

> From the point of view of propaganda, a serious mistake was made. In front of our speakers there was in essence an amorphous political mass which had very little idea of its own ultimate aims. Yet they [the Bolsheviks] regarded it as Liberationist, as people of a definite bourgeois-liberal frame of mind – they addressed themselves as if to an opponent who had to be defeated and destroyed. Many did not understand what was required of them; they saw only that they were being spoken to 'severely', something which they honestly believed they did not deserve. Hence their accusation of 'narrowness' in the Social Democrats, of 'impatience' and 'tyranny' which one often heard after the first congress, and which

---

29   ibid.
30   Pokrovskii 1905a.

in great measure prepared the atmosphere of the second. The mythical 'Liberationist' did our party an enormous disservice.[31]

At the end of Pokrovskii's article, Lenin added a note expressing some sympathy for Pokrovskii's views but attributing them to political inexperience. According to Lenin:

> Extremes are bad everywhere, but if the choice lay with us, we should prefer narrow and intolerant definiteness to mild and limp diffusiveness. It is only feeble and flabby characters who will be frightened away from us by fear of 'tyranny'. Anyone who has a bit of 'spirit' in him will soon see for himself, and will be shown by events, that clear-cut and sharply expressed political opinions concerning 'mythical' 'Liberation members' are fully justified and that he himself considers this typical Liberation member 'mythical' only because of lack of political experience.[32]

Although Lenin was favourably impressed by Pokrovskii, the feeling was not entirely reciprocated, as Pokrovskii did not consider Lenin's political perspectives at all realistic. He reported:

> Lenin spoke almost exclusively of armed insurrection. I had only just then arrived from Russia, immediately after the most lamentable failure to organise a general strike in Moscow. 'What utopians these foreign leaders are', I used to remark going home along the Geneva streets in the pouring rain after a meeting. 'You can't so much as get our workers to come out on strike, and there he is talking about an armed uprising!'[33]

4   The 1905 Revolution in Moscow

On returning to Russia, however, Pokrovskii was to be won round to Lenin's point of view by the development of events themselves. 'When I got back to Moscow in September', Pokrovskii recalled:

> ... coming back quietly from some meeting of the literary group, I came across a skirmish on, I remember, Tverskoi Boulevard. Cossacks galloped

---

31   ibid.
32   Pokrovskii 1905a; Lenin 1958f-65, p. 177.
33   Pokrovskii 1929a, p. 9.

past me and stones were flying through the air. The crowd was no longer afraid of the Cossacks. This was not the same crowd I had left in June. And yet only a month after this, in October, I myself ended my 'subversive lectures' ... with the slogan: 'Long live the armed uprising!'[34]

However, before the insurrection materialised, Pokrovskii first extended his activities to the field of political journalism. From October 1905 the first legal Social-Democrat newspaper *Novaia zhizn'* began to appear in St Petersburg. In addition to Lenin, Bogdanov and Gorky, its contributors included people who had written for *Pravda* and members of the Moscow literary-lecturing group, such as Rozhkov, Lunacharskii, Bunin and Veresaev. The initiative for publishing an equivalent newspaper in Moscow came from the literary-lecturing group, and this project was approved at a meeting of the party Central Committee held in Gorky's flat at the end of November. Gorky was enthusiastic about the project. He told V.A. Desnitskii:

> A newspaper in Moscow and precisely the kind which the comrades have in mind is very necessary. We must try to win over the intelligentsia and put an end to the dominance of the Moscow liberals ... Pokrovskii, Stepanov and Rozhkov are doing a fine job of work routing them at meetings. It would be excellent if they could continue that useful service in print.[35]

The newspaper in which the offensive against the liberals took place was *Bor'ba*, which appeared weekly from 27 November 1905. The finance for the newspaper was provided by the Moscow publisher S.A. Skirmunt, who was so convinced of the success of the revolution that when he secured premises for *Bor'ba*'s editorial board he took out a five-year lease. Funds were also contributed to the newspaper by the writer N.G. Garin-Mikhailovskii. To overcome bureaucratic and censorship problems Skirmunt undertook to be the newspaper's responsible editor.[36] The actual editorial board of *Bor'ba* consisted entirely of members of the Moscow literary-lecturing group.[37] During

---

34   ibid.
35   Desnitskii 1940, p. 103.
36   ibid.
37   The members of the editorial board are listed on the front page of *Bor'ba*: Pokrovskii, Skvortsov-Stepanov, Rozhkov, Desnitskii, P.G. Dauge, S.I. Chernomordik (P. Larionov), V.Ia. Kanel', D.I. Kurskii, M.G. Lunts, L.L. Nikiforov, M.A. Sil'vin (Taganskii), Lunacharskii, Ol'minskii, A. Bogdanov, V. Bazarov, V. Friche, N. Nikol'skii, S. Suvorov, P. Maslov.

its short life Pokrovskii contributed two articles to *Bor'ba*, 'Marxists who ...' and 'The Revolutionary Bourgeoisie'. It fell to the lot of Pokrovskii as editor in charge to issue the final number of *Bor'ba*, containing a call to armed insurrection.

From its first number, which appeared just a week before the December uprising, the headquarters of *Bor'ba* at the Nikitskii Gates had become an organisational centre for the Moscow proletariat – a fact which did not escape the notice of the Moscow police authorities. The ninth, and last, issue of the newspaper was the most noteworthy. In place of a leading article, it contained the proclamation of the Moscow Committee and Moscow Soviet *To All Workers, Soldiers and Citizens!* with the summons to begin a general political strike and the armed uprising. The document had been distributed to most other Moscow newspapers, but it was published in *Bor'ba* alone. On 8 December the police laid an injunction on *Bor'ba*, and its patron Skirmunt was fined 15,000 roubles and imprisoned for three years.[38]

During the December uprising in Moscow Pokrovskii gave up his flat in the house in Dolgorukov Street to the local militia to use as a first-aid post for the wounded, though, as Pokrovskii recalled, most of the casualties who were brought there were not combatants, but by-standers caught in the crossfire. As it turned out, leaving his flat was a fortunate thing to do, because during the fighting on 9 December the house came under artillery fire, and when it was stormed by troops its owner, I.I. Fidler, was wounded and arrested.[39] After the defeat of the uprising, on 23 December, Pokrovskii was taken into custody and his flat searched, the police having had reports from one of their agents that he had a secret hoard of firearms. The search yielded nothing incriminating, and after a few days Pokrovskii was set free.[40]

Following the demise of *Bor'ba*, the next undertaking of the literary-lecturing group was a collection of articles under the general title of *Tekushchii moment*, which appeared at the end of January 1906. Rozhkov supplied the title and the introductory article, which established the context in which the collection appeared. This was:

> The barricades have been smashed, the shooting has died down, the bodies have been buried, the prison population has been increased, the fires have been put out. Free speech has gone quiet in the press, at meetings,

38   Kuznetsov and Shumakov 1968, pp. 69–70.
39   Levin 1906b, p. 6.
40   Gorelov 1990, p. 302.

gatherings and lectures, and all that is heard are the calls to the black-hundred Duma by the knights of trade and industry of the 17th of October ... .[41]

The armed uprising in Moscow had ended with the formal victory of the government, it was true, but, Rozhkov insisted, the struggle was not over, and the task in hand was to prepare for a new armed insurrection in the light of the lessons that had been learnt.

Pokrovskii submitted two articles to the collection: 'Idealism and the Petty Bourgeoisie' and 'Military Technique and the Question of the Militia'. The first of these was a short polemical essay against ethical objections that had been raised in the Russian press to a socialist revolution. Such objections, Pokrovskii considered, were a sign of the times. While the revolution had triumphed, it had many enthusiastic supporters, but after its defeat these were much less in evidence.

Pokrovskii's other contribution to *Tekushchii moment*, 'Military Technique and the Question of the Militia', was of greater significance. It was inspired by the observation that the insurrectionaries in the December uprising, armed with a few revolvers, had acquitted themselves well against the regular troops equipped with machine-guns and artillery. In a survey of the increasing sophistication of weaponry in modern times, and the corresponding need for more educated soldiers, Pokrovskii argued that the most efficient fighting forces were militias. The Russian army was not efficient or even particularly well disciplined, but it served the government's purpose of quelling internal disturbances. He concluded that the question of political freedom related to that of abolishing the standing army.[42]

Pokrovskii had obviously done some serious research into military affairs, as emerges from a recollection by Meshcheriakov, who got to know Pokrovskii in 1906, when he was a member of the literary-lecturing group. According to Meshcheriakov:

> I dropped in at M.N.'s flat for some reason or other, and I was amazed to see him writing at his work desk, surrounded by all kinds of books – handbooks on the operation of machine-guns, on the construction of some kind of trench, and similar types of military manuals. I asked him: 'Why is all this necessary?' 'Well', he said, 'You see, events have posed the question

41   Rozhkov 1906, p. 3 There is no overall pagination in the volume; all of the articles begin
       from page one.
42   Pokrovskii 1906b.

of an insurrection; an armed insurrection is inevitable, we must prepare ourselves for it, we must study this question.'[43]

Pokrovskii's article earned for him the reputation of something of a military specialist, and as a result he was invited to join the fighting group of the RSDRP's Moscow Committee. Although his theoretical military expertise was never called upon for the intended armed uprising, it did not go to waste. In several articles in *History of Russia in the XIX Century*, such as 'The Crimean War', 'The Conquest of the Caucasus' and 'The Eastern Question', Pokrovskii demonstrates an impressive knowledge of types of weaponry, tactics and military doctrine. Military history was a branch of knowledge for which he clearly had a passion.

Among other noteworthy contributions to *Tekushchii moment* was the essay on 'The Political and Social Views of the Decembrists' by Kirik Levin, with whom Pokrovskii would later collaborate in writing the chapter on the Decembrists in *History of Russia in the XIX Century*. Levin also contributed a day-by-day account of the December uprising in Moscow. Also significant was S.I. Mitskevich's article 'At the Dawn of the Workers' Movement in Moscow', a valuable first-hand source on the history of Social Democracy in Moscow, which the author would republish several times in the Soviet era, and an article by the Latvian Social Democrat Dauge on the peasant movement in the Baltic provinces.

After the December uprising in Moscow and the unrest throughout the country, it had become more difficult to find commercial undertakings who were willing to publish revolutionary tracts. As a result of this, and encouraged by the success of *Tekushchii moment*, each of the authors contributed one third of the royalties he had received to a 'publishing fund' in preparation for the compilation of a new volume, *Voprosy dnia*.[44]

The material for *Voprosy dnia* was ready by April 1906, but due to circumstances 'beyond the control of the publishers' the book did not appear until June. The circumstances in which the collection appeared were characterised by Taganskii's article 'The War of the Ruling Caste against the People', which catalogued the atrocities perpetrated by the government against the peoples of the Russian Empire. Pokrovskii's contribution 'The Victors' was an analysis of the evolution of the Kadet party from the Union of Liberation and the left wing of the zemstvo liberalism. The article contains an element of autobiography,

---

43   *Na boevom postu marksizma* 1929, p. 51.
44   Skvortsov-Stepanov 1925, p. 8.

and one can discern in it why Pokrovskii might have become disillusioned with the liberalism that he had so recently supported. In his opinion, the campaign the liberals conducted against state oppression was not for any high ideal, but merely to bring about a more equitable distribution of rights and privileges within the noble estate.[45]

Yet, however successful and influential these collections might have been, the literary-lecturing group was acutely conscious that they were no real substitute for a regularly published newspaper. The opportunity came in May when, as the revolutionary tide reached new heights, it was again possible to produce a legal newspaper as a successor to *Bor'ba*.

Rozhkov was able to raise funds for the new paper *Svetoch*. It was edited by him and was run by the same members of the group who had edited *Bor'ba*. Its regular contributors were Taganskii, Lunts, Pokrovskii and Ol'minskii. As in all of the group's publications, Skvortsov-Stepanov was one of the chief organisers. Since the main political task of this newspaper was the critique of the First Duma, all the four articles which Pokrovskii contributed to *Svetoch* became the object of a campaign by the police and censors, which led eventually to the confiscation of almost every issue. At the end of May 1906 *Svetoch* disappeared from the scene, or more accurately, from 1 June its name was changed to *Svobodnoe slovo*.[46]

Under this new title the newspaper appeared only four times and carried no articles by Pokrovskii. The reason for this may be easily surmised. The literary-lecturing group had decided to issue a series of pamphlets, 'Lectures and reports on the question of the programme and tactics of Social Democracy'. The third volume in this series was Pokrovskii's pamphlet *Economic Materialism*. The title of the pamphlet, Pokrovskii stated, was chosen to mislead the censor. The censor, however, was not misled, and, noting passages which advocated social revolution and the violent overthrow of the existing order, on 17 July sent a report to the prosecutor to confiscate the book and to arrest those responsible for its publication. At the beginning of August, threatened with arrest, Pokrovskii had to 'disappear over the horizon'. He spent some time in the Caucasus, returning to Moscow in October.[47]

By that time the tactics of the party on the question of participation in the State Duma had changed. It had been decided to take part in the election campaign, and for this purpose to issue a legal weekly newspaper, *Voprosy dnia*. This paper had no greater longevity than its predecessors: its first issue appeared

---

45   Pokrovskii 1906a, p. 6.
46   Kuznetsov and Shumakov 1968, p. 100.
47   Redaktsiia 1932, p. 11.

on 11 November 1906, and the last, on 10 December 1906, making five numbers in all. The editing of this paper was in the hands of Pokrovskii and Skvortsov-Stepanov, aided by Lunts, Taganskii and A.V. Shestakov. The introductory editorial article in the first issue on the contemporary political situation in Moscow was written by Pokrovskii. To No. 3 he contributed the article 'The Opposition Parties: The Constitutional Democrats', and to No. 4, 'Kadets and Capitulation', both of which were an examination of the class composition of the Kadet party. On 13 December 1906 *Voprosy dnia* was closed down by order of the Moscow Department of Justice for its 'subversive activities'. Among the contents of the newspaper upon which this charge was based, pride of place was given to Pokrovskii's editorial in the first issue entitled 'Moscow, 11 November'.[48]

In the by now classic fashion the same newspaper reappeared, this time under the title of *Istina*, even going so far in continuity as to complete some items which *Voprosy dnia* had left unfinished. Of this paper only five numbers appeared, twice monthly, from 14 January to 14 March 1907, and to it Pokrovskii contributed two articles, 'Our Friends on the Right' in No. 1 and 'Mr Kizevetter in Face of the Red Peril' in No. 2.[49]

In the autumn of 1906 Pokrovskii was elected as a delegate to the Fifth Congress of the RSDRP which was held in London in May–June 1907. Before the Congress itself he attended the preparatory meetings of the Bolshevik fraction in Kuokkala in Finland, presided over by Lenin. At the Congress itself Pokrovskii, using the pseudonym of 'Domov', spoke at several of its sessions. The first of these was the discussion on the Congress agenda. Pokrovskii was insistent that the question of armed uprising was the most pressing, and that Congress should pay it the attention it deserved. In the session devoted to discussing the attitude of the RSDRP to the bourgeois parties he gave an analysis of the Russian bourgeoisie that would later be incorporated into his historical writings. It was that:

> Our grande bourgeoisie is not a unified whole. One section has moved to European forms of appropriation, the other, constituting the upper bourgeoisie, is fed by subsidies, by protective tariffs, dues, etc. It still belongs to the category of exploiters of the period of 'primary accumulation'.[50]

Pokrovskii made several forceful speeches against the Mensheviks at the Congress, showing that his sympathies were with the Bolshevik fraction. At a separ-

---

48   Kuznetsov and Shumakov 1968, pp. 110–11.
49   Kuznetsov and Shumakov 1968, p. 113.
50   Iaroslavskii 1935, p. 69, p. 497.

ate meeting of Bolshevik deputies Pokrovskii was elected to the editorial board of *Proletarii*, the Bolshevik newspaper, and to the Bolshevik Centre, which functioned as the clandestine Bolshevik Central Committee.

The Russian authorities were made aware of Pokrovskii's participation in the London Congress, and even of the pseudonym he had used. After Pokrovskii returned from London at the end of May, orders went out for his arrest, and his flat was searched on 2 June. The police officer in charge described what he found there in the protocol of the search. The flat in the former Fidler building, now owned by the 'Rossiia' insurance company, consisted of five rooms, a kitchen, a hall and a toilet. Present were Pokrovskii's wife Liubov', his baby son Iurii, a maid and a student who was staying overnight on the way to the Crimea, but no Pokrovskii. Liubov' denied any knowledge of the whereabouts of her husband.[51] Having seen his spacious accommodation, the police officers must have reflected that Pokrovskii seemed an unlikely revolutionary.

For a time Pokrovskii lived in secret in the outskirts of Moscow, and at the end of August 1907 he moved to Terijoki in the Vyborg province of Finland, which enjoyed a degree of autonomy within the Russian Empire. There he joined other Bolshevik exiles in Finland, living in Kuokkala near the Russian border, among them Lenin, Krupskaia, Bogdanov and his wife Natalia, Rozhkov, I.P. Goldenberg, and I.F. Dubrovinskii. It was at this time that serious disagreements began to emerge between Lenin and Bogdanov on philosophy and on participation in the Duma. At the end of November the Bolshevik colony learnt that the Vyborg province would be placed under martial law and that the tsarist government would empower the Okhrana to conduct searches and arrests of fugitives in Finland. Along with many other Social Democrats and Socialist Revolutionaries, Lenin and Bogdanov left Finland for Western Europe. Pokrovskii helped Lenin leave Kuokkala unobserved by police spies.[52]

Pokrovskii himself contrived to remain in Finland for a further six months. Together with Goldenberg he tried to arrange the publication of a party journal in St Petersburg but was unsuccessful. He did manage to engage in his academic work, spending days on end at the Helsingfors public library. In this period Pokrovskii wrote chapters for the multi-volume work *Russia in the XIX Century*. He had been invited by the Granat publishers to take part in this project in 1904, both to write chapters, and to edit the volumes. He expressed his delight at the invitation in a letter to his wife on 25 September of that year. In all, Pokrovskii contributed 11 chapters to the book, comprising more than 700 pages. He had

51   Redaktsiia 1932, p. 6.
52   Chernobaev 1992, p. 47.

to find time for his writing when not involved in the hectic events of the 1905 revolution. Some of the chapters were written in 1907 when he was in hiding from the police in the outskirts of Moscow. 'I never worked so hard as in these "illegal" months', he later recalled. 'I had to keep my nose to the grindstone and sit down and write'.[53]

In Finland Pokrovskii was constantly threatened by arrest, and in August 1908 he was warned by a friendly Finnish police officer that this was imminent. On 28 August, three days before he was to be apprehended, Pokrovskii, Liubov' and Iurii sailed on a British steamer to Stockholm, and from there made their way to Berlin. While in Berlin Liubov''s health deteriorated, and she was forced to return to Moscow to recuperate. Pokrovskii and Iurii went on to Paris, where they were joined by Liubov' eighteen months later.[54]

5   *Economic Materialism*

Two years after the publication of his review of Rickert's book, in 1906, Pokrovskii expounded his conception of the Marxist interpretation of history in a popular pamphlet entitled *Economic Materialism*. The pamphlet was the third volume in the series 'Lectures and reports on the question of the programme and tactics of Social Democracy'. Between 1906 and 1924 it was republished six times. *Economic Materialism* was intended for a mass audience and is correspondingly written in an accessible form, though it does contain some complex philosophical ideas. It is an important work for the study of Pokrovskii's intellectual development, and contains some themes which would reappear in his later writings.

One can discern in *Economic Materialism* a number of distinct elements:

1)   Knowledge gained from researching his contributions to *Readings in Medieval History* and the chapters for the *Beseda* volumes.

2)   Arguments deployed in the review of Rickert's book published in *Pravda*.

3)   The Marxist texts with which Pokrovskii was familiar, notably the *Communist Manifesto*. From reading *Economic Materialism* one has the impression that the works of Marx and Engels do not form its essential core, and that these works are interpreted in the light of Positivist philosophy, that of Ernst Mach in particular. As regards the pamphlet's title, Pokrovskii stated in 1930:

---

53   Chernobaev 1992, pp. 48, 51.
54   Chernobaev 1992, p. 57.

You know very well that 'economic materialism' was a censor's term for
Marxism, a censor's label which we used in the days of the first revolution. At that time I entitled my pamphlet *Economic Materialism* precisely
because the censor doubtless would have allowed neither 'Marxism' nor
'historical materialism' to pass. The censorship could already distinguish
between terms. Why was this title acceptable? Because this was Marxism
minus dialectics, i.e. Marxism minus revolution. Such a purely economic
interpretation of the historical process was in itself quite acceptable to
the tsarist censor.[55]

The censorship motive may be partly the reason for the title of the pamphlet, but this is almost certainly not the chief one. 'Economic materialism' was
then the generally accepted synonym for Marxism, both in revolutionary and
in learned publications. It was improbable, therefore, that the censor would be
greatly deceived. As late as 1922 Nechkina could entitle her study of Marxist
historiography *Russian History in the Light of Economic Materialism*.

In fact, a discussion of the terms 'economic materialism', 'historical materialism' and 'Marxism' is the way Pokrovskii begins his pamphlet. He states:

'Economic' or 'historical materialism' is that conception of history by
which the chief, the predominant, significance is attached to the economic structure of society, and all historical changes are explained by
the influence of material circumstances, the material needs of man. This
concept of history was enunciated in a fully developed form in the Communist Manifesto written by Marx and Engels in 1847. Therefore economic materialism is still often called 'Marxism'.[56]

But, Pokrovskii hastens to add that these two concepts – 'economic' or 'historical materialism' and 'Marxism' – are not entirely identical. The difference is
that whereas it is possible for a peaceful evolutionist to be an economic materialist, Marx and Engels called for a social revolution. They viewed history not
as a peaceful development, but as a struggle – a constant ruthless struggle
– between classes. 'Marxism', therefore, was more complex than 'economic
materialism': it not only explained history according to economic factors but
represented these economic factors in the definite form of the class struggle.
Marxism was the 'revolutionary historical materialism', as distinct from the
peaceful evolutionary economism espoused by many bourgeois writers.

---

55   *Trudy pervoi vsesoiuznoi konferentsii istorikov-marksistov* 1930, p. 302.
56   Pokrovskii 1920, p. 3.

Thus, for Pokrovskii, what distinguishes Marxism from 'economic materialism' is the combination of the economic interpretation of history with the doctrine of the class struggle as the moving force of history. But, Pokrovskii points
out, Marxism is not unique in this combination. Long before the *Communist
Manifesto* was written, over 300 years ago, the Italian writer Niccolo Machiavelli
explained the changes in the political structure of his native Florence by economic causes – and precisely by the class struggle. In Pokrovskii's view, the early
economic maturity of Florence accounted for the maturity of Machiavelli as a
writer. Although a pioneering work in the field of social science, Machiavelli's
Florentine Histories were not appreciated by contemporaries, and remained
known only to specialist historians. The *Florentine Histories* were of course
known to Pokrovskii through his research for the chapter on 'The Rule of the
Medicis in Florence' for *Readings in Medieval History*.

From Machiavelli Pokrovskii traced the materialist approach to history
through Descartes, Hobbes, Spinoza to Holbach, who in his *System of Nature*
argued that if one knew the past and understood the laws which governed
human history, one could predict the future. Pokrovskii included Kant among
those thinkers who viewed human affairs in a materialist light. Using the statistics that had been collected on such things as the growth in population,
criminality, mortality etc. Kant found that one could predict in which month
there would be the most suicides, and in which the least. He concluded that
the force driving historical development was the struggle for survival. In Pokrovskii's view, Kant had come close to the 'economic interpretation of history'. From his survey of intellectual history Pokrovskii could state that: 'the
ideas of the *Communist Manifesto* are deeply rooted in that view of the world
which came to replace medieval Catholicism in the XVII and XVIII centuries'.[57]

But, Pokrovskii enquired, if economic materialism was so in keeping with
the march of human progress, why had it not become the main interpretation of history? Despite all the scientific progress of the past century, not a
year passed without the appearance of some book saying how narrow and
inadequate the economic interpretation of history was. What motivated the
opposition to economic materialism was the class interest of the bourgeoisie
to maintain its dominant economic position. It opposed materialism in the
same way that the feudal regime had opposed the cosmology of Copernicus
and Galileo. The feudal aristocracy wished to believe that serfdom was eternal,
and the bourgeoisie wished to be assured that private property would never be

---

57   Pokrovskii 1920, p. 7.

abolished. Whereas the feudal lords had found their ideological support in the Catholic church, the bourgeoisie found its in idealist philosophy.

Pokrovskii did not intend to dwell on the philosophical (epistemological) bases of idealism; he was concerned with its application to history. The tactic of historical idealism was to detach the human personality from the connected mechanical causality of the world process. In this way some authors – here Pokrovskii has Rickert in mind – completely deny the possibility of making human history a science. They agree that a poorly developed personality, like a peasant or a worker, can be the subject of science. But the personalities of a university professor or a highly paid banker are above the laws of scientific history, which are only obligatory for inferior beings.

From Pokrovskii's point of view, the history of the formation of general concepts provided convincing proof of the validity of economic materialism. This was because the formation of general concepts was determined by 'interest', be this personal or class. As he explained: every generalisation presupposes a choice from a variegated mass of reality of what is 'necessary' for us. What determines this choice? This was explained by the French scholar Théodule Ribot: 'It must not be forgotten that perception is pre-eminently a practical operation, that its mainspring is interest or utility, and that in consequence we neglect – i.e. leave in the field of obscure consciousness – whatever at the moment concerns neither our desires nor our purposes'.[58] To illustrate this point Pokrovskii added:

> For a vet, horses are divided into those that are healthy and those that are sick, for a riding master – into placid and restive, for a sportsman – into fast and slow, for an artist – into beautiful and ugly. And each of them looks on a horse from their own point of view. The vet's description of a horse would be of no use to an artist. We see only what our attention is directed to: and the direction of our attention is always adapted to a given purpose – there is no such thing as disinterested attention.[59]

Pokrovskii stressed that the economic interpretation of social phenomena by no means exhausted the thought of Marx and Engels. This was only the *statics* of Marxism; its *dynamics* was the theory of class struggle as the driving force of history. It was in the dynamics of Marxism that Pokrovskii thought that its dialectical character, its Hegelian heritage, consisted.

---

58   Ribot 1899, p. 4.
59   Pokrovskii 1920, p. 16.

Pokrovskii found the concept of class struggle particularly useful for explaining the actions of the state, which he regarded as an instrument of the class struggle. This was a logical extension of the campaign he had conducted in his *Beseda* articles against the idea of a 'supra-class state', that historians such as Chicherin propounded. In *Economic Materialism* he contests the anarchist Peter Kropotkin's contention that the city states of the past were democratic institutions. Pokrovskii demonstrates that this was not the case by once again drawing on his knowledge of Florentine history derived from Machiavelli. In the case of monarchies that had newly arisen out of social conflict, he shows the class character of the regimes of Henry IV and Louis Bonaparte in France, and Cromwell in England. As for traditional monarchies of the feudal era, the connection of these with the nobility was so obvious that it had not been denied by most bourgeois historians.

The subject of monarchs led Pokrovskii to the question of the role of the individual in history. For if an individual person, such as Bonaparte, Cromwell, or Henry IV, could act as some kind of regulator of social relations, it implied that such a person could introduce something of 'their own' into the course of history. In that case 'historical determinism' would have its limitations, and individuals could influence the course of history.

Pokrovskii conceded that of course history acted through the mediacy of people; that if there were no people, no human individuals, there could be no history. But every feature in the character of some historical actor or other could be explained from the general conditions of the age in which they lived. Napoleon I, for example, hated England. All his foreign policy revolved around one main task: to crush the 'perfidious Albion'. This was his individual peculiarity. But if one looked at the general sweep of France's foreign policy from the end of the seventeenth century, one could see that a constant theme was hostility towards England. The interests of France and England in the realm of foreign policy were diametrically opposed through colonial rivalry. On colonial enterprises, moreover, the capitalism of the time grew. Hence, Pokrovskii could argue that Napoleon and other historical individuals were not unique, and, albeit indirectly, reflected the material processes of the times. In this way his approach to the individual and the unique in history was the exact opposite of Rickert's.

Although *Economic Materialism* is ostensibly a pamphlet intended to popularise Marxism, it is clear that Pokrovskii only partially at best owes his historical conceptions to the writings of Marx and Engels. These have come largely from Pokrovskii's own researches in Russian and medieval history, and from the arguments deployed in justification of a constitutional regime in Russia. The philosophical dimension of the pamphlet comes principally from his debate with Rickert on the pages of *Pravda*.

One might have expected that a writer on the Marxist interpretation of history would sift through the works of Marx and Engels and attempt to reconstruct what their doctrine on history was, as later generations of Marxologists were to do. Pokrovskii did not do this, and for two main reasons. One was that the few writings by Marx and Engels that were available to him by 1906, and which he mentions in his pamphlet, gave a poor insight into what a 'Marxist' interpretation of history might be. It was only in the 1930s that writings such as *The German Ideology* and the *Grundrisse* became available.

The other reason was that in 1906 Pokrovskii would feel no compulsion to make his ideas conform to those of Marx and Engels. The requirement of 'orthodoxy' was the product of a later period in history of Bolshevism. In 1894 Peter Struve had set the tone by proposing to supplement the perceived lack of a philosophical dimension in Marx's doctrines with neo-Kantianism. For writers of Pokrovskii's generation, the ideas of Marx and Engels were elements which might be used in combination with others. His associates on the editorial board of *Pravda*, Lunacharskii, Bogdanov, Bazarov, did exactly that. Bogdanov in fact was insistent that the writings of Marx and Engels, or indeed those of anyone else, should not be regarded as 'authorities' and their opinions taken as gospel. The idea that one should make one's theoretical writings conform with some other writer's works would never have entered Pokrovskii's head in 1906.

Exile

1   Vpered

The assumption behind the publications of the literary-lecturing group had been that the defeat of the December uprising in Moscow was a temporary retreat for the revolution, and the task ahead was to prepare for an armed uprising against the tsarist regime. Lenin's perspective, however, was entirely different. In an article entitled 'Against the Boycott' published in June 1907 he argued that the tactic of boycott of the Duma was the correct one while the revolution was on the ascendancy, as had been the case during the year 1905. But in the subsequent period 1906–1907, beginning with the defeat of the December uprising, the revolutionary tide had receded, and in the new circumstances the boycott tactic was no longer appropriate.[1]

In July 1907 the RSDRP had held a conference in the Finnish town of Kotka where the tactic of participation in the Duma was debated. All the members of the Bolshevik delegation were in favour of boycotting the Third Duma, with the exception of Lenin. Bogdanov's argument for retaining the boycott echoed the views of the literary-lecturing group. This was that all the factors which had brought about the 1905 revolution continued to operate. The disconnect between the political structure of the country and the demands of its economic development still existed. The ruination of the peasantry and the impoverishment of the proletariat remained as before. Moreover, the forces of the revolution had not been fundamentally weakened and were being gathered for a new and decisive revolutionary struggle.

Lenin, however, was of the opinion that the period 1906–1907 had been one in which the reaction advanced and the revolution retreated. In these conditions to continue with the boycott would be pointless. He consequently urged that the party participate both in the election campaign and in the Duma itself. In order to avoid the adoption of the resolution proposed by the Mensheviks and the Bund, the Bolsheviks, with the support of the Poles and Latvians, passed Lenin's resolution. In this way the Bolshevik fraction committed itself, against its will, to participation in the elections and the proceedings of the Third Duma. In a separate statement the Bolshevik delegates made it plain that

---

1   Lenin 1958a–65, pp. 1–36.

they considered the decision to end the boycott mistaken and explained that they had only voted for Lenin's resolution as the lesser evil.[2]

Pokrovskii was not present at the Kotka conference, but he was a delegate to the conference that was held in Helsingfors in November 1907 where the performance of the Social-Democratic fraction in the Duma was discussed. This served to confirm the forebodings of those who had favoured the boycott. The need to form alliances with other opposition groups in the Duma prevented the fraction from following consistent Social-Democratic policies. Moreover, since the Duma fraction was mostly Menshevik in composition, it would not willingly subordinate itself to the demands of the predominantly Bolshevik Central Committee. From this situation two schools of thought emerged among the Bolsheviks: one was that the fraction should be issued with an ultimatum, to follow party policy; the other was that if the fraction did not submit to the directives of the Central Committee, it should be recalled. Lenin objected vehemently both to the 'ultimatumists' and the 'recallers' (*otzovisty*), and defended the Duma fraction.

In April 1909 Pokrovskii was summoned to Paris for a session of the Bolshevik Centre. The message he received was in invisible ink, and not all of it was legible, so he did not know when the meeting was to take place. In order not to miss it he left for Paris immediately. On arrival, however, he discovered that the meeting would be in June. It was impossible for him to wait for three months in Paris, but he took the opportunity to discuss the question of Duma participation with Bogdanov supporters. As Krupskaia wrote to one of her correspondents: 'Today Domov came: he saw Nikolai Nikolaevich and Cherepnin. He has been sufficiently stuffed by them with all kinds of gossip, but he still has to find his feet ... It is a pity that there are no protocols. Obviously, it was "they" who invited him'.[3]

Pokrovskii made use of his time in Paris to make his views known to Lenin. He recalled:

> I went to Il'ich and had a long talk with him – perhaps the longest talk I ever had with him. I pointed out that the course on which he had embarked would lead straight into the marsh of reformism and revisionism, that he was pushing the Russian workers away from revolution towards Bernsteinism. Il'ich replied that Russian history completely guaranteed the Russian worker against such a turn of events. 'In Russia', he

2   Institut marksizma-leninizma pri TsK KPSS 1983, pp. 290–8.
3   Sokolov 1963, p. 33.

said, 'class contradictions are so sharp that one can rest assured that the Russian worker will never follow the reformists'. At the same time he defended the legal press and the Duma fraction. 'We shall make use of the Duma', he said. I was unable to agree with him, and went off to join the Vpered group.[4]

In a letter to I.F. Dubrovinskii dated 23 April 1909 Lenin gave his version of the encounter. He began by saying: 'Pokrovskii came to visit us. A philistine of the purest water'. Lenin then gave the gist of what Pokrovskii had said. This was:

Of course otzovism is nonsense, of course it is syndicalism, but for moral considerations both I, and probably Skvortsov-Stepanov, will be on the side of Bogdanov.[5]

Lenin implies that Bogdanov advocated recalling the Social Democrat deputies from the Duma, which he did not. But otherwise, Lenin's account of the conversation has the ring of truth. Both Pokrovskii and Skvortsov-Stepanov were close associates of Bogdanov from 1903 and would naturally take his side against Lenin.

A casualty of the disagreements between Pokrovskii and Lenin was a projected two-volume Bolshevik history of the 1905 revolution. Lenin had written to Pokrovskii in Finland proposing that he write such a work, and when he was in Paris Pokrovskii presented Lenin with the outline of the book. Pokrovskii recalled:

In 1909, when in Paris, I composed a plan for the projected two-volume work. I must admit that it did not meet with Lenin's approval – and rightly so. Two ideas were developed in the plan: the first of these was not my own; it was that each social class makes its own revolution. This idea was quite widespread amongst us in those days ... The second idea for this abortive plan was that the Russian revolution could only be successful as a socialist revolution. This idea was connected with the first one. I did not say that a bourgeois revolution was impossible, but I predicted that it was doomed to failure, because, it seemed to me, all the cards of the bourgeois revolution had been played in 1905.[6]

---

4 Pokrovskii 1929a, p. 15.
5 Lenin 1958d-65, p. 174.
6 Pokrovskii 1925d, pp. 3–4.

The plan for a Bolshevik history of 1905 was abandoned, leaving the field to the Mensheviks, who, by 1907, had already produced four monograph studies on the social forces in the Russian revolution, and would go on to publish the four-volume *The Social Movement in Russia at the Beginning of the xx Century* between 1909 and 1914.[7] It is unlikely that Pokrovskii had any regrets about the abandonment of the project; his time was entirely taken up with the completion of the chapters for *History of Russia in the xix Century*.

In an attempt to bring forward the meeting of the Bolshevik Centre, on 21 April Pokrovskii, Bogdanov and Shantser sent a letter to the editorial board of *Proletarii* demanding the immediate convocation of the available members of the Bolshevik Centre to decide when the plenum of the BC should be held. The reply came in a letter signed by Kamenev, Lenin, Zinoviev and Taratuta, saying that the plenum would take place at the appointed time – in June. The exchange served to exacerbate the animosity between the Bogdanov and Lenin camps.[8]

The need for Pokrovskii to return to Finland caused him to miss the meeting of the Bolshevik Centre, which took place between 21 and 30 June, in the guise of the extended editorial board of *Proletarii*. For his alleged support of otzovism and ultimatumism Bogdanov was expelled from the Bolshevik Centre.

On 16 July Pokrovskii, along with Bogdanov, Krasin and Shantser, circulated a pamphlet entitled *Report to the Comrade Bolsheviks of the Expelled Members of the Expanded Editorial Board of Proletarii*, which analysed the factors that had brought about Bogdanov's expulsion. The authors recalled that at the Kotka conference only Lenin was in favour of participation in the Duma, the Bolshevik contingent being outvoted. Since that time the pro-Duma current among the Bolsheviks had transformed what should have been a question of tactics into a matter of principle. They had made Duma activity the main focus of party life, and adopted the quasi-Menshevik standpoint of 'parliamentarianism at any price'. The result had been a split in the party and a frenzied struggle against the otzovists. The authors declared that they regarded Bogdanov's expulsion as illegal, since he had been elected to the Bolshevik Centre at the Fifth Congress of the RSDRP.[9]

In the spring of 1909 Bogdanov was occupied organising the party school for workers on the island of Capri, where Maxim Gorky lived at the time. The need for such a school arose from the fact that, following the defeat of the 1905

---

7   On the Menshevik historiography of 1905 see Thatcher 2021.
8   Sokolov 1970, p. 68.
9   White 2019, p. 233.

revolution there had been an exodus from the ranks of the party, both of workers and intellectual elements. The exodus of the latter was especially felt in all party organisations because they had acted as secretaries, treasurers, propagandists and agitators. With their departure these functions had been taken over by the workers themselves, who felt the need to acquire more knowledge and training to carry out these essential party tasks.

Bogdanov took up this cause with enthusiasm because it was entirely in keeping with his view that it was essential to prepare the workers for the next revolutionary upsurge, which must inevitably come. Conversely, it was contrary to the opinion, held by Lenin, that the revolutionary tide had subsided, and that the chief focus of the party should be on parliamentary tactics. It was through this conflict of political perspectives that the project of training some workers in a party school generated such bitter controversy. The school was also being organised at a time when Bogdanov was suspected of planning to establish a new Social-Democratic fraction to rival the Bolsheviks, and it was believed that the party school for workers would be a convenient platform from which to launch it.[10]

At the beginning of August 1909, the First Higher Social-Democratic Propagandist and Agitational School began to function. It had 15 workers from Russia, with an additional 12 émigré workers living on Capri who planned to return to Russia and engage in party work. The lecturers were Bogdanov, Lunacharskii, Liadov, Gorky, Aleksinskii and Desnitskii. Invitations were sent to several prominent figures in the workers' movement, including Lenin, Trotsky, Plekhanov, Rosa Luxemburg and D.B. Riazanov, but only Pokrovskii agreed to attend. He taught a course on the history of Russia.[11]

One of the students, V.M. Kosarev, recalled that Pokrovskii gave seven lectures on Russian history in all. 'Always witty, talented and simple, he explained to us the incomprehensible, far-off events and their significance, adopting the Marxist approach in explaining the course of social events in old Russia'.[12]

Although most of the students were in sympathy with Bogdanov and his associates, a minority were Leninists, causing tension between the two groups. Lenin, for his part, did what he could to foment dissension among the students and disrupt the functioning of the school, which he accused of forming a new political fraction whose ideological inspiration was 'otzovism' and 'god-building'.

---

10   White 2019, pp. 225–6.
11   Livshits 1924, p. 58.
12   Kosarev 1922, p. 71.

In view of the deep division in the party, Bogdanov's supporters among the lecturers and students of the school decided to form themselves into an ideological group, whose main task was to campaign for the restoration of Bolshevik unity. The group, which took the name 'Vpered', drew up a Platform, which set out its assessment of the current situation of the country and the prospects for revolution. It was in the Platform of 'Vpered' that Bogdanov first introduced his conception of proletarian culture. Although Pokrovskii put his name to the Platform, it is probable that even at this stage he had his reservations about proletarian culture. He later wrote that 'when at the extended meeting of the *Proletarii* editorial board Bogdanov was expelled from the party and formed the 'Vpered' group, I joined the group with the reservation that I subscribed to its political programme only in part'.[13]

Among the questions discussed by the RSDRP Central Committee when it met in Paris in January 1910 was that of party schools for workers. Recognising the success of the school on Capri, the Central Committee resolved to establish a second school, but this time organised by the entire party, rather than by the 'Vpered' group alone. For this purpose, a nine-member School Commission was set up, with representatives from the Bolsheviks, Mensheviks, Poles, Latvians, the Jewish Bund and the 'Vpered' group. The 'Vpered' group was represented by Pokrovskii and G.A. Aleksinskii. However, as the Central Committee allocated a miserly amount of money to finance the school, suggesting it did not take the undertaking seriously, Pokrovskii and Aleksinskii left the School Commission and joined other members of the 'Vpered' group in making arrangements to hold a party school for workers in Bologna.

The school, which opened on 21 November 1910, had better success in securing people from outside the 'Vpered' group, such as Trotsky, Alexandra Kollontai, P.P. Maslov and M.P. Pavlovich, to come and lecture to the students. On this occasion Russian history was divided between two lecturers: I.M. Kheraskov gave 9 lectures on the pre-Petrine period, while Pokrovskii gave 6 on the period from Peter I to the liberation of the peasants in 1861. Pokrovskii would of course have abundant material for these lectures from his work on *History of Russia in the XIX Century*.[14]

As with the Capri school, Lenin attempted to disrupt the school at Bologna, and tried to discredit it by hinting to the editors of the Menshevik publication *Golos Sotsial-Demokrata*, that the school had been financed by 'expropriations', the proceeds of bank robberies. Bogdanov and Lunacharskii wrote to the journal to give their assurances that the story was a fabrication.

---

13   Sokolov 1970, pp. 69–70.
14   White 2019, pp. 264–8.

Although ostensibly a non-fractional institution, the party school organised at Longjumeau near Paris in the summer of 1911 was largely a Bolshevik affair since a majority of the lecturers and students were Bolsheviks. For appearances' sake some members of the 'Vpered' group were invited to lecture at Longjumeau. Lunacharskii accepted the invitation and lectured on the history of Russian art and history. Pokrovskii, on the other hand, refused on principle to participate. This would not be forgotten in Soviet times when Pokrovskii came under attack.

It had been the intention of the 'Vpered' group to publish a popular newspaper for workers, but as the group did not have the financial resources to put this into practice, its publication activities extended only to some pamphlets and a few issues of the journal *Vpered*. In the 1910 issue of *Vpered* Pokrovskii published an article on 'The Finnish Question', in which he accused the tsarist government of abolishing the Finnish constitution in revenge for the help the Finns gave to Russian revolutionaries. Here of course Pokrovskii could draw on his own personal experience of seeking refuge in the Grand Duchy after the defeat of the 1905 revolution.[15]

To the 1911 issue of *Vpered* Pokrovskii contributed the long article 'The Peasant Reform of 19 February 1861: For the fiftieth anniversary'[16] This was the second work Pokrovskii had written on the history of the 1861 reform, the first one being for the *History of Russia in the XIX Century*. A comparison of these two works reveals a progression in Pokrovskii's thinking. Whereas the early one is almost purely factual in its approach, the second one provides a broader historical context, and supplies an economic motivation for events. It is probably the interpretation of 1861 that Pokrovskii presented in his lectures in Bologna and would later give in his *Russian History from the Earliest Times*.

In the 1910 issue of *Vpered* Bogdanov developed the concept of proletarian culture that he had outlined in the 'Vpered' Platform. His argument was that although the complete socialist transformation of society could only be achieved following a proletarian revolution, the element of socialism that could develop within the existing capitalist society was socialism's most essential element – comradely cooperation. In Bogdanov's view, this was the prototype of socialism, its real beginning. The more it grew and developed within the confines of capitalist society, the more acutely it would come into conflict with the capitalist system. These conflicts would culminate in a series of revolutions that would lead to the establishment of a socialist society.[17]

15   Pokrovskii 1910, pp. 10–15.
16   Pokrovskii 1911.
17   Bogdanov 1990, pp. 99–103.

Bogdanov's ideas on proletarian culture were contested in the same number of *Vpered*, by S. Vol'skii, who found Bogdanov's conception of the working class completely divorced from reality. Pokrovskii was also critical of Bogdanov's conception of proletarian culture. In November 1910 he wrote to Bogdanov protesting that:

> If in the Platform there were incautious expressions such as 'proletarian science' and elements of socialism in the present, now there appears an article specially devoted to this, where the same unfortunate expressions are repeated in a widely disseminated way and with deadly clarity.

In other letters Pokrovskii described Bogdanov's article 'Socialism of the Present' as 'revisionist'. On the insistence of Pokrovskii, Aleksinskii and V.P. Menzhinskii, the 'Vpered' group adopted a resolution declaring that 'proletarian culture and science' were not the views of the journal's editorial board. This, however, did not prevent Pokrovskii from resigning from the group in May 1911.[18]

One can infer that what was objectionable to Pokrovskii about Bogdanov's conception of proletarian culture was that it implied that there could not be a proletarian revolution until such times as the working class had developed its own culture and its own science. The time required for this to take place could be enormous. This was something that Bogdanov could countenance, but not Pokrovskii, who thought of the socialist revolution as being 3–4 years away.

Dissatisfaction with the concept of proletarian culture was not the only reason for Pokrovskii's leaving the 'Vpered' group. He also disliked its sectarianism and paranoia. As he explained in 1925:

> My personal joining the 'Vpered' group was motivated not so much by disagreements with Lenin's political line as circumstances of a more organisational character – because of course a dispute about the time scale of the coming revolution alone was too little to cause a rift. I joined the 'Vperedists', as many others did, assuming that by doing this I would preserve the link with those sections of our party which were freest from any suspicions, and which also set out to achieve objectives for the whole party. As soon as I saw that the fabled 'party school' was nothing more than a fractional 'Vperedist' pen, and that, as far as the clearing out

---

18   Kin 1929, pp. 388–9.

of police spies was concerned, Bogdanov was every bit as bad as his opponents – I shook the dust from my feet and had nothing more to do with 'Vpered' from the spring of 1911.[19]

It is probable that a number of considerations influenced Pokrovskii both in joining and in leaving the 'Vpered' group. But by 1925 the political climate was such that he would feel it expedient to emphasise his more principled differences with the 'Vperedists'. In 1920 Lenin instigated a campaign to discredit Bogdanov and his ideas, which culminated in Bogdanov's arrest and imprisonment by the OGPU in 1923. Subsequently Bogdanov was generally referred to disparagingly in Soviet publications, when he was mentioned at all. In Soviet times Pokrovskii was not usually forthcoming about his association with Bogdanov. However, when Bogdanov died in 1928 Pokrovskii's obituary in the *Bulletin of the Communist Academy* acknowledged Bogdanov as one of the outstanding philosophers Russia had ever produced.[20]

2   Writing Russian History

Pokrovskii's exile in Paris began in September 1909. Life in France did not impress him very favourably. In 1924 he wrote that it was only at this time, when he saw Western democracy in practice, that his liberal illusions were shattered. On the whole he found that France compared rather unfavourably with the Russia he had left.[21]

In Paris Pokrovskii's chief activity, and also his main means of livelihood, was the writing of his major work *Russian History from the Earliest Times*. While still living in Finland, P.N. Sakulin, a specialist in the history of Russian literature and a contributor to *History of Russia in the XIX Century*, had put him in touch with the recently established 'Mir' publishing firm based in Moscow. 'Mir' intended to publish a book on Russian history for self-study, with an exposition of the facts, with general evaluations illuminating individual periods and 'revealing their basic mechanisms', written in an interesting and lively fashion. The 'Mir' publishers preferred the book to be written by Marxists who were specialists in the relevant fields. The kind of book that 'Mir' had in mind was one that would compete with Kliuchevskii's *Course of Russian History*. Pokrovskii

---

19   Morozova 2020, p. 205.
20   Pokrovskii 1928a.
21   Pokrovskii 1924d, p. 210.

undertook to take charge of the project and to do most of the work; he would
select topics to write himself, and delegate a few others to his associates. It was
eventually agreed that N.M. Nikol'skii would contribute a section on the history
of religion and the church, and that V.K. Agafonov would supply an introductory historico-geographical chapter on 'The Great Russian Plain in the Past'.

Although Pokrovskii was enthusiastic about 'Mir''s project, he did not agree
with some aspects of the book's specification. Whereas 'Mir' wanted the book to
set out the facts of Russian history, Pokrovskii resisted this factual approach. He
was more inclined to favour the thematic approach that Miliukov had adopted
in his *History of Russian Culture*. Pokrovskii argued that those who read for self-
study could acquaint themselves with the basic facts of Russian history from
any good textbook. In support of his contention Pokrovskii could draw upon
his teaching experience. He told the publisher:

> As a former lecturer and participant in various 'self-education institu-
> tions' like the 'Commission for Home Reading' I know from experience
> that this audience values 'a holistic approach to the world'. Nor have I ever
> noticed in it any special affection for a recital of facts.[22]

'Mir' was reluctant to accept that students who wanted to know the facts of
Russian history would have to consult a textbook, but in this matter Pokrovskii
largely got his way. Nevertheless, even after the publication of the first volumes,
the problem of the book's lack of appeal to the general reader had arisen in correspondence between Pokrovskii and 'Mir' in November 1911. Pokrovskii's reply
was:

> To a certain extent I cannot but agree with such reproaches. But the prob-
> lem is not because I cannot write in a popular way, but entirely due to
> the circumstances I am working in: the complete lack of groundwork for
> a general materialist course in literature, so that in many cases I have to
> carry out original research work, the rapidity of the writing itself (to write
> clearly and concisely and to write quickly, are mutually exclusive), finally
> to the scale of the book itself: you cannot write 5 volumes in the style of a
> textbook for senior pupils, and you cannot fill it up with anecdotes in the
> style of Waliszewski.[23]

---

22   Gukovskii 1968a, p. 125.
23   Gukovskii 1968b, p. 135.

Another point of contention between Pokrovskii and 'Mir' was on the physical character of the book. 'Mir' intended that the book's five volumes should be purchased by subscription, that it should be luxuriously bound and printed on good-quality paper, and that it should be richly illustrated. Pokrovskii objected that this kind of publication would be beyond the means of the kind of self-study audience that the book was meant to cater for. On these matters, however, the publishers had their way.

In his letter to Ol'minskii of 22 September 1909 Pokrovskii complained that it was an unfavourable time to be publishing books:

> The old intelligent readership is completely scattered – some in prison, some in emigration, some holed up in some god-forsaken corner, and don't want to see the light of day. A new kind of consumer has emerged, one who takes up a book for its appearance: that it should be thick, that it should have illustrations, that its binding should be 'sumptuous'. They sit it on a shelf and imagine that they have become educated people. The Granat Brothers, 'Mir' and others live more and more at the expense of these people – and the likes of us have to prostitute ourselves, act as fodder for such editions, in the secret hope that maybe this readership has children, and that the young people, even of the bourgeoisie, will not be lacking in the signs of humanity.[24]

Pokrovskii's jaundiced view of the book's illustrations belied their role in increasing the educational value of the book. Whereas *History of Russia in the XIX Century* had featured sepia portraits of historical figures of the times, *Russian History* had monochrome reproductions of paintings, mainly from the Tret'iakov and Rumiantsev Galleries in Moscow. The illustrations often depicted scenes from Russian social life of the particular period. They were chosen and provided with explanatory comments by V.M. Storozhev. The illustrations were a distinct asset to the book.

Contrary to Pokrovskii's forebodings, the sales of the book exceeded all expectations and 'Mir' was satisfied with the swift rise in subscriptions. The first volume came out at the beginning of 1910, and subsequent volumes appeared in succeeding years. Pokrovskii was entitled to five author's copies, and their distribution gives good indication of which personal relationships he most valued. Copies went to his mother, his wife, Skvortsov-Stepanov, Bogdanov's wife Natalia and Ol'minskii. Of Ol'minskii he said:

---

24   Chernobaev 1992, p. 69.

This is an old Marxist author who has for some reason relinquished his pseudonym which, therefore, I shall not mention, and under his own name wrote the book *The State, Absolutism and Bureaucracy in Russian History*. Here, without mentioning my name, he fearfully attacked my articles in *History of Russia in the XIX Century*. He sent me his book, and I should like to repay him, especially since he is one of the very few Marxist historians of Russia.[25]

The work on *Russian History* was extremely arduous, and complicated by the lack of resources on Russian history in the Bibliothèque Nationale in Paris. But the popularity of the book and its consequent high sales ensured that Pokrovskii and his family were able to live relatively comfortably in Parisian exile, on a standard well above what was usual for Russian émigrés.[26] The spring of 1910 was spent on holiday in Jersey, a welcome escape from the bustle of the French capital. To give Liubov' the tranquillity she needed for her health, the family moved from their flat in the city to a spacious house in the small village of Sceaux on its outskirts. Pokrovskii then commuted each day between his home at 39 Rue des Imbergères in Sceaux and the Bibliothèque Nationale.

It was only when Pokrovskii had almost completed his book that a serious setback occurred. In September 1912, when he was already making plans for future works, the tsarist Press Committee appeared at the premises of the 'Mir' publishers and confiscated the fifth volume of the book. The charge made against it was 'audacious disrespect towards the supreme power'. The offending passages included a quotation from Marquis de Custine's *La Russie en 1839* and various uncomplimentary expressions relating to Nicholas I.[27]

In September 1913 Pokrovskii began the fifth volume anew, this time with a more 'academic' approach, though he protested to the publishers:

> ... to give an academic description of Nicholas I is something of a Platonic hope. This is something that Kizevetter would be able to do ... but for me it goes against the grain ... .[28]

It was a task made increasingly difficult, as by now Pokrovskii had contracted a stiffness of the fingers, and in consequence wrote slowly and with great difficulty. It was only by March 1915 that the fifth and last volume of *Russian History*

---

25 Gukovskii 1968a, p. 132.
26 Gukovskii 1968a, pp. 131–2.
27 Gukovskii 1968b, p. 137.
28 Gukovskii 1968b, p. 141.

was finally completed, his 'academic' treatment having been found fully satisfactory by the Russian censor.[29]

While the efforts to salvage volume 5 were being made, Pokrovskii began negotiations with the 'Mir' company for the publication of a new work on Russian history – the two-volume *Study in the History of Russian Culture*. The book drew upon the same material as *Russian History from the Earliest Times*, but with a thematic rather than a chronological arrangement of the material. In this respect it had the same structure as Miliukov's *Studies in Russian Culture* and shared the same kind of themes. But Pokrovskii would probably see his book as a counter to Miliukov's interpretation of Russian history. Whereas Miliukov viewed the state as the moving force behind history, Pokrovskii was adamant that the Russian state was an organisation which represented economic interests. In *Study in the History of Russian Culture* Pokrovskii introduced what he regarded as the main economic interest behind state power in Russia: that of merchant capital. The first volume of *Study in the History of Russian Culture* was published in 1914, and the second – in Soviet times – in 1918.[30]

3   Trotsky

Pokrovskii's position outside any fractional grouping within the RSDRP caused him to gravitate towards Trotsky, who also stood outside any of the political fractions. *Pravda*, the newspaper Trotsky edited in Vienna, was non-fractional and had been recognised as such by the Tenth Plenum in 1910. In 1912 Pokrovskii collaborated with Trotsky in producing a joint volume, occasioned by the tricentenary of the Romanov dynasty. The work consisted of two essays under the general title of *Three Hundred Years of Our Disgrace (1613–1913)*. Pokrovskii contributed the essay 'Three Hundred Years of Romanovs and Pseudo-Romanovs', and Trotsky – 'Most Exalted, Most Autocratic!'

Pokrovskii's essay is a condemnation of hereditary monarchy; the system throws up monarchs who are insane, alcoholics, or incapable of producing heirs. Peter III belonged to the last category, so that the father of the Emperor Paul was one of Catherine II's many lovers. Hence Pokrovskii's contention that some of the dynasty was not genuinely Romanov.

The interpretation of Russian history in the essay follows that in *Russian History from the Earliest Times*. In explaining the rise of the autocratic state

---

29   Gukovskii 1968b, p. 142.
30   Pokrovskii 1914b; Pokrovskii 1918a.

Pokrovskii emphasises that the original form of government in Rus' was democratic, that a sovereign in the modern sense of the word was unknown in ancient Rus'. In the time before the Tatar invasion the real sovereign was the *veche* – i.e., the people. The Tatars invariably supported the prince against the *veche*, until such time as one of the princes, the prince of Moscow, became stronger than the Tatars themselves, and became the tsar and autocrat of all Russia. In Pokrovskii's view, the power of the tsar was perpetuated because it favoured the interests of the landowning class. It was the power of the tsar which enabled the nobility to enserf the free peasants, take their land and make them perform labour and other services.[31]

In view of the later controversy between Pokrovskii and Trotsky on the nature of the Russian state, the collaboration between them in 1912 is remarkable. However, because both authors were writing on a popular level for a mass audience, theoretical conflicts did not surface. Nevertheless, the grounds for the polemic of 1922 were present in works already in existence.

It is possible that Pokrovskii's break with the 'Vpered' group was not as absolute as he liked to maintain in Soviet times. On 7 July 1914 Lunacharskii wrote to the Geneva 'Vpered' group that several leftist Bolsheviks who sympathised with 'Vpered' wanted to gather together their scattered forces to publish a newspaper. He said that all the 'Vperedist' and former 'Vperedist' writers had been invited. The people Lunacharskii named were, besides himself, Bogdanov, Aleksinskii, Pokrovskii and Menzhinskii. Lunacharskii considered Bazarov and Skvortsov-Stepanov as 'Vperedist' sympathisers who might be interested in the project. The outbreak of the war put paid to the idea, but it is significant that Lunacharskii viewed Pokrovskii as being within the 'Vperedist' orbit.[32]

In fact, the 'Vperedists' at that time already had access to a publication which shared their aims: this was Trotsky's journal *Bor'ba*. At the end of 1913 Pokrovskii was approached by Trotsky, who was then planning to publish the workers' journal, *Bor'ba*, which appeared in St Petersburg between February and June 1914. Trotsky intended to use the new publication to combat the sectarianism that reigned in the RSDRP in the wake of the Leninist dominated Prague Conference of January 1912, and the subsequent unsuccessful efforts of the Vienna 'August Bloc' to restore unity to the party.[33]

Trotsky believed that the need for unity was now especially urgent. After the defeat of the 1905 revolution many of the former workers' leaders – the Marxist intelligentsia – had deserted the movement. In this situation, their place

31   Pokrovskii 1912, pp. 3–16.
32   Morozova 2020, p. 212.
33   Thatcher 1994, pp. 113–14.

was being taken, and would increasingly be taken, by the most advanced section of the workers. However, in this transitional period the intelligentsia who remained loyal to Marxism would continue to provide an important political and cultural service. It was, consequently, incumbent on these members of the intelligentsia to refrain from fractional wrangling, which was liable to confuse workers entering the political arena for the first time.

It was, Trotsky argued, essential that the workers arm themselves with a theoretical understanding of the conditions and course of the class struggle and have a consciousness free from fractional narrow-mindedness. In educating the advanced workers in the non-fractional spirit the function of *Bor'ba* would be to serve as their 'theoretical counsellor'.[34]

As contributors to *Bor'ba* Trotsky aimed to attract those members of the intelligentsia who had remained loyal to Marxism, and who did not belong to any of the fractional groupings, particularly to the Leninists, and the followers of Martov. He viewed the 'Vpered' group as a potential source of contributors to his paper. While Bogdanov welcomed the appearance of a political current that was akin to that of 'Vpered', he thought that the timing of a publication like *Bor'ba* in Petersburg was inopportune. Lunacharskii, on the other hand, was enthusiastic about the project. The issue of *Bor'ba* for May 1914 carried a letter signed by the Geneva, Paris and Tiflis 'Vpered' groups, saying that in the future they hoped to be able to express their opinions on the pages of *Bor'ba*, along with other intellectual currents. The groups stressed, however, that they remained Left Bolsheviks, and at the present time their closest affinity was with the Leninists, who had turned leftwards in response to the rising tide of the workers' movement in Russia. In reply Trotsky enlarged on his vision of an RSDRP with fractions within it and reassured the 'Vperedists' that *Bor'ba* would welcome the expression of their views on the pages of the journal.[35]

As the 'Vperedists' had implied in their letter to *Bor'ba*, the relations between the 'Vperedists' and Leninists had changed following the upsurge in the workers' movement in Russia after the massacre on the Lena goldfields in 1912. The episode was a vindication of the 'Vperedist' perspective for the coming revolution. Since the Leninists had become more radical as a result, the differences between them and the 'Vperedists', the Left Bolsheviks, had diminished, opening the way for a possible rapprochement of the two groups. It was in this context that Pokrovskii made contact with the Bolshevik Centre at the beginning of 1914 through the journals *Sotsial-demokrat* and *Prosveshchenie*. It was at

---

34   ibid.
35   Lapina 2010, p. 53.

this time that he contributed the article 'Russian Imperialism in the Past and Present' to *Prosveshchenie*, the Bolshevik theoretical journal.[36]

As a writer associated with 'Vpered', Trotsky approached Pokrovskii to contribute to *Bor'ba*. In doing this Trotsky combined extolling the virtues of the journal with flattery of its intended contributor. In his letter dated 27 December 1913 Trotsky promised Pokrovskii:

> In our journal you will have the possibility to be in constant contact with worker readers and your fine talent as a scholarly populariser will not be hidden under a bushel.[37]

As an incentive, Trotsky enumerated the distinguished figures from the Marxist world that he would be approaching to write for his journal – Rudolf Hilferding, Otto Bauer, Max Adler and Gustav Ebert. He said he also intended to recruit Pokrovskii's colleague Rozhkov to be a contributor.

Trotsky's letter of 1 January 1914 is of particular interest because its emphasis is not only on persuading Pokrovskii to contribute to *Bor'ba*, but also to remain a member of the RSDRP. The implication must be that Pokrovskii's aversion to sectarian infighting had inclined him to abandon party politics altogether. Trotsky promised Pokrovskii a key position on the journal and suggested the kind of contribution he might make:

> We hope that your collaboration will be systematic, that in our journal there will be, so to say, a permanent M.N. Pokrovskii section. Would you not agree to give us a series of articles, of which each one would be a 'thing in itself' – on the history of the development of Russian estates and classes of the Russian state? From the collection of such articles there could be compiled an indispensable book, which we in advance lay claim to publish.[38]

Pokrovskii's contribution to *Bor'ba* was exactly as Trotsky suggested. It was a series of articles entitled 'From the History of the Social Classes in Russia'.[39] The series, which was unfinished due to the demise of *Bor'ba*, was based on *Russian History from the Earliest Times*. It gave a concise account of the slave trade in Kievan Rus', the emergence of the *dvorianstvo* estate under Ivan the

---

36   'Tribuna', *Bor'ba*, 5, 16 May 1914, pp. 24–6.
37   Lapina 2010, p. 55.
38   Lapina 2010, p. 56.
39   Pokrovskii 1914a.

Terrible, and the resistance to serfdom during the Time of Troubles. The series
ended with the promise to explain the rise of merchant capital and its influence
on the course of Russian history.

Pokrovskii's correspondence with the Bolshevik journals encouraged Lenin
to think that he might detach Pokrovskii from Trotsky. On 20 May 1914 Lenin
wrote to A.A. Troianovskii: 'I should like you to send me Pokrovskii's letters
for perusal. Your proposal to correspond with him is very interesting, to take
him away from the indecent *Bor'ba*'.[40] In the same year Pokrovskii contributed
five articles to Trotsky's *Golos* published in Paris. In 1915 after *Golos* had been
closed down by the French police and had been succeeded by *Nashe slovo*, he
wrote three articles for the new paper. In 1922 Pokrovskii could recall with some
humour: 'How we, the staff of the Parisian *Nashe slovo* would have laughed if
someone at our meetings had predicted that in four years' time our editor, comrade Trotsky, would hold a military review on the Red Square. And nowadays,
who but ourselves could imagine comrade Trotsky not leading an army?'[41]

4   War

Pokrovskii's series of articles for *Bor'ba* was curtailed by the outbreak of war
in the summer of 1914. In the new situation the old fractional boundaries were
effaced by the more fundamental division into those who supported the war,
and those who opposed it. Pokrovskii was firmly in the latter, the 'internationalist', camp. This was a position he shared with the members and former
members of the 'Vpered' group with the exception of Aleksinskii, who took the
side of the Entente against the Central Powers.

Pokrovskii's first wartime articles, including 'Historical Tasks', which placed
Russia's war aims in historical perspective, were contributed to *Golos*, whose
editorial board consisted of Martov, D. Manuil'skii, M. Vladimirov and V.A. Antonov-Ovseenko. The board was joined by Trotsky when he moved to Paris in
November 1914. For its anti-war stance the paper was shut down by the French
government at the insistence of the Russian Embassy in January 1915.[42]

From January 1915 *Golos* was replaced by *Nashe slovo*, with the same editorial board. Like *Bor'ba*, *Nashe slovo* had the material and moral support of the
Geneva 'Vpered' group. Pokrovskii wrote three articles for *Nashe slovo*, among

---

40   Lenin 1958e–65, p. 292.
41   Pokrovskii 1922b, p. 35.
42   Getzler 1967, p. 141.

them 'The Life-Guards of the Romanovs' in which he castigated Russian historians for their fawning attitude to the tsarist regime in time of war.[43]

During 1915 most of Pokrovskii's time was spent writing not political articles, but encyclopaedia articles on topics in Russian history for the Granat encyclopaedia, to whose publishers he felt a debt of gratitude. As he told the editors of *Sotsial-demokrat*:

> Unfortunately, I cannot promise you anything for the May issue … I have a mass of accumulated work, among it, for the Granat dictionary … The turn of these people to the left is worthy of note. I am unable to forget that they commissioned *History of Russia in the XIX Century* from me in the autumn of 1904 – and it was no fault of theirs that the 'days of freedom' proved so short, and the book ended up with new editors.[44]

Although Lenin did not succeed in drawing Pokrovskii away from the Trotskyist camp, there are signs that Pokrovskii was not happy with the left-centralist orientation of *Nashe slovo*, and that he would have preferred to see an alliance between it and Lenin's *Sotsial-demokrat*. In the spring of 1915 a dissident left wing began to form in the editorial board, consisting of Pokrovskii, Lunacharskii, S. Lozovskii, D. Manuil'skii, V. Antonov-Ovseenko and K. Zalewski. In June of 1915 the group published a manifesto in *Nashe slovo* which called for a complete break with 'social-chauvinism' and a rapprochement with Lenin's *Sotsial-demokrat*. This was a move which was received very favourably by the Paris Bolsheviks, and must have done much to further the reconciliation between Pokrovskii and Lenin.[45]

In a letter dated 20 October 1915, Trotsky wrote to Pokrovskii to counter the latter's dissatisfaction with *Nashe slovo*, and possibly with Trotsky himself. The letter is worth quoting at length for the insight it gives into Trotsky's attitude to Pokrovskii, and Pokrovskii's attitude to *Nashe slovo*.

> Dear Mikhail Nikolaevich!
> For a long time I have wanted to talk to you about your attitude to *Nashe slovo*. I cannot for the life of me account for the causes of your alienation from the newspaper. If these causes are ones of principle – they cannot be anything else – then, as you well know, given the attitude of the editorial board to your contributions, you will always find a full and unlimited

---

43   Morozova 2020, p. 244.
44   Tikhomirov 1966, p. 18.
45   Temkin 1968, pp. 44–5.

possibility to express your point of view in the newspaper, and subject to criticism the point of view of the editors. If the matter is in some awkwardnesses of a personal nature, then it would be no trouble to get rid of them.

Allow me to say some words from myself personally. You know, I hope you know, how I regard you, that I value your enormous talent as a materialist historian, which you bring to your publicistic writings. I hope that you never doubt the full sincerity of my attitude, as you should not doubt that I have no reason to change it.

Now more than ever the newspaper needs your contributions – after the right wing has begun openly or clandestinely to boycott it.

Dear Mikhail Nikolaevich! Come back to *Nashe slovo*, write for it more often. I hope that we shall not have any conflicts or misunderstandings. At least, I on my part, as one of the chief editors, shall do everything I can to eliminate them.[46]

We do not know how Pokrovskii responded to Trotsky's plea, because he destroyed his side of the correspondence, but it was not by writing more articles for *Nashe slovo*. His next important article, one on the history of Russian foreign policy, appeared in Gorky's journal *Letopis'*.

A further step in the rapprochement between Pokrovskii and Lenin came when Lenin was attempting to consolidate the ranks of the internationalist wing of the socialist movement. To this end, Lenin proposed that a new journal should be issued to promote the internationalist line. The journal *Kommunist* was to appear twice a month. A circular was sent out by Krupskaia on 22 May 1915 to various leading left-wing socialists – Franz Mehring, Rosa Luxemburg, Karl Liebknecht, F.A. Rothstein, D. Blagoev, A. Pannekoek, Trotsky and Pokrovskii.[47]

Trotsky refused to participate in the project, but in the summer of 1915 Pokrovskii worked on an article for *Kommunist* entitled 'Those Responsible for the War'. It was based on a paper he had given to the Internationalist Club in May, where it evoked a prolonged and heated debate. What caused controversy, Pokrovskii says, was the basic idea of the paper that the imperialist bloodbath was a symptom, not of the recent progress of capitalism, but of its disintegration and collapse. This idea was in marked contrast to the influential conception of Rudolf Hilferding, elaborated in his book *Das Finanzkapital*, published in 1910,

---

46   Lapina 2010, p. 57.
47   Temkin 1968, p. 185.

that finance capitalism, with its centralisation of economic systems nationally and internationally, laid the foundations of a socialist society. Because Pokrovskii's article did not hold out the prospect of socialism emerging inevitably and smoothly in this way, it was prevented from appearing in *Kommunist* and other socialist publications of the time.[48]

Lenin and Zinoviev read the article before passing it on to Bukharin, who thought that it could not be published in its present form. Lenin decided to reject the article and drafted a tactful letter to Pokrovskii advising him to discard the section dealing with imperialism. In the event only one issue of *Kommunist* appeared, and that contained Bukharin's article 'The World Economy and Imperialism' written in the Hilferding spirit. Pokrovskii's article first appeared in 1918 in a collection of his articles on foreign policy. By that time Pokrovskii could feel vindicated, because the revolution in Russia had not followed the Hilferding model but had been more in keeping with the process that Pokrovskii had predicted.[49]

In the spring of 1916 Pokrovskii received a letter from Gorky with the suggestion that he should draw upon the forces of the exiled Russian writers to organise the production of a series of popular pamphlets under the general heading of 'Europe before and during the War'. It was intended that the series should explain to the workers what kind of countries the belligerent powers were. What Gorky also intended – though this was not stated openly because of the military censorship – was that an analysis of the essence of the war itself should be made.[50]

No time was lost in working out the actual themes for the pamphlets – descriptions of separate countries. Lunacharskii was to write on Italy, Zinoviev – on Austro-Hungary, Pokrovskii together with Lozovskii – on France. Britain it was proposed to entrust to Rothstein, but he refused, and that booklet was instead written by Kheraskov. Gorky had proposed Iu. Larin as the most suitable person to write on Germany, but it proved impossible to get in touch with him until just before the February revolution – which rendered the whole series finally obsolete.

As a general introduction to the series, it was proposed to have a pamphlet on imperialism. Skvortsov-Stepanov and Bukharin had already published works on this subject, but perhaps for political reasons, the choice fell on Lenin. Pokrovskii accordingly contacted Lenin through Zinoviev, who was his link with *Sotsial-demokrat*.

---

48 Pokrovskii 1918c, p. 162.
49 Chernobaev 1992, pp. 87–8.
50 Pokrovskii 1979, p. 372.

By July Lenin had completed the work and delivered the manuscript to Pokrovskii. Gorky and his associates, however, judged Lenin's manuscript too long, and demanded that it be substantially shortened. It fell to Pokrovskii to make the requisite cuts, and in particular, to remove the note which criticised Kautsky, to which Lenin attached great importance, but which Gorky found objectionable.

On 8 December Pokrovskii received Lenin's reaction – milder than expected. Reproaching Pokrovskii for having given his assent to the cuts, Lenin said he would have to deal with Kautsky elsewhere, as in fact he was later to do. According to Pokrovskii, he did not see the first edition of Lenin's book *Imperialism The Highest Stage of Capitalism*, because it came out in Russia after the February revolution, in a 'non-mutilated form', while Pokrovskii was still in exile in France.[51]

5   The 1917 Revolution

At the time of the February revolution in Petrograd, Pokrovskii was working in the Biblothèque Nationale in Paris. As he recalled:

> It was there that comrade Vladimirov brought me the first tidings of the February revolution. He brought in and placed before me on the table the issue of *Information* with the news of Nicholas's abdication and all the other things. I think I shall never forget that moment.[52]

Pokrovskii's flair for organisation was mobilised in arranging the passage of the Russian émigrés in France back to their native country. This was a major undertaking, considering that there were about 600 émigrés in Paris alone. Money had to be raised for their journey, passports obtained, and transport arranged. The task was made more difficult by the obstruction of the Provisional Government in Russia, and by the governments of the Allied Powers.

It was not until the autumn that Pokrovskii and his émigré committee had two steamers, the *Dvinsk* and the *Tsaritsa*, placed at their disposal. In the middle of August 1917, the Pokrovskiis, in a group of 350 political émigrés, travelled to Brest to begin their perilous voyage to Russia. Having avoided German air attack, after two weeks at sea, the ships reached Archangel. There

---

51   Pokrovskii 1979, pp. 373–5.
52   Pokrovskii 1924c, p. 220.

Pokrovskii and his party were put under arrest for four days before being sent under convoy to Moscow.[53]

At the end of August 1917 Pokrovskii's ten years of exile were at an end, and he found himself once again in his native Moscow, and in the company of what remained of the literary-lecturing group of 1905. When on 27 February news had been received in Moscow of the revolution in Petrograd, the local Social Democrats, among them Skvortsov-Stepanov, Ol'minskii, and P.G. Smidovich, had met in the flat of V.A. Obukh. The group put out a leaflet expressing solidarity with the insurgents in Petrograd and calling for the creation of a Soviet of workers' deputies. When the Soviet was established on 1 March, Skvortsov-Stepanov became the editor of its *Bulletin* (*Izvestiia Soveta rabochikh deputatov*).[54]

After returning to Russia Pokrovskii resumed work on the second volume of *Study in the History of Russian Culture*, which was published in 1918. In September he wrote the introductory chapter for a proposed collective work on 'The History of the Emancipation of Russia'. The project was never completed, but Pokrovskii's introduction was published as a separate volume, entitled *Tsarism and Revolution*, at the beginning of 1918. Academic work had to be paused in October of 1917, as political events demanded the undivided attention of Pokrovskii and the other authors in the project.[55]

Thereafter, his chief function during 1917 was editing the *Bulletin* of the Moscow Soviet, along with Skvortsov-Stepanov. He was also a deputy of the Moscow Soviet and was chosen to stand for election to the Constituent Assembly. Commenting on Pokrovskii as a candidate for the Constituent Assembly, Lenin wrote at the end of September:

> As for the candidature of M.N. Pokrovskii? In 1907 he left the ranks of the Bolsheviks and for years stood on the sidelines. It would be excellent if he were to return to us for good. But for this he must prove himself by hard work.[56]

Of course, very little in this characterisation is accurate. Pokrovskii did not leave the Bolsheviks in 1907. He did not stand on the sidelines. He was not 'returning' to the Leninists, because he had never been one of them. Clearly, this was

---

53   Chernobaev 1992, pp. 87–8.
54   Lukashev 1973, p. 29.
55   Chernobaev 1992, p. 98.
56   Lenin 1958b-65, p. 345.

a more palatable presentation of the events than to admit that Pokrovskii was a newcomer to the Leninist fold.

In Moscow the October revolution came later than that in Petrograd, and was much more bloody, as serious resistance was mounted by the military cadets, the 'Iunkers'. Towards the end of October Pokrovskii joined the Moscow Military Revolutionary Committee (MRC), the organisation that directed the street battles in the city. In relation to the October revolution in Moscow, Pokrovskii writes:

> As for those events, I could not be a memoirist: I was not present at most of them. I very quickly entered the new organ of power which incarnated the victory of the Soviets in Moscow almost literally on the day after its appearance: but I had no part in its formation. I lived through the October battles in Moscow, not as a member of one of its leading collectives, but as a Soviet journalist, a 'war correspondent', as the others jokingly referred to me – and as I did as well – of *Bulletin of the Moscow Soviet*, which was at that time edited by I.I. Skvortsov-Stepanov ... In this capacity I saw and heard a great deal, sometimes from very close quarters ... But in the matter of leading the Moscow revolution I am unable to claim the slightest credit.[57]

Communications between Petrograd and Moscow had been broken, as the telegraph was controlled by the anti-Bolshevik Railwaymen's Union (Vikzhel). There were only vague rumours about what had taken place in the capital, and local moderate socialists gave the impression that a government of 'all socialist parties' had been formed, and that the same thing should happen in Moscow. The MRC, however, did not adopt this suggestion.

The Iunkers, surrounded by the insurgent armies and the Red Guards, who had all the heavy artillery at their disposal, had no choice but to surrender. It was decided that the Iunkers should be disarmed and allowed to return to their units. In fact, what the vast majority of them did was to join the Volunteer Army and fight on the side of the Whites in the Civil War.

Pokrovskii recalls that at the time the Iunkers were being disarmed, he had become chairman of the Moscow Soviet, which had taken over from the MRC. In this capacity he had become the arbiter of what became of the Iunkers. Reflecting on his actions at that time Pokrovskii wrote:

---

57   Pokrovskii 1929a, pp. 207–8.

It is painful to recall how the Iunkers came to us in the Soviet for passes to travel out of Moscow, and how quickly those passes were granted … But, on the other hand, what else could we do? To organise concentration camps at that time was physically absolutely impossible. There was some attempt to imprison the Iunkers – at least the most dangerous – in the Butyrki prison … but even this had to be abandoned – who would guard them?[58]

Pokrovskii was writing in 1927, after the Red Terror, after the Civil War, after the Kronstadt mutiny, when such acts of apparent magnanimity would seem the height of folly. Four years later they would be deemed treasonous.

Once the Soviet had taken power in Moscow, it was confronted with the problems of running the city. The most acute of these was the shortage of food, as promised shipments of grain failed to arrive from Siberia, and rations had to be severely reduced. The bank employees had gone on strike, making it impossible to pay wages. On 3 December the Moscow Union for the Defence of the Constituent Assembly organised a mass demonstration to protest against the postponement of the opening of the Assembly from 28 November to 5 January. Despite the appeals of the *Bulletin* of the Moscow Soviet not to attend, a hundred and fifty thousand people assembled on Red Square.[59]

6   Brest-Litovsk

On 3 December 1917, the day of the mass strike in Moscow, Pokrovskii received an urgent telegram from Trotsky with a summons to Petrograd to take part in the peace negotiations in Brest-Litovsk. In Trotsky's opinion, Pokrovskii's participation was 'absolutely necessary'. He was one of the very few Bolsheviks with expertise in international relations, albeit of those in the past. Pokrovskii recalls that he was flattered by this invitation, and also eager as a historian to witness the first momentous meeting of a socialist and an imperialist power. He kept a journal recording his impressions of events as they unfolded before him.[60]

Although he had a great deal of important business to attend to in his capacity as Chairman of the Moscow Soviet – the deteriorating economic situation in the city, mass demonstrations and strikes – he hurried to Petrograd, where

---

58   Pokrovskii 1929a, p. 212.
59   Koenker 1981, p. 349.
60   Esina 1993, p. 153.

he expected to be briefed on the Soviet delegation's negotiating strategy. He was disappointed to discover from Lenin and Trotsky that there was no such strategy: the plan was simply to draw out the negotiations for as long as possible in the expectation of revolution in Germany and Austro-Hungary. They were also of the opinion that Germany desperately wanted peace.

Pokrovskii thought it advisable to include in the Soviet delegation experts in international relations from the Ministry of Foreign Affairs, but this idea had no traction with Lenin or Trotsky. He did, however, manage to take with him to Brest-Litovsk M.P. Pavlovich, who had lectured on international politics at the Bologna party school.[61]

When Pokrovskii and Pavlovich arrived in Brest-Litovsk on 6 December, neither the German nor the Soviet negotiators had arrived. It increasingly seemed to Pokrovskii that his time was being wasted. He reported his impressions in a letter to Liubov':

My dearest friend, yesterday I arrived in Brest – and am now sitting with not a thing to do, cursing human folly. So far there have been no negotiations with the Germans, but even the members of the Russian delegation have been unable to confer amongst themselves, because Kamenev succumbed to hysterics and departed for Warsaw to visit Russian prisoners-of-war and got stuck there. Time is going by in the most absurd way. Last night I had supper with Prince Leopold of Bavaria, the Commander-in-Chief of the German Eastern Front, chatting with him in French about Sceaux (he was stationed there in 1870). I drank in sequence Moselle (very good), champaign and Munich beer (the order was exactly that – but don't worry I had very little of each); in a word, God knows what it was all about. Was it for this that I had to leave Moscow at the most critical juncture! If I had longer hair I would tear it out, but failing this I picture Kamenev's beard with sadistic pleasure. To crown it all, we don't know what is happening back home – the Hughes telegraph machine that connects us with Petrograd is broken. I wanted to send you a telegram yesterday – but no chance. At breakfast later today we shall inquire what kind of Russian radio messages they have intercepted. About our arrival, i.e. my arrival, here they found out precisely from an intercepted radio message of Trotsky's. It hadn't occurred to this great statesman that he should use the telegraph. Nevertheless, we shall probably still go to Stockholm. But when? How? All this is extremely vague. Outwardly, we are prospering –

---

61   Esina 1993, p. 154.

it's warm. The food is great. The room is much better than what I have in Moscow. Regards to Mother. Wishing you all the best of sane things.[62]

Pokrovskii spent two months in Brest-Litovsk, for the most part in inactivity. On 10 February 1918 he wrote to Trotsky formally asking that he be allowed to return to Moscow. Three days later the negotiations came to an end, when the Germans refused to agree to Soviet proposals for the line of demarcation between the armies. The Soviet delegation drew up a lengthy protest to present to the Germans, which Pokrovskii signed, but Trotsky simply made the declaration that: 'Russia is ending the war and demobilising its army'. In Pokrovskii's opinion, this declaration was intended not for the participants in the negotiations, but for the Russian, German and Polish workers. After Trotsky had made his declaration, the Soviet delegation left Brest-Litovsk.[63]

Pokrovskii was back in Moscow during the German advance, and the subsequent signing of the Brest-Litovsk Treaty on 3 March. The opposition to the treaty was most resolute in Moscow, the Moscow Regional Bureau of the Bolshevik party being the stronghold of the 'Left Communists'. On 2 March an expanded Plenum of the Bureau voted in favour of carrying on a revolutionary war against imperialism. Some attempts were made to recruit workers into a revolutionary army, but without success. Recognising that the Soviet state had no forces to fight a revolutionary war with, Skvortsov-Stepanov concluded that the German peace terms would have to be accepted. Pokrovskii, however, was reluctant to concede that this was the case. On 3 March when Sverdlov put the case for accepting the peace treaty to the Moscow Soviet, Pokrovskii made an impassioned speech condemning the immoderate demands of the Germans as an unacceptable plundering of the young Soviet state.[64] He later recalled:

The Central Committee were all along officially in favour of a revolutionary war. This was the spirit in which they had brought us up ... we were in a 'suicidal' mood. We knew that in the revolutionary struggle many of us would lose our lives. We did not know that Il'ich at this time had already protested in the Central Committee against revolutionary phrases, that there was to be no war of any kind against anyone, and that it could bring about nothing save the destruction of Soviet Russia. Therefore it came upon us like a bolt from the blue when, at Lenin's insistence, the Central Committee accepted the German ultimatum. I remember that I was

---

62   Pokrovskii 1995, pp. 220–1.
63   Esina 1993, p. 159.
64   Varlamov and Slamikhin 1964, pp. 119–20.

so confused that I had no heart to go and pay my respects to Il'ich at the Ekaterininskii Hall in the Tauride Palace. It seemed to me that a moral outrage of the most colossal proportions had been committed.[65]

At the Fourth Congress of the Moscow Regional Soviet, which opened on 11 March 1918, it was decided to establish a Moscow Council of People's Commissars (Sovnarkom). Pokrovskii was elected president of the Council, with the Left Socialist Revolutionary A.A. Bitsenko as vice-president. The commissariats in Moscow replicated those in Petrograd, though they existed largely on paper. As there was a shortage of personnel at the Moscow Sovnarkom's disposal, on 12 April it resolved that its president would not be permitted to take up the post as Deputy People's Commissar for Education. The situation was rationalised when the Soviet government moved from Petrograd to Moscow and eliminated the duplication of functions.[66]

Like most Left Communists, Pokrovskii had become reconciled to the Leninist party line by the spring of 1918. His protest against the Brest-Litovsk Treaty was the last time that he would be in opposition to the party leadership. For the rest of his life, he would be, at least outwardly, one of its most loyal supporters. In 1924 Pokrovskii published an article on Lenin as a revolutionary leader in which he reviewed the occasions when he had had disagreements with Lenin, and now conceded that in these cases Lenin had been right:

> I often argued with him about practical matters, and every time got myself into a mess. After repeating this procedure about seven times, I stopped arguing with Lenin and gave in to him, even when logic dictated that I shouldn't act in that particular way. But I reckoned that he understood things better than I did; that he had remarkable perspicacity.[67]

What Pokrovskii admired in Lenin was his political courage, his ability to act according to his convictions in the face of any opposition, or even ridicule. Victor Chernov, the SR leader, had not had this political courage, and he was unable to put his policy of socialising the land into practice. Pokrovskii rated Lenin higher than Cromwell and Robespierre as a revolutionary leader. It is significant that in 1924 Pokrovskii viewed Lenin as a great revolutionary leader rather than as an outstanding Marxist theoretician.

---

65 Pokrovskii 1929a, p. 16.
66 Serebriakova 1977, pp. 94–5.
67 Pokrovskii 1929a, p. 18.

7   Deputy Commissar of Education

In May 1918 Pokrovskii was appointed deputy People's Commissar of Education under Lunacharskii, a post which he held until his death in 1932. When he took up his post, the atmosphere in which he operated was still hostile. The civil servants and bank employees had responded to the Bolshevik accession to power with strikes and sabotage, which the new government had countered with the creation of the Cheka headed by Feliks Dzierżyński. Even when this initial resistance had been overcome, the academic and teaching establishment that Pokrovskii had to deal with were loath to cooperate with the Soviet authorities. An example of this was the attitude of Iu.V. Got'e (Gautier), an eminent history professor at Moscow University, that emerges from his diary entry from 18 January 1918. He writes:

> Today I reached the firm conclusion that the Bolsheviks are going to remain in power for a very long time. Evidence for this is the compromise of the bank employees, who are yielding to the Bolsheviks and going back to work; the collapse of the strike of the finance-administration employees and of the city teachers ....[68]

The universities were centres of resistance and obstruction to the new regime. In its work of re-organisation, Narkompros came into conflict both with the existing professors and with the student body. Among the professors opposition came not only from the more conservative, but from the liberals as well. Their objective in the past had been full autonomy for the universities, and this they refused to forego.[69]

In an article written in 1918, Pokrovskii set out the ambition of Narkompros for its reform of the universities. It was to democratise them, open them up to the workers, and make them less institutions reserved for the privileged classes in society. The obstacles to realising this aim were not just the resistance of the intelligentsia, but the privations caused by the disruption to the economy by the Civil War. There were shortages of food and fuel as well as of suitable accommodation to hold classes. It was only after the Civil War ended in 1921 that the reform of the educational system could be undertaken in any systematic way. Before then the measures taken were short-term and improvised.

---

68   Got'e 1988, p. 102.
69   Pistrak 1932, p. 5.

In view of the unstable situation of the Soviet regime, it was essential that the universities produce graduates who would not simply accept Soviet power, but who would actively promote it. To this end Narkompros saw as a priority the reform of the way in which the humanities and social sciences were taught. It decreed that faculties of law should be abolished, since the teaching of law and economics, as well as philosophy, theology and history, were 'imbued with an ideology hostile to the proletariat'. In April 1919 the Law and the Historico-Philological Faculties at Moscow University were merged to form a new Faculty of Social Science (FON). It was headed by Pokrovskii, and a number of existing staff were recruited to teach in the FON. To exercise control over the ideological content of the courses taught in the universities Pokrovskii established the State Academic Council (GUS) within Narkompros in 1919.[70]

In his diary entry for 5 March 1919, Got'e viewed this development with evident disapproval. He remarked:

> They say the fate of the history professors will be decided on Friday. The Bolsheviks have set up some sort of commission of fifteen communists (including Storozhev) and fifteen non-communists, who are supposed to decide which of the professors of the Law Faculty and the History Department of the Historico-Philological Faculty are worthy of entering the Faculty of Social Sciences. From among us, Boguslovskii, Savin, Petrushevskii, and Vipper are obliged to go there. I am very sorry for them ...[71]

As it happened, Got'e too was recruited to teach in the FON, but it did nothing to assuage his hatred and contempt for the new regime, and for Pokrovskii, its most visible representative. This is clear from the entry in Got'e's diary for 21 May 1919. It reads:

> Pokrovskii was present today at the saloon faculty of social sciences; I was amazed by his wish – and it seems a sincere one – to somehow draw near to his old comrades. This could be felt in all his words and actions. I think that he would be quite amazed if he could read the absence of such reciprocal feelings in the hearts of those present.[72]

In the first years of Soviet power, the universities changed very little. The organisation of courses and the staffing remained basically the same, so that the

---

70   Lagno 2009, p. 298; Pistrak 1932, p. 8.
71   Got'e 1988, p. 246.
72   Got'e 1988, p. 270.

historian N.M. Druzhinin, for example, who began his university education in tsarist times, could complete it in the twenties without any loss of continuity; the same regulations remained in force, and he retained his previous teachers, Boguslovskii and Vipper.[73] This policy of Narkompros was in line with what Lenin recommended. He advised 'smashing as little as possible', and using the existing university staff to teach in the FON, though with some restrictions on the subject matter of their lectures.[74]

In March 1921 the FON was reorganised into seven separate institutes. As it was considered that the people who taught them were unlikely to be able to deliver courses in history from a Marxist viewpoint, the history courses were abandoned altogether. The discipline of history was no longer taught at Moscow university, courses in social science being given in its place. The measures taken to protect the FON against the alien ideology of its teaching staff were ineffective in isolating the university from the influence of Trotskyism, which engulfed centres of higher education throughout the country in the spring of 1924.[75]

Before the FON at Moscow University was closed down in 1925, it became the focus for a new institution, the Russian Association of Social Science Research Institutes (RANION), which was launched by Narkompros in May 1924. In addition to the seven institutes that had been included in the FON, RANION brought together scholarly and research institutes dealing with social and economic studies in different parts of Russia. The idea behind RANION was that the training of Soviet functionaries would be concentrated within a single institution, so that best use could be made of the most highly qualified staff and the small number of Marxist lecturers that Narkompros had at its disposal. Pokrovskii served as chairman of RANION until 1927.[76]

The ambition of Narkompros to open up the universities to the working class had to reckon with the fact that the educational level of working class university entrants tended to be very low. One academic complained of an entrant to a French language course, for example, who had no idea of what grammar was.[77] It was necessary to arrange some intensive preparatory courses, to bring entrants up to the required level. According to Pokrovskii, the suggestion had come from students at the Plekhanov Institute and Moscow metal-workers that the courses be held, not outside, but inside Moscow University; that they

73 Druzhinin 1967, p. 115.
74 Pokrovskii 1967d, pp. 11–12.
75 Lagno 2009, pp. 299–304.
76 Ivanova 1968, pp. 94–5.
77 Lagno 2009, p. 308.

should constitute a faculty, like other faculties, in the University. Pokrovskii accepted the idea, and the workers' faculty (*rabfak*) was duly established. The first *rabfak* was opened in February 1919, staffed by the small number of teachers and students sympathetic to the Bolsheviks. *Rabfaks* then became competitors with the FON for teaching space and fuel for heating at the University.[78]

In the dire economic conditions of the Civil War years a *rabfak* could be a rather makeshift affair, as one *rabfak* student complained:

> There is no definite programme. At lectures, together with grammar, they talk about ethics and psychology. For lack of accommodation the *rabfak* is divided into several groups and scattered throughout different parts of the city ... It is no better in the hostel. Besides bare bunks, of which there are not enough to go round, and broken windows, there is nothing. Instead of a blanket to sleep in, there is a sack that you crawl into before going to bed, covering your head at the top against a sudden attack by rats.[79]

In the early years of the Soviet regime workers' education was not only the province of Narkompros, but also of the Proletkult, which was inspired by Bogdanov. Bogdanov's idea of a Proletarian University came from his experience teaching workers in clandestine study circles, and from the party schools on Capri and in Bologna that both Pokrovskii and Lunacharskii had taught in. For Bogdanov, a Proletarian University should be a democratic institution in which staff and students would be on an equal footing, and in which the students would not be the passive recipients of knowledge but would actively participate in the learning process.

A Proletarian University was opened in Moscow on 23 March 1919. P.I. Lebedev-Polianskii chaired the meeting, which was attended by a large audience of workers and Red Army men. Pokrovskii addressed the meeting on behalf of Narkompros, saying that, besides its role as a disseminator of higher learning among the workers and peasants, the Proletarian University also had an important part to play in training instructors for the Red Army, for whom a great need was felt.[80]

Bogdanov's Proletarian University, which offered a broad education, however, did not prove viable in a situation where there was an urgent need for the

---

78   ibid.
79   Chagin and Klushin 1975, p. 57.
80   White 2019, pp. 401–2.

training of Communist organisers and propagandists. An institution which better met these needs was the Central School of Soviet and Party Work, which had been established by Ia.M. Sverdlov, the party secretary, in 1918.[81] In the summer of 1919 the Proletarian University was merged with the Central School to form the Sverdlov Communist University, with V.I. Nevskii as its rector.[82] It was at the Sverdlov Communist University that Pokrovskii gave the lectures which would be published in 1920 as the *Brief History of Russia*.

In respect of teaching methods, Narkompros was no different from Proletkult, as Pokrovskii made clear when he addressed the Proletkult conference in September 1918. In speaking of the preparatory courses for workers, he stressed that the idea that the workers should sit passively and listen to lectures was an unacceptable legacy of the old system of education. The Proletkult conference was an occasion when Pokrovskii avowed his adherence to the methods employed in the Capri and Bologna party schools. After the campaign against Bogdanov and his ideas, launched by Lenin in 1920, Pokrovskii was much less forthcoming about the provenance of his teaching methods.[83]

Although the Proletarian University itself was short lived, the teaching methods that it employed – the active participation by students, the use of seminars, laboratories and excursions, were ones espoused by Pokrovskii, most notably in the Institute of Red Professors (*Institut krasnoi professury*, IKP), which was established in February 1921. The intention behind IKP was to produce a new generation of academics who could teach in Soviet educational institutions and replace the existing staff, who were in the main unsympathetic to the Soviet regime. Pokrovskii was the overall rector of IKP, and head of its history department, in which the first cohorts of Soviet historians were trained.

An important institution founded by Pokrovskii was the Socialist Academy of Social Sciences (SAON). He recalls that the idea came to him while drafting the Soviet constitution, along with M.A. Reisner, in the spring of 1918. The purpose of the Academy, which was instituted in October 1918, was to raise

---

81   The first teaching programmes at the Sverdlov University were drawn up by Sverdlov himself. The courses he envisaged were:
      Labour and Capital in the History of the Class Struggle – Lenin.
      The Agrarian Question – Iaroslavskii.
      The Organisation of Soviet Power – Vladimirskii.
      Parliamentarianism and the Dictatorship of the Bourgeoisie – Pokrovskii.
      The Structure of the Soviets – Petrovskii.
      The National Question – Stalin.
      The Soviets and Primary Education – Lunacharskii. Sverdlova 1960, p. 390.
82   White 2019, p. 402; Sverdlova 1960, p. 390.
83   Lebedev-Polianskii 1918, pp. 7–14.

the level of theoretical discussion in the country. Writing in the first issue of
the Academy's *Bulletin* in November 1922, E.A. Preobrazhenskii described the
status of the Academy thus: 'Marxism in Russia is the official ideology of the victorious proletariat. The Socialist Academy is the highest institution of scholarly
research in Marxist thought'.[84]

The Socialist Academy, renamed the Communist Academy in 1924, was the
forum in which the main theoretical debates of the 1920s took place. Its *Bulletin* attracted contributions from leading Marxist thinkers of the day, both
from inside and outside the Soviet Union. Its contributors included Bogdanov,
Bukharin, Preobrazhenskii, Riazanov, Pokrovskii, Trotsky, Lunacharskii, and
the Hungarian philosopher Georg Lukács.

SAON was divided into two sections: one concerned with research, and the
other with teaching. The main attention in this first period of its existence was
concentrated on the teaching side. There was no formal entrance qualification to study at SAON; it accepted all applicants over the age of 16. But since
in the first intake there were very few proletarians, it was decided to abandon the SAON's teaching function and to concentrate on research. In November
1919, SAON was reorganised into a number of 'cabinets', or subject areas, each
supervised by a commission of members of the Academy. Bogdanov headed
the section on the history of ideology, Pokrovskii on history of the Russian
revolutionary movement, Rothstein on foreign policy and Sh.M. Dvolaitskii on
economics.[85]

As a historian, one of Pokrovskii's most pressing concerns was the preser-
vation of archives. Between 1918 and 1920, the organisation which managed
the archives was Glavarkhiv, whose director was Riazanov. Riazanov regarded
the archives as a resource that should be freely available, and the staff he
employed in Glavarkhiv came from a wide social spectrum. It included members of the aristocracy, former civil servants and military men. They were
chosen by Riazanov for their competence and skills, rather than for their political reliability. Pokrovskii deeply disapproved of Riazanov's approach, arguing
that archives were a weapon in the armoury of the Soviet state. In 1920, while
Riazanov was on a trip abroad, Pokrovskii took over his position as head of
Glavarkhiv, and introduced a number of reforms. One was to transfer Glavarkhiv from Narkompros, where Riazanov had placed it, to the purview of the
Soviet Government. In 1922 Pokrovskii established a new institution to replace
Glavarkhiv. This was Tsentrarkhiv, a body which was responsible for the admin-

---

84   Preobrazhenskii 1922, p. 7.
85   Udal'tsov 1922, pp. 13–7.

istration of archives throughout the country. Pokrovskii was director of Tsentrarkhiv, and so was the person in charge of Soviet archives from 1920 until his
death in 1932.[86]

One use to which Pokrovskii put the archives was to publish collections
of documents on a number of themes. These included the correspondence
between tsar Nicholas II and his wife Alexandra, the Decembrist movement,
the 1905 revolution in Russia, and the origins of the Great War. The documents
from the tsarist Ministry of Foreign Affairs had a special significance for Pokrovskii, since the main focus of his research in the Soviet era was on the origins
of the 1914–18 War.

At the beginning of 1920 the cabinet of the theory, history and practice of
Marxism detached itself from SAON to become Institute of Marx and Engels
(IME), headed by Riazanov. Riazanov was well qualified for the position. Before
the war he had published a collection of Marx's early writings, and had collaborated with August Bebel and Marx's daughter Eleanor in bringing out a four-
volume collection of Marx-Engels correspondence. As in the case of Glavarkhiv,
Riazanov employed people in IME for their abilities, rather than for their loyalty
to the Soviet regime. On his staff were the young scholars such as A.M. Deborin,
I.I. Rubin and I.K. Luppol. IME also attracted scholars from outside the Soviet
Union, including Georg Lukacs. IME quickly became a centre for Marxist studies of international standing. It acquired an extensive library, supplemented by
the purchase of books from abroad. It acquired unpublished manuscripts by
Marx and Engels and, in collaboration with the Frankfurt School, began the
publication of the complete works of Marx and Engels (MEGA).[87]

IME also brought out the journal *Arkhiv K. Marksa i F. Engel'sa* which published hitherto unknown works by Marx and Engels, as well as scholarly articles
on socialist thought, and the history of the international labour movement.
It also published the journal *Letopisi marksizma*, and the collected works of
Plekhanov. By the mid-1920s, IME had overtaken the Communist Academy, its
parent body, as the most authoritative arbiter of Marxist doctrine.

On the international arena, IME brought prestige to the Soviet regime, but
from the point of view of Pokrovskii and the Soviet leadership, IME posed two
related problems. One was that it rendered Marxism, 'the official ideology of
the victorious proletariat', unpredictable. One could not know what Marx or
Engels might say in documents still unearthed, that might undermine existing
conceptions of what Marxism was. The first volume of the *Marx and Engels
Collected Works* in Russian only appeared in 1928.

---

86   Rokitianskii and Müller 1996, pp. 61–2; Chernobaev 1992, pp. 155–6.
87   Rokitianskii and Müller 1996, pp. 67–8.

The other problem was that Riazanov was not a person who could be relied upon to refrain from publishing items that would be awkward for the regime's official ideology. Riazanov's loyalties were not to the Soviet authorities, with whom he disagreed profoundly on many issues, but to the international community of scholars. According to Riazanov, on the insistence of Pokrovskii and Skvortsov-Stepanov, in 1927 a commission of the Central Committee strictly prohibited Deborin and his team of philosophers at IME from studying Marx's ideas, or theory of any kind. They were allowed to study only pre-Marxist philosophy, and that only from a factual-historical point of view.[88]

In view of his many teaching, administrative and literary commitments, Pokrovskii had a punishing workload. In one of his articles O.D. Sokolov reproduces a document in which Pokrovskii listed the many and varied demands on his time.[89] Some were teaching commitments, such as his seminars at IKP, and lectures at the Sverdlov Communist University and RANION. He was head of the Communist Academy, Tsentrarkhiv, and IKP. He edited the *Great Soviet Encyclopaedia* and a number of scholarly journals, including *Istorik-marksist*, *Krasnyi arkhiv* and *Vestnik Kommunisticheskoi Akademii*. In addition, there were occasional tasks to perform, such as arranging events to mark the anniversaries of Chernyshevskii, and the October revolution. All told, Pokrovskii had somewhere in the region of twenty jobs. Being one of the few qualified academics that the Soviet regime had at its disposal, it was inevitable that he was called upon to carry out so many functions. Even when suffering from cancer, Pokrovskii was only able to divest himself of some of them.

---

88   Rokitianskii and Müller 1996, p. 318.
89   Sokolov 1969, p. 41.

CHAPTER 4

Pre-revolutionary Historical Works

1 History of Russia in the XIX Century

The *History of Russia in the XIX Century*, published by Granat, consisted of nine volumes, which appeared between 1907 and 1911, covering, in chronological order, economic, social, political and cultural developments in the Russian Empire. Like *Readings in Medieval History*, the authors who contributed chapters to the project were specialists in the various fields. They included Pokrovskii's academic colleagues: Rozhkov, Kizevetter, and Miliukov; fellow members of the literary-lecturing group: Friche, Kanel', Tseitlin, Levin and Taganskii; prominent Social Democrats: L. Martov and Lenin.

A notable feature of the work was its geographical scope, which included not only Russia proper, but territories acquired during its expansion, particularly Poland and the Baltic provinces. Z. Lenskii wrote about Poland, and Karl Lander contributed three chapters on the Latvian and Estonian provinces. In his chapter on the history of Russian Social Democracy Martov included both the Polish and the Latvian parties.

Vladimir Medem of the Jewish Bund mentions in his memoirs that Pokrovskii commissioned him to take charge of a section on the Jews in Russia. To discuss the details, he had met Pokrovskii, whom he describes as a 'congenial, serious, modest person'. It was on his visit to Pokrovskii that Medem encountered Lev Kamenev, who explained that as a standard-bearer for the Social-Democratic party it would not be appropriate for Lenin to participate in the project, and in fact no contribution by Lenin appeared in *History of Russia in the XIX Century*. As it happened, Medem did not contribute to the work either. The publisher later told him that, as other contributions had increased in length, there was a shortage of space, and, as Medem ruefully remarked: 'Who gets thrown out? Naturally, the Jews'.[1]

The main contributor, however, was Pokrovskii, who wrote almost a quarter of the 50 chapters in the volumes, some of these constituting substantial monographs. His organising role can be seen from the fact that the first four chapters are his; they are on Russia at the end of the XVIII century, Paul I, Alexander I, and the Decembrists. These chapters are written in the same style as

---

1 Medem and Portnoy 1979, pp. 415–16.

those Pokrovskii contributed to *Readings in Medieval History* and were probably intended for the same kind of audience. They assume very little or no
previous knowledge of the subject; they are accessible, readable, and highly
informative. The ideological dimension in them is slight, or entirely absent.
They are essays which can still be read with profit in the present day.

The chapter entitled 'Russia at the End of the XVIII Century' serves as an
introduction to the entire work, setting the scene by characterising the kind of
country Russia was as it entered the XIX century. This was a country, according to Pokrovskii, which still had a natural economy, where commerce was yet
in its infancy. Trade was little developed because communications were poor.
The transportation of goods was so expensive that it was unprofitable to export
grain; it was better to process it locally by using it to brew vodka. Brewing was
one of the privileges enjoyed by the landowning nobility. All such local enterprises employed mainly serf labour, wage labourers being still a rarity.

In Pokrovskii's view, the landowning nobility were sovereigns in miniature.
The peasants on their estates were completely at their mercy, the landowner
being able to punish them in a variety of ways. The serfs could be flogged, sent
as recruits into the army, or exiled to Siberia, without the government's thinking to question the landowner's judgement.

As in his earlier, liberal, articles Pokrovskii insists that the state is an instrument of class rule and does not stand in the same relation to the nobility as the
nobility do to their peasants. He concedes that it might seem to do so, in the
light of the personal power that sovereigns such as Catherine II appeared to
wield. The illusion was created, however, because, as Catherine admitted, she
only decreed what she knew would be popular. She, for example, did not try
to liberate the peasants, although she genuinely wanted to at the beginning of
her reign, because she doubted that this would meet with the 'general approval'
of those who owned the peasants. In Pokrovskii's view, the Russian tsar of the
XVIII century could only rule with the consent of the nobility. Paul I did not
understand this, and paid with his life for his mistake.

According to Pokrovskii, the nobility had control of the local institutions of
government, which was where their interests lay. They were not, however, represented in the central government, and did not wish to be. This was because:
'The central power was still so little active, so rarely and sporadically intervening in the life of the people, that a constant participation in it still did not
represent a great value in the eyes of the nobility of the XVIII century'.[2] This
was an idea of Pokrovskii's that did not go uncontested.

---

2 Pokrovskii 1907d, p. 13.

The chapter on the Emperor Paul I begins with a disquisition on the impact that the development of a capitalist economy has on the power of the central government. The passage is significant, because in it Pokrovskii comes close to admitting that the state can stand above society, an idea that in all his subsequent writings he contested vehemently. Pokrovskii argues that in a natural economy the power of the sovereign is limited by the need to appease the landowning nobility, whose support was indispensable. But with the emergence of a capitalist economy the picture changes: central government acquires a reliable and constant source of income and is now in a position to purchase services that it formerly had to beg for. In place of unreliable vassals with whom it was necessary to negotiate and bargain, there were now impersonal obedient civil servants. The fate not only of persons, but of whole social groups begins to depend on the caprice of the ruler. At the start of the XIX century, it was the Russian nobility who were subjected to the eccentricities of the Emperor Paul.[3]

According to Pokrovskii, Paul was prone to nervous instability, a condition that modern psychiatrists would call hysteria. Paul himself stated that in his youth he had suffered from hallucinations, and his contemporaries testified that, like his father Peter III, he was an alcoholic. His main preoccupation was drilling soldiers, and he brought a military ethos into the court in St Petersburg.

By acting on impulse and ignoring their privileged status, even making them subject to the same corporal punishment as the peasants, Paul antagonised the nobles. Although he did not set out to do so, he became the enemy of the ruling class, and the incarnation of the hopes and aspirations of the common people. In foreign relations, he sided with Napoleon against Britain, Russia's main trading partner. The resulting economic disruption, which undermined the nobility's material well-being, increased the hostility towards Paul, and strengthened the determination to oust him from power. A palace coup was organised on 11 March 1801 in which Paul was assassinated, probably with the connivance of his son, the future Alexander I. For Pokrovskii, the lesson to be drawn from the episode was that the function of the tsarist autocracy was to represent the class interests of the landowning nobility. If the incumbent ruler did not act accordingly, he or she would be replaced, by lethal force if necessary.[4]

For Pokrovskii, the account of Paul I's reign serves as a background to that of Alexander I. Unlike his father, Alexander was well aware that his power depended on the good will of the nobility, so that whatever course of action he might subjectively wish to take would have to be abandoned in favour of one

---

3   Pokrovskii 1907c, p. 21.
4   Pokrovskii 1907c, p. 30.

that would meet with the nobility's approval. Influenced by his enlightened tutor La Harpe, Alexander would have liked to abolish serfdom in the country but knew that this would not be approved by those to whom the serfs belonged. Nevertheless, in 1803 Alexander did issue an edict on 'free cultivators', which allowed serfs to buy their freedom on payment of a sum of money agreed with the landowner. He judged that such an arrangement would not evoke opposition from the nobility, because it could only be implemented with the landowner's consent.[5]

It was also Alexander's ambition to make Russia a constitutional monarchy, and to this end he had his secretary, Speranskii, draw up proposals for reform. Although these were relatively moderate, Alexander surmised that the nobility might see them as a threat to its privileged position and hesitated to introduce a constitution. In the event, he adopted only one of Speranskii's proposals: the establishment of a State Council. This was a body which had the functions that in constitutional states would be assigned to assemblies of people's representatives. But with the State Council there was the important difference that its members were not elected but appointed by the sovereign.[6]

After the 1812 campaign against Napoleon, Alexander increasingly fell under the influence of conservatives within Russia and abroad, and forever abandoned the ideals of his youth. The last years of his reign were marked by oppression and despotism, and it was in this atmosphere that secret societies which plotted the overthrow of the autocracy began to emerge.

Pokrovskii's chapter on the Decembrists is the length of a short monograph. It deals with all aspects of the movement: the emergence of secret societies after the Napoleonic war, their membership, and the relations between them; the plans of the societies for the transformation of Russia after a successful revolution; the ideological currents within the Decembrist movement; the uprising in St Petersburg in December 1825, and its defeat; the interrogation of the Decembrists by Nicholas, and the sentences imposed on them. The work forms a logical continuation and is a point of culmination of the three previous chapters.

The chapter on the Decembrists was written in conjunction with Kirik Levin, who had contributed an essay on 'The Political and Social Views of the Decembrists' to the collection of articles *Tekushchii moment* in 1906.[7] Levin's essay had argued that the programmes for reform drawn up by the Decembrists were not

---

5   Pokrovskii 1907a, pp. 38–9.
6   Pokrovskii 1907b, pp. 49–53.
7   Levin 1906a, pp. 1–13.

the products of their selfless idealism, but the reflection of their aristocratic and bourgeois class interests. This argument, along with some of the material Levin had used, was enlarged upon, and modified in the jointly written chapter on the Decembrists.

Pokrovskii begins his analysis by pointing out that the memoirs of the Decembrists give a false impression of what their thinking at the time of the insurrection had been. They were writing at a time when the liberation of the peasants was in the offing, and they wanted to believe that their movement had prepared the way for the legislation of February 1861. Were this the case, then their sacrifice would not have been in vain. But in fact, the emancipation of the peasants played only a minor part in the Decembrists' plans. Of much more concern to them was the defence of their privileges as members of the nobility. In this way, Pokrovskii argued, there was continuity between the palace revolutions of the XVIII century and the Decembrists.[8]

The explanation is not entirely convincing. What is lacking is some indication of how exactly Alexander I's actions at the end of his reign had so antagonised the Russian nobility, particularly as he had previously been careful to avoid doing so. Moreover, an alternative rationale for the action of the Decembrists is given in the opening section of the article. There it is explained that the young officers who had taken part in the 1812 campaign against Napoleon returned from France bringing with them liberal ideas and the aspiration to reform Russian institutions on the Western-European model. To counter the interpretation that the Decembrists might have been motivated by liberal convictions, rather than by conservative self-interest, Pokrovskii has to argue that the Decembrist plans to introduce constitutional government in Russia are not to be taken seriously. He accordingly indicates the ways in which Nikita Muraviev framed his constitution to ensure the preponderance of noble interests. This allows Pokrovskii to declare that: 'no phrases taken from bourgeois constitutions can mask that the Decembrist movement was in essence a nobles' movement'.[9]

Pokrovskii's insistence that the motives of the Decembrists were self-interest, rather than a genuine wish for constitutional reform, was motivated by the need to find a materialist explanation for their actions. But there is also a more personal explanation for his interpretation. The Decembrists were the forerunners of the zemstvo liberals, who had given rise to the Union of Liberation, and then to the Kadet party. At the turn of the century Pokrovskii had

8 Pokrovskii 1907b, p. 105.
9 Pokrovskii 1907b, pp. 108–9.

given this political current his support, but as emerges from his 1906 article 'The Victors', he became convinced that the zemstvo liberals were inspired not by any high ideal, but merely by the wish to bring about a more equitable distribution of rights and privileges within the noble estate. The antagonism Pokrovskii felt towards the liberals of his day was extended to their Decembrist predecessors.

There were ways in which the chapter on the Decembrists looked towards the future. It was, according to the authors, the first political society in Russia which put the slogans of armed insurrection, and a constituent assembly, on its banners, though this aspect of the movement was not emphasised in the Decembrists' memoirs. A more ominously prophetic aspect of the Decembrists' thinking was the perceived necessity to eliminate the Emperor and his entire family to ensure the success of a new republican order. In that way the danger of the emergence of pretenders to the throne, seen in earlier Russian history, would be avoided.

Like that on the Decembrists, Pokrovskii's chapter on the peasant reform of 1861 is a lengthy work of over a hundred pages. Also, like the chapter on the Decembrists, it has a mainly narrative structure, taking the reader through all the various stages in the preparation of the legislation. The description of the provincial committees, in which the landowning nobility discussed proposals of reform, gives Pokrovskii the opportunity to show the differences of opinion among the serf owners, how the progressive minority is outnumbered by those who are determined to free the peasants with as little loss to themselves as possible.

What was the motivation for the liberation? This question was an important one for Pokrovskii in the light of his clash with Struve in 1898 on this particular issue. As opposed to Pokrovskii's conception that the peasants were liberated because serfdom had become unprofitable, and it had become advantageous to the landowners to employ free labour, Struve had demonstrated that on the eve of 1861 serf labour in fact was on the increase. For Struve, therefore, the emancipation of the serfs had not been for economic reasons. In his chapter Pokrovskii nowhere mentions Struve, but one can see that he has taken Struve's findings on board.

In posing the question why the landowners allowed the emancipation, Pokrovskii finds that there are two possible explanations. One of them is that the matter was decided by the intervention of a kind of *deus ex machina*, the supra-class state, which for purely political motives, decided to abolish serfdom. But, Pokrovskii argues, this explanation is unsatisfactory. There was initiative from above with Catherine II, but there was no peasant reform. The same was true with Nicholas I, and again no reform ensued.

In place of this 'idealist' explanation Pokrovskii proposes a 'materialist' one. This explanation is that in the 1850s the owners of serf labour themselves understood that peasant reform was in the interests of the self-preservation of the nobility as a class. In the long-run, the management of the landowners' estates would be on a capitalist basis, using free hired labour. In the meantime, in order to increase productivity for the wheat market, the landowners made greater use of serf labour, putting old, feudal, 'extra-economic compulsion' to new, bourgeois, ends.

The snag was that the intensification of serf labour increased the likelihood of peasant disturbances, which had become endemic in the 1850s. The danger was that serfdom would be eliminated from below, in a revolutionary way, that would destroy the social order as well. The famous dictum of Alexander II in March 1856 that it was better to abolish serfdom from above than to wait until it abolished itself from below, was not just empty words – it described the reality of the situation. Pokrovskii summarised his argument in the following way: 'We have seen that the main driving force behind the peasant affair at the end of the 1850s was the fear of a Pugachev rebellion: without this, we would have had a slow evolution of economic relations, and not the revolution from above of 19 February'.[10]

In this interpretation of the 1861 liberation of the peasants Pokrovskii succeeds in taking into account Struve's finding that in the 1850s the use of serf labour increased, and at the same time showing that the reform was in the class interests of the landowning nobility. He had provided a 'materialist' explanation for what, in spite of his aversion to the idea of a supra-class state, he referred to as a 'revolution from above'.

2   Chapters on Russian Foreign Policy

Five of the chapters Pokrovskii contributed to *History of Russia in the XIX Century* were on Russia's foreign policy. Taken together, they form a continuous narrative, and in 1918 they were published in a volume entitled *Diplomacy and Wars of Tsarist Russia in the XIX Century*. In character, the chapters resemble those in *Readings in Medieval History*, in that they are substantial works of scholarship, with very little in the way of ideological colouring, beyond the propensity to focus on the economic aspects of a given topic, where these can be found.

---

10   Pokrovskii 1908, p. 115.

In the case of the chapter entitled 'Russia's Foreign Policy in the First Decades of the XIX Century', Pokrovskii examines the economic consequences of Russia's alliance with France following the Peace of Tilsit in 1807. By the terms of this treaty, Alexander I agreed to join Napoleon's 'Continental System', and to impose high tariffs on British goods. This measure benefited countries which had the beginnings of heavy industry, like Saxony, Belgium and northern Italy, but was ruinous for countries living by the export of raw materials, such as Sweden, Prussia, Poland, and Russia. In this way, the action of Napoleon's tariff policy ensured that Prussia, Sweden and Russia would be members of the future anti-French coalition. It was Alexander's refusal to continue to adhere to the 'Continental System' that made war with Napoleon inevitable.[11]

Because Polish landowners, like their Russian counterparts, exported grain, Alexander believed that he could count on the support of the Poles against Napoleon. With Polish forces on his side, Alexander planned to launch an offensive against the French in 1811. The Poles, however, considered that they had much more to gain from siding with Napoleon, as a French victory over Russia held out the hope of a reconstituted Polish state. The Polish army, consequently, went over to Napoleon, who now decided on the invasion of Russia, a campaign that Pokrovskii describes at some length.[12]

A major part of the chapter is devoted to 'The Eastern Policy of Nicholas I', which introduces the topic of Russia's aspiration to gain control of Constantinople and the Straits, that was to figure prominently in Pokrovskii's writings on Russian foreign policy. The objective could be gained only with the partition of Turkey, in which Russia hoped to participate. The European powers, principally Britain and France, however, did not look favourably on this prospect.

The theme of Russia's desire for the acquisition of Constantinople and the Straits was taken up in the following chapter in the series entitled 'The Crimean War'. In this chapter Pokrovskii recounts how Nicholas I provoked a war with Turkey and its allies Britain and France, ostensibly for religious motives, but in reality to extend Russian influence to European Turkey, the Balkan peninsula and Constantinople. Pokrovskii not only provides a narrative of the campaigns of the Crimean war, but also analyses the reasons for the Russian defeat. According to Pokrovskii, the weaponry and the tactics of the Russian army were out of date, and while Russian warships were sailing vessels, those of the Allies were propeller driven. Moreover, Russian communications were poor. Whereas

---

11 Pokrovskii 1923, p. 32.
12 Pokrovskii 1923, p. 38.

a country like Austria had a well-developed railway network and could quickly concentrate its armies at any chosen point, Russia had to manoeuvre its armies and its waggons along primitive dirt roads. Russian medical facilities were dire, and more men were lost through disease than were killed in battle.[13]

Nicholas died in 1855, and it was Alexander ii who attended the Congress of Paris, which brought the war to an end. The terms of the peace reflected Russia's defeat, the most important of these being the closure of the Dardanelles to the warships of all nations, which of course was most onerous for Russia. Alexander's attempts to revise the terms of the Paris Peace are recounted in the chapter of *The History of Russia in the xix Century* entitled 'The Eastern Question (from the Peace of Paris to the Congress of Berlin)'.

The chief focus of this chapter is Russia's war against Turkey in 1877–78, which took place against the background of Panslavist support for the revolt of the Balkan Slavs against Turkish rule. Despite the stern resistance put up by the Turks at Plevna, the Russians eventually prevailed. They were not able, however, to continue their offensive to the Turkish capital. This was prevented by the Turkish navy, which was still intact, and by the presence of the British Mediterranean fleet, which would have come into action as soon as the Russians threatened the Straits. Lord Derby, the British Foreign Minister, warned Shuvalov, the Russian ambassador, that the seizure of Constantinople by Russian forces, even temporarily, would meet with British resistance. The Russians made their headquarters at San Stefano, outside Constantinople, where they dictated the terms of the peace. By the Treaty of San Stefano, Bulgaria, Serbia and Montenegro became independent states, and Russia made some territorial gains at Turkey's expense. At the Congress of Berlin in the spring of 1878, the terms of the San Stefano Treaty were modified to take into account the interests of the European powers, of Austria in particular, who objected to the creation of a Bulgarian state. On the insistence of the British, who feared a Russian threat to the Mediterranean route to India, the neutral status of the Straits remained unchanged.[14]

The chapter 'Russia's Foreign Policy at the End of the xix Century' covers developments in the reign of Alexander iii. Its first section deals with the emergence of the Franco-Russian Alliance. The obstruction shown by Prussia and Austria to Russia's Bulgarian policy had disillusioned Alexander with Russia's traditional alignment with Prussia against France. Alexander felt that Bismarck had not sufficiently rewarded Russia for the help it had given Prussia in the

13   Pokrovskii 1923, pp. 117–78.
14   Pokrovskii 1923, pp. 264–98.

Franco-Prussian War of 1870. The Franco-Russian alliance, which was signed in 1894, was an expression of the military and financial common interests of the two countries.[15]

Having helped to bring about the emergence of Bulgaria as an independent state, the Russians expected to be able to influence its political and economic orientation, and in particular, to exploit it as a market for Russian goods. They tried to persuade the Bulgarians to link their railways to the Russian network. Anticipating that few benefits would accrue from a Russian connection, the Bulgarians opted to operate within the Austrian orbit, and to construct their railways accordingly.[16]

Failing to extend its influence in the Balkans, Russia turned its attention to the Far East. This resulted in the construction of the Trans-Siberian Railway, Russia's seizure of Manchuria in 1900 during the Boxer uprising in China, and the conflict with Japan, leading to the Russo-Japanese War of 1904. With this chapter Pokrovskii brought his narrative up to the eve of the 1905 revolution in Russia.[17]

One of the sections in this chapter entitled 'In Search of an External Market', deals with the Russian conquest of Central Asia. This, and the chapter 'The Conquest of the Caucasus', form a distinct category in Pokrovskii's contribution to *History of Russia in the XIX Century*, in which he examines the incorporation of non-Russian peoples into the Empire. In both cases Pokrovskii approaches the subject from the point of view of the native populations and shows the heavy-handed way in which the Russian authorities dealt with them.

In his chapter on the Caucasus, Pokrovskii explains that not all the peoples who inhabit the area are homogeneous either linguistically or in social and economic development. The factor they had in common was their Islamic faith, so that the Russians had to resort to communicating with them in Arabic. Whereas the social relations of the Cherkes resembled those of feudal Europe in the XI–XII centuries, Chechen society was like the Germany in the times of Caesar and Tacitus.[18]

Until the beginning of the nineteenth century, the Russian government did not attempt conquest of the Caucasus, merely defending itself from raids by the mountain tribes. Colonisation by Russians began at the start of the nineteenth century, accompanied by a more aggressive approach towards the native peoples. If a raider or his family were not given up, the Russians would burn the

---

15   Pokrovskii 1923, pp. 302–13.
16   Pokrovskii 1923, pp. 346–50.
17   Pokrovskii 1923, pp. 355–78.
18   Pokrovskii 1923, p. 200.

entire village. Hostages would be taken, and in the event of insubordination, these would be hanged or sent to Siberia.

According to Pokrovskii, armed resistance to the Russian conquest was inspired by the religious movement which bore the name '*muridism*' (one who seeks), a form of mystic Sufi Islam, which was brought to the Caucasus from Central Asia in the 1820s. In its asceticism Pokrovskii thought it comparable to the teaching of the Franciscan order. The resistance movement was led by the Daghestani Imam Shamil, who invoked Sharia law in the organisation of the mountain tribes into a formidable fighting force. The Caucasian War lasted throughout the reign of Nicholas I, and it was only in 1859 that Shamil fell into Russian captivity. As reasons for his downfall Pokrovskii cites the adoption of rifles by the Russian army, the opposition to Shamil by the Caucasian aristocracy, and by the attempt of Shamil to concentrate power in his own hands and make his position hereditary.[19]

Pokrovskii's account of the Russian conquest of Central Asia in the chapter 'Russia's Foreign Policy at the End of the XIX Century' is comparable to his chapter on the Caucasus. Here too the Russians sought to subject the native peoples to their rule, and encountered resistance, though here the resistance was not so difficult to overcome as that in the Caucasus. The methods the Russians employed were no less brutal. Central Asians were killed needlessly in order that Russian commanders could claim brilliant victories and be entitled to decorations. If a Russian soldier was killed whole villages would be burnt to the ground in reprisal.[20]

According to Pokrovskii, the Russians came to exploit the country, so that, as soon as the guns fell silent, Russian capitalists swiftly emerged to make the country their own. At the time of the Russian conquest, the handicraft industry of Turkestan specialised in producing fine silk and cotton yarn, which was used in the production of textiles in the Moscow and Vladimir provinces, for the local and Russian markets. The rise in the price of cotton at the end of the 1880s prompted Russian manufacturers to use the climatic conditions of Central Asia to deprive America of its monopoly in cotton. The success of cotton growing caused the price of bread in Turkestan to more than double in the years 1890–1894, as the more profitable cotton crop ousted that of the less profitable wheat. However, in the opinion of Pokrovskii, the penetration of Russian capitalism into Central Asia was a progressive phenomenon, in comparison with the primitive system it replaced.[21]

---

19   Pokrovskii 1923, pp. 206–21.
20   Pokrovskii 1923, pp. 323–7.
21   Pokrovskii 1923, pp. 340–5.

The two works by Pokrovskii on the Russian conquest of native peoples suggest an indebtedness to Vinogradov and the Germanist school for their insights into pre-capitalist social and economic systems. They are also reminiscent of the chapters Pokrovskii had submitted to Vinogradov's *Readings in Medieval History*, for the way they approach religious movements from within, and attempt to convey the spirit of the doctrines they profess.

3   *Russian History from the Earliest Times*

Russian History from the Earliest Times was published between 1910 and 1913 in five volumes. The first edition of the work was written by Pokrovskii in collaboration with N.M. Nikol'skii, Pokrovskii being the main author, while Nikol'skii supplied the chapters on the history of religion and the church. From the second edition of 1918, the number of volumes was reduced to four, and from the fourth edition, published in 1922, the chapters by Nikol'skii were omitted. Thus, the Soviet editions of *Russian History from the Earliest Times* appeared as a four-volume work written entirely by Pokrovskii. Running to well over a thousand pages, it was the most substantial piece of historical writing that Pokrovskii produced.

In their Preface to the book *Russian History from the Earliest Times* Pokrovskii and Nikol'skii explained that, although the title of their book might remind readers of S.M. Soloviev's monumental *History of Russia from the Earliest Times*, they had no intention of emulating Soloviev's ground-breaking research. Their task was much more modest; it was to act as an intermediary between, on the one hand, the historians who conducted original research and, on the other, those sections of the reading public who wanted to be informed about the findings of recent historical scholarship, but who had not the time or the ability to do so for themselves.

However, Pokrovskii and Nikol'skii hastened to assure their readers that simply because they had renounced any claims to originality, it did not mean that they saw themselves as mere compilers of other people's material. Far from it. They could not take the existing historical generalisations as they found them, because these generalisations contained misconceptions arising from the idealist viewpoint of existing historians. The research of these historians required to be re-worked and refined from a materialist, (i.e., from a Marxist) point of view. It was in the presentation of modern scholarship on Russian history from a Marxist viewpoint that the authors of *Russian History from the Earliest Times* claimed that the originality of their work lay.

Chronologically, the scope of *Russian History from the Earliest Times* is comprehensive, extending as it does, from primitive society to the end of the nineteenth century. But the book does not set out to acquaint its readers with the events of Russian history. It assumes in them quite an extensive existing knowledge. In this respect it is quite unlike Kliuchevskii's *Course*, which had in mind a student audience who had, at best, been taught some Russian history at school. For Pokrovskii, the ideal audience would be readers who were well acquainted with Kliuchevskii's *Course*, so that they might better appreciate how Pokrovskii had gone beyond Kliuchevskii in the depth of his analysis. The aspects of Russian history which Pokrovskii chooses to concentrate on in *Russian History from the Earliest Times* are those in which he believes he can contribute something new and interpreted afresh. While the book is a work of impressive scholarship, it lacks the cohesion of a cogent narrative.

Skvortsov-Stepanov remarked on how Pokrovskii's *Russian History* could best be appreciated in comparison with earlier works. In a letter to Pokrovskii written on 24 February 1913 he observed:

> You know, it turns out that one doesn't appreciate your *History* all at once. I liked your beginning of the xvii century earlier. But I didn't really understand it until last month when I read it in conjunction with Platonov and Kliuchevskii.[22]

In his review of *Russian History from the Earliest Times* for *Prosveshchenie* published in November of 1913 Skvortsov-Stepanov wrote:

> Pokrovskii's book presupposes an acquaintance with the most important facts of Russian history. For those who are new to the subject, Kliuchevskii is probably still useful as an introduction. But for real scholarly depth on the subject Pokrovskii's work is the only textbook.[23]

In its coverage of the nineteenth century, *Russian History from the Earliest Times* goes over some of the same ground as the chapters in *History of Russia in the XIX Century*, so that it is possible to compare the two versions of the same episode. The main difference between them is that in the earlier work Pokrovskii focuses on showing that the real power behind the autocracy is the landowning nobility, and that, consequently, the Russian state is not a force which is independent of society. In the later work, on the other hand, the focus has shifted. Pokrovskii is now concerned to demonstrate that the actions of

---

22   Chernobaev 1992, pp. 71–2.
23   Skvortsov-Stepanov 1930, p. 315.

Russia's rulers have been determined by an economic force, such as the fluctuation in grain prices. Thus, in *History of Russia in the XIX Century* Catherine II did not liberate the serfs because the nobility would not allow it. In *Russian History from the Earliest Times* – she could not liberate the serfs because the idea of liberating the peasants was killed by the grain prices.

In keeping with this economic explanation, Pokrovskii traces the initial stimulus for the emancipation of the peasants in 1861 to the rise in grain prices, whereas in his earlier work the motivation had been to avoid a repeat of the Pugachev rebellion. In *History of Russia in the XIX Century*, Paul I had acted irrationally, and on impulse; in the later work his actions were explained by his anxiety to forestall peasant discontent, and in this way safeguard the long-term interests of the serf-owners. In speaking of the Decembrists in *History of Russia in the XIX Century*, Pokrovskii had referred to their defence of noble privilege, and continuity with the palace revolutions of the XVIII century. *Russian History from the Earliest Times* also mentions this continuity, but notes that the Decembrists also had contacts with the merchantry of St Petersburg, implying a wider social base and economic reasons for the movement.

Rather than describe how Pokrovskii approaches each historical period in its chronological sequence, it is more instructive to survey the main features of the interpretation he brings to his historical material. These features can be considered under the following heads: 1) the economic forces behind the historical events; 2) the relationship of the State to society; 3) the part played in events by individuals; 4) the relationship of Russia to Western Europe; 5) the Russian revolutionary movement. Of course these features of Pokrovskii's interpretation of Russian history are inter-connected and reinforce each other in the presentation of events.

1) The economic forces behind the historical events.

In *Russian History from the Earliest Times* Pokrovskii never uses the term 'economic materialism', characterising his approach to history as 'materialist', in contrast to the 'idealist' presuppositions of his predecessors. Fundamental to his interpretation of Russian history, however, is the need to find an economic explanation of the events he recounts. These economic explanations vary over time, and define the successive eras in Russian history. In the early period, it is trade that accounts for the rise of Kiev as the centre of Russian civilisation. Its commercial relations with Constantinople, including the trade in slaves, were the source of its prosperity. The capture of Constantinople by the French and Italian crusaders in 1204, causing the trading routes to shift, to the detriment of Kiev, led to the city's decline. The rise of Moscow as the new centre of the

Russian state was due to its favourable position on the intersection of trading routes, running from north to south and from east to west.[24] The quest for trading routes with Western Europe through the Baltic in the interests of merchant capital motivated Peter the Great's Northern War against Sweden, which lasted from 1700 to 1721.

From the reign of Catherine II onwards, the chief determinant of Russian internal and external policy for Pokrovskii was the fluctuation in grain prices. While the prices of grain were low on the European market Russian landowners had no incentive to abolish serfdom. It was for this reason that Catherine's plans to free the serfs came to nothing.[25] Instead, labour service (*barshchina*) was intensified, leading to the mass peasant uprising of Emilian Pugachev (1773–74). To avoid a repetition of the Pugachev uprising, Catherine's successor Paul I limited the amount of *barshchina* a landowner could demand of his serfs to three days in the week.

In Pokrovskii's view, the development that spelled the end of the serfdom system was the rise in grain prices brought about by the abolition of the Corn Laws in Britain, and the famine in Western Europe in the 1840s. This increased the opportunities for grain producers to export their product. The obstacle to increasing production for the market was that serf labour was extremely inefficient. In this connection, Pokrovskii quotes the A.I. Koshelev who in 1847 wrote as follows:

> Let us have a look at *barshchina* labour. The peasant comes to work as late as possible, looks about him and stares into space as often and as long as possible, and he works as little as he can. He is concerned not so much with working as with getting his day in ....[26]

The solution was clearly to replace serf labour by hired workers. But this was not so simple to accomplish. The landed estates lacked capital for investment, and they were very often heavily in debt to the State Bank. To overcome these difficulties, Koshelev proposed to sell to the peasants their freedom together with the allotments which they had cultivated under serfdom. With the money they received the landowners could pay off their existing debts and acquire capital, not as a debt, which they would have to repay, but as the proceeds of a sale. Koshelev's idea of liberation of the peasantry with land was the essence of the

---

24   Pokrovskii 1967a, p. 211.
25   Pokrovskii 1967b, p. 113.
26   Pokrovskii 1967b, p. 313.

actual legislation of 1861. This was a liberation not motivated by any legal or moral considerations, but by a purely economic calculation.[27]

As Pokrovskii points out, by no means all Russian landowners were able to run their estates on commercial lines and preferred to retain their serf labour. The modifications introduced to the Koshelev version of the liberation to cater for this 'feudal' element, made the terms more onerous for the peasantry, and ensured that this was not a real liberation, but one in appearance only.

The high grain prices which accompanied the era of reforms lasted into the 1870s. The 1880s were a period of low grain prices and reduced export of grain, and these phenomena underpinned the onset of reaction and counter-reform under Alexander III.[28] Nevertheless, the 1880s saw the further growth of industrial capitalism that had begun to develop under Nicholas I. It was stimulated by railway construction and the associated metal-processing industries.[29] As Pokrovskii indicates, Alexander III's policy of reversing the reforms of the 1860s may have worked in the countryside, but not in the towns, where the proletariat was emerging as a significant social force.[30]

With the peasant reform of 1861 there is the opportunity to compare Pokrovskii's interpretation with Marx's treatment of the subject. In 1948–1952 the journal *Arkhiv K. Marksa i F. Engel'sa* published manuscripts written by Marx, summarizing his reading on the reform. The outline Marx composed of the history of the reform and its economic consequences begins with Alexander II's Emancipation Manifesto and the convocation of the committees to discuss the reform.[31] Marx does not trace the origins of the emancipation to any economic motivations in Russian society which might have prompted the measure. His approach to the reform is 'from above', from the viewpoint of the governing bodies.[32] It is consequently at variance with the approach taken by Pokrovskii, who believed he was following the Marxist interpretation of history.

2) The relationship of the State to society.

In *Russian History from the Earliest Times* Pokrovskii continues to voice his opposition to the school of historical thought which sees the State as the driving force of developments, and society as its passive object. In this respect,

27   Pokrovskii 1967b, p. 321.
28   Pokrovskii 1967b, p. 485.
29   Pokrovskii 1967b, pp. 539–40.
30   Pokrovskii 1967b, p. 499.
31   Koniushaia 1952, pp. 3–9.
32   See White 1996, pp. 211–80.

there is complete continuity between *Russian History from the Earliest Times* and Pokrovskii's earlier articles written in the liberal cause. In discussing the powers of the *veche* assembly in XIII century Novgorod *vis à vis* the prince, for example, Pokrovskii intends to show that there was no great gulf between the ruler and the ruled, that early Russian society was democratic. As evidence he cites a chronicle in which it is stated that between the prince and his elected official 'there was no essential difference; both the one and the other enjoyed authority only by virtue of its delegation by the town, and only until such time as the town deprived them of it'.[33]

In a passage which equates the doctrine of the State standing above society with the idealist approach to history, which he opposes, Pokrovskii writes:

> The conventional antithesis of 'boiars' and 'the State' as centrifugal and centripetal forces respectively in the young state of Moscow is one of the most unfortunate survivals of the idealistic method, which represented the 'State' as some independent force, acting upon society from above. In actual fact, the State in appanage Rus' was, as always, simply a certain form of organisation of the dominant social elements, and the princes of Moscow, for their part, did not think of denying the fact that they ruled their principality, not alone, but jointly with the boiars, as 'first among equals'.[34]

In describing Russia's political structure in the reign of Ivan the Terrible in the sixteenth century, Pokrovskii states that the sovereign could not rule without the consent of his boiars. But significantly, he retreats from the contention he had made in the article 'Zemskii sobor and Parliament' that the *zemskii sobor* was an early form of representative institution. It was now his opinion that: 'It would, of course, be very naive to imagine that this "*zemskii sobor* of 1566" ... even remotely resembled modern popular representative bodies'.[35] He goes on to explain that the heat has now gone out of the controversy that surrounded the *zemskii sobor* on the eve of the 1905 revolution. At the present time, hardly anyone wanted to argue about whether it resembled a representative institution of the Western European type, or whether it was a 'consultation of the government with its own agents'. It was probably neither, but something unique that did not fit neatly into any modern political category.[36]

---

33   Pokrovskii 1967a, p. 196.
34   Pokrovskii 1967a, pp. 215–16.
35   Pokrovskii 1967a, p. 324.
36   Pokrovskii 1967a, p. 444.

For the more modern period, from Peter the Great onwards, Pokrovskii depicts the ruler as representing the interests either of merchant capital or of the landowning class, and only at his peril pursuing independent policies. The Emperor Paul I antagonised the nobility in this way and paid for it with his life.

Pokrovskii paid particular attention to the question of the role of the State in modern Russian history in *Russian History from the Earliest Times*. His treatment of it in *History of Russia in the XIX Century* had come in for criticism by M.S. Aleksandrov (Ol'minskii) in his book *The State, Bureaucracy and Absolutism in Russian History*, published in 1910. The book was a critique of how Russian historians had viewed the relationship of the State to society, their tendency to see the autocracy as standing above, and shaping society. He was particularly dismissive of the theory that the autocracy had 'enserfed' and subsequently 'disenserfed' the estates composing Russian society. Ol'minskii disputed Pokrovskii's claim that: 'The central power was still so little active, so seldom and sporadic in interfering in the life of the people, that constant participation in it was still little valued in the eyes of the nobility of the XVIII century'. In Ol'minskii's view, the nobility would hardly agree with the idea that participation in the central power was of little value, if, for example, the central power was taken out of the hands of the nobility and placed in those of the merchantry.[37]

On reading Ol'minskii's book while he was in the process of writing *Russian History from the Earliest Times*, Pokrovskii sent the author the following rather petulant letter:

> The theory of 'enserfment' and 'disenserfment' has not enjoyed any credit among younger Russian historians for about the last ten years. If we did not come out against it specially, then you may easily see that we have systematically ignored it. We have not written to refute it simply because there has been no external pretext; none of us has so far undertaken such a large comprehensive work as, for example, *Russian History* [*from the Earliest Times*] which is now being published. In it I shall, of course, take this prejudice into account, and I hope that the corresponding chapters will meet fully with your satisfaction.[38]

Whether or not Ol'minskii's book influenced Pokrovskii in the way he approached the question of the State and society in *Russian History from the*

---

37   Aleksandrov 1919, p. 160.
38   ibid.

Earliest Times it is impossible to tell. But certainly, from this time he never again suggested that the Russian State could be anything other than the expression of class interests.

3) The part played in Russian history by individuals.

As Pokrovskii had indicated in his pamphlet *Economic Materialism*, the question of the State and society and that of the role of the individual in history were closely related. For if individuals, such as the ruler of the country, could introduce something of 'their own' into the course of history, this would be a phenomenon that could not be explained by the materialist method. It was therefore important for Pokrovskii to show that every feature in the character of some historical actor or other could be explained from the general conditions of the age in which they lived. Consistently in *Russian History from the Earliest Times* there is the determination to deny any of the personalities in it anything that is in any way unique to them.

Although historians had considered cruelty and barbarity the distinguishing feature of Ivan IV, hence his appellation of 'the Terrible', Pokrovskii argued that this feature was one common to people in his day. As evidence of this he cites the opinion of the publicist Ivan Peresvetov, who believed that unjust judges should be flayed alive, and their skins nailed up in the law courts with the inscription: 'without such terrors justice cannot be brought into the realm'.[39] The implication was that the cruelties which Ivan the Terrible visited on the country were no worse than the measures a contemporary recommended in order to encourage the judiciary to follow best practice. Pokrovskii does not suggest that any judges were treated in this way, but he makes a valid point about the cruelty of the times, which he does not balk at describing.

In speaking of the Emperor Paul I, Pokrovskii expresses satisfaction that he has been able to account for his actions without resorting to the favourite method of the majority of historians of his reign – to psychology. He admits, however, that he himself in *History of Russia in the XIX Century* had been guilty of explaining much in Paul's policy by his hereditary morbidity. Pokrovskii now considered that everything that the 'mad' Paul did would have been done also by a normal person of comparable intellectual development and inclinations, placed in a similar position. These inclinations, moreover, were not deviations from the norm, but only exaggerations of the habits and customs of the social group to which he belonged.[40]

---

39   Pokrovskii 1967a, p. 315.
40   Pokrovskii 1967b, p. 168.

Even prominent figures such as Peter I, Catherine II, Alexander I, Nicholas I and Alexander III are all treated simply as the vehicles through which economic forces operated, or as examples of the occupant of a particular type of political institution, rather than as living individuals with eccentricities. For Pokrovskii, personalities did not contribute anything to the historical process. In his opinion: 'The individualist method, which attributes all historical changes to the actions of individual persons, is at a loss when confronted with the fact that even when there are no persons on the stage, changes are obviously still taking place'.[41] History for Pokrovskii is impersonal and, seemingly, rational, since it proceeds without the interference of human beings whose actions might, albeit unintentionally, change its course.

4) The relationship of Russia to Western Europe.

Not only did Pokrovskii deny uniqueness to people; he denied it to nations. It is a principle for Pokrovskii that any phenomenon in Russian history will be replicated in some way in the history of Western European countries. This was an idea which was basic to the Positivist approach to history that Vinogradov and Kovalevsky espoused, and there is continuity in this respect between Pokrovskii's liberal and his Marxist works.

One example of this doctrine is in his description of society in early Russian history where Pokrovskii reminds his readers that the ancient Roman 'familia' denoted 'slaves of one master', and that, similarly, in the ancient Russian household the term for 'children' applied not only to the relatives of the master of the house, but also to his servants.[42]

Pokrovskii was firmly of the opinion that feudalism existed in Russia on the Western European model. In this he had the support of the historian N. Pavlov-Sil'vanskii, who argued that the boiars' service to their superior was equivalent to the vassalage of Western feudalism and found that even the terminology employed to convey the relationship between vassal and suzerain was very similar.[43]

It was in terms of Western European feudalism that Pokrovskii conceived the ruling institutions of ancient Russia. Just as at the head of every feudal state in Western Europe there stood a group of persons – king or duke, the 'suzerain', with the 'curia' of his vassals – so at the head of the Muscovite state there like-

---

41   Pokrovskii 1967a, p. 209.
42   Pokrovskii 1967a, p. 95.
43   Pokrovskii 1967a, p. 127.

wise stood a group of persons: the prince, later grand prince, and tsar, with his boiar duma. And just as the Western European feudal sovereign, in unusual and in especially important matters, was not content with the counsel of his immediate vassals but convoked the representatives of all feudal society – the 'estates of the realm' – so also in Russia the prince, in early times, occasionally took counsel with his *druzhina*, and the tsar with the *zemskii sobor*, the assembly of the land. Both the duma and the *sobor* embodied the feudal principle that from a free servitor can be demanded only that service for which he has been contracted, and that he can abandon this service whenever he finds it disadvantageous.[44]

A more surprising parallel that Pokrovskii draws is that between the reign of Peter the Great and the Italian Renaissance. The festivals and masquerades that Peter's contemporaries engaged in, together with the hedonism and the mockery of established religion, had, in his view, their counterparts in Italy two centuries before. In Pokrovskii's view, the account of Peter's reign written by Prince Kurakin is comparable to the history of Florence written by Machiavelli. In his *Russian History from the Earliest Times* Pokrovskii repeats his contention that, in the way Machiavelli depicts individuals as being representatives of classes or social groups, he is one of the forerunners of 'economic materialism'. The evidence of his *Russian History from the Earliest Times* shows that, in his treatment of individuals, Pokrovskii himself might be seen as a disciple of Machiavelli.[45]

In his chapter on the Decembrist revolt of 1825 Pokrovskii here too shows that the liberal ideas that inspired it were not unique to Russia. He points out that in Germany, and especially in Italy and Spain, the bearers of liberal ideas were participants in the 'wars of liberation' against Napoleon, and that the first revolutionary movements of the 1820s took the form of armed uprisings.[46] For Pokrovskii, therefore, the Decembrist uprising was not a phenomenon unique to Russia.

Pokrovskii considered Russia's relationship with Western Europe to be not just a shared or parallel history, but Russia's active involvement in Western European affairs, even to the extent of aggression towards Western European countries. In the case of the 1812 war against Napoleon, Pokrovskii rejects the idea of a French invasion. He argues that Alexander I's letters leave not the slightest doubt that Russia was preparing to attack France already in 1810.

---

44   Pokrovskii 1967a, pp. 128–9.
45   Pokrovskii 1967a, pp. 601–2.
46   Pokrovskii 1967b, p. 231.

It was only when Alexander discovered that the Poles would not be on his side, but on Napoleon's, that he abandoned his plans for an aggressive campaign.[47]

Similarly, in the case of the Crimean War, Pokrovskii disputes the opinion of historians who believed that Russia was not prepared for the war, and that it came as a surprise. In fact, he contends, soon after the conclusion of the treaty of Hünkâr İskelesi in 1833, Nicholas I wrote to General Ivan Paskevich about war with Britain as a distinct possibility. Not only did Nicholas contemplate this possibility, but he took practical measures to prepare for it. It was around 1833 that Russia embarked on an extensive programme of shipbuilding to equip the navy. The defences of the Kronstadt and Sevastopol fortresses were reinforced. However, despite these preparations, Russia was defeated by the Western European powers, because of its economic weakness.[48]

Looking ahead to the way Pokrovskii would approach the outbreak of the First World War in his Soviet-era writings, one can see that here too he follows the same principles as he had in his depictions of the 1812 campaign and the Crimean War. He regards Russia as the initiator of the war, and he maintains that the social forces that had driven Russia to war were replicated in other European countries. For Pokrovskii, Russia was seldom the victim of war, but often the perpetrator.

5) The Russian revolutionary movement.

Much of the final chapter of *Russian History from the Earliest Times*, on 'The End of the XIX Century', deals with the revolutionary movement. At the time Pokrovskii was writing there were very few sources on this subject; these would be published in any considerable number only in Soviet times. From the text of Pokrovskii's chapter it emerges that he is basing his conception of how the Russian revolutionary movement developed on the writings of Plekhanov, one of the pioneers of Social Democracy in Russia. Plekhanov's writings, such as *Socialism and the Political Struggle*, *Our Differences* and *The Monist View of History* were extremely influential in how the intellectual currents within the Russian revolutionary movement were conceived.

Plekhanov, however, was not a dispassionate observer of the movement, but a polemicist, intent on undermining his ideological opponents. In the 1880s the early followers of Marx, such as Danielson and Vorontsov, deplored the

---

47   Pokrovskii 1967b, p. 217.
48   Pokrovskii 1967b, pp. 307–8.

emergence of capitalism in the country, because it uprooted the peasants from the land, without creating occupations for them in industry. Famine, disease and starvation were the result, particularly in the years 1891–92. Plekhanov, however, took the view that the development of capitalism in Russia was a positive development that would lead eventually to the emergence of a pro-letariat, and the triumph of a socialist revolution. He believed that Russia's economic development would be no different from that of the countries of Western Europe.

In order to discredit those socialists who thought that the development of capitalism was detrimental to Russia, Plekhanov accused them of being not Marxists, but 'Narodniki' (Populists), followers of a doctrine with Slavophile antecedents, who believed in Russia's uniqueness. The founders of the 'Nar-odnik' current, according to Plekhanov, were Herzen and Chernyshevskii. This conception of the intellectual history of the Russian revolutionary movement was taken up by the historian Bogucharskii, and subsequently became the accepted version both in Soviet and in Western historiography. A reading of the relevant texts is sufficient to show that 'Narodism' is the product of Plekhanov's invention.[49]

Pokrovskii was convinced by Plekhanov's arguments, and, correspondingly, believed that there was a 'Narodnik' phase in the revolutionary movement, and that it was initiated by Herzen and Chernyshevskii. Pokrovskii would be recept-ive to Plekhanov's ideas, because Plekhanov's Marxism was a doctrine which held that all countries pass through the same stages of development. This of course was in keeping with Pokrovskii's principle in *Russian History from the Earliest Times* that there are no phenomena in Russian history that do not have their counterparts in the history of Western European countries.

Pokrovskii was familiar with Lenin's book *The Development of Capitalism in Russia*, which embodies the assumption that Russia already had a capitalist economy. He did not, however, draw upon any of the theorising it contains, cit-ing it mainly to illustrate the process of economic stratification undergone by the Russian peasants.[50]

Russian History from the Earliest Times is a work which shows Pokrovskii as a historian who is capable of writing on all periods of Russian history. Although he is less confident in his coverage of the Russian revolutionary movement, as a whole, Pokrovskii treats most topics knowledgeably and in some detail.

---

49   White 1996, pp. 316–18.
50   Pokrovskii 1967b, pp. 488–9.

The price he pays for his extensive chronological span is dependence on the work of other historians since it would be impossible to conduct first-hand research on each and every topic. This emerges in his letter to Ol'minskii, where he says that 'The theory of "enserfment" and "disenserfment" has not enjoyed any credit among younger Russian historians for about the last ten years'. For a truly original historian it should not matter what the scholarly consensus is at any given time, because that historian would investigate the topic in question independently, from primary material, and arrive at a finding. Because he worked on a broad chronological scale, this path was not open to Pokrovskii. As he implied in the Preface to *Russian History from the Earliest Times*, his claim to originality was the way in which he interpreted other people's historical writings. Kliuchevskii had been able to avoid any such dependence on secondary works in his *Course of Russian History* because the topics he had specialised in spanned a wide time scale and had many applications in his general *Course*.

Because of his dependence on the writings of others, it was particularly important for Pokrovskii to be able to assess these writings critically, hence the attention he paid to the question of historiography. Pokrovskii's lectures on Russian historiography, which are a key element in his scholarly output, can be considered as a by-product of his ambition to produce a comprehensive account of Russian history.

4   *Study in the History of Russian Culture*

Pokrovskii completed the first volume of *Study in the History of Russian Culture* in France before the outbreak of the World War, and the second volume – in Moscow in 1918. Unlike *Russian History from the Earliest Times*, the arrangement of the work's material is not chronological, but thematic, or, as Pokrovskii described it, 'vertical'. There are sections on the economy, the political structure, the judiciary, and religion. Because to some extent *Study in the History of Russian Culture* goes over the same ground as *Russian History from the Earliest Times*, Pokrovskii was at pains to reassure his readers that *Study in the History of Russian Culture* was not simply a summary of what was contained in *Russian History from the Earliest Times*, but an independent work in its own right. There were, he said, topics in *Study in the History of Russian Culture* that did not appear in *Russian History from the Earliest Times*, and vice versa. This is certainly true, and one important feature of *Study in the History of Russian Culture* that is absent in the longer work is the introduction of merchant capitalism as a driving force of Russian history.

There is every likelihood that *Study in the History of Russian Culture* had its origins in the lectures on Russian history that Pokrovskii delivered at the Capri party school in 1909. V.M. Kosarev, one of the students at the school, states that the lectures were subsequently published as *Study in the History of Russian Culture*.[51] What gives Kosarev's statement credibility is that, although the book as a whole is pitched at the same level as *Russian History from the Earliest Times*, it begins with an introduction to historical methodology, which clearly started out as a lecture to students.

It is significant that Pokrovskii's main argument in this introductory section is that in terms of methodology there is no essential difference between history and the social sciences. He is concerned to refute those scholars who maintain that history cannot be the object of science, because science is concerned only with things which can be repeated, whereas history has to do with individual facts, which occur only once. Here Pokrovskii repeats the case he made against Rickert in his 1904 review article in *Pravda*, though in this instance simplifying Rickert's position appreciably.[52]

In the introductory section too, Pokrovskii proclaims his opposition to the Hegelian school of historical writing, which views all developments as emanating from the State. Nor does he leave any doubt that he rejects entirely the conception that the Russian State created the classes in Russian society, 'enserfed' them, and, when it deemed it convenient, 'disenserfed' them.

The new factor that Pokrovskii introduces in *Study in the History of Russian Culture* to account for developments in history is 'merchant capitalism', which was to become a distinguishing feature of his interpretation of Russia's past. It was not widely deployed for that purpose in *Study in the History of Russian Culture* itself but would increasingly feature in works written in the Soviet period. In *Study in the History of Russian Culture* Pokrovskii shows how merchant capitalism emerged in the Russian context, and how it related to the later-developing industrial capitalism.

According to Pokrovskii, the earliest form of trade in Muscovite Rus' appeared in small local markets, when the products of agriculture were exchanged for those of handicraft industry. These exchanges were direct transactions between the producer and the consumer. A feature of these early markets was the cheapness of their goods. A foreign writer in the XVII century remarked on the cheapness of silver buttons, which were sold for little above the value of the silver which composed them. The Moscow artisans did not demand any

---

51   Kosarev 1922, p. 66.
52   Pokrovskii 1914b, pp. 9–10.

profit on their goods. They only wanted paid for the raw materials and the cost of their labour time. They were satisfied to earn enough from their work to maintain themselves.[53]

In this period, trading middlemen, merchants, did not exist, or, if they did, they dealt in goods imported from abroad. But here too the activities of such men had an artisan character. The old Russian merchant was generally a small trader, travelling around the country with his cart, or simply with a pack on his back. The fact that there were thousands of such traders does not signify, as some scholars believed, that trade in ancient Rus' was especially well developed. It simply meant that there was not a concentration of trade and merchant capital. Those 'merchants' did not think of profit, but only how to support themselves by their efforts.

The situation began to change by the first half of the XVII century, when economic relationships in Moscow became more complex. In the 1620s the Moscow government, alarmed by the rise in grain prices in the capital, tried to impose a tax on bread. The civil servants to whom this task was entrusted were artisans in outlook. They calculated the price of flour, added to this the cost of maintaining the baker, and arrived at what they considered was a fair price. But the Moscow bakers protested that they had nothing left after the tax was levied. The authors of the tax accused the bakers of not being content with a fair price for their loaves, and with wanting to make a profit on them. But the bakers answered that without their profit there was no point in baking bread at all. Certainly, Pokrovskii concedes, this was capitalism in a very limited form. But the petition the bakers presented reveals a secondary, higher, stage in the concentration of capital. It mentions certain 'bread and pastry dealers' who bought bread and pastry wholesale in order to sell it at retail prices.[54]

If, Pokrovskii concludes from this episode, the bakers of Moscow in the 1620s were the beginnings of industrial capitalism, the bread and pastry dealers were the representatives of merchant capital. Merchant capitalism is much older than industrial capitalism, the desire for profit appearing among the merchants much earlier than among artisans. In *Study in the History of Russian Culture* Pokrovskii goes on to speak of the conflict between merchant and industrial capitalism. It was this dynamic that he later used to explain the developments that historians of the Hegelian school attributed to the actions of the State.

Writing in 1924, Pokrovskii described himself as 'the person, one might say, who discovered the role of merchant capitalism in Russian history'.[55] This was

---

53   Pokrovskii 1914b, p. 88.
54   Pokrovskii 1914b, pp. 89–90.
55   Pokrovskii 1924c, p. 6.

a contentious claim, because other people had written on the subject of merchant capitalism previously. The most obvious example was Kliuchevskii, who referred to it in several places in his *Boiar Duma*. Other pioneers in this field were Peter Struve, Tugan-Baranovskii and Rozhkov.

One finds many references to the importance of trade in Russia's historical development in Struve's book *Critical Notes*. He is of the opinion that: 'All economists who are historians by training or by inclination are united in recognising that trade has an enormous role in history'. He credits Kliuchevskii with having shown in his *Boiar Duma* the part played by trade in the formation of the Russian state.[56]

In his book *The Russian Factory Past and Present*, Tugan-Baranovskii leaves no doubt that the part played by merchant capitalism in Russian history, at least in the earlier period, has been well examined. He informs his readers that he will 'not dwell upon the enormous significance of merchant capital, both on the economic and on the political structure of pre-Petrine Russia', since 'this question has been sufficiently illuminated by our historians – Soloviev, Kostomarov, Kliuchevskii and others.'[57]

Rozhkov's essay *Town and Country in Russian History* is a work which ascribes a prominent place to the role of merchant capital. While playing down the importance of internal trade, Rozhkov finds great significance in Russian foreign trade from the time of the *Russkaia Pravda* and thinks that Peter the Great's conquest of the western seaboard was carried out in the interests of merchant capital.[58]

Critics of Pokrovskii in the Soviet era were inclined to accuse him of having taken his conception of merchant capitalism from Alexander Bogdanov. Because by that time Bogdanov's ideas were considered heretical, Pokrovskii naturally denied any intellectual debt to his former associate. Nevertheless, Bogdanov was a source from which Pokrovskii might have derived his conception of merchant capitalism, since this figures prominently in Bogdanov's *Short Course of Economic Science*. Bogdanov devotes a section of his book to the era of merchant capitalism, which he saw as the precursor of the era of industrial capitalism of modern times. However, Pokrovskii's conception of merchant capitalism differed significantly from Bogdanov's. Whereas for Bogdanov merchant capitalism constituted a particular period in European economic evolution, for Pokrovskii it extended throughout Russian history, from the earliest times to the present day.

---

56   Struve 1894, pp. 88–9.
57   Tugan-Baranovskii 1898, p. 2.
58   Rozhkov 1918 [1904], p. 11.

It is unlikely that Pokrovskii took his conception of merchant capitalism from Bogdanov or any other particular writer. Pokrovskii was one of a number of historians of the day who appreciated the importance of trade in Russian history. One can observe too that in elaborating his ideas on the subject he draws not upon existing works, but upon his knowledge of Russian chronicles and other primary sources. For that reason, one may conclude that in his conception of merchant capitalism Pokrovskii had some claim to originality.

CHAPTER 5

Istpart

1 Trotsky's *From October to Brest-Litovsk*

It was during the negotiations at Brest-Litovsk that an important event took place for the subsequent evolution of Soviet historiography. This was the publication of Leon Trotsky's pamphlet *From October to Brest-Litovsk*.[1] In his memoirs Trotsky recalls the circumstances in which the work was written.

> We had with us a good many stenographers who had been on the staff of the State Duma, and I began dictating to them, from memory, a historical sketch of the October Revolution. From a few sessions there grew a book intended primarily for foreign workers. The necessity of explaining to them what had happened was most imperative; Lenin and I had discussed this necessity more than once, but no one had any time to spare. And I had been farthest from supposing that Brest-Litovsk would become a seat for my literary work. Lenin was very happy when I brought back with me a finished manuscript on the Russian Revolution. In it we both saw one of the modest pledges of a future revolutionary recompense for the harsh peace. The book was soon translated into a dozen European and Asiatic languages.[2]

From October to Brest-Litovsk was therefore a work intended primarily for foreign consumption, and it was this which determined how the revolution of 1917 was presented. Being written at Brest-Litovsk, and at a time when the Bolsheviks were pinning their hopes on a revolution in Germany, it was the German workers that Trotsky had most in mind. In fact, the first foreign language into which the pamphlet was translated was German. It was therefore a work which strove to present the acquisition of power by the Bolsheviks in the way most acceptable and worthy of emulation to workers in Germany in the spring of 1918.

This circumstance goes to explain why this first history of the October revolution was written by Trotsky, and not by Pokrovskii, who was a trained

---

1 Trotsky 1919.
2 Trotsky 1970a, pp. 369–70.

historian, well capable of writing a short history of 1917, and, presumably, had the same amount of leisure time as Trotsky. The reason is likely to be that Trotsky's pamphlet grew out of a strategy of which Pokrovskii did not approve and would not be a party to. Whereas Lenin and Trotsky were staking everything on encouraging a revolution in Germany, Pokrovskii was intent on deploying his expertise in foreign policy to have serious negotiations with the Germans. What Pokrovskii wanted to achieve was a just peace with the Central Powers; what Lenin and Trotsky wanted was a German revolution.

In trying to achieve his objective, one factor that Trotsky had to reckon with was the reaction to the revolution which had so far appeared in the German press. This had been generally unfavourable, and even the socialist press had been unenthusiastic about the new government in Russia. The *Leipziger Volkszeitung*, for example, on 17 December 1917, had accused the Bolsheviks of having fomented a civil war, of dividing the working class against itself, and of establishing a dictatorship, ostensibly of workers and peasants, but in reality of the Bolshevik party itself. Karl Kautsky, the most influential figure among the German socialists, castigated the Bolsheviks in a similar way, accusing them of having infringed democratic principles by dispersing the Constituent Assembly, and deplored their refusal to broaden the base of the government by coming to terms with the other socialist parties, or even by surrendering power altogether to 'democratic elements who had the support of the majority of the common people'.[3]

In view of these charges against the Bolsheviks, Trotsky in a pamphlet intended for a German audience, had to show that the Bolsheviks had not carried out a coup d'etat behind the backs of the Russian working class, that they had not established a party dictatorship, and that they had done everything possible to draw all the socialist parties into the government. These are all themes which figure prominently in Trotsky's pamphlet, in addition to the explicit polemic against Kautsky's accusation that the Bolsheviks had violated the principles of democracy.

The purpose for which Trotsky's pamphlet was written explains the striking difference between the presentation of the Russian revolution embodied in it, and the kind of interpretation which would later become usual. The most obvious difference is in the periodization of the events covered: it does not begin with the February revolution and describe events as they unfolded during 1917 to culminate in the Bolshevik seizure of power on 25 October. Instead, the events from February until the autumn of 1917 are severely foreshortened,

---

3 Mehring 1966, pp. 755–7; Waldenberg 1972, pp. 342–3.

and the real starting point of Trotsky's account is the aftermath of the Kornilov Affair. On the other hand, 25 October is not treated as the end of one historical phase and the beginning of a new one, but as part of a continuum, which included the unsuccessful negotiations the Bolsheviks conducted with the Mensheviks and Socialist Revolutionaries after 25 October with a view to forming a coalition government.

The effect of Trotsky's periodization is to emphasize the continuity of events before and after 25 October, and to show that what took place on that day was part of a prolonged process which resulted in the shift of state power to the Bolshevik party. From such a presentation of events one could hardly draw the conclusion that there had been a Bolshevik 'coup d'etat' or a 'seizure of power'. The quite extensive account of the Bolshevik attempts to form a coalition government makes it clear that the negotiations failed, not through lack of will on the Bolsheviks' part, but through the intransigence and treachery of the Mensheviks and Socialist Revolutionaries.

Although it was soon superseded as a work of history, Trotsky's pamphlet had enormous political significance. In answering the Bolsheviks' critics, Trotsky was at the same time providing a legitimation of the Bolshevik regime. This existed not because it had come to power by force, but because it had been put there by the Russian working classes, because it had a popular mandate. Trotsky's pamphlet highlights the importance of the history of the October revolution: it was on how this event took place that the legitimacy of the Soviet regime depended. This continued to be true during the whole of the Soviet era and set apart the history of the October revolution from the rest of Russian history.

Already embodied in Trotsky's pamphlet was the programmatic feature that would be characteristic of later Soviet works of the kind. Because of its importance as a means of legitimising the regime, it was essential that all other works on the October revolution should adhere to the same interpretation as Trotsky's. One can see this in John Reed's book *Ten Days that Shook the World* published in 1919.

Although Trotsky did not mention the fact in his memoirs, the production of literature like *From October to Brest-Litovsk*, which was intended for propaganda purposes abroad, was one of the functions of the Commissariat of Foreign Affairs, which Trotsky headed. In December 1917 there was attached to the Commissariat a Department of International Revolutionary Propaganda, specially concerned with the production of propaganda for foreign consumption. The Department had various foreign-language sections staffed by Bolsheviks, who having lived abroad, knew a foreign language, and by foreigners who were sympathetic to the Bolshevik cause. John Reed, for example, was put in charge of the English-language section of the Department. When Reed returned to the USA, he was succeeded by Albert Rhys Williams who, in March 1918, became Commissar of the entire Department.[4]

A comparison of *Ten Days that Shook the World* with *From October to Brest-Litovsk* shows that Reed adopted Trotsky's interpretation of the October revolution. This can readily be established by observing how all the features which distinguished Trotsky's interpretation are also present in Reed's *Ten Days that Shook the World*. Thus, the chronological framework of both works is the same; both concentrate on the time-span from the period following the Kornilov Affair to the defeat of Krasnov and Kerenskii at Gatchina. Reed, like Trotsky, treats the events of 25 October as part of an extended process in the transference of power to the Soviets, not as the decisive day on which the Bolsheviks seized power. This approach, indeed, is emphasized by the title Reed chose for his book.

Most significant of all is the identity of view of Reed and Trotsky on the cardinal point of interpretation – the role of the Bolshevik party in the October revolution. Both are agreed that the initiative for the insurrection did not come from the party, but from the workers themselves. Reed conveys this idea in a graphic account of the meeting of the Bolshevik Central Committee on 10 October. This is as follows:

> There were present all the Party intellectuals, the leaders – and the delegates of the Petrograd workers and garrison. Alone of the intellectuals Lenin and Trotsky stood for insurrection. Even the military men opposed it. A vote was taken. Insurrection was defeated!
>
> Then arose a rough workman, his face convulsed with rage. "I speak for the Petrograd proletariat", he said harshly. "We are in favour of insurrection. Have it your own way, but I tell you now that if you allow the soviets to be destroyed, we're through with you!" Some soldiers joined him ... And after that they voted again – insurrection won ....[5]

Reed's anonymous 'rough workman' helps to establish that in taking power the Bolsheviks were not acting against the desires of the workers, but with their full approval. One may enquire in vain after the identity of Reed's 'rough workman' and what subsequently became of him. His existence was not confirmed by any documents relating to the meeting of 10 October which appeared later,

---

4 Iakushevskii 1976, p. 65.
5 Reed 1919, p. 38.

and these, in fact, depict a meeting quite unlike the one Reed describes. One must suspect that the entire scene was invented by Reed in order to make the points his interpretation required.

2   Istpart

By the time the Second Congress of the Communist International met in July 1920 the tide had turned in favour of Soviet Russia in the Civil War. The regime no longer felt itself on the defensive but poised to carry the revolution into Western Europe. The Russian communists felt, moreover, that they were entitled to enjoy predominance in the Comintern because they – and they alone – had proved that they knew how to make a successful revolution. They were able to insist that their tactics were a model on which all socialist method must be based. This new, confident, stance demanded a fresh interpretation of the October revolution, and from 1920 onwards there emerged one which contrasts strongly with that elaborated by Trotsky in 1918.

     The basic proposition of this new interpretation was that the initiative for bringing about the October revolution had been taken by the Bolshevik party. It held that the party, by its theoretical and organisational expertise, had led the Russian workers, overthrown the capitalist system and established the dictatorship of the proletariat. It had accomplished, in fact, what every socialist party strove to achieve, and in so doing had become an example for them all. The basic tenets of this interpretation were set out by Lenin in his pamphlet *'Left-Wing' Communism. An Infantile Disorder*, which was distributed to delegates to the Second Congress of the Comintern.

     The very first page of the pamphlet establishes the requisite periodisation of Lenin's interpretation of the revolution: he speaks of 25 October as marking 'the conquest of political power by the proletariat in Russia'.[6] The finality of this act was reinforced by the absence of any mention by Lenin of the negotiations between the Bolsheviks and the other socialist parties on the formation of a coalition government. This change of emphasis transformed the transfer of power in October 1917 from the extended process Trotsky had described to a more defined and deliberate action. The presentation of the October events in this form was more consistent with attributing to the Bolshevik party the role of having organised and led the seizure of power.

     Although Lenin's periodisation conflicted with Trotsky's and John Reed's, it is easy to see why it could gain acceptance. For it was an accusation levelled

---

6   Lenin 1958c–65, p. 3.

against the Bolsheviks by their opponents that they had planned and executed a coup d'etat and usurped power in the country. Although evaluations might differ, Lenin, and the Bolsheviks' adversaries, were agreed on the basic premiss.

The fact that the events of 1917 were brought nearer in this way to the abstract concept of a 'proletarian revolution' had the very important result that henceforth the history of the Russian revolution would be written in a way that did not give prominence to factors which reflected Russian national peculiarities. The Soviet Union's leading position in the Comintern could hardly be justified if the October revolution were shown to have been brought about by causes which could not be replicated elsewhere.

The proposition that the Bolshevik party had organised and led the first successful proletarian revolution was one principle upon which Lenin's interpretation of the October revolution was based. The other was that the success of the revolution was due to the experience of 'Bolshevism', which 'as a trend of political thought – and as a political party – had existed since 1903'. Bolshevism, which consisted in 'the strictest centralisation and iron discipline', had arisen on the 'granite theoretical foundation' of Marxism, had passed through 15 years (1903–17) of practical history, which, in wealth of experience, 'had had no equal anywhere else in the world'.[7]

In a few introductory passages of *'Left-Wing' Communism* Lenin had established by assertion two points which had far-reaching consequences for how the Russian revolution was subsequently to be interpreted. Both of these stemmed from the linking of the October revolution to the origins of the Bolshevik fraction in 1903. The first was that the victory of the Bolshevik party in the October revolution had vindicated the Leninist concept of party organisation elaborated in *What is to be Done?* The second point, without which the first would have been negated, was that the Bolshevik party between 1903 and 1917 had been organised on Leninist principles, that is, of 'strict centralisation and iron discipline'. This is what, in Lenin's view, gave the historical experience of Bolshevism its particular value, and rendered it so instructive to the international communist movement.

At the time Lenin outlined his interpretation of the Russian revolution in *'Left-Wing' Communism*, it was not supported by any historical works published up to that date by the Soviet government; in fact, it was contradicted by the accounts of Trotsky and John Reed, and by collections of documents which had been published to support the presentation of events they had adopted. For Lenin, the next logical step was to find a means by which historical works

---

7   Lenin 1958c–65, pp. 6, 8.

supporting his point of view could be published, or at least to prevent the publication of works which contested it.

He began to explore ways of doing this in the summer of 1920 in discussions with Pokrovskii and V.V. Adoratskii on the possibility of establishing an organisation concerned specifically with the collection and distribution of materials on the history of the Bolshevik party and the October revolution. The organisation's terms of reference were meant to correspond to the scheme elaborated in 'Left-Wing' Communism.

Pokrovskii objected that the history of the October revolution ought to be treated separately from the history of the party. His argument was that the October revolution was a complex series of events, which could be approached like any other subject in history. The person in charge of the project would require having a historical training, but, because it would involve working with documents, the people employed might even be non-party. The history of the party, on the other hand, especially in the period when it operated clandestinely, would not be based on documents, but on the reminiscences of the direct participants in the events.[8]

Lenin would not hear of treating the history of the October revolution and the history of the Bolshevik party separately and insisted that both functions be given to the same organisation, in this way building into its very structure the idea that the Bolshevik party was responsible for the success of the first proletarian revolution. The new organisation was called the 'Commission on the History of the Russian Communist Party and the October Revolution', or 'Istpart'. It was chaired by Ol'minskii, with Pokrovskii as vice-chairman and Adoratskii as secretary. It was staffed mainly by Bolshevik party veterans, some of whom had written on the history of the party or would shortly do so. Such people included: N.N. Baturin, A.S. Bubnov and V.I. Nevskii. These were later joined, among others, by, S.I. Mitskevich, M.N. Liadov, both of whom had written on party history, and Lenin's sister Anna Elizarova, whose main interest was the publication of a volume dedicated to the memory of her brother Alexander.[9]

Istpart's Chairman, Ol'minskii, although not a historian by training, had published some works on the early history of Russian social democracy. These included his memoirs of the social-democratic movement in St Petersburg in the 1890s, which appeared in the journal Byloe in 1906.[10] He would go on to edit a collection of reminiscences by members of the first social-democratic groups

---

8   Pokrovskii 1930b.
9   Komarov 1958, p. 154.
10   Ol'minskii 1906.

in St Petersburg, entitled *From the Blagoev Group to the 'Union of Struggle'*, published in 1921.[11] Under his own name of Aleksandrov, Ol'minskii was also the author of *The State, Absolutism and Bureaucracy in Russian History*, which had criticised Pokrovskii's articles in *History of Russia in the XIX Century*. There is no doubt that academically Ol'minskii was well qualified to head Istpart, but because of the importance of the October revolution to the Bolshevik regime, Ol'minskii's political skills were needed even more.

The status of Istpart rose swiftly. When it was first set up in August 1920, it was attached to Gosizdat, the state publishing house. As, however, Istpart was to be concerned not only with the publishing, but also the collection and processing of historical materials, it was transferred a month later to Narkompros. Along with this transfer, the functions of Istpart were more formally defined in a governmental decree of 21 September 1920. These were: 'The collection, editing and publishing of materials relating to the history of the October revolution and the Russian Communist Party'. Its responsibilities for collection and custody of materials were especially stressed. Istpart was to collect 'all types of materials, both printed and manuscript ... in Russia as well as abroad, and organise special archives and libraries for their safekeeping and use'. The serious political purpose of the Commission was reflected in the clause which stated that:

> All Soviet and social organisations, and also private persons, who have in their possession such materials, are obliged to surrender them to the Commission which, in case of necessity, may demand these materials from institutions and private persons, and in so doing may call upon the support of the appropriate authorities.[12]

Istpart was thus given teeth, the power to requisition any documents it chose.

Alexander Berkman[13] relates in his memoirs how the documents on the history of the Russian revolutionary movement that he had collected on a special expedition through provincial Russia for the Museum of the Revolution in Petrograd were seized by Istpart. According to Berkman, Istpart was a 'special body ... with exclusive authority to collect material relating to the history of the

---

11   Ol'minskii 1921.

12   Sovnarkom 1920.

13   Alexander Berkman was an American Jewish anarchist of Russian origin. In 1919, along with Emma Goldman, he was deported from the United States for anti-war activities. He returned to Russia and worked for the Bolshevik regime, with which he quickly became disillusioned. He left Russia at the end of 1921.

Russian Communist Party'. It claimed control over the Museum, and insisted on placing a political commissar in charge of future expeditions. Berkman found the attitude of Istpart inimical to free effort, and would not consent to being supervised by a commissar, whose duties were 'identical with spying and denunciation'.[14]

To enforce a particular interpretation of history, however, the power to requisition particular materials was insufficient; it was essential that all the relevant material without exception should be in its possession. This demanded a scale of operation well beyond the scope of Narkompros, and from 1 December 1921 Istpart became attached to the Communist party Central Committee as one of its departments. The transfer was initiated by Lenin's sister Anna Elizarova and supported by Pokrovskii and Ol'minskii. It was expedited by Stalin in his capacity as head of the Central Committee's Agitprop department.[15]

Two months later Istpart was extended to cover the entire country by an instruction from the Central Committee obliging all oblast' and guberniia party committees to set up Istpart organisations in their areas. These were to be departments of local parties and were to function under the supervision of the central Istpart, with which they were to maintain direct communication. Ultimate responsibility for the activities of Istpart rested with the Central Committee, and all decisions it took which had political or ideological implications, had to be sanctioned by the Secretariat, the Politburo or the Orgburo. This arrangement provided the mechanism for exercising party control over what was written on the history of the revolution and the Bolshevik party throughout the entire country.

The expansion of the Istpart organisation was accompanied by the rigorous enforcement of the Commission's powers to acquire historical archives and materials, especially the records of the tsarist authorities relating to the revolutionary movement. Ol'minskii warned in 1923 that any person who neglected to hand over such records to Istpart was committing a punishable offence and would be subject to the full force of the law.[16]

The establishment of Istpart had the effect of designating an area of special ideological significance and removing it from the province of academic historical study. The people on the staff of Istpart, therefore, were not chosen for their historical scholarship, but for their political reliability, a fact noted with

---

14   Berkman 1989, p. 279.
15   Elizarova 1930, pp. 157–8.
16   Ol'minskii 1923, p. 267.

some annoyance in 1923 by Rozhkov, who, though a former Menshevik, was a historian of some standing, and with an interest in the history of the Russian revolutionary movement.[17] By the same token, however, the remainder of Russian history, including the social and economic conditions which led up to the 1917 revolution, was left for scholarly study. This was an area in which Pokrovskii's post-1917 academic activity was concentrated.

Pokrovskii, who was the only historian by training on the staff of Istpart, seems to have played a rather minor part in its activities.[18] He never himself wrote a history of the October revolution – something one would have expected the only professional historian among the Bolsheviks to do – nor a history of the Bolshevik party. Apart from an odd article on an individual aspect of the Russian revolution or the history of Bolshevism, Pokrovskii's main efforts were devoted to areas of Russian history which lay outside Istpart's terms of reference.

Pokrovskii's presence on Istpart was probably necessary, however, to give the Commission some academic respectability. His name also featured on the historical journal of Istpart, *Proletarskaia revoliutsiia*, which first appeared in 1921. After writing the introductory article to the first number, his contributions to the journal were extremely meagre.

The interpretation of the October revolution which emerged from the pages of *Proletarskaia revoliutsiia* was the one which Lenin had advanced in '*Left-Wing*' *Communism*. Materials were published showing that the Bolsheviks had not simply followed the mood of the workers in October 1917, but had taken the initiative in planning and organising the insurrection. The second number in 1921 printed a series of hitherto unpublished letters by Lenin written in 1917, such as 'The Bolsheviks Must Seize Power', and 'Marxism and Insurrection', urging the party to make immediate preparations for an uprising.[19] The October issue in 1922 published the minutes of the Bolshevik Central Committee meeting of 10 October 1917 when the decision to prepare for an armed insurrection was taken. These minutes showed that the meeting in question had been quite different from the way John Reed had described it. It had been a closed session of the Central Committee; no 'rough workmen' had been present, and only two Central Committee members had been in opposition. It was emphasized, however, in an editorial note, that such opposition was not to be taken as a lack of cohesion in the party; for, on the contrary, 'from these experiences and

---

17   Rozhkov 1923, p. 71.
18   Ol'minskii 1930, pp. 154–5.
19   Lenin 1921, pp. 94–114.

moments of hesitation our party always emerged stronger, more integrated and more disciplined than ever'.[20]

The October 1922 issue of *Proletarskaia revoliutsiia* also contained Trotsky's reminiscences of the October revolution. These accord completely with the Leninist interpretation and tell a very different story from *From October to Brest-Litovsk*. In these memoirs Trotsky no longer presented a picture of the Bolshevik party in 1917 as simply reacting to the manoeuvres of its opponents. It now appeared that the way the Bolsheviks had come to power had been planned beforehand, and that they had executed a carefully prepared insurrection.[21]

In this version the question of power had been decided finally by 25 October; there was no reference to any attempts to form a coalition government with other socialist parties. Neither was there any suggestion that a significant part during events had been played by the Second Congress of Soviets, nor any hint that the Bolsheviks had hoped to come to power by gaining a majority at the Congress. In fact, very little remained of the interpretation Trotsky had elaborated at Brest-Litovsk.

The need to respect the politically determined interpretation of the October revolution constrained Istpart's scope for the kind of historical materials it could publish. Nevertheless, it did bring out some valuable sources. These included the protocols of party congresses and conferences, chronologies of events of 1917, biographical dictionaries, memoirs by participants in the Russian revolutionary movement, and the collected works of Lenin, Trotsky, Zinoviev and Kamenev.[22] In general, one could say that Istpart published sources for a history of the Russian revolution, but not the history itself.

3   Iakovlev

The Istpart interpretation of the October revolution rendered Trotsky's *October to Brest-Litovsk* obsolete, so that a fresh programmatic book was needed. The responsibility for producing this was also given to Trotsky, who clearly was regarded by Istpart as someone who had the authority to safeguard the legitimacy of the Bolshevik regime.

Trotsky himself reproduces the actual document sent to him by the Orgburo. This read as follows:

---

20   Pozitsiia Ts.K. partii v oktiabr'skie dni 1917 g. 1922, pp. 459–65.
21   Trotsky 1922b, pp. 43–93.
22   Komarov 1958, p. 164.

Excerpt from the report of the session of the Organisation Bureau of the Central Committee for 22 May, 1922 No. 21: Comrade Iakovlev is commissioned to compose, by the first of October under the editorship of Comrade Trotsky, a textbook on the history of the October Revolution.[23]

The resulting work by Ia.A. Iakovlev, an official in the party's Agitation and Propaganda department,[24] was a short pamphlet entitled *On the Historical Significance of October*.[25] It was the first work to deal with the February as well as the October revolution.

Iakovlev began his account by considering what the causes of the 1917 revolution had been. The main ones he thought to be popular demands for land, peace, and an end to national oppression. These had led to the overthrow of the tsar in February 1917. The Provisional Government, however, had been incapable of carrying out the necessary bourgeois-democratic reforms, leading to its downfall in October 1917, when the well-organised Bolshevik party had carried out an armed insurrection. The Bolsheviks had immediately issued decrees on peace, land, and national equality, thus carrying out the bourgeois-democratic revolution that the Russian bourgoisie itself had been incapable of implementing. According to Iakovlev, this bourgeois-democratic revolution was inseparably connected with Russia's revolutionary exit from the imperialist war, which transformed the war of workers against workers, waged in the interests of finance capital, into a war of the worker against capitalists, in the name of socialism. This peculiarity of the October revolution determined its inevitable 'growing over' from a bourgeois-democratic into a socialist revolution. This formulation was, in effect, a restatement of Trotsky's theory of 'permanent revolution'.

Iakovlev argued that the workers could have come to power in February 1917 if they had been led by the kind of disciplined organisation the Bolshevik party provided. For Iakovlev, the events of the February revolution demonstrated that the efforts of workers, acting independently, were doomed to failure; to achieve their aims they required to be organised. According to Iakovlev:

> February showed that it was one thing to bring down the tsarist regime in street battles, but quite another to organise revolutionary workers' power in its place. For the latter task the workers lacked the organisational basis ... The fact that the class which had carried out the revolution lacked

---

23 Trotsky 1962, p. 16.
24 Sivolapova 1976, p. 216.
25 Iakovlev 1922.

an organisation which would have enabled it to take power into its own hands not only explained why Miliukov came to power on the backs of the workers, but also defined the cardinal contradiction of the whole February revolution.[26]

In this way, Iakovlev drew a contrast between the February and the October revolutions. Both had been bourgeois-democratic, but only the October revolution had been successful in bringing about the required transformations, its success being due to the operation of Bolshevik methods of party organisation.

The interpretation of the October revolution which stressed that its success was due to the organisation and discipline of the Bolshevik party had a significant corollary. This was that because it did not deliver political power into the hands of the working class, the February revolution could not have been led by the Bolshevik party, and consequently could not have been organised. From this point of view, the suggestion that the Bolsheviks in Petrograd had given direction to the movement during the February days would have implied that a revolution with Bolshevik leadership had failed to secure victory for the workers. This would have undermined the legitimacy of Bolshevik party rule and was therefore unacceptable to the regime. Iakovlev's and subsequent Soviet interpretations of the February revolution in the 1920s maintained that the February revolution had been spontaneous.

Thus, in his memoirs on the February revolution, V.N. Kaiurov takes care to mention that: 'In the course of three days of street fighting the masses had been led exclusively by worker-Bolsheviks: absolutely no guiding initiative was felt from the party centres'.[27] This statement, which has been taken by historians as a candid admission of the Bolshevik party's organisational failings, is actually an expression of party doctrine by a member of Istpart.[28]

The dissenting voice was Alexander Shliapnikov's. His memoirs, *The Year 1917*, published in 1923–25, left no doubt that 'the parties of the underground, and especially the Bolshevik party, were extremely active in instigating the revolution'.[29] Shliapnikov describes the part he and the members of the Vyborg District Committee had played in the street battles in the February days. They had not managed to take power, because when the revolution began to triumph on the 27th, the movement had been joined by groups of intelligentsia, who formed the Petrograd Soviet. This development changed the character of the

---

26   Iakovlev 1922, p. 10.
27   Kaiurov 1923, p. 169.
28   White 1979, pp. 475–6.
29   Shliapnikov 1923, p. 47.

movement from one that was anti-war to one that favoured its continuation. Shliapnikov and the Petrograd Bolsheviks continued to maintain their anti-war stance in *Pravda*, but they had been overruled, when they returned from Siberian exile, by Kamenev, Muranov and Stalin, who gave *Pravda* a 'defencist' orientation.

Istpart published Shliapnikov's book, but reluctantly, as Shliapnikov indicated. The editors of Istpart, he remarked, 'are happier accepting documents than memoirs with evaluations and analyses. As for my memoirs, they certainly do have evaluations and analyses, and have always caused the editors worry and alarm'.[30] The two volumes of Shliapnikov's book were reviewed hostilely in 1927 by D.Ia. Kin. Besides questioning the factual accuracy of *The Year 1917*, Kin compared it to Trotsky's 'Lessons of October'. He wrote:

> It is highly symptomatic that the volumes of comrade Shliapnikov's book on *The Year 1917* should appear – one before the publication of comrade Trotsky's 'Lessons of October', and the other one directly after. Comrade Shliapnikov seems to have set himself the aim of facilitating comrade Trotsky's task, by reflecting in the distorting mirror of his *The Year 1917* the real year 1917.[31]

The discomfort of the Soviet leadership with Shliapnikov's memoirs occasioned an article by Iakovlev in *Izvestiia* on the tenth anniversary of the February Revolution. In it Iakovlev reproached Shliapnikov with having 'immeasurably exaggerated the degree of organized leadership by the Bolsheviks in the February Revolution'. There were, he insisted, no definite leaders, no definite organizers; the Bolshevik inspiration of the February Revolution was, Iakovlev stated, of a more general kind, and lay in the fact that:

> ... hundreds of thousands of workers who were schooled by the Bolshevik *Pravda* in 1912–14, who had undergone the lesson of 1905, who knew of the implacable position of the Bolsheviks in relation to the war ... formed spontaneously the spontaneous movement of hundreds of thousands, uttering genuinely revolutionary slogans, lifting the red flags aloft, leading the crowd against the police and the officers. Such was the type of Bolshevik leadership in the February days.[32]

---

30   Shliapnikov 1927, p. 101.
31   Kin 1927, p. 55.
32   Iakovlev 10 March 1927.

Being a mere seventeen pages in length, Iakovlev's pamphlet of 1922 gave no more than an outline history of 1917. It was nevertheless an important document because, like Trotsky's *From October to Brest-Litovsk*, its function was to set out the approved interpretation for other historians to follow. This can readily be observed in the history of the Russian revolution by S.A. Piontkovskii, *The October Revolution in Russia: its Pre-Conditions and Course of Development*. Although the book was published in 1924, it had gone to press before Trotsky's 'Lessons of October' had appeared. It thus occupies an important place in the development of Soviet historiography, being the last work to come out before the anti-Trotsky campaign was launched.

Piontkovskii's book in fact represents the height of Trotsky's influence in the Soviet historiography of the Russian revolution. Although considerably fleshed out with factual material, its interpretative framework is that taken from the pamphlet written by Iakovlev and edited by Trotsky. The October revolution is classed as bourgeois-democratic, though with socialist features arising from soviet power. In February the working class is said to have lost power to the bourgeoisie through lack of party organisation, whereas in October success was achieved through the planning and organisation of the Bolshevik party. Piontkovskii gives great prominence to Trotsky himself. The account of the October revolution follows exactly that given in Trotsky's memoirs published in 1922, and often quotes them directly. The events of October are therefore presented as deliberately orchestrated by the Bolshevik party, within which, apparently, there were no disagreements. The seizure of power was accomplished on 25 October, and, in Piontkovskii's view, everything had been decided by the time the Petrograd Soviet met at 2 p.m. on that day. This allowed Trotsky as Chairman to make the speech marking the culmination of the revolution.

> So far, Trotsky declared, no blood has been spilt; we do not know of a single casualty. I do not know in the history of the revolutionary movement a case where such great masses of people have been involved and which has taken place so bloodlessly. The power of the Provisional Government which Kerenskii headed was moribund and only awaited the broom of history to sweep it away.[33]

This prominence given to Trotsky was linked to the main theme of Piontkovskii's book: the need for party organisation. He argued as follows:

---

33   Piontkovskii 1924, p. 78.

The October revolution was remarkably peaceful in character. The workers and peasants came to power almost bloodlessly. In contrast to the February events, in October the masses acted in a planned and organised way. In October everyone knew what had to be done, how to do it, and why it had to be done. The October revolution was meticulously prepared.[34]

Piontkovskii's interpretation was quickly overtaken by events. Within a few months 'Lessons of October' had been published, and the machinery to promote Trotsky's reputation was put into reverse.

The interpretation of the October revolution promoted by Istpart justified the status of the Bolsheviks as the ruling party in the country. It followed that those in power were the people who had organised and led this October revolution. In other words, the status of figures in the Soviet leadership depended on the role they had played, or alleged to have played, in the October revolution. These were the presuppositions that underlay the discourse of the political struggles of the 1920s. The obvious example here is the reputation of Trotsky. While Trotsky was in favour, he was credited with being a principal organiser of the October revolution. Thus, in an article in *Pravda* of 6 November 1918 Stalin could write of Trotsky:

All the work of practical organisation of the insurrection was conducted under the immediate leadership of Comrade Trotsky, the Chairman of the Petrograd Soviet. It can be stated with certainty that the party is indebted primarily and principally to Comrade Trotsky for the rapid going over of the garrison to the side of the Soviet and the efficient manner in which the work of the Military Revolutionary Committee was organised.[35]

After he fell from grace, not only was Trotsky stripped of the honour of being a leader of the October revolution but was accused of having striven to obstruct the accession of the Bolsheviks to power.

With the emergence of the Lenin cult, it became obligatory for members of the Soviet leadership to demonstrate their Leninist credentials. This was especially the case after Lenin's death in 1924, when Leninism became the official ideology of the Soviet regime. As in the case of participation in the October revolution, those in favour were credited as 'Leninist'; those out of favour were

---

34   Piontkovskii 1924, p. 79.
35   Stalin 1918, p. 2.

held to be 'anti-Leninist'. These were attributions which had little to do with the actual ideological outlook of the people concerned.

The Ninth Party Congress in September 1920 had resolved that Lenin's writings should be published in a collected edition. Until the creation of the Lenin Institute in 1923, most of the work for this edition, which appeared between 1920 and 1926, fell upon Istpart. The purpose of this publication was more political than academic, an approach first employed by Lenin himself, when in September 1920 he arranged for the reissue of his polemical philosophical work *Materialism and Empiriocriticism*, to combat the influence of Bogdanov and the Proletkult movement. The new edition contained a preface by V.I. Nevskii, shortly to become the head of the section on party history in Istpart, denouncing Bogdanov in terms as virulent as any encountered in the Stalin era.

The publication of Lenin's writings was indispensable, if events were to be interpreted from a Leninist point of view. K.N. Ostroukhova, for example, in recalling her work for Istpart, revealed the method employed when she had written a series of articles for *Proletarskaia revoliutsiia* on Lenin's campaign against the boycott of the Second and Third Dumas. This was an important subject because it formed part of the argument in Lenin's *'Left-Wing' Communism*. According to Ostroukhova:

> I was worried about my ability to expound these complex themes correctly. M.S. Ol'minskii gave me advice: first of all, study Lenin's works, his pronouncements on the question of intra-party struggle in these years ... I remember that in writing the article 'Social Democracy and the Elections to the Third State Duma' I took my guidance chiefly from Lenin's article 'Against the Boycott' ....[36]

By structuring historical events around Lenin's writings in the way Ostroukhova describes there was inevitably produced a version of history proving that events had confirmed the correctness of Lenin's views. The logic of the situation eventually led to the history of the Bolshevik party and the October revolution becoming a kind of exegesis on Lenin's writings. In the course of the 1920s, Lenin's pronouncements were to become the criterion of truth for Soviet scholars in all historical events.

---

36   Ostroukhova 1967, p. 94.

4   Pokrovskii's Debate with Trotsky

When Istpart began its operations, it was not only Lenin's works which were thought to be suitable for providing the approved interpretation of party history; so too were those of other party leaders. Trotsky, Zinoviev and Kamenev all had collected works, Trotsky's being especially voluminous. These publications of course served to enhance the prestige of the Soviet leaders. As one contemporary writer remarked:

> Look through the list of our leading activists and you will see that every one of them has more than one volume of writings to his credit, not to mention the central figure. I ask you, when was it that any bourgeois minister had collected works in 20 volumes as Comrade Lenin has?[37]

The converse of this position of course was that persons who were not in favour, far from having their works republished, would have them suppressed, as was the case with Bogdanov.

Not only Lenin's works, but also those of Trotsky were regarded by Ol'minskii as programmatic. In October 1921 he wrote to Trotsky as follows:

> Why not begin to prepare a complete collection of your writings? ... It is high time it was done. The new generation, not knowing, as it should, the history of the party, unacquainted with old and recent writings of the leaders, will always be getting off the track.[38]

These in fact began to appear, with volumes arranged according to themes, such as the 1905 revolution and the October revolution of 1917.

Besides the collected works, Ol'minskii suggested that Trotsky should publish a Russian translation of his book *1905*, that had appeared in German in 1909. Ol'minskii wrote to Trotsky recommending that he, Trotsky, should personally undertake the translation into Russian for the publication. The completed work was duly published in 1922, much to Pokrovskii's consternation, because it embodied the theory of 'permanent revolution', which predicated both Russian economic backwardness and a supra-class autocracy, both of which Pokrovskii had argued against for most of his academic career.

---

37   Lemke 1923, p. 435.
38   Trotsky 1962, p. 24.

Trotsky's scheme of Russian history was the diametrical opposite of what Pokrovskii had long been teaching, and the contrast caused some disturbance amongst the university students. The problem, as Pokrovskii saw it, was that:

> Trotsky's book will be studied. And since we are dealing with an author whose every word carries extraordinary weight, every pronouncement of the book will be imprinted on thousands of young minds. And due to the lapidary-artistic style in which the book is written, that impression will be so lasting that it will not be erased by the dozens of books that are written with less artistic talent, and by authors who carry less authority.[39]

'It was natural', Pokrovskii states, 'that the students should turn to their professors of history, not without anger (Trotsky's authority in 1922 was still great), and demand "What are you telling us? Read what Trotsky writes: you are all wrong."'[40] It was incumbent upon Pokrovskii to produce some kind of reply, and this he did in a review article on Trotsky's book, entitled 'Is it True that in Russia Absolutism Existed in Spite of Social Development'.

Pokrovskii opened this review with the declaration that: 'Like every scheme which is clear and distinct, Trotsky's scheme is easily memorised and assimilated. And this is a great pity. For, first, this scheme is not ours; and second, it is objectively wrong'.[41] What, he asks, is this scheme but that which Miliukov put forward without, and Struve with, Marxist terminology, and which has been so recently resurrected by Plekhanov's Introduction to the *History of Russian Social Thought*? According to Pokrovskii, the theory of the supra-class state was in keeping with the liberal policies of Kadets like Miliukov, or with Mensheviks who sympathised with the Kadets, like Plekhanov. But how was the theory to be reconciled with Bolshevik calls to the proletariat to seize power from the bourgeoisie, when the bourgeoisie didn't have power? It seemed to Pokrovskii that: 'We must fight most decisively against this theory, no less energetically than we now fight against religious prejudices. I say further: it is less important to prove that there was no historical Jesus Christ than that a supra-class state never existed in Russia'.[42]

For Pokrovskii, the case against the supra-class state is more easily made for the most recent times. Not even Kadet historians, Pokrovskii notes, would deny the bourgeois reforms of Alexander II, the anti-bourgeois counter reforms of

---

39 Pokrovskii 1925c, p. 21.
40 Pokrovskii 1925c, p. 41.
41 ibid.
42 Pokrovskii 1925c, p. 23.

Alexander III, or the class nature of the electoral system of the State Duma. He adds that his own account of the 1861 reforms from a class point of view had been praised by Vladimir Semevskii, a recognised authority in the field.

On the other hand, Pokrovskii readily admits that, as far as the origins of the autocracy are concerned, the position is much less favourable. For here there has been no assistance from bourgeois historians in acknowledging the material factor for this phenomenon. For, continues Pokrovskii, they require a political explanation, and they find a completely satisfactory one from their own point of view – the interests of military defence from an external enemy. 'Why did Rus' form itself around Moscow? For defence against the Tatars. Clear and simple'.[43]

It is to Trotsky's merit, Pokrovskii considers, that he has not simply reproduced the argument about the Tatars, but has substituted 'the pressure of Lithuania, Poland and Sweden'. But, Pokrovskii enquires, what could their motives have been for attacking Russia? Citing memoirs of visitors to Russia in the sixteenth century, Pokrovskii argues that Russia in the period was a country in which trade was well developed, and in which the tsar and the ruling classes were involved. To Pokrovskii, the conflicts with Lithuania, Poland and Sweden that Trotsky had mentioned were ones to secure trade routes for Russia, and it was for this purpose that military modernisation was needed.

From the facts adduced, Pokrovskii concludes that to speak of Russia's backwardness misses the point; Russia was 'a new country seized with the development of merchant capitalism', and it was necessary for it to find a place in the sun, along with other, well-established, competitors. For this Russian merchant capitalism had to rule the country with 'iron discipline and form a veritable dictatorship. The incarnation of this dictatorship of merchant capital was the Muscovite autocracy'.[44]

Trotsky's reply to Pokrovskii's review appeared in two parts, in *Pravda* for 1 and 2 July 1922. It took the form of an article entitled 'Concerning the Peculiarities of Russia's Historical Development'. It was an article which he later reproduced as an appendix to the second edition of *1905*, and later still, to all editions of his *History of the Russian Revolution*. Trotsky, with reason, obviously, considered the question of very great importance, for, in his own words: 'In 1922 Pokrovskii came down upon the historic conception of the author which lies at the basis of the theory of Permanent Revolution'. Trotsky, no doubt, answered Pokrovskii at such length, because it was an opportunity to re-state his theory,

---

43 Pokrovskii 1925c, pp. 23–4.
44 Pokrovskii 1925c, p. 29.

this time following the successful October revolution, which he took to be a vindication of his ideas. Now he was able to pose the question in terms of how it came about that the proletariat could come to power in a backward country like Russia.

Trotsky conceded that Plekhanov's presentation of Russia's historical development was very close to his own, but thought it false to claim that Plekhanov had used this scheme to justify a bloc with the Kadets. Plekhanov had not drawn the conclusion from it that it was possible for the proletariat to come to power in Russia. But then neither had he drawn any conclusion from another of his unquestionably correct propositions, namely: 'The Russian revolutionary movement will triumph as a working-class movement or it will not triumph at all'.[45]

For Trotsky, Pokrovskii's arguments showed that he thought in rigid categories and absolutes: the autocracy was either completely independent or completely dependent; the bourgeoisie either had complete power or it had none; Russia was either completely backward or not backward at all. Trotsky considered that in the process of emphasising Russia's similarities with the West, Pokrovskii had completely forgotten that significant differences did exit, the most significant of which was Russia's economic backwardness. As Trotsky observed: 'Pokrovskii ... flatly denies the primitiveness and backwardness of our economic development, and therewith consigns the peculiarities of Russian historical development to the realm of legend'. In Trotsky's view, the reason for this oversight was that Pokrovskii was completely hypnotised by the comparatively extensive development of trade, noticed by him, and also by Rozhkov, in sixteenth century Russia.[46]

Perhaps the most telling, and certainly the most vivid, part of Trotsky's refutation of Pokrovskii was his way of challenging the validity of the assumption that a high development of trade necessarily denoted economic progress. This he did, not by reference to history, but to his own experience of trading during his exile in Siberia, and his acquaintance with a 'dictator of merchant capitalism'.

> My Siberian employer (in whose office ledger I entered poods and arshins for a period of two months), Iakov Andreevich Chernykh ... was in practically unlimited control of economic life in the Kirensk district by virtue of his trade operations. He bought furs from the Tungus natives, he bought

---

45   Trotsky 1922a, p. 298.
46   Trotsky 1922a, pp. 299–300.

church lands from priests in remote districts, and he sold them cotton and, especially, vodka … He was illiterate, but a millionaire (in the currency of the time). His dictatorship as a representative of merchant capital was unquestioned; he even spoke of the local indigenous population as 'my little Tungus folk'. The town of Kirensk … was a place of residence for police officers of various rank, kulaks, in a state of hierarchical dependence on one another, a variety of petty government officials, and a handful of wretched artisans. I never found any organised artisanal trade there as a basis of urban economic life – no corporations, no guilds, although Iakov Andreevich was officially listed as a 'merchant of the second guild'.[47]

By his personal reminiscence Trotsky made the point that his former employer, who was the living embodiment of the 'dictatorship of merchant capital' that Pokrovskii spoke of, operated in conditions of extreme economic backwardness.

Trotsky expressed surprise that Pokrovskii had only objected to the first chapter of his book, which dealt with tsarism, and not the second, which was concerned with the Russian capitalism, that was also a product of Russia's economic backwardness. Russian capitalism did not develop from artisanal trade via the manufacturing workshop to the factory, because European capital, first in the form of merchant capital, and later in the form of financial and industrial capital, flooded the country at a time when most Russian artisanal trade had not yet separated itself from agriculture. Hence the appearance in Russia of modern capitalist industry in a primitive economic environment, the dominant role of Western European capital in Russia's economy, and the consequent political weakness of the Russian bourgeoisie. It was these factors that made the defeat of the Russian bourgeoisie in 1917 inevitable.

Now, in the aftermath of the revolution, Trotsky could add to his theory that Russian economic backwardness had left its mark on the proletariat. It did not have the traditions that Western workers had derived from the guilds; Russian workers had been hurled into the factory boiler straight from the plough. Hence their illiteracy, their lack of technical knowledge, of organisation, of culture. These were problems the young Soviet government had to face.[48]

Trotsky concluded by pointing out to Pokrovskii an important aspect of Russian backwardness that had contributed to the downfall of tsarism. This was the inability of the economy to respond adequately to the demands of milit-

---

47   Trotsky 1922a, pp. 301–2.
48   Trotsky 1922a, p. 304.

ary operations during the war. With the help of the Allies, tsarism was able to deploy the most modern weaponry. But it did not have, and could not have, the means to reproduce these weapons. Nor did it have the means of transporting them with sufficient speed by rail or waterway. In this respect Russia was operating on a more primitive economic base than its enemies or allies.[49]

Following this exhaustive reply by Trotsky, the rest of the polemic became more repetitive, and more concerned with clarifying the respective standpoints, particularly on the question of whether tsarist Russia was a colony of the Western powers. This question was to be a problem of major importance for Soviet historians later in the decade.

That Pokrovskii's work played a great part in the struggle against 'Trotskyism' is acknowledged by Trotsky himself. In 1937 he recalled:

> The most prominent part in the struggle against 'Trotskyism' was accorded to historical questions. These involved both the history of the development of Russia as a whole, as well as the Bolshevik party and the October Revolution, in particular. The deceased M.N. Pokrovskii must unquestionably be acknowledged as the most authoritative Soviet historian. For a number of years he waged, with a vehemence peculiar to him, a struggle against my general views on the history of Russia, and especially my conception of the October Revolution. Everything written by the other 'communist' critics on this theme was merely parroting the ideas of Pokrovskii.[50]

In September 1924, in response to the attacks made on him by Lenin's successors in the Soviet leadership, Kamenev, Zinoviev and Stalin, Trotsky took the opportunity of the publication of the third volume of his collected works to write an introductory essay entitled 'Lessons of October'. Under the pretext of analysing the lessons that the younger generation and foreign communists could learn from the experience of the Bolsheviks in the October revolution, Trotsky gave prominence to the mistakes made in 1917 by Zinoviev and Kamenev, and, by implication, Stalin.

In introducing his subject with a survey of what had been published on the October revolution to date, Trotsky in effect gave an assessment of the activities of Istpart. There was, he observed, not a single work which would give a general picture of the October revolution, and identify its most important political

---

49   Trotsky 1922a, p. 308.
50   Trotsky 1962, p. xxx.

and organisational aspects. Moreover, even the source materials with a direct bearing on the different aspects of the preparation of the revolution, and on the revolution itself – including the most important documents – had still not been published. A considerable number of documents had appeared on the history of the revolutionary movement and on the history of the party, as well as materials relating to the pre-October and post-October periods, but to October itself much less attention had been paid.[51]

It would appear from the tone of Trotsky's survey of literature on the subject that he thought Istpart remiss in neglecting to publish an analytical history of the October revolution, and source material on its central aspects. What he was actually criticising was the function that Istpart had been set up to carry out: to legitimise the Soviet government, burnish the reputations of the people who composed it, and to perpetuate the primacy of the Russian party within the Communist International. Trotsky would know this full well and would be aware that by questioning the accepted interpretation of the October revolution, he was posing a serious challenge to the Soviet leadership.

Because of this absence of a substantial historical account of the October revolution, the version proposed by Trotsky was to have a profound and lasting impact. Of all the 'lessons' Trotsky might have drawn about the October revolution, the ones he drew attention to were those which involved the actions of his political opponents, Zinoviev and Kamenev. These concerned two main episodes. The first of them was in the period before Lenin returned to Petrograd in April 1917. At that time Kamenev advocated conditional support to the Provisional Government and urged that the war effort be maintained, since the war that Russia was fighting was a 'defensive' one. These positions were roundly condemned by Lenin on his return to Russia. The second episode was in October 1917 when Zinoviev and Kamenev had argued in print that the attempt of the Bolsheviks to take power was a reckless and dangerous adventure. Lenin had reacted furiously and demanded that the pair be expelled from the party.

In 'Lessons of October' Trotsky declared that his intention was not to criticise individuals, but to analyse objectively the experience of the October revolution. But given the dynamics of Istpart, Trotsky would be aware that what he was doing in fact was to undermine the status and the reputations of Zinoviev and Kamenev as Soviet leaders. The ruling triumvirate reacted in kind, unleashing what was known euphemistically as the 'literary debate', in which Trotsky's former Menshevik affiliations and his past conflicts with Lenin were unearthed.

---

51   Trotsky 1924–7, p. xi.

To illustrate the latter point Ol'minskii brought out a collection of Lenin's anti-Trotsky writings. In an article entitled 'Leninism or Trotskyism' Stalin denied that Trotsky had played any special part in the October revolution, in this way deploying the same device as Trotsky had used to diminish the political standing of Zinoviev and Kamenev.

The 'literary debate' redounded to the benefit of Pokrovskii. In 1924 his polemic against Trotsky's view of the Russian autocracy became part of the anti-Trotsky campaign. Trotsky's book *1905* was no longer held by Istpart to be programmatic, and it was Pokrovskii's interpretation of Russian history that emerged victorious. As a counterpoise to Trotsky's book, Pokrovskii included a section on the 1905 revolution in his *Brief History*, in which he laid bare Trotsky's failings as a revolutionary leader.

5   Local Istparts

Along with the central Istpart organisation in Moscow, subsidiary local bureaus of Istpart were established to carry out the collection and publication of materials on the October revolution in their respective areas. There were local Istpart organisations in Petrograd, Moscow, Viatka, Kaluga, Tula, Voronezh, Ivanovo-Voznesensk, Nizhnii Novgorod, Baku, Barnaul and other places.[52] As the focal point of the October revolution, Petrograd had a well-resourced Istpart organisation. It was headed by the old Bolsheviks V.A. Bystrianskii, V.I. Nevskii and P.F. Kudelli, and published the journal *Krasnaia letopis'*. The Moscow Istpart had among its members S.I. Mitskevich, the memoirist of the revolutionary movement in Moscow. There were also Istpart organisations in Ukraine, Belorussia, Turkestan, Georgia, and other national areas. By the end of 1921 there were over twenty local Istpart organisations on the territory of the former Russian Empire. In 1922 there were 44, and in 1923 there were 82.[53]

Research on the history of local Istpart organisations shows that during the 1920s much was done to collect the reminiscences of wide sections of the population. Scholars went 'to the people', gathering oral testimony, distributing questionnaires and conducting surveys. There was a focus on collecting data from the agrarian population, and this was done with some urgency, as it was realised that the spread of education and contact with urban centres would

---

52   For a detailed account of the Istpart organisation in Viatka and its relations with the central Istpart see Holmes 2021.

53   Komarov 1958, p. 157; Ivanova 1968, p. 152.

erase the features of peasant life, the language, the customs and the attitudes that had been prevalent at the time of the revolution.[54]

Questionnaires asked witnesses about six main themes: 1) the revolutionary movement of 1905–06; 2) the revolution and the Civil War; 3) the history of the Bolshevik party organisation; 4) the history of counter-revolutionary organisations; 5) the biographies of prominent revolutionaries; 6) the life and activities of Lenin. Pokrovskii was eager that as much memoir material as possible should be collected while participants and eye-witnesses of events were still alive. His student, Anna Pankratova, was among those involved in recording the reminiscences of people who were unable to express themselves in writing.[55]

Some of the memoirs collected were published in such journals as *Proletarskaia revoliutsiia, Letopis' revoliutsii, Katorga i ssylka*, and in local journals. But, as a rule, they were heavily edited, both for their form and their content, before they were allowed to appear. Most of the material that was collected was never put to any use. By the mid-1930s all social organisations concerned with the collection of materials on the history of the revolution and the Civil War were dissolved.[56] The collectivisation of agriculture put paid to any attempt to capture the atmosphere of the villages that had produced the peasant movement of 1917. The purges of the 1930s removed many of the participants in revolutionary events, as well as the scholars who recorded them.

One outcome of the proliferation of Istpart organisations throughout the country was the publication of the book *Studies in the History of the Russian Communist Party* by V.I. Nevskii in 1924.[57] Nevskii took advantage of the wealth of material that had appeared in the publications of the local Istpart organisations, to show how social democracy in Russia had been formed in local groups up and down the country, each one with distinctive characteristics, and composed of distinctive personalities. It showed, for example, how members of the St Petersburg Brusnev group, described by Ol'minskii in his book *From the Blagoev Group to the Union of Struggle*, had extended their activities to Moscow, Nizhnii Novgorod, Tula, and Dorpat. It showed the contribution of Martov's group in Vilna in initiating the tactic of 'agitation', which was then implemented in social-democratic groups throughout the country. From Nevskii's book one could see how the various local groups inter-acted to form a social-democratic movement that extended throughout the Russian Empire. It was an approach that was entirely appropriate to the subject.

---

54   Shcheglova and Drozhetskii 2014, p. 256.
55   Shcheglova and Drozhetskii 2014, pp. 257–8.
56   Shcheglova and Drozhetskii 2014, p. 259.
57   Nevskii 1925.

Unfortunately for Nevskii, and indeed for the study of Russian social democracy, his book was condemned by Ol'minskii, and the approach he had adopted was discontinued. The reason for Ol'minskii's distaste is not hard to find.
The account of the rise of social democracy in Tula gives prominence to the
activities of Alexander Bogdanov, against whom Lenin had waged a vicious
campaign, with, as it happened, the collaboration of Nevskii. In other connections Bogdanov's name was no longer mentioned.

Even worse was that in the section of Nevskii's book dealing with the revolutionary movement in Nikolaev, a great deal of attention was devoted to Trotsky,
who had begun his political career there. As in his treatment of Bogdanov, there
was nothing condemnatory in Nevskii's account of Trotsky's activities. There
was a picture of Trotsky, and a long quotation from him about the Southern
Workers' Union, the organisation to which he belonged. As objective treatment
of Bogdanov and Trotsky was no longer acceptable in the current political climate, Nevskii's book was severely criticised by Ol'minskii, and consigned to
oblivion. Nevskii's approach to party history was not repeated, and subsequent
books on the subject adopted a more unilinear structure. This was probably
what Pokrovskii had in mind, when in 1926 he remarked, in a personal letter
to E.M. Iaroslavskii, who was then editing a four-volume history of the Russian
Communist Party:

> Your book takes the well-trodden path of the history of congresses, con-
> ferences, pre- and post-congress polemics. That is the way in which one
> could write the history of the party in our own days, when political initi-
> ative is centralised. But even in 1905, due to the objective circumstances,
> organisations on the ground had to be incomparably more independ-
> ent.[58]

Istpart survived as a distinct entity until August 1928, when it was merged with
the Lenin Institute, so giving institutional recognition to the fact that conformity with Lenin's writings was the factor which determined interpretations of
the history of the Bolshevik party and the Russian revolution. In the words of
Ol'minskii, 'The question of a merger arose naturally: one cannot imagine the
history of the party without Lenin, or the history of Lenin without the party'.[59]

---

58   Govorkov 1976, p. 173.
59   Komarov 1958, p. 165.

CHAPTER 6

Institute of Red Professors

1   Institute of Red Professors

The Institute of Red Professors (IKP) was Pokrovskii's 'brain-child' (*detishche*), the institution in which he invested much of his time and attention. It was an elite graduate school, which produced the first cohorts of Soviet-trained historians. For Pokrovskii, IKP represented a decisive departure from the pre-revolutionary system of producing academics, the 'retaining for the profess-orial vocation', which demanded from the aspiring academics subservience to their supervisors, who were in a position to bestow their patronage. In Pok-rovskii's opinion, it was the most obsequious, rather than the most talented students, who came through this system. IKP provided an entrance to the aca-demic profession in which applicants would be judged on their merits.[1]

The idea of establishing a special centre for the training of highly qualified Marxist cadres of social scientists was raised in the Commission, chaired by Fedor Rothstein, (December 1920–January 1921) to effect the radical transform-ation of the teaching of the social sciences in institutions of higher education. In the opinion of the Commission, such a transformation was impossible so long as the existing teaching staff remained in the universities. The Commis-sion considered replacing them with Marxist intellectuals from the ranks of the Bolshevik party. This, however, turned out to be impracticable, because such people found it impossible to combine teaching with the other party and governmental functions they performed. The alternative that was adopted was to train up young Communists to supplement, and, eventually, to replace the existing Communist academics.[2] To implement the policy the Council of People's Commissars on 11 February 1921 adopted a resolution calling for the establishment of institutes for the training of red professors, who would teach in the Republic's institutions of higher education such subjects as 'theoretical economics, historical materialism, the development of social forms, modern history and Soviet construction'.[3]

Pokrovskii recalled that the initiators of the project would count themselves lucky if they managed to attract 25 entrants to the new institute, so it was

---

1   Pokrovskii 1922a.
2   ibid.
3   *Dekrety sovetskoi vlasti* 1989, pp. 62–3.

decided not to insist on party membership in case they were left with unfilled places. As it turned out, they needn't have worried; in the first year there were 289 applicants, of whom 81 were finally accepted, after going through the selection procedures for academic and political suitability; 75 of them were party members. When IKP was established, the Civil War was ending, enabling young people who had been serving in the Red Army to resume the education that the war had interrupted. Some of the applicants to IKP belonged to this category. Among them 30% were graduates of institutions of higher education, while 37% had incomplete higher education. In terms of social composition, 62% belonged to the intelligentsia, and only 12% were workers, the remainder being artisans. The Institute of Red Professors opened on 3 October 1921 in Moscow.[4] The first cohort graduated in 1924 and included in its number S.M. Dubrovskii, S.M. Monosov, A.V. Shestakov, N.N. Vanag, B.B. Grave, G.E. Meerson, Kh.G. Lur'e, A.P. Taneev, A.N. Gusev, A.N. Slepkov, S.D. Kuniskii – people who would form the first generation of Soviet-era historians.

For entrance to IKP there was an admissions committee of three people, one from the party Central Committee, usually the head of the Agitprop section, one from the IKP management, and one representing the IKP students. The entrance requirements for IKP were high. Applicants had to show an acquaintance with the works of Marx, Engels, Lenin, Adam Smith, Kautsky, Hilferding, Tugan-Baranovskii, and of Pokrovskii himself. A.I. Gukovskii recalls that when he was waiting at the door of Pokrovskii's office with other candidates, one of them advised him: 'Whatever he asks you, just say it has something to do with the change in grain prices'.[5] With or without the advice, Gukovskii was able to pass muster and was duly admitted to study at IKP.

The IKP came under the control of the Agitation and Propaganda Department of the Central Committee. It was the party which approved the teaching plans, the entrance requirements, the choice of the teaching staff, and the students. At the head of the IKP was the rector, under whom the management operated. Although there were changes in the composition of the management, Pokrovskii remained rector throughout the 1920s, while at the same time serving as head of the IKP's history department.

4   Genkina 1984, p. 259; Pokrovskii 1922a, p. 2.
5   Gukovskii 1965, p. 82.

2   Departments

The study of Marxism formed the core of the IKP programme. As initially conceived, the first of the three years' study would be the acquisition of the basic
principles of Marxist doctrine, which would involve the simultaneous study of
Marxist philosophy, political economy and history. However, as this ambitious
curriculum overloaded the students with work, the scheme was abandoned,
and in the second year the students were allowed to specialise in philosophy,
economics or history. Until 1924 IKP had three departments: philosophy, economics and history. In 1924 a natural science and a law department were added,
and in 1927 a literature and a party-history department.

    In order to make the student body more proletarian, by the decision of the
Thirteenth Congress of the RKP(b) in 1924, there was established a two-year
preparatory department, which would coach workers for entrance to the IKP.
This was to become the IKP's main source of recruitment, and IKP graduates
figured prominently among its teaching staff. The management of IKP hoped
that by increasing the proletarian presence, the student body would become
less prone to Trotskyist influence. In the event, the policy proved unsuccessful.
Although the number of worker entrants rose steadily year by year, very few
of them managed to complete the course. In the period 1924–29 IKP produced
236 graduates, of whom there were 19 workers, 8 peasants and 209 white collar
workers.[6]

    The departments of IKP were headed by Marxists who were specialists in the
various fields. Thus, in 1928 the history department was headed by Pokrovskii
(his deputy being the IKP graduate I.I. Mints), the economics department by
Sh.M. Dvolaitskii, the philosophy department by A.M. Deborin, the natural science department by A.A. Maksimov, the law department by E.B. Pashukanis,
the party history department by B.N. Astrov (later by V.V. Adoratskii), and the
literature department by V.M. Friche. The head of the preparatory department
was N.S. Berezin. In the 1930s on the basis of the departments of IKP, a number
of independent Institutes of Red Professors were formed: Institute of History,
Institute of Economics, Institute of Philosophy, Institute of Natural Science,
Institute of World Economics and Institute of World Politics.[7]

    In addition to their academic studies – preparing papers for discussion and
writing articles – students at the IKP had also to engage in party-pedagogical
work. This was an integral part of the course. It included teaching in district
party schools, leading Marxist study groups at factories, making agitational

6   Solovei 1990, p. 93.
7   Nikulenkova 2015, p. 162.

speeches, and taking part in political campaigns. The idea was to produce a new type of scholar, who would be highly qualified academically, but also committed politically.[8]

The great demands on time made by the practical activities led to students falling behind with their academic work, and not being able to give enough attention to the learning of foreign languages and the writing and defending of dissertations. As a result, in 1924 the period of study at IKP was extended to 4 years, the final year being intended for the writing of a dissertation. Although, as E.B. Genkina recalls, nobody wrote a dissertation while she was at IKP, some monographs of a high academic standard were produced, including ones by Mints, A.M. Pankratova, and by Genkina herself.[9]

Teaching at IKP was by seminar; lectures were only used as introductions to topics, and attendance at them was not compulsory. In instituting the seminar system, Pokrovskii was re-creating the method by which he himself had been taught history by Vinogradov at Moscow University in the 1890s. One can also see in the seminar method a reflection of Bogdanov's conception of a proletarian university, one in which students would take an active part in the learning process, and not simply assimilate knowledge, inculcated into them by authorities. At IKP seminars the students would prepare papers, using, as far as possible, primary sources in the original languages, and present these in the seminar group, where they would be discussed and criticised, sometimes extremely forcefully.

The teaching staff at IKP consisted largely of Bolshevik party intellectuals: Adoratskii, Nevskii, Riazanov, Rothstein, V.P. Volgin, A.D. Udal'tsov, N.M. Lukin, Iaroslavskii and Pokrovskii. Despite the shortage of teachers, Pokrovskii was extremely reluctant to make use of pre-revolutionary academics. This was despite the fact that Lenin had specifically recommended that their expertise should be utilised.[10]

Pokrovskii was most in his element teaching the graduate history students of IKP, and formed close relationships with some of them. Bukharin had many supporters among the IKP students, but Stalin was not highly regarded, and his lectures on 'The Foundations of Leninism' at the Sverdlov Communist University in 1924 did not attract great attention. Trotsky, however, had enormous influence among the IKP students, as among Soviet students in general. His *New Course* pamphlet of 1923 recognised this, and in it Trotsky regards the party

8   Nikulenkova 2015, p. 161.
9   Genkina 1984, p. 262.
10   Pokrovskii 1967d, p. 9.

youth as the force to counter the bureaucratisation of the party, perpetrated by the old guard. The students rallied to Trotsky's support, but they were unable to overcome the party apparatus that Stalin controlled. In May 1924 a purge of IKP students was carried out in which 15% were expelled. For the authorities it was an opportunity to get rid of the non-party students, and those who did not do party-pedagogical work.[11]

The anti-Trotsky campaign at IKP had particularly tragic consequences for Anna Pankratova, whose husband G.Ia. Iakovin – also an IKP graduate – became a leading figure among the Leningrad Trotskyists. Instead of supporting Iakovin in his political convictions, Pankratova dissociated herself from him and denounced him publicly. After a number of spells in prison and exile, Iakovin was shot in 1938, along with a number of other Trotskyists.[12]

IKP continued to be a centre of oppositionist activity, and in 1927–28 around 10% of IKP graduates were expelled from the party for Trotskyist sympathies. In 1928–29 a considerable number of IKP staff and students sided with Bukharin against Stalin, evoking a further round of purges, to remove Bukharinists from the Institute.

3   Russian Historiography

The seminar papers produced by the IKP students were often of a quality that was suitable for publication. This was the case with two seminar topics led by Pokrovskii, one on Russian historiography, and one on the history of the October revolution. The papers on Russian historiography were published in 1927 as *Russian Historical Literature from the Class Point of View*, with an introduction by Pokrovskii. Pokrovskii's approach to historiography was an extension of the way he had approached the question of historical knowledge in his 1904 article on Rickert. Historians, he believed, did not, and could not, reproduce the past as it had actually existed. What they did was to reconstruct a selection of that reality, and in doing so they would order their material and their conceptions in accordance with their class interests. Pokrovskii's fullest account of his approach to historiography is in the lectures he gave on the subject at the Sverdlov University in 1923.

---

11   Ivanova 1968, p. 34.
12   Zelnik 2005, p. 17.

3.1   Ideology

Pokrovskii believed that the idea of the student as the passive receptacle of the professor's wisdom was a relic of the old, bourgeois school and should be left behind. Lectures were an unsatisfactory means of conveying knowledge and should be replaced by independent study. This would expose the students to the works of historians from pre-revolutionary Russia, and they should be made aware that reading a book of history was not like reading one on electricity. For historians did not deal in facts, but in ideology. Ideology, Pokrovskii explained, was the reflection of reality in people's minds, seen through the prism of interests, mainly class interests. Pokrovskii's lectures on historiography were designed to show how the class interests were reflected in the works of the historians the students were likely to encounter.[13]

3.2   Karamzin

Pokrovskii begins his survey of Russian historiography with N.M. Karamzin's *History of the Russian State*, published at the start of the nineteenth century, in the reign of Alexander I. He recounts how Karamzin had written to tsar Alexander I pleading with him to provide him with a livelihood, so that he could devote his time to writing his *History*. Alexander consented, and in return received a historical work which eulogised his rule.

The main feature of Karamzin's work was that, in deference to the policies of Catherine II and Alexander I of territorial expansion – acquiring territories in Poland, Finland and the Caucasus, his *History* regards the mainspring of Russian history as the gathering of lands, from Rurik through Ivan the Terrible to the present day. This process, according to Pokrovskii, was driven by merchant capital, which required an expansion of territory on which it could enforce its monopoly of trade.

Karamzin was a supporter of serfdom, because the interests of merchant capital required maintenance of the serf economy as a means of squeezing the surplus product for the market out of the peasants. For Pokrovskii, merchant capital was the directing power behind tsarism, the force which created both serfdom and the Russian Empire.

According to Pokrovskii, by the time Karamzin finished writing his *History*, industrial capitalism was beginning to form in Russia, and this economic system demanded new ideological viewpoints, including on history. Industrial capitalism was more revolutionary than merchant capitalism. Merchant capitalism was based on the exchange of goods rather than on their produc-

---

13   Pokrovskii 1925a, p. 10.

tion, it did not interfere in production, but left the existing economic system unchanged – the peasant with his allotment, the craftsman with his workshop, and the merchant with his wares. Industrial capitalism, on the other hand, demanded social change; it required that the peasants be turned into proletarians to work in the factories, and to form an internal market for the commodities that were produced there.[14]

Industrial capital had to have a hammer with which it could break up all the social obstacles which stood in its way. That hammer in the hands of industrial capital was the new bourgeois State, whose mission was to turn the whole population into two groups: on the one hand, the owners of the means of production, and on the other – the proletariat. The needs of industrial capital gave rise to the school of historiography in Russia which regarded the State as the driving force of historical progress. Its chief representative was B.N. Chicherin, but among its many adherents were Trotsky and Plekhanov; only Rozhkov had resisted its influence.[15]

3.3   Chicherin

Chicherin, as a follower of Hegel, considered the institutions of Russian society to be the creations of the State. It was, in his view, the State which had created the social classes or 'estates' (*sosloviia*). It was due to this that in Russia the relations between State and society were entirely different from those in the West. Whereas in the West the social classes acted as a limitation on State power, this was not the case in Russia. There the estates could not limit the power of the State, because they themselves were the creations of State power. For this reason there could be in Russia no class struggle like that which occurred in the countries of Western Europe. This made Russian history less eventful and more uniform than that of the West.

As a Tambov landowner in the era of Alexander II's great reforms, Chicherin was fearful that the emancipation of the Russian peasantry might lead to social revolution. This fear was at the root of the particular form that Chicherin's Hegelianism took. Chicherin wanted to show that all the great social changes in Russia took place from above, by force of the all-powerful State, and that this would also be true of the current changes in the relations between peasants and landowners. He also wanted to show that the will of the State would not meet resistance, and that the changes would take place peacefully, without revolution. The disenserfment of the peasants would be the completion of the

---

14   Pokrovskii 1925a, pp. 25–34.
15   Pokrovskii 1925a, p. 35.

process that had been begun by Catherine II's emancipation of the nobility in the eighteenth century.

In Chicherin's scheme of Russian history, the State created estates, and imposed a burden on each of them: the nobility – military service; the merchantry – trade; the peasantry – agriculture for the benefit of the State and the nobility. Subsequently, when the State no longer demanded this enserfment of the estates, it began to disenserf them. In the eighteenth century the obligations of the nobility were removed; at the beginning of the nineteenth century the merchants were given equal civil rights, and in the middle of the nineteenth century – in 1861 – the peasants were liberated. Thus, the whole of Russian society, which had been enserfed by the State, was disenserfed by the State.[16] This was the theory that Pokrovskii had gone out of his way to disown in his letter to Ol'minskii in 1910.

In his day, Chicherin became well known also for his explanation of the origins of the peasant commune. He took issue with historians who believed that the commune was of great antiquity and was a spontaneous creation of Russian society. In the creation of this institution too Chicherin saw the hand of the State. In his view, the peasant commune in its present form dated only from the end of the sixteenth century and had been created by the State to ensure the collection of the poll tax, and to allocate the duties imposed on the peasants by the landowner.

3.4   *Shchapov*

Pokrovskii contrasted Chicherin's theory of the peasant commune with that of Afanasii Shchapov, a contemporary of Chicherin's, who had a more materialist view of history. Shchapov was the son of a village sexton from the Siberian town of Irkutsk, educated at the Kazan' Theological Seminary. His short academic career at Kazan' University was brought to an end in 1861, following a revolutionary speech he made in support of the peasants shot during the disturbances at Bezdna. He was arrested, and in 1864 exiled to Siberia, where he died in 1876. Shchapov saw the peasant commune as a primeval Russian institution which had come into being naturally, through the necessity for the people to pool their limited resources in the face of a severe northern climate, and the difficulties of making a living from the land. For Shchapov the commune was a social, and not a State creation.

Whereas Chicherin saw the driving force of Russian history in the centralised State, Shchapov held it to be in the common people. He believed that the

---

16   Pokrovskii 1925a, p. 36.

future well-being of Russian society consisted in the cultivation of people's initiative and self-expression, and looked forward to the time when there would be a system of local self-government in Russia.

Like Karamzin, Shchapov saw territorial expansion as an important feature of Russian history. But whereas Karamzin attributes this expansion to the success of the princes, Shchapov's explanation was in economic terms. The extensive method of agriculture carried on by Russian peasants called for ever-increasing territory as the population grew. In this way the Russian Empire extended, so that its northern border marked the point at which agriculture was still possible in the climatic conditions. The reason for Russia's eastward expansion beyond the Urals, according to Shchapov, was the quest for furs. The beaver and the sable had been eliminated in European Russia, so hunters moved to the Urals, and thence into Siberia. It was in the process of hunting sable that the whole of Siberia was conquered.

Pokrovskii expresses his approval of Shchapov's democratic approach to history, and in particular his materialistic explanation for Russia's territorial expansion. But he does not subscribe to the way Shchapov accounts for the mood swings in the Russian national character in terms of the slow blood circulation of northern peoples. Pokrovskii thinks that Shchapov's misapprehension here is that nature acts on society directly, and not through the mediacy of its economic system. In this respect Pokrovskii views Shchapov as an ancestor of Marxism, and not its direct teacher.

3.5   Soloviev

In Pokrovskii's view, Chicherin's theory had left one very interesting question unanswered. The Russian State had created society, enserfed the nobles, the peasants and the townspeople – everyone. But why was this done? Why was it necessary? It was Soloviev who supplied the answer to this question.

Pokrovskii considered Soloviev to be unquestionably the greatest Russian historian of the nineteenth century. But he too represented a class. Whereas Chicherin was a Tambov landowner, Soloviev was a city dweller. He belonged to the circle of wealthy clerics who led a bourgeois way of life and was imbued with the views and sympathies characteristic of the wealthy urban intelligentsia.

In an article published in 1856 Soloviev presented his views on the origins of the Russian State. It was, he wrote, Russia's geographical position on the frontiers of Europe that necessitated its constant struggle with the nomads from the East. The settled populations were threatened with conquest and enslavement by Asiatic peoples. It was only with the foundation of the Russian State in the thirteenth century that the liberation of the Slavonic tribes from the yoke of the nomadic Asians could begin. The new State took upon itself the blows of the steppe raiders. It bent before them but did not break. It gathered its strength, and at the time Byzantium fell to the Turks, the Muscovite State triumphed over them, and began, in its turn, an offensive movement on Asia.

Soloviev returned to the subject in an article published in 1877, in which he characterised the Russian State's struggle with the nomads from the East as a conflict between the 'forest' and the 'steppe', the steppe representing the mobile life of the nomadic tribes, and the forest representing the settled life of the Russians. Since the forest was a place to which the people of the steppe would not venture, it was a refuge for the settled Russians.

Pokrovskii draws attention to the fact that when both articles were written Russia was at war with Turkey. This suggests that the struggle with the steppe related to the wars against Turkey which Russia waged in the nineteenth century. The motivation for these wars provided the materialist explanation of the ideology that Soloviev represented. Why were these wars waged?

The reason lay in the slow development of the internal market for Russian industry. It was impeded because the interests of the industrial capitalist conflicted with those of the landowner. Industrial capital needed the swift transformation of peasants into proletarians, to work in the factories, and to become consumers of the goods that the factories produced. This process, however, was artificially obstructed by the landowners, who delayed the abolition of serfdom, though this was insistently demanded by industrial capital. Though the Crimean War forced the abolition of serfdom, it was a half-hearted reform which left the peasant attached to the land, as was indeed intended by the framers of the legislation.

The slow expansion of the internal market compelled Russian industrial capital, almost from its inception, to look for external markets. The economic significance of the Turkish wars was that they were necessary for the expansion of Russian industrial capital. The intention was that they would enable Russian manufactures to compete successfully with England in the Asiatic trade. In his conception of the struggle between the forest and the steppe, Soloviev was constructing a theory that would provide a historical justification for wars against Turkey. Thus, Pokrovskii concludes:

> ... the theory bears a particular class character, despite the fact that, seemingly, there is nothing in common between the moisture of the forest and the cotton factories of the Vladimir Province.[17]

3.6   Kliuchevskii

When Pokrovskii begins his discussion of Kliuchevskii, one realises that his account of Chicherin, Shchapov and Soloviev has been in preparation for his treatment of Kliuchevskii. They are regarded as component parts of Kliuchevskii's approach to Russian history. Pokrovskii intends to show that his former teacher was an eclectic, and these historians of the nineteenth century are the elements which Kliuchevskii will bring together.

Pokrovskii begins his lecture on Kliuchevskii by reproducing the way that Kliuchevskii himself formulated his conception of the historical process. For Kliuchevskii, the three basic forces which formed human existence were: human personality, human society, and the nature of the country. All three of them, according to Pokrovskii, were taken from other historians. Human society, as one could observe from the role it played in Kliuchevskii's writings, was roughly what Chicherin called the State. The conception of human personality was taken from P.L. Lavrov's idea of critically-thinking individuals, people who formulated ideas which went on to have an impact on society. Kliuchevskii's conception of the influence of external nature on the national character came from Shchapov's idea of how the climate acted on personality. This was an idea which belonged to the old, pre-Marxist, economic materialism.

Pokrovskii concedes that Kliuchevskii had great artistic talent, that as a writer he could compare with Turgenev. But his talent would not have saved him if he had displayed a one-sided approach to the historical process. Russian intellectuals abhorred one-sidedness, and for that reason they had no sympathy for Marxism, which they judged to be one-sided. Kliuchevskii, however, could give them several influences at once. If they wanted personality, Kliuchevskii had Lavrov; if they wanted State theory, Kliuchevskii had Chicherin; if they wanted the natural factor, Kliuchevskii had Shchapov. Pokrovskii speculated that intellectuals reading Kliuchevskii would be in their glory: here was no narrow Marxist, but a profusion of theories. Of course, Pokrovskii observes, these theories were mutually exclusive, though Kliuchevskii's skill as a writer obscured this inconvenient fact. Kliuchevskii's eclecticism, designed to appeal to an audience of intellectuals, made him a typical representative of the Russian intelligentsia.

In Pokrovskii's view, Chicherin's theory of enserfment and disenserfment lay at the root of Kliuchevskii's scheme of Russian history. For Kliuchevskii, Russian society had been formed by the State, and in the manner most in keeping with its needs. Characteristic in this respect were Kliuchevskii's views on the *zemskie sobory* (a topic which Pokrovskii had written on in his article 'Zemskii sobor and Parliament' in 1905). In fact, in his articles on *zemskie sobory* Kliuchevskii continually refers to Chicherin. There is a striking similarity between Chicherin's theory of the peasant commune and Kliuchevskii's theory of the *zemskie sobory*, which are regarded as a form of mutual responsibility (*krugovaia poruka*). For Kliuchevskii, *zemskie sobory* were simply meetings of the government with its own agents. Instead of issuing a decree from the centre, as would be done in the nineteenth century, the government convened the heads of localities in Moscow and gave them instructions on what had to be done in their particular areas. Since *zemskie sobory* were purely governmental institutions, they did not become centres of political opposition; nor did they, or could they, become the origins of parliament on the Western model.

Like Chicherin, Kliuchevskii maintains that the estates – the nobility, the merchantry and the peasantry – were the creations of the Russian State. And like Soloviev, Kliuchevskii explains why the State did this with reference to defence from an external enemy. To protect the country from the external danger the Moscow rulers united the formerly fragmented Russian lands under a single power. In Kliuchevskii's words: 'Great Russia was united under the power of the Moscow sovereign, not as a result of conquest, but under pressure from external danger which threatened the existence of the Great Russian people'. In Pokrovskii's view, Kliuchevskii's account of the origins of the Russian State consisted of Chicherin's theory supplemented by that of Soloviev – defence against the Tatars from the steppe.

But, as Pokrovskii pointed out, the flaw in Chicherin and Soloviev's scheme was that it did not correspond to the facts. The most intense struggle with the steppe took place in the thirteenth and fourteenth centuries, when Rus' was finally conquered by the Tatars. Yet at that time there was no unified State; the princes were constantly at war with each other. Nor was there any enserfment at that time; the nobility went freely from one prince to another. But in the sixteenth and seventeenth centuries, when both serfdom and the Muscovite State came into being, the Tatars had been so much weakened that they could not even dream of the conquest of Russia and could only plunder it. In other words, there could be no connection between defence against the steppe and the emergence of the Russian State, because at the time when the centralised State was most needed the country was most divided.

The content of Pokrovskii's lectures appeared not only in his Introduction to the collection of essays on historiography by IKP students, but also in an appendix to his *Brief History* entitled 'The Writers of Russian History Before the Marxists and How They Wrote it'. The approach Pokrovskii adopted in these lectures gave rise to the saying attributed to him that history was 'politics projected into the past'. The origin of this phrase comes from an article published in 1928 where he states: 'All these Chicherins, Kavelins, Kliuchevskiis, Chuprovs,

Petrazhiskiis – they all directly reflected a distinct class struggle which was taking place in the course of the nineteenth century in Russia and ... the history written by these gentlemen is nothing, but politics projected into the past'.[18]

4   Stalin's Judgement

The lectures on Russian historiography form the background to an interchange between two of Pokrovskii's students and Stalin, in which Stalin passed judgement on the 1922 polemic between Pokrovskii and Trotsky. On 2 March 1927 two IKP students, S.A. Alypov and P.S. Tsvetkov, wrote to Stalin to ask him for clarification about the official position on the origins of the Russian State. From their letter it is clear that the students had followed the polemic between Pokrovskii and Trotsky on the subject of the supra-class State, and had attended Pokrovskii's seminar on Russian historiography. The letter also reflects the way in which the students experienced the seminar system of teaching practised at IKP. It is worth quoting at some length.

> Comrade Stalin!
>
> At the Russian history Department at the Institute of Red Professors (1st year) we have to study the origins of the autocracy in Russia.
>   In preparing for the seminar, we came across in your speech at the Tenth Party Congress the statement that the centralised State in Russia (the autocratic order) was formed, not as a result of the country's economic development, but in the interests of the struggle against the Mongols and other peoples of the East ...
>   A number of queries occurred to us, and so we are approaching you with the following questions:
> 1)   What struggle against the Mongols was it – after all, the height of this struggle falls in the period of feudalism, but when the centralised State was formed the struggle against the Mongols was already over.
> 2)   In that case, wasn't the historian Soloviev right, when he traced our State back exactly to the struggle with the steppe (Mongols etc.)?
> 3)   How does this fit in with the class nature of the State and its economic base?

---

18   Pokrovskii 1928, p. 5.

4)   Does it turn out that comrade Trotsky was right when he stated that
     our State in its development overtook economics?

5)   But then, why were comrade Pokrovskii's articles defending the
     opposite point of view, and directed against Trotsky (precisely on
     this question), printed without any comments in the journals *Kom-
     munisticheskii Internatsional, Pod znamenem marksizma*, and *Vest-
     nik Kommunisticheskoi Akademii, Pravda* etc.?

6)   Then Pokrovskii very prominently expounded and defended his
     point of view in his *Brief History*. Lenin read it and in a letter to Pok-
     rovskii called the book good and made no objections to Pokrovskii's
     conceptions. At the present time Pokrovskii's conception on this
     question is, as it were, considered orthodox, and is considered to be
     right in his polemic against Trotsky.

And so it is in fact: in this question and in Marxist theory our historical
'practice' is certainly on the side of Pokrovskii.

However, your statement basically contradicts Pokrovskii's conception
(see Pokrovskii's books: 1) *Marxism and the Peculiarities of Russia's Historical Development*; 2) *The Class Struggle and Russian Historical Literature*;
3) *History* ... etc.)

We are about to embark on pedagogical work. But, irrespective of this,
we would like to orientate ourselves in controversial questions. That is
why – before working on this question in the seminar – we felt obliged to
put our queries to you and request an explanation.

With communist greetings: First year students of the History Department, Tsvetkov, Alypov.[19]

To this query Stalin replied on 7 March that the two students had based their
questions on a misunderstanding: Stalin had not been speaking of the formation of the 'autocratic system' in Russia, but of the formation of centralised and
multi-national states in Eastern Europe (Russia, Austro-Hungary). He denied
that he had said that a centralised state was formed in Russia 'not as a result of the country's economic development, but in the interests of the struggle
against the Mongols and other peoples of the East', as the students had claimed
in their letter. What he had said was that, owing to the requirements of defence
against these peoples, the process of formation of centralised states in Eastern Europe was more rapid than the process of the constitution of peoples
into nations, as a result of which multi-national states were formed in these

---

19   Nechkina 1990, pp. 242–3.

parts before the abolition of feudalism. For Stalin, therefore, the requirement for defence against Eastern peoples had only accelerated a process already in existence but had not initiated the process itself. This was, he declared, a view quite different from the one attributed to him by the students.[20] Stalin concluded his reply to Alypov and Tsvetkov with the statement:

> As for the theory of 'autocratic structure', I must say that basically I do not share comrade Trotsky's theory, whereas I consider Pokrovskii's theory correct in the main, although it is not without its overstatements in simplifying the economic explanation of the rise of the autocracy.[21]

In the light of his replies to the questions, Stalin saw no need to discuss the conceptions of Soloviev.

Stalin would not wish to be aligned with Soloviev, and even less with Trotsky, so that his reply to Alypov and Tsvetkov was, in general, predictable. Nevertheless, his explanation of the formation of the Russian State given at the Tenth Party Congress in 1921 is not all that different from those of Soloviev and Trotsky, and one can understand why the two students should see a similarity. In fact, in the 1930s Stalin would adopt exactly the interpretation of the formation of the Russian State advanced by Soloviev and Trotsky, though not of course explicitly.

5 Genkina

The tenth anniversary of the October revolution in 1927 was a landmark that could not be missed by Soviet historians and demanded some form of commemoration. At IKP Pokrovskii devoted a series of seminars to the history of the October revolution, the students involved preparing papers on various aspects of 1917. E.B. Genkina wrote on the February Revolution, M.S. Iugov – 'The Soviets in the first period of the Revolution', O.A. Lidak – 'The July Days', N.L. Rubinshtein – 'The Foreign Policy of the Provisional Government under Kerenskii', A.L. Sidorov – 'The Influence of the Imperialist War on Russia's Economy', K. Sidorov – 'The Workers' Movement during the Imperialist War' and D. Baevskii – 'The Bolshevik Party during the Imperialist War'. Each of the contributions was the length of a short monograph.

---

20   Stalin 1954b, pp. 179–80.
21   Nechkina 1990, p. 243.

In her memoirs of IKP Genkina recalls that, contrary to later Soviet practice, she wrote her seminar paper on the February revolution without any supervision, though she was given some helpful suggestions by Mints. The presentation of the paper went well, with no serious criticisms from her fellow students. Pokrovskii, however, while conceding that the paper was well written, and was the equivalent of a master's thesis under the pre-revolutionary system, objected that it was not really research, since it did not use archival sources. Genkina goes on to say that subsequently Pokrovskii took her to the building where the archives were housed in his car, and there she supplemented her paper with materials from the Northern Front and Stavka archives.

In her paper and in the published chapter Genkina argues that even if Lenin and the Bolshevik leadership had been in Petrograd at the time, the February revolution would still not have been socialist. She explains that this argument is an implicit polemic against Pokrovskii, who had claimed that if Lenin and the Bolshevik leadership had been in Russia, and if the revolution had not taken them by surprise, they could have established in February the regime that was later established after October 1917.[22]

This had been Pokrovskii's position in 1924, but in an article written in 1927 he had modified his ideas on the subject. He now conceded that, although it was absolutely true to say that February was not a socialist revolution, it did not follow from this that it was not an episode in the proletariat's struggle against the bourgeoisie. One could not say that February was only a bourgeois revolution and October only a socialist one. This was simply untrue, because October was the completion of the bourgeois revolution (the decree on land), and February was the embryo of October, the start of the transfer of power to the working class. Although one could not say that February was 'necessarily' a socialist revolution, one could say that it necessarily 'led' to a socialist revolution.[23]

The two volumes of papers were sent to press at the end of 1926, and duly appeared in print at the start of the anniversary year. Genkina was surprised by the speed with which the operation was carried out, and marvelled in retrospect that the volumes were published as they had been written, without any editing or reviewing processes taking place.[24]

The resulting work, *Studies in the History of the October Revolution*,[25] was an important landmark in Soviet historiography. It was the nearest that Soviet his-

---

22   Genkina 1984, p. 264; Pokrovskii 1924c, p. 213.
23   Pokrovskii 1927a.
24   Genkina 1984, pp. 263–4.
25   Pokrovskii 1927b.

torians of the 1920s got to producing a history of the Russian revolution. But, as the title implies, it was a number of separate studies, rather than a systematic history of the period. The title was also a misnomer; the episode of the 1917 revolution that was not covered in the collection of essays was the Bolshevik accession to power in October. In this way the work adhered to the policy of not encroaching on the province of Istpart. Nevertheless, the title page, which declared the collection to be the work of an IKP historical seminar, also bore the stamp of Istpart, implying that the *Studies* had been published with Istpart's approval.

It may well be true that Genkina did not experience any political direction when writing her paper on the February revolution. But she could not escape knowing what the accepted interpretation of the February revolution was at that time, and it is clear that she followed it. Her interpretation was that the February revolution was a spontaneous event but carried out by workers who had been propagandised in a general way. In other words, Genkina was adopting the formula that Iakovlev had enunciated previously.[26]

In his essay on the Bolsheviks during the war, Baevskii too accepted that the workers' movement during the February days had had a 'semi-spontaneous or spontaneous character'. He went on to say, however, that since the movement had proceeded under the Bolshevik slogans of 'Down with the tsar!' and 'Down with the war!' one could and must speak of the directing role of the party on the eve and at the moment of the fall of tsarism.[27] Baevskii adopts Iakovlev's formulation that 'the transformation of the revolution against tsarism in the conditions of 1917 implied the growing over of the bourgeois revolution into a proletarian one', since 'the struggle against tsarism was connected with the struggle against imperialism'. Throughout his essay Baevskii conducts a polemic against Trotsky, contrasting Trotsky's attitude towards the war with Lenin's, and arguing that very little separated Trotsky from the position of the social-chauvinists, who supported the war.[28]

Despite the impression that Gekina gives that the IKP students could write what they liked, their contributions to the *Studies* conformed to the programmatic guidelines laid down in Iakovlev's 1922 pamphlet *The Historical Significance of October*. Thus, we find in these contributions the assertion that the February revolution was spontaneous, and the doctrine that, because the October revolution was anti-imperialist, it was thereby necessarily socialist. Though the latter doctrine had Trotskyist origins, this fact was obscured by the hostile

26   Pokrovskii 1927b, p. 59.
27   Pokrovskii 1927b, p. 507.
28   Pokrovskii 1927b, pp. 506–7.

attitude towards Trotsky adopted by the contributors to *Studies in the History of the October Revolution*.

6   The Society of Marxist Historians

On 5 February 1925 Pokrovskii brought together representatives of the IKP, the Sverdlov Communist University, the Communist University of the Toilers of the East and the Communist University of the Western National Minorities, with the aim of founding a Society of Marxist Historians. In March a meeting of university lecturers was held, and on 1 June the Society of Marxist Historians was formally inaugurated, with Pokrovskii as its chairman and P.O. Gorin as secretary.

The aims of the Society were: 1) to unite all Marxists engaged in academic work in the field of history; 2) the scholarly elaboration of questions of history and the Marxist methodology of history; 3) the struggle against distortions of history by bourgeois scholarship; 4) the critical elucidation of current historical literature from a Marxist point of view; 5) the provision of help for members of the Society in acquiring scholarly literature, access to archives, and undertaking research trips etc.; 6) propaganda and popularisation of the Marxist method, and informing the broad masses about Marxists' achievements in the historical field.[29]

Pokrovskii insisted that the name of the organisation should be the 'Society of Marxist Historians', rather than the 'Society of Communist Historians', in order for it to be more inclusive, and to aim at extending the Marxist influence to all academics.[30] An important stimulus for the creation of the Society was to overcome the isolation felt by Marxist historians, both in the capital and in the provinces, not only from other historians in the Soviet Union, but also abroad.

The Society's creation was at a singularly appropriate time. 1925 was the 150th anniversary of the Pugachev uprising, the jubilee of the 1905 revolution, and the 100th anniversary of the Decembrist uprising. This provided the opportunity for organising lectures devoted to these events, which attracted audiences from the Communist Academy, IKP, RANION and the Communist Universities. The Society quickly grew: on 1 January 1926 there were 40 members, by 1 January 1929 there were 345. The majority of its members were lecturers from the universities of Moscow, Leningrad and the provinces.[31]

---

29   Gorin 1926, pp. 317–18.
30   Levshin 1974, p. 99.
31   Ivanova 1968, p. 187.

A major activity of the Society of Marxist Historians was the publication of the quarterly journal *Istorik-marksist*. A need was felt for a journal specially devoted to history, because, although there were other historical journals, such as *Proletarskaia revoliutsiia, Krasnyi arkhiv, Krasnaia letopis'* and *Katorga i ssylka*, these, for the most part, published documents and materials on the history of the party and the revolutionary movement, and did not give sufficient attention to methodological questions. While one could publish historical articles in journals like *Krasnaia nov'* and *Vestnik Kommunisticheskoi akademii*, these would be swallowed up in the general mass of non-historical material. *Istorik-marksist* was the first Soviet journal to publish a wide range of articles covering not only Russian history, but also the history of the countries of Western Europe and the East. The journal also aspired to have an international profile. This was reflected in G.S. Fridliand's proposal that an approach be made to historical societies and individual historians in Western Europe to establish contacts, so that articles by foreign scholars could be printed in the Society's journal. It was also desirable that Western academics should know about the achievements of Soviet historiography.[32] The first number of *Istorik-marksist* appeared in June 1926, with an editorial board of Pokrovskii, Gorin, V.P. Polonskii, M.P. Pavlovich, A.V. Shestakov, Fridliand, and S.M. Monosov. Its first item was Pokrovskii's opening address to the Society of Marxist Historians.

When *Pravda* reviewed the first number of *Istorik-marksist*, it made the observation that a deficiency in it was the lack of any attention given to historical methodology, apart from what was contained in Pokrovskii's address to the Society.[33] This was a serious criticism, considering that the elaboration of a Marxist methodology of history was one of the Society's cardinal aims. In this light, one can view Pokrovskii's address as a statement of what he – and in all probability his associates – understood the Marxist approach to history to be in the mid-1920s.

An important point that Pokrovskii makes in his address is that the Marxist approach to history is not simply economic materialism. It is not sufficient to look for an economic explanation for events, however useful this may appear. History is made by living human beings who need not be directly motivated by economic factors. Whereas formerly it had seemed possible to explain the origins of the 1914 war in terms of the fluctuation of grain prices, revelations about great power diplomacy had shown that grain prices were beside the

---

32   Levshin 1974, pp. 101–3.
33   Levshin 1974, p. 104.

point. International relations had taken on a life of their own in the pre-war period and were not simply the politics of finance capitalism.

The other feature of the Marxist approach to history that Pokrovskii was able to indicate arose from his experience of the 1905 revolution, when he witnessed the creativity of the masses. From this he became aware that pre-revolutionary Russian historians were accustomed to look upon the masses as the object of actions from above, never as the subject of actions. A Marxist historian, on the other hand, would represent the past, not as the preserve of the upper classes, but as the concerns of workers and peasants.[34]

These two features of what Pokrovskii believed to be a Marxist approach to history were very far from being a practical guide for working historians. Just how difficult it would be to come up with a clearly defined Marxist approach to history was indicated by the young, but extremely industrious, graduate of Kazan' University, M.V. Nechkina in her monograph *Russian History in the Light of Economic Materialism*, published in 1922. This surveyed the evolution of Marxist historiography of Russian history to date, including works by Rozhkov and Pokrovskii. In it she observed that debates about what constituted Marxism, or 'economic materialism', were still going on, and there were the most diverse interpretations, even of its most fundamental principles. The reason for this was that most of the literature on the subject was polemical, and there was no basic work on the subject, no 'gospels' with which one could begin. There were a few references to history in the *Communist Manifesto*, and in the *Contribution to the Critique of Political Economy*, and beyond that, some scattered references in Marx's polemic with Proudhon, Engels's polemic with Dühring, and Kautsky's polemic with Bax. But there was nothing that could be considered definitive, or that could serve as a guide on how to write 'Marxist' history.[35]

In the light of the prominence later given to Lenin in Soviet historical works, it is significant that in 1922 Nechkina gave Lenin only a passing mention. Posing the question whether Lenin's book *The Development of Capitalism in Russia* applied the theory of economic materialism, Nechkina considered that it did not. The period it covered was too short, and it dealt exclusively with economic history.[36]

At the time Nechkina wrote, there was no prospect that Marxism would become a well-defined doctrine. In the following year Riazanov delivered an

---

34   Pokrovskii 1926d, pp. 8–9.
35   Nechkina 1922, pp. 26–8.
36   Nechkina 1922, p. 47.

address to the Socialist Academy in which he reported on his progress in finding hitherto unknown drafts of Marx's *Capital*, unpublished manuscripts, and
correspondence. Deciphering, editing and publishing the material would be a
long-term enterprise. Consequently, despite the pressure put upon Riazanov
by students of IKP to do so, the production of a complete edition of Marx's
works still lay in the future. The implication was that 'Marxism' was a work in
progress, and that it was uncertain what it might finally turn out to be. Not only
was Marxism an elusive entity for scholars, but it was also unsuitable as a ruling
ideology for the Soviet state.[37]

The solution to the problem was to regard Lenin's pronouncements as authentic interpretations of Marxism, and to substitute Leninism for Marxism.
There were several advantages in doing this. The obvious one was that Leninism was stable; there was an identifiable corpus of writings, which were, for the
most part, clear and unambiguous, and needed little interpretation. Because
Lenin had spent most of his adult life as a journalist, he had commented on
all the important political events of his times. Most of his writings had a direct relevance to the Russian situation. The drawback here was that since these
writings had no identifiable unifying thread, one could not say in advance what
Lenin's attitude to a particular issue might be, hence the perennial hunt for
Lenin quotations to cover particular topics.

But even with the emergence of the Lenin cult immediately after his death,
it was by no means inevitable that the Soviet leader would be accepted as a theoretician on the level of Marx and Engels. Lenin was revered as the organiser of
the first successful proletarian revolution, not as a Marxist thinker. The case for
Lenin as a worthy successor to Marx and Engels was put by Nikolai Bukharin
in a talk to the Communist Academy in February 1924, the month after Lenin's
death. In it Bukharin conceded that while it was widely accepted that Lenin
had been an incomparable activist of the workers' movement, his standing as
a theoretician was much lower. An indication of this was the maxim current at
IKP which stated 'Marxism in science, Leninism in tactics – this is our motto'.[38]

This attitude, Bukharin argued, was quite mistaken. The impression that
Lenin was not a theoretician was created by the fact that his theoretical pronouncements were scattered throughout his writings, and not concentrated
in any one place. Lenin still awaited his systematiser. In time, however, Lenin
would be recognised for the great theoretician he was, and Leninism would
be regarded as the culmination and the further development of Marxism.

---

37   Riazanov 1923, pp. 251–376.
38   Bukharin 1924, p. 32.

Moreover, according to Bukharin, Lenin's Marxism was more relevant to the modern era than the Marxism of Marx. This was because after Marx's death there had been developments that lay outside Marx's experience, such as the monopoly stage of capitalism, the World War, the successful proletarian revolution, and the practice of the proletariat in power. All these were new areas for theoretical investigation that were beyond the scope of the Marxism of Marx and his generation of thinkers.[39]

The case that Bukharin makes for Lenin as a Marxist theoretician is special pleading. As an intellectual, and well versed in Marx's writings, Bukharin would know that Lenin came nowhere near Marx's level as a thinker, that Lenin's talent was as a journalist, and political maneuverer. Bukharin is arguing on grounds of expediency. What is more doubtful is whether he appreciated the consequences of his elevation of Lenin. The popularisation of what passed for Marxism would encourage dogmatism, and the harrying of those whose opinions did not conform to the Leninist template.

From the mid-1920s, when the Society of Marxist Historians was founded, Leninism became the dominant ideology, when it became obligatory to quote Lenin as an indication of ideological orthodoxy. Stalin showed great perspicacity in making himself the curator of this aspect of the Lenin heritage. His lectures delivered at the Sverdlov University in April 1924 on 'The Foundations of Leninism' echoed Bukharin's arguments and defined 'Leninism' as a new stage in Marxism, Marxism in the age of imperialism and proletarian revolution.[40]

In her memoirs Genkina illustrates why Leninism was popular with IKP students. In the early 1920s, while she was still studying at the Sverdlov University, she and her friends spent days, and even sleepless nights, trying to master the works of Marx and Engels. By the time she entered IKP in 1925, the emphasis had shifted to Lenin's writings, and these she found easy to understand, so that they became a guidebook for all her later historical studies.[41]

In March 1923 the Lenin Institute was founded, with Kamenev as its head. The Institute took over the publication of Lenin's works from Istpart, and from 1925 issued its own journal *Leninskii sbornik*, which published documents relating to Lenin which had not been included in the *Collected Works*. With the growing prominence of Lenin in Soviet ideology, the Lenin Institute increased in importance, absorbing Istpart in 1928, and the Marx-Engels Institute in 1931.

---

39   Bukharin 1924, pp. 32–7.
40   Stalin 1953, pp. 16–17.
41   Genkina 1984, p. 265.

The Marx-Engels Institute was a casualty of the adoption of Leninism as the ideology of the Soviet state. Under Riazanov's directorship the Institute had become a renowned centre of Marxist scholarship, not only within the country, but internationally as well. So long as the Soviet State laid claim to Marxist credentials, it was IME which would function as the arbiter of authentic Marxism. It was inevitable that in time IME would collide with the party leadership. During the 1920s attempts were made to undermine IME's standing, but these were resisted by Riazanov, who defended his right to free thought and expression. He refused to recognise the doctrine of a Leninist stage in the development of Marxism. On 16 February 1931 Riazanov was arrested and charged with Menshevism, and the underestimation of Lenin's contribution to the development of Marxism. He was sent into exile in Saratov, and IME was merged with the Lenin Institute to form the Marx Engels Lenin Institute (IMEL), which was attached to the party's Central Committee.[42]

The increasing adoption of Leninism as the criterion of intellectual rectitude caused serious difficulties for Pokrovskii. His books and articles had been written before Leninism had become obligatory and were now out of keeping with the new orthodoxy. Teachers and lecturers in Soviet educational institutions were the first to become aware of the problems raised by the divergencies between Pokrovskii's historical conceptions and passages in Lenin's works. In the second half of the 1920s Pokrovskii became noticeably less creative, and more defensive, as he admitted to mistakes, and made attempts to show that what he had written was in accord with the Leninist canon. Because Riazanov's arrest had been preceded by smear campaigns against his colleagues, the economist I.I. Rubin and the philosopher A.M. Deborin, orchestrated by the IKP graduates P.F. Iudin and M.B. Mitin, Pokrovskii feared that he too might be subjected to the same treatment by people bent on making a reputation for themselves as unimpeachable Lenin loyalists. In February 1931 Pokrovskii wrote to the Central Committee seeking reassurance that this would not happen.[43] Since Pokrovskii enjoyed the support of Stalin, he did not suffer that particular fate.

---

42   Rokitianskii and Müller 1996, pp. 96–104; Riazanov 2018, pp. 30–40.
43   Ivanova 1968, p. 180.

CHAPTER 7

Post-revolutionary Historical Works

1 Tsarism and Revolution

The Bolshevik revolution of 1917 gave Pokrovskii a new perspective on Russian history. He now knew how tsarism would be brought to an end, and how the Russian revolutionary movement would culminate. Now too Pokrovskii had a new objective: to explain Russian history to a mass audience, many of whom would have had no previous knowledge of the subject. The pamphlet *Tsarism and Revolution* was his first attempt at a work on Russian history that was brief, accessible, and had a Marxist approach. The attempt cannot be said to be entirely successful, because in explaining the economic forces behind the tsarist regime – the conflict between merchant and industrial capital, and the various phases of the Russian revolutionary movement – the work lacks both a chronological and logical sequence. It is an illuminating commentary on Russian history, but not sufficiently systematic for the purpose of instruction. What makes the work unusual, and gives it special significance, is its focus on the faith of the Russian peasants in the mystique of tsarism, and the misapprehensions of the Russian revolutionary currents about what would make the peasants rise in rebellion.

By way of introduction, Pokrovskii poses the question: why did tsarism so easily give way to the new republican order? Why should it be that after forty years of vain uphill struggle to limit the tsar's powers, it took less than forty minutes to be rid of the autocracy altogether? It was not, Pokrovskii argues, because the common people hated the tsar, or that the republican ideals of ancient Rus' had suddenly surfaced after 500 years. It was because the belief of the workers in mythical tsarism had been shattered by the experience of 'Bloody Sunday' in January 1905.[1]

In Pokrovskii's view, the belief of the common people in the mystique of tsarism was remarkably persistent, even among people opposed to the existing social order. By the beginning of the XVII century mystic tsarism had become a revolutionary peasant ideology. However, the tsars who were the objects of this ideology were the illegal ones: the False Dmitrii of the Time of Troubles, and the peasant rebel Emilian Pugachev, who claimed to be the Tsar Peter Fedorovich.

---

1 Pokrovskii 1918b, p. 2.

On the other hand, the peasants had no great liking for the legitimate tsars. They detested the reformer Peter the Great, and, more surprisingly, hated the 'Tsar Liberator' Alexander II.

The revolutionaries failed to move the peasants to new Razin and Pugachev rebellions, because they were unable to comprehend the real ideology of the peasantry. For the peasants, the tsar was the incarnation of their earthly ideals. Their wishes, their concepts of justice, the peasants transferred to the tsar, as if these were his wishes, his concepts. It was indicative that the only mass movement of peasants in the 1870s that the revolutionaries managed to produce, the so-called Chigrin affair, was brought about with the help of a false tsarist manifesto.[2]

In *Tsarism and Revolution* Pokrovskii introduces the theme of the conflict between merchant capitalism and industrial capitalism that he would deploy extensively in his later works. The two systems had very different requirements for their functioning. In the case of merchant capitalism, where the merchant dealt in the goods produced by serf labour using its own means of production, it was simply a matter of taking the greatest possible quantity of these articles from the countryside, transporting them to the town as cheaply as possible, and selling them where most money for them would be paid.

Industrial capital, on the other hand, presupposed the employment of free workers in a factory owned by the industrial capitalist. It required an internal market of people able to purchase the goods it produced, to ensure that accumulation took place rapidly, and was capable of attracting capital into industry. And whereas merchant capital was quite content with the system of serfdom and the abuses of the bureaucracy, industrial capitalism demanded the abolition of serfdom and the introduction of a constitutional regime.

Serfdom was a necessary concomitant of merchant capital, since the whole system of merchant capitalism required 'extra-economic compulsion' for it to function. Tsarism was the natural crowning of this edifice, just as the despotism of the Tudors and Stuarts had been in England in the XVI and XVII centuries, and the absolutism of Louis XIV had been in France. In order to compel the peasants to give up their product, it was necessary to deprive them of all political autonomy.[3]

Behind the ritual facade of tsarism was the economic interest which animated it: tsarism expressed the interests of merchant capitalism. As Pokrovskii put it in a memorable phrase: 'merchant capital ruled in the cap of Mono-

---

2   Pokrovskii 1918b, p. 10.
3   Pokrovskii 1918b, p. 12.

makh'. He cites the observation of Samuel Collins in the XVII century that the tsar was 'the chief Merchant in all the Empire'. The success or failure of individual Russian rulers depended on how well they represented the interests of merchant capital, the real power behind the throne. In the nineteenth century merchant capitalism had determined the fates of both Paul I and his son Alexander I.[4]

It was the emergence of industrial capital that began to undermine the foundations of the tsarist regime, because industrial capital was incompatible with serfdom. However, in Russia, the industrial bourgeoisie did not try to destroy the existing order, as the French bourgeoisie had done. The Russian bourgeoisie regarded the tsarist regime as an ally, though one that would be dispensed with when the necessity arose, as indeed happened in 1917.

Since in Russia the bourgeoisie did not wish to fulfil its revolutionary role, this had to be taken on by the Russian working class. But, Pokrovskii argues, although the Russian workers had always been objectively revolutionary, the mystique of tsarism died hard with them. It was characteristic that even the most advanced workers in Russia were reluctant to confront tsarism, and still felt it necessary to mention Christ and the apostles. The reverence of the Russian working class for the tsar explains the hopes that were placed in the petition to him that was intended to be presented in January 1905.[5]

Pokrovskii concludes *Tsarism and Revolution* by recounting an episode surrounding Bloody Sunday. At one meeting, before the pilgrimage to the Winter Palace, following the reading of the petition, the chairman put the question to the workers: 'But what if the tsar does not receive us and doesn't want to read our petition, what will we do then?' The reply that came from the workers was: 'Then we don't have a tsar!' On the following day, after the shooting, speakers from the Social Democrats could report of the workers: 'They're listening now ...' The significance of the Bloody Sunday massacre was that it dispelled the long-held regard of the common people for the tsar. It was now understood that there was no point in petitioning him for reforms. Change would have to come about by revolution.[6]

---

4 Pokrovskii 1918b, p. 13.
5 Pokrovskii 1918b, p. 31.
6 Pokrovskii 1918b, p. 32.

2   *Brief History of Russia*

Pokrovskii's most famous work, his *Brief History of Russia*, was first published in 1920, and went through 15 editions, 10 of them in the lifetime of the author.[7] It was the most widely read textbook on Russian history in the Soviet era and was translated into several foreign languages. Its translation into English by D.S. Mirsky appeared in 1933,[8] while Pokrovskii's reputation was still intact.

According to Pokrovskii, the idea for the book grew out of the propaganda lectures that he gave in 1906, but the actual text came from lectures given at the Sverdlov Communist University in 1919. The book derived its character from the circumstances in which it arose. For the audience he addressed Pokrovskii explained:

> ... we had to pump them up with Marxism in a great hurry to send to the front. And the *Brief History* emerged because there was no time for idle chat. It was necessary in the shortest possible form to convey the greatest possible quantity of facts in the most vivid light. For in front of me were people who on the morrow would be going to the front, and for whom we had to connect the Russian past with the present day, to show them the historical significance of that struggle to which they were going, and in which they would, perhaps, lay down their lives.[9]

The theme that runs through the *Brief History* is the conflict between merchant capitalism and industrial capitalism that Pokrovskii had introduced in *Tsarism and Revolution*. The dynamic of this conflict was that the two types of capitalism needed very different kinds of environment in which to exist. Merchant capitalism needed serfdom and could co-exist with the autocratic regime; industrial capitalism, on the other hand, aspired to abolish serfdom and to establish a constitutional regime. Whereas *Tsarism and Revolution* had described this dynamic in general terms, the *Brief History* applied it to the actual events of Russian history.

The mere description of the conflict between the two types of capitalism already suggests how Pokrovskii structured his book: he divides it into two sections, one covering the era of merchant capitalism, and the other devoted to

---

7   Pokrovskii 1967c, p. 611.
8   Pokrovskii 1933a.
9   Pokrovskii 1933c, p. 301.

the era of industrial capitalism, though, as Pokrovskii makes clear, in this latter era the influence of merchant capital still made itself felt.

As was already evident in *Tsarism and Revolution*, Pokrovskii believed that the conflict between merchant and industrial capitalism was not only a Russian phenomenon but was a feature of Western European history as well. For that reason, one does not find in the *Brief History* the themes of Westernisation and modernisation that are typical of most histories of Russia. This approach was in keeping with the Positivist view of history represented by Vinogradov and Kovalevsky, which held out the hope of there being a parliamentary democracy in Russia. In Soviet times Pokrovskii's universalist view of history took on a new significance: it was that the Russian revolutionary experience was applicable to all countries and was a pattern that foreign communist parties should strive to emulate. Russian leadership in the Communist International presupposed the approach to world history that Pokrovskii espoused.

The treatment of Russian history in the two parts of the *Brief History* is uneven. Because it covers a period from Kievan Rus' to the eighteenth century, the section on merchant capitalism is necessarily terse and concise. The section on industrial capitalism, on the other hand, begins in the nineteenth century and extends to the 1890s, and so Pokrovskii is able to give more space to the various topics of the period.

Drawing on the *Primary Chronicle*, Pokrovskii introduces merchant capitalism at the very beginning of his narrative. According to this source, the founders of the kingdom that was to become Russia were not Slavs, but Varangians, people who had migrated from Scandinavia. The names of the first princes of Kiev were of Swedish origin. As Pokrovskii points out, these Swedish princes were slave owners and slave traders, their chief pursuit being the capture of, and trade in, slaves. The prisoners taken in the incessant internecine wars would be enslaved and traded in Constantinople, which was at that time the chief slave market.

In this way Pokrovskii contrives to bring together slave ownership and merchant capitalism, which might be assumed to belong to different epochs. It stands to reason, however, that if human beings are bought and sold, they must be considered commodities, just as any other goods brought to market. For the early rulers of Kievan Rus' the goods which they traded in were obtained by conquest; for them, trade and robbery went hand in hand. Such was the economic basis on which the Kievan state flourished.

One factor which undermined the prosperity of Kiev and other Russian towns was the fall of Constantinople to the Crusaders in 1204, and its occupation by Italian merchant capital, which now dominated trade with the Orient, a development which ruined Russia's principal customer for slaves. The other factor was the Tatar/Mongol invasion, which had a disastrous effect on Russian towns, from which they never recovered.[10]

According to Pokrovskii, it was trade that accounted for the rise of the Muscovite state. Moscow stood at the intersection of two trading routes, one from north to south, and the other from east to west. The ruler of Moscow also benefited from being entrusted to collect tribute on behalf of the Tatar sultan.[11]

Pokrovskii regards the emergence of feudalism in Russia as co-existent with merchant capitalism. A feudal structure in Russia arose as the smaller lords became dependants of the larger ones. Since society rested on brute force, even a lord with an armed retinue was always in danger of being attacked by a more powerful neighbour. He might be made a slave, or at the very least be driven out of his house, which would be burnt down, and his peasants and their cottages would become the possession of the assailant. Pokrovskii emphasises that this phenomenon was not purely Russian, but also characteristic of feudalism in Western Europe.[12]

The main events which Pokrovskii deals with in the first part of his *Brief History* are the reign of Ivan the Terrible, the Time of Troubles and the Northern War. Pokrovskii sees Ivan as a particularly good example of a ruler who personified the interests of merchant capital. His conquest of Kazan' from the Tatars opened up a trading route to the East. To establish trading outlets on the Baltic coast, he embarked on an unsuccessful war in Livonia. He blamed this failure on the cowardice and treachery of the nobility, the boiars, and, with the help of the smaller gentry and merchant capitalists, launched a campaign of terror, the *oprichnina*, against them. This was the occasion for giving Ivan the nickname of 'the Terrible'. But, in keeping with his refusal to elevate the role of individuals, Pokrovskii emphasises, this did not mean that Ivan himself was exceptionally cruel, or that his part in the anti-boiar campaign was particularly prominent.[13]

In his account of the Time of Troubles, Pokrovskii describes Boris Godunov as 'the incarnation of merchant capital, which ruled in Russia'.[14] He attributes major significance to the period, since it witnessed a popular revolution against the feudal order. The false Dmitrii was supported by the peasants because he passed edicts to mitigate the oppression they experienced. For this reason, Dmitrii was extremely unpopular with the landowners and merchants, who

---

10   Pokrovskii 1967c, p. 34.
11   Pokrovskii 1967c, p. 41.
12   Pokrovskii 1967c, p. 38.
13   Pokrovskii 1967c, p. 57.
14   Pokrovskii 1967c, p. 619.

engineered his downfall. However, the peasant insurrection spread further, led by Ivan Bolotnikov, a fugitive slave. The insurrection was put down with extreme ferocity.

Out of the conflicts of the Time of Troubles the Romanov dynasty emerged. Having crushed the peasant masses with the aid of the small gentry and sections of the Cossacks, the Romanovs laid the foundations of a political order based on serfdom, officialdom, and a standing army, which survived until the revolution of 1917. The Romanovs were the representatives of the new feudal aristocracy, and of merchant capital. They not only served the interests of merchant capital but became identified with it. Ivan the Terrible's court had taken part in commercial affairs. Ivan's son Theodore was a share-holder in the English Company, which traded with Muscovy. It was in those times that an English writer could say that the tsar was 'the chief merchant in all the Empire'.[15]

The first part of the *Brief History* concludes with a mention of Peter the Great's Northern War against Sweden, which brought Russia ports on the Baltic seaboard, the trade routes desired by merchant capital. In view of its importance in Russian history, most historians devote particular attention to the reign of Peter the Great. In this respect it is remarkable how fleeting an appearance Peter makes in Pokrovskii's *Brief History*.

The second part of the *Brief History*, which deals with the era of industrial capitalism, begins with developments in the early nineteenth century. Pokrovskii traces the beginnings of industrial capitalism in Russia to the peace that Alexander I made with Napoleon in 1807. The terms of the peace required Alexander to join the French boycott of English goods. The demand was unpopular with the merchant capitalists, but it was a stimulus for native Russian industry. Freed from English competition, factories, especially those producing textiles, sprang up in Russia like mushrooms after rain. After the resumption of trade with England, Russian manufacturers demanded, and got, tariff barriers to protect native industry from foreign competition.[16]

As Pokrovskii points out, these industries were not of the modern industrial type, using machinery, and employing free workers. The workers of these manufactures were serfs, and the techniques which they used belonged to the pre-machine age. Unlike in England, or in the United States, in Russia industrial capital never became completely dominant; it always had to share its place with merchant capital. An important juncture in the development of industrial capitalism with its free labour, should have been the liberation

---

15   Pokrovskii 1967c, p. 75.
16   Pokrovskii 1967c, p. 102.

of the peasants in 1861. This liberation, however, was deliberately only partial in order to prevent the formation of a proletariat, and only partially and
gradually gave rise to a contingent of free workers who could be employed in
industry.[17]

With the rise in world grain prices in the 1870s, Russian merchant capitalism attained its highest development through the export of wheat to Western
Europe. This had its implications for foreign policy, since it was more profitable
to transport the wheat from its growing-area in the southern steppes to ports on
the Black Sea, rather than on the Baltic. The long-held aspiration of merchant
capital to control the Dardanelles was the reason for Russia's going to war in
1914.[18]

Pokrovskii structures the second part of the *Brief History* to imply a steady
radicalisation of Russian society in the nineteenth century. It was a radicalisation that was accompanied by a widening of the revolutionary movement's
social base. The participants in the Decembrist revolt in 1825, 'the first and
last revolution of the bourgeoisie', had been guards officers, with an admixture
of nobility. The radicals of the 1860s and 1870s, on the other hand, who composed the 'Narodnik revolutionary movement' were, in Pokrovskii's view, petty-
bourgeois intellectuals. They included such figures as Chernyshevskii, Herzen
and Lavrov, people who thought that capitalism was impossible in Russia, and
whose socialist ideal was the peasant commune.

However knowledgeable Pokrovskii might be on Russian history up to the
eighteenth century, he had no special insight into the history of the revolutionary movement. As a result, he took as his main source for the 'Narodniki'
Plekhanov's pamphlet *Our Differences*.[19] Ironically for someone who emphasised the need to examine sources critically, Pokrovskii did not notice that 'Narodnik' was merely a polemical label that Plekhanov attached to his opponents;
in reality no such intellectual current existed. Because, however, Lenin had
used the term, it was accepted into Soviet discourse.

The final chapter of the *Brief History* is that on the workers' movement. It
contains graphic descriptions of the wretched conditions that Russian workers lived in before the revolution: the dangerous and unsanitary conditions of
the factory, the irregular payment of wages, and the fines for the pettiest violation of factory regulations. These passages are paralleled by the descriptions
of the lives of peasants on landed estates under conditions of serfdom. In the

---

17   Pokrovskii 1967c, pp. 107–8.
18   Pokrovskii 1967c, p. 101.
19   Pokrovskii 1967c, p. 624.

Brief History only a fleeting suggestion remains of *Tsarism and Revolution*'s contention that, until it was dispelled in January 1905, the Russian people had a mystical regard for the tsar.

Having read the *Brief History*, Lenin sent his opinion of it to Pokrovskii in a letter dated 5 December 1920. It read as follows:

> Comrade Pokrovskii,
>
> I congratulate you on your success: I like your new book *Brief History of Russia* immensely. The construction and narrative are original. It reads with tremendous interest. It should, in my opinion, be translated into European languages.
>
> I shall permit myself one minor remark. To make it a textbook (and this it must become) it must be supplemented with a chronological index. This is, roughly, what I am suggesting: 1st column, chronology; 2nd column, bourgeois view (briefly); 3rd column, your view, Marxism, indicating the pages in your book.
>
> The students must know both your book and the index so that there should be no skimming, so that they should retain the facts, and so that they should learn to compare the old science and the new. What do you say to such an addition?
>
> With Communist greetings,
>
> Yours,
>
> Lenin[20]

Lenin had noticed the two main drawbacks of Pokrovskii's book. One was that since the exposition was largely thematic, it would be impossible for someone who was new to the study of Russian history to know what happened when. To remedy this fault, in subsequent editions of his book Pokrovskii introduced a chronological table, with dates of events in Russian and European history.[21] Nor, as Lenin implied, would a beginner appreciate the novelty of the book's Marxist approach if there was no indication of what the non-Marxist interpretations were. To this problem Pokrovskii had the simple solution of adding

20   Pokrovskii 1967c, pp. 3–4.
21   Pokrovskii 1933a, pp. 252–80.

an appendix containing a modified version of his lectures on Russian historiography, which he called 'The writers of Russian history before the Marxists and how they wrote it'. Despite these additions, the *Brief History* still proved something of a challenge for Soviet students of the 1920s.

In 1923 Pokrovskii published the third part of his *Brief History*, which covered the period 1896–1906. This was, for the most part, a straightforward narrative of the events of the 1905 revolution, without recourse to an explanation in terms of merchant or industrial capital. In the earlier editions it only touched upon the part played in the revolution by the Bolshevik party. This was because, separately from Pokrovskii's lectures, another course of lectures was being given at the Sverdlov University on the history of the Bolshevik party, and Pokrovskii tried to avoid duplicating these. In later editions of the book, and in separate histories of 1905, Pokrovskii tried to make good this omission. In doing so, he had made his treatment of the subject more political by including in it criticisms of Trotsky's theory of 'permanent revolution', and of his leadership of the Petersburg Soviet. Unlike most historians of the 1905 revolution, however, Soviet or Western, Pokrovskii gave credit to Alexander Bogdanov for having been the Bolshevik leader in St Petersburg during the 1905 revolution.[22]

Although Pokrovskii never refers explicitly to himself, there is an autobiographical element in the section of the book dealing with the December 1905 uprising in Moscow. He mentions, for example, how the last issue of the newspaper *Borb'ba* published the manifesto calling for an armed uprising but does not say that he himself was the editor in charge.[23] Neither does he make any mention of the literary-lecturing group which produced the newspaper. It can be observed too that some passages in Pokrovskii's account of the armed conflicts during the uprising echo those in the article 'Military Technique and the Question of the Militia', published in *Tekushchii moment* in 1906.

3   *Studies in the History of the Russian Revolutionary Movement*

In 1924 Pokrovskii published a series of lectures on the history of the Russian revolutionary movement in the nineteenth and twentieth centuries, beginning with the Decembrist revolt of 1825, and ending with the February revolution in 1917. The lectures do not encroach on the territory of Istpart, because they steer clear of any mention of the Bolshevik party, or of the October revolu-

---

22   Pokrovskii 1967c, pp. 602–5.
23   Pokrovskii 1967c, p. 453.

tion. In general, the lectures deal with the alignment of social forces in the last years of the Russian Empire that gave rise to the revolutions of 1905 and 1917. As sources for his lectures, Pokrovskii could draw on archival materials that were now available to him, the memoirs of participants, and, as he himself had taken part in the politics of the period, he had the insight that came from personal experience.

The book, especially in its first chapters, goes over much the same ground as *Tsarism and Revolution*, and the *Brief History* had done. In fact, Pokrovskii assumes that his audience have read his textbook, and would know about the conflict between merchant and industrial capital. In *Studies in the History of the Russian Revolutionary Movement in the XIX and XX Centuries*, Pokrovskii interprets the main developments in the period in question in the light of the struggle between merchant and industrial capital.

The liberation of the peasants was a measure demanded by industrial capital to obtain free labour to work in the factories, and consumers to form an internal market for the goods the factories produced. But it was merchant capital that dictated the terms of the legislation and did so in such a way as to further its own interests, rather than those of industrial capitalism. The peasants were not free to leave their villages and go to work in factories, because they had been liberated with land, which was intended to guarantee their subsistence, and they were attached to communes, in which they were collectively responsible for their taxes. The legislation had been specifically designed to prevent the growth of a proletariat, whose power had been demonstrated in the revolutions of 1848. Pokrovskii quotes Kankrin, Nicholas I's Minister of Finance, who assured the tsar that in Russia unemployed workers would not go on strike, as happened in the countries of Western Europe; they would go back to their villages, and there find food and shelter. As Pokrovskii goes on to show, things did not go exactly as Kankrin had predicted. By the end of the nineteenth century, there were over two and a half million unemployed workers, because the peasants were being uprooted from their villages faster than urban industry developed. Wages were so depressed that the workers had no choice but to go on strike.[24]

In order to establish what kind of revolution took place in Russia, Pokrovskii discusses whether or not Russia was an imperialist country before 1917. In doing this, he compares the definitions of imperialism given by Hilferding, and Lenin. According to Hilferding, imperialism was the foreign policy of finance capital, whose domination of the economy was indicated by the growth of syndicates

---

24   Pokrovskii 1924c, pp. 46–50.

and trusts. By this definition, one could not say that Russia was an imperialist country, even in 1914, because, although there were syndicates and trusts, these did not dominate the economy. However, one could say the same thing about France and England. There too syndicates and trusts existed but did not dominate. Under Hilferding's definition of imperialism, only two countries satisfied the conditions: Germany and the USA.

Pokrovskii added that in his book *Imperialism: the Highest Stage of Capitalism* Lenin had introduced an important corrective to Hilferding's formulation. He had regarded imperialism, not only as the special foreign policy of finance capital, but also as the general tendency of finance capital to establish monopolies. The essence of the matter was not in the formation of syndicates and trusts, but the aspiration towards monopoly, in whatever form it took.

In order to evaluate whether a country had entered the imperialist stage, one had to examine, not whether it had a sufficient quantity of trusts and syndicates, but whether there were present two indicators, which were also noted by Hilferding. These indicators were, first: high tariff barriers which made the territory of the country the monopoly sphere of the home industry, and second: the impulse to extend the tariff barriers in order to encompass within their boundaries as much territory as possible. From the 1880s these two indicators of imperialism were present in Russia.[25]

In Pokrovskii's view, during Sergei Witte's term of office as Finance Minister (1892–1903) the hegemony of industrial capital was consolidated. He saw the introduction of the gold standard by Witte in the 1890s as a victory of industrial capital over merchant capital. Merchant capital preferred the unexchangeable paper money, because its purchasing power was greater inside the country than on the international market, something that suited the landowning exporters of grain. The gold rouble, on the other hand, did not fluctuate, and so was of benefit to Russian industrialists, who had to buy machinery and cotton abroad.

Witte continued his predecessor Vyshnegradskii's practice of maintaining high tariff barriers for foreign goods. One consequence of this was that in order to avoid the customs dues foreign firms set up branches inside the country. Witte encouraged this practice, seeing it as a way to introduce modern industries into Russia. By the turn of the century there were many foreign firms, such as Siemens, Renault, Singer, Ericsson, operating in the country, but mainly centred in St Petersburg. These foreign firms would of course benefit from the gold standard, since it would enable them easily to repatriate their profits.

---

25   Pokrovskii 1924c, pp. 118–19.

In Pokrovskii's view, the interests of the Russian industrial bourgeoisie were so well catered for by the Witte regime that they had no cause to be radical and co-existed gladly with the tsarist autocracy. The landowners, on the other hand, during the Witte ministry were inclined to be more liberal since the government was less indulgent towards them. But even the most left-wing among the landowners went no further than the demand for a consultative representation.[26]

But the victory of industrial capital did not last long. When Witte left office in August 1903, merchant capital again gained the upper hand, in the person of his replacement Plehve, who was detested by the liberals. Following the 1905 revolution, when Stolypin became Prime Minister, he made some major concessions to industrial capital by his agrarian reform. For Pokrovskii, Stolypin's policies represented a compromise between merchant and industrial capital.[27]

Stolypin intended to dissolve the peasant agrarian commune, by encouraging the separation out of individual holdings, held as private property. Most historians have tended to stress the limitations of this reform, both in terms of the number of individual farms created, and the fact that the biggest uptake was in the western provinces, where the commune was already weak, leaving Central Russia as the bastion of communal landownership. Pokrovskii, however, saw the Stolypin reform differently, emphasising that it managed to dissolve a third of all peasant communes, and would have destroyed even more, had it not been curtailed by the World War.

The Stolypin reform performed a valuable service for industrial capital, first, by ending the system of mutual responsibility (krugovaia poruka) by which the communes were collectively responsible for the payment of taxes and other financial obligations owed by their members. This measure facilitated peasant mobility, and enabled those who had given up their allotments to leave the villages and seek employment in what industry there was. On the other hand, the wealthier peasants, who had separated out of the commune to become independent farmers, expanded the internal market for industrial goods. According to Pokrovskii, it was these kulaks who bought the sugar, roofed their huts with corrugated iron, and wore clothes made of cotton.[28]

In Pokrovskii's view, the objective economic result of the dissolution of the commune and the creation of a kulak stratum was positive. The fertility of the land and the intensity of agriculture increased, and correspondingly there was an increased use of agricultural machines by Russian agriculture. Due to the

---

26   Pokrovskii 1924c, pp. 125–9.
27   Pokrovskii 1924c, p. 141.
28   Pokrovskii 1924c, p. 147.

policy pursued by Stolypin, the years following the 1905 revolution witnessed a strong upsurge in industrial capitalism. And whereas industrial development at the end of the nineteenth century, during Witte's term in office, had depended mainly on the influx of capital from abroad, after 1909 foreign capital played a decreasing role in Russian industry, and Russian capital – an ever-larger part in the process of native accumulation.[29]

As a result of its growing role in the national economy, Russian industrial capital became bolder politically. In 1912 it formed its own opposition party, the Progressist party. This was led by Konovalov, a Moscow industrialist, who became Minister of Trade and Industry in the Provisional Government in 1917. Prior to the foundation of the Progressist party, the Russian industrialists had been represented by the Octobrist party, led by Alexander Guchkov, who became, briefly, Minister of War in the Provisional Government.[30]

At the beginning of the war, it was merchant capital which dominated; the objective of capturing the Straits was one that merchant capital dictated, as an episode in Russia's struggle for trading routes. Industrial capital, on the other hand, was initially rather lukewarm towards the war. But in the course of hostilities these attitudes were reversed. The curtailment of exports seriously reduced the attraction of the war for the merchant capitalists, but for the industrial capitalists the war held out the promise of increased profits. A situation then arose in which merchant capital wanted to end the war, whereas industrial capital wanted to continue it.[31]

In order to forestall the efforts of the tsarist government, on behalf of merchant capital, to make peace with Germany, industrial capital hatched a plot to intercept the Emperor's train and arrest him. Before the plot could be put into operation, however, the February revolution had erupted in the streets of Petrograd, and power did not pass smoothly to Guchkov and his co-conspirators but had to be shared with representatives of the workers. Pokrovskii did not think that the Bolsheviks in Petrograd in February 1917 led the uprising, and in support of this contention he cites the memoirs of Alexander Shliapnikov, the Bolshevik leader, who admits that he opposed the arming of the workers. To the question: could there have been a workers' government in Petrograd in February? Pokrovskii answers: Yes, there could, if Lenin and the rest of the Bolshevik leadership had been present.[32]

---

29 Pokrovskii 1924c, p. 161.
30 ibid.
31 Pokrovskii 1924c, p. 201.
32 Pokrovskii 1924c, pp. 207–15.

4   *The Imperialist War*

The final chapter in Pokrovskii's *Studies in the History of the Russian Revolu-tionary Movement in the XIX and XX Centuries* is one on foreign policy. It is to a large degree a summary of the articles that Pokrovskii had written on Rus-sia's external relations in the previous decade. These articles, and ones written in the Soviet period, were published in the collections entitled *Foreign Policy*[33] and *The Imperialist War*,[34] published in 1918 and 1928 respectively. Inevitably, most of these articles were devoted to the history of the 1914–1918 war, as the most important event in modern European history, and the context in which the Soviet state emerged. Pokrovskii's studies of Russian history led him to view the war from the perspective of earlier directions in Russian foreign policy. He was far from thinking that in 1914 Russian statesmen blundered into war; in Pok-rovskii's view, the war was the culmination of trends in Russian foreign policy that went back as far as the eighteenth century.

Although Pokrovskii started to write about the politics of the World War soon after it began, most of his works on the subject were made possible by the October revolution in 1917. The first act of the Commissariat of Foreign Affairs under Trotsky was the publication of documents from the former For-eign Ministry.[35] These provided Pokrovskii with valuable source material for his research. In addition to this archival material, the memoirs of the states-men who had been involved in the run up to the war were being published in the 1920s. He makes use, for example, of the memoirs of Sir George Buchanan, the British Ambassador, and of the French Ambassador Maurice Paléologue.

Pokrovskii believed that the main objective of the war on Russia's part was to gain control of Constantinople and the Straits, and that this objective was determined by the economic interests of merchant capital. In the struggle between merchant and industrial capital, in Pokrovskii's view, the war was an episode in which merchant capital had the upper hand, and this was the case not only in Russia, but in all the belligerent countries.

In an article entitled 'Historical Tasks' published in Trotsky's paper *Golos* in January 1915, Pokrovskii set out his historical perspective on the war. In it he rebuts the idea that the motivation for the conquest of Constantinople was religious – the intention to restore the Orthodox Christianity of the Byzantine Empire. He does this by arguing that the further the Russian rulers drifted away

33   Pokrovskii 1918c.
34   Pokrovskii 1928b.
35   Pokrovskii 1928b, pp. 295–6.

from Orthodoxy, the greater attention they gave to Constantinople in their foreign policies. This began with Peter I's Pruth military campaign in 1711, and
Catherine II's extensive plans for the re-establishment of the Byzantine Empire.
Both Peter I and Catherine II were confronted with the need to find trading
routes for Russia's produce. Peter's efforts had been mainly concentrated on
the Baltic area, but already in 1750 south Russian landowners were complaining that they had no outlet for their wheat, because Russia did not have a single
port on the Black Sea.

As Pokrovskii explains, it would have been possible to export Russian wheat
through the Black Sea even then, but since the Turks had a monopoly of Black
Sea shipping, paying them would have made the grain trade unprofitable. Catherine II's military campaigns against Turkey resulted in the treaty of Küçük
Kaynarca (1774) which gave Russia equal rights with Turkish shipping on the
Black Sea. There remained, however, the question of the freedom of navigation in the Straits, and this was finally resolved by the peace of Adrianople
(1829), which made navigation from the Mediterranean to the Black Sea and
back absolutely free for merchant vessels of all powers at peace with Turkey.

In 1833 Nicholas I forced the Turkish Sultan to conclude the Treaty of Hünkâr İskelesi, in a secret clause of which the Sultan undertook to close the
Straits to foreign (English and French) warships. The prospect of a Russian
navy based in Sevastopol and Nikolaev, capable of commanding the eastern
half of the Mediterranean, alarmed English and French statesmen, and they
did not rest until the possible base of the Mediterranean Russian navy was destroyed – until in the Crimean War Sevastopol itself was captured. Pokrovskii
concludes his article by reminding his readers that the reign of Nicholas I
was the first spring of Russian manufacturing capitalism. Restricted in the
internal market, which was growing slowly because of serfdom, it looked for
foreign markets and found them, it seemed, in the backward areas of Western
Asia.[36]

For Pokrovskii, Russia's expansionist foreign policy was a corollary of its economic backwardness, its inclination towards extensive rather than intensive
development. In an article published in Gorky's *Letopis'* in 1916, he made this
argument by drawing a parallel between peasant migration to Siberia, and the
aspiration to gain Constantinople. The former was driven by the impossibility
of the peasants to conduct an intensive form of agriculture, so that they were
compelled to seek out new areas for cultivation. In the latter case, Russian man-

---

36   Pokrovskii 1928b, pp. 26–9.

ufactures were forced to seek external markets because the development of the internal market was retarded by the out-dated landowning economy. Object-ively, Pokrovskii concluded, the Turkish wars and peasant migration served one aim: the maintenance of an outmoded economic system.[37]

Most of Pokrovskii's pre-revolutionary articles on the war were focused on Russia, but in the essay entitled 'Those Responsible for the War' he extended his analysis to the other belligerent powers. There too he found that the forces which drove the various countries to war were not those associated with the most advanced sector of the economy, but the most backward and conser-vative. In this approach Pokrovskii had found himself at odds with his fellow members of the Parisian Internationalists' Club, where he presented his paper in May 1915. Pokrovskii's ideas were controversial, because they disputed Hil-ferding's conception of imperialism, as the policy of finance capitalism, the effort to protect its monopolies by erecting tariff barriers and extending the territory protected by the tariffs. The present war had been caused by the colli-sion of finance capitals seeking territorial expansion. For Hilferding, therefore, the war was the product of the most advanced form of capitalism; for Pok-rovskii it was of the most backward. For Pokrovskii too it meant that there was no connection between finance capital and socialist revolution, an idea that Pokrovskii's fellow socialists were reluctant to accept.[38]

In the case of Germany, Pokrovskii found no evidence that it was trying to extend its economic territory or to erect tariff walls. On the contrary, German policy over the past forty years had not been to extend territory, but to conclude trade treaties, such as the ones with Russia in 1894 and 1904. Moreover, German policy had a peaceful character, as evidenced by its attempts to prevent the out-break of war during the annexation of Bosnia Hercegovina by Austria, and the Agadir crisis. Contrary to Hilferding, Germany was not trying to annex territory; it began the war because it believed that it was going to be attacked by Britain and France.

In France the most advanced branches of the economy were inclined to-wards closer ties with Germany since French industry needed German coal and machinery. A more traditional French economic activity was lending money, including foreign loans. It was in this sector that the advocates of war were to be found. The popular French press demanded war against Germany.

In Russia heavy industry had prospered in the pre-war years, and its repres-entatives had no desire for war. The more traditional textile industry, however,

---

37   Pokrovskii 1918c, p. 25.
38   Pokrovskii 1918c, p. 162.

had recently experienced a slump, and suffered from the competition of Łódź. The Moscow merchants demanded a 'war to a victorious conclusion', but they were few in number, and had little political influence. A more serious point of conflict was the competition between Russian and Prussian landowners. At the end of the 1870s the prices on the world grain market began to fall, causing severe financial loss to the Prussian Junkers. To protect Prussian agriculture, in 1880 the German government imposed import tariffs on grain, a measure which disadvantaged Russian landowners. The dispute was settled by the Russo-German trade treaty of 1894, but tensions remained. The class interests of the landowners not only led Russia towards a war with Germany, but also towards the acquisition of Constantinople and the Straits, the 'door of one's own house', to be able to export grain through the Black Sea.[39]

In Britain the social grouping which advocated war with Germany was not that associated with modern industry. It was a mythical idea that Germany and Britain were in industrial competition. The war party in Britain, headed by Edward Grey and Winston Churchill, was the equivalent of the Junkers in Germany. True, Pokrovskii conceded, Britain had no peasantry, but it did have an Empire, with subject peoples, who were treated as inferior beings. Britain benefited enormously economically from its colonial possessions, especially from India, whose loss would be a severe blow. For that reason, the British viewed as a serious threat to their interests any attempt to interfere with their route to India. On the eve of the war, they had been alarmed by the German domination of the Straits, and by German plans for a Berlin to Baghdad railway.[40]

However, in Pokrovskii's view, most of the bourgeois world would never have gone to war only for the economic conflicts he had described. It was the growing influence of the labour movement, and the threat of socialist revolution, that pushed the industrial bourgeoisie under the yoke of the rightist groups – of agrarian capitalism in Russia, colonial in England, and money-lending in France.[41]

When in the Soviet period Pokrovskii returned to the subject of who was responsible for the war, he had the benefit of access to the archives of the Russian Foreign Ministry and knew in much greater detail the events that had preceded the outbreak of war. These revelations did not simply add to Pokrovskii's factual knowledge but involved a revision of his historical methodology. He

---

39   Pokrovskii 1928b, pp. 47–8.
40   Pokrovskii 1928b, pp. 42–52.
41   Pokrovskii 1928b, p. 73.

now became acutely conscious of the insufficiency of economic explanations of historical events. From the vantage point of 1925 he observed:

> In the 1890s it might have seemed a discovery of genius to explain the outbreak of the 1914 war by fluctuations in the price of wheat (as I did in an article published seven years ago), but now that we know in the most minute detail about such things as the Russo-French military and the Anglo-Russian naval conventions, now that we know with complete exactness about the complex machinations behind the assassination of Franz Ferdinand, we realise that wheat prices are neither here nor there.[42]

Pokrovskii continued to treat the acquisition of Constantinople and the Straits as a central aim of Russian diplomacy. As before, he saw the greatest obstacle to the accomplishment of this aim the British determination to safeguard their route to India.[43]

The situation, as Pokrovskii saw it, was that Britain would not tolerate an attack by Russia on Turkey. But if Germany became involved in the struggle for the Straits, Russia would get the cooperation of the British. Therefore, to control the 'door of its own house', it was necessary to arrange such a war that the Germans would necessarily be involved. This, Pokrovskii considered, had been the tactic deployed in the Russian mobilisation in 1914. Having satisfied themselves that Britain would fight on the side of Russia and France, the Russians had to draw Germany into the conflict. The means to accomplish this was for Russia to attack Austria or create a situation where this attack would seem inevitable to Germany. In this way the Russian mobilisation achieved the desired alignment of forces for the Russian government.[44]

In August 1914 tsarist diplomacy was confronted with a delicate task: the war was being conducted for Constantinople and the Straits. But Turkey was not fighting, and, moreover, there was a danger that it might become an ally. Turkey had offered to put its army at Russia's disposal, and even offered to dispense with the presence of the German officers. In return Turkey wanted Western Thrace, the Aegean Islands and a defensive alliance with Russia lasting 5–10 years. This was far from what was desired by the Russians; they wanted Constantinople, and the war with Turkey would provide the best excuse to occupy it. The situation was saved, however, when two German warships, the *Goeben* and the *Breslau*, had entered the Dardanelles, and were not disarmed by the

---

42   Pokrovskii 1926d, p. 9.
43   Pokrovskii 1928b, p. 98.
44   Pokrovskii 1928b, p. 96.

Turks. Within a few weeks a Turkish-German agreement had been concluded, and in October Turkey abandoned its neutrality and entered hostilities on the side of the Central Powers.[45]

There was, in Pokrovskii's view, another obstacle to Russia's acquisition of Constantinople and the Straits. This was that the British promise of Constantinople to the Russians was simply a bait to keep them in the war; they had lost none of their reluctance to see Russian control of the Straits, and the consequent threat to the route to India. The British were also fearful that the Russians might agree to a separate peace with Austria, if by that means they could achieve their aim. To forestall this possibility was, in Pokrovskii's opinion, the rationale behind the Gallipoli campaign. He thought that:

> The prospect of an Austro-Russian peace confronted the British with a well-defined political objective: to arrange it so that Nicholas II could receive Constantinople only from the hands of the British. And this led in practice to the strategic aim: to be at the Straits before the Russians. On 19 February the British fleet began to bombard the Dardanelles forts.[46]

The situation, as Pokrovskii saw it, was that Russia had entered the war without a firm guarantee of getting the Straits. It had to obtain this in the course of the war, relying on France against England, who remained unsympathetic to the prospect of Russia's occupying Constantinople. The March 1911 agreement on the Straits was signed by Britain with such unwillingness that Russian diplomats never fully believed in its sincerity. Hence the attempts to confirm it with a separate peace deal with France, guaranteeing the latter the left bank of the Rhine, in exchange for the Dardanelles. The last such agreement took place almost on the eve of the February revolution.[47]

In a short article written in 1927 Pokrovskii reflected on the impact that the events of 1917–1918 had had on Russia's international relations. He believed that the war had strengthened the subjection of Russia to the Entente powers, to such an extent that Sir George Buchanan had become a force in the country to rival the Emperor. Following the February revolution, the Allied Ambassadors influenced the personnel of the Provisional Government. According to Pokrovskii:

---

45   Pokrovskii 1928b, pp. 170–6.
46   Pokrovskii 1928b, p. 187.
47   Pokrovskii 1928b, p. 259.

The diaries of Buchanan and Paléologue leave no doubt as to the fact that Kerenskii was selected and approved by the Entente incomparably earlier than the Mensheviks and SRs 'elected' him ... It is less well known – and it is well worth mentioning – that Miliukov was ousted so easily because he did not suit the Entente, because of his irksome references to the Dardanelles, which gave England cause to wince at every mention.[48]

The implication of what Pokrovskii says is that the slogan of the parties in the Petrograd Soviet 'peace without annexations and indemnities' played into the hands of the British, because by it Russia renounced its aspiration to acquire control of Constantinople and the Straits. With its principal war aim unrealised, Russia would have been fighting for nothing.

The accession to power of the Bolsheviks had brought about a major realignment in foreign relations, as Russia left the war. In Pokrovskii's view, making peace with the Central Powers was the Bolsheviks' trump card. The whole country needed peace, and this recognition had lessened opposition to the Bolshevik government. He also thought it a wise move of the Bolsheviks to have cancelled the debts incurred to the Allied powers, since this had the effect of freeing Russia from their financial domination.

By 1924 Pokrovskii's conception of the war had become more complex as a result of the researches carried out by former IKP students, in particular by N.N. Vanag. In the article 'How the World War Came About' Pokrovskii cited figures from Vanag's still unpublished book, which revealed that in Russia on the eve of the war 55% of the iron industry was in the hands of the French, 22% in the hands of the Germans, and 10% in the hands of Franco-German concerns. Apart from the textile industry, which was owned by Moscow merchants, the whole of Russian industry was dominated by foreign finance capital.[49]

The dominance of finance capital determined Russia's participation in the imperialist war. However, Pokrovskii insisted, this did not contradict the fact that the war was connected with the interests of Russian merchant capital, its attempt to secure the 'key to its own house'. Seen from this perspective, the war that brought an end to the Romanov dynasty also brought an end to its 'historical mission': to open up trading routes on the Baltic, and on the Black Sea.[50]

A serious challenge to Pokrovskii's conception of international relations in the period of the World War came from E. Tarle's book, *Europe in the Age of Imperialism*, published in 1927. To Pokrovskii's mind, Tarle's book, although it

48   Pokrovskii 1928b, p. 285.
49   Pokrovskii 1928b, pp. 122–3.
50   Pokrovskii 1928b, pp. 123–4.

had the trappings of a Marxist approach, was a work which took the side of the Entente powers against Germany. It sought to maintain the fiction that 'Germany started it', while avoiding any suggestion that the Allied powers had any aggressive designs. He thought the book dangerous, because there were very few works published in Russia on the origins of the war, and it was likely that for those interested in the subject, Tarle's was the only book they would read.[51]

Pokrovskii was especially incensed at the way Tarle interpreted the Treaty of Brest-Litovsk as a measure which prolonged the war, and determined the harsh terms dictated to Germany at Versailles. Tarle's reasoning was that the working classes of France, Britain and Italy had initially thought that their governments should follow the Russian example, and open negotiations with the Germans for an end to the war. But after the terms of the Brest-Litovsk Treaty became known, the mood changed. Then the imperialist impulses of the Entente governments were able, with renewed energy, to return to their old theme of 'war to a victorious conclusion', and the resolve not to let the Germans enjoy their spoils.[52]

To show that the Peace of Brest-Litovsk had nothing to do with the Allies' vindictive attitude to Germany at the Versailles peace conference, Pokrovskii directed Tarle to the book *Tsarist Russia and the War*, published in 1924, which documented the fact that as early as September 1914 the British were insisting that no peace was possible while Germany's military hegemony remained intact. What Germany would forfeit following its defeat was agreed between the respective Russian, British and French ambassadors. In other words, in Pokrovskii's estimation, the programme of the Versailles Peace was prepared by the Allies as early as the autumn of 1914.[53]

In a short article in *Istorik-marksist* Tarle answered Pokrovskii's criticisms, point for point. He denied that his book was pro-Entente, pointing out that in many places he repeated that Britain and Germany were as bad as each other, and that it would be a pointless exercise to try to decide who was more to blame for the war. Tarle continued to insist that the terms the Germans demanded in the Treaty of Brest-Litovsk had prolonged the war and had made the conditions imposed on Germany at Versailles more severe. He agreed that the plans for the peace with Germany might well have been laid in 1914, but it needed the experience of Brest-Litovsk to carry them out.[54]

---

51   Pokrovskii 1931a, p. 10.
52   Tarle 1958, pp. 389–90.
53   Pokrovskii 1928d, p. 16.
54   Tarle 1928, pp. 101–7.

At the end of Tarle's article Pokrovskii added an editorial comment. This did not contest Tarle's arguments, but claimed credit for the Soviet regime in publishing Tarle's works, although he was not a Marxist. Pokrovskii refused to apologise for the harsh tone he had used regarding Tarle, because, he maintained, it was in this tone that one addressed one's class enemies. If Tarle did not like it, he should not get involved in the class struggle, or defend the point of view of imperialists against a Marxist analysis. For Pokrovskii the subject of Europe in the age of imperialism was not one in which academic differences of opinion were acceptable; it was a matter of taking sides in a clash of ideologies.[55]

---

55   Pokrovskii 1928f, pp. 108–9.

CHAPTER 8

Debates on Imperialism

1 Slepkov

Studies in the History of the Russian Revolutionary Movement in the XIX *and* XX *Centuries* proved to be the most controversial of Pokrovskii's works. There were several reasons for this. The first was that it covered the most recent period of Russian history, one that Pokrovskii had never been comfortable with, and was dissatisfied with its treatment in the fifth volume of *Russian History from the Earliest Times*.[1] The second reason was that in *Studies* Pokrovskii had interpreted all the major events of the period in terms of the struggle between merchant and industrial capital, resulting in the treatment appearing schematic and artificial. The third reason for the controversy surrounding the book was that its conception of 'imperialism' was at variance with that of Hilferding, and Lenin. Whereas previously this would not have mattered, by 1924 the demand for ideological conformity was being increasingly felt.

A.N. Slepkov, a recent graduate of IKP and follower of Bukharin, reviewed *Studies* in the November 1924 issue of the journal *Bol'shevik*. The review is especially interesting, because it goes beyond its ostensible subject, to discuss other aspects of Pokrovskii's scheme of Russian history. Slepkov acknowledges that in the literary debate with Trotsky Pokrovskii was indisputably in the right. He thinks, however, that Pokrovskii has over-stated his case. The whole of Russian history is replete with merchant capitalism. It extends throughout the ages – from Ivan the Terrible, through Peter the Great, right to the time of the last tsar, who lived in the era of the domination of world finance capital. Only with the triumph of the workers' revolution in February 1917 did the rule of merchant capital come to an end. This homogeneity of approach to the question of the character of the autocracy took no account of its internal dynamic, its dialectic of development, and was therefore unacceptable.[2]

A related error of Pokrovskii's, Slepkov considered, was his placing of landowners and merchants into the single category of merchant capitalists. It was an impossible combination, because merchants and landowners had different roles in the production process, and therefore different sources of

---

1 Pokrovskii 1924c, p. 3.
2 Slepkov 1924, p. 114.

income. In the time of Peter I, when the landowner might also be a merchant, the interests of the two might coincide, but they would diverge when, in the second half of the XIX century, a social transformation of the landowner and the autocracy took place. This came about as a result of the increasing connection with the world market, through the export of grain, and the tendency of the landowner to run his estate on capitalist lines. To facilitate the transportation of grain, the state built railways, which stimulated the development of industries connected with railway construction. In this way, the autocracy, which represented landowner interest, inevitably displayed in its policy aspects of a bourgeois capitalist order. It could not be otherwise, since it existed in an environment of 'world capitalist encirclement'.[3]

Added to this, was the fact that in the XX century industrial capital was transformed into finance capital, and the landowning autocracy came into contact with finance capital. One also had to take into account that the property of the landowner was mortgaged to the banks, so that the landowner was economically a prisoner of bank capital. In this situation it could not be maintained, as Pokrovskii did, that the autocracy was 'politically organised merchant capitalism'.[4]

Slepkov then proceeds to a critique of Pokrovskii's conception of imperialism in Russian history. He gives Pokrovskii credit for having been among the first to analyse Russia's motives for participation in the World War. He thought particularly valuable Pokrovskii's investigation of the part played by the competition between the Russian landowner and the German Junker in the trade in grain as a factor leading to the confrontation. But Slepkov believed that Pokrovskii's vague conception of what imperialism was had prevented him from seeing the whole picture. Even in the collection of articles *Foreign Policy*, Pokrovskii had not made the necessary distinctions between the foreign policies of merchant, industrial, and finance capitals. For Pokrovskii the term 'imperialist' seemed to signify no more than 'aggressive', so that by this measure all wars were 'imperialist'.[5]

Slepkov takes issue with Pokrovskii's idea of how Lenin's conception of imperialism differed from that of Hilferding, who, as Slepkov indicated, was regarded as an authority by all Marxists, including Lenin. Although Slepkov conceded that the differences between the two conceptions were merely semantic, he nevertheless provided a barrage of quotations to show how Pokrovskii had misrepresented Lenin.

---

3 Slepkov 1924, pp. 114–5.
4 Slepkov 1924, p. 115.
5 Slepkov 1924, pp. 115–16.

Since, Slepkov argued, Pokrovskii regarded the Russian revolution not simply as a national, but as a world phenomenon, it demanded an explanation of Russia's motives for participation in the World War, that would take account of the influence of Allied finance capital on the Russian economy and policies. It demanded that Russia be regarded as a component element of the world economy. To do this Pokrovskii would have to broaden the scope of his investigations.[6]

A third area of Slepkov's disagreement with Pokrovskii was on the peasant movement. Again, Pokrovskii had failed to show how this had developed over time, and was no longer just the anti-feudal movements of the Bolotnikov and Pugachev uprisings. Now, after the proletariat had come to power, the peasant movement had new perspectives: the kulaks were no longer dominant, and the middle peasants were the allies of the workers. In this situation it was not appropriate to call for the state control of peasant capitalism, but to conduct a campaign for the social cooperation of the peasantry.[7]

In replying to Slepkov on the question of the class nature of the autocracy, Pokrovskii produced a quote from Hilferding, whom, he noted, Slepkov recognised as an authority, and with whom all Marxists were in agreement. This was that:

> The large landowners have a direct interest in the expansion of industry. They must sell their products, and capitalism creates a large domestic market for them as well as giving them the opportunity to develop agricultural industries, such as distilling, brewing, starch and sugar etc. production. This interest of the large landowners has a great significance for the development of capitalism: it provides support for capitalism in its early stages, and also ensures the support of the state. Mercantilist policy is also always supported by the landed proprietors, who are the product of the capitalist transformation of landownership.
>
> A further development of capitalism soon destroys this community of interests as a result of the struggle against *mercantilism and its executive agent, the absolutist state*. The struggle is waged directly against the landed proprietors who largely dominate the state and occupy the highest posts in the army, the bureaucracy and the judiciary, and who increase their income by economic exploitation of the state, and are the direct representatives of state power in the rural areas.[8]

---

6 Slepkov 1924, pp. 116–19.
7 Slepkov 1924, pp. 119–21.
8 Pokrovskii 1924b, p. 251.

The quotation provided the useful service for Pokrovskii of showing that he was in agreement with Hilferding on the class nature of the absolutist state, though he admitted that Hilferding's formulation 'the executive agent of mercantilism' was more elegant than his own 'the political organisation of merchant capital'. The quotation also showed that Hilferding, like Pokrovskii, regarded landowners and merchant capitalists as having interests in common, and that these only became separated with the further development of capitalism. It was from this further development, Pokrovskii stated, that there emerged the duel between the two types of capitalism – merchant and industrial – that he had depicted in his *Studies*.

Turning to the second part of Slepkov's review, the section dealing with imperialism, Pokrovskii agrees that here Slepkov's position is much stronger, as the pages of his *Studies* cited by Slepkov are among the least successful in the book, and do not provide any understanding either of imperialism in general, or of its specifically Russian variety. He concurs with Slepkov that his own characterisation of the Russian revolution as a world phenomenon obliges him to give an analysis of Russia's connections with world finance capital, an explanation of Russia's participation in the World War, and the effects of Entente finance capital on the Russian economy and politics.

In reply to this, Pokrovskii states that the obligation has already been partly met, in that his article 'How the World War Came About' contains figures for the foreign investment in Russian industry. These figures, however, were not included in his *Studies*. The reason for this, Pokrovskii explains, was that when he gave the lectures, he had fallen between two stools – the Hilferding conception, and that of Lenin, which differed in quite important details.[9]

Pokrovskii embarked on a comparison of the way in which Hilferding and Lenin defined imperialism. Whereas Hilferding believed that an imperialist country erected high tariff barriers and tried to increase its territory, Lenin thought that these phenomena were particular instances of the domination of banking capital. The failure to mention banking capital Pokrovskii considered to be the principal defect of his characterisation of imperialism in his *Studies*.

Misled by Hilferding's formulation when in 1915 he wrote his paper on 'Those Responsible for the War', printed in *Foreign Policy*, which Slepkov mentioned, Pokrovskii denied that the war was imperialist. It was only a year and a half later, after reading Lenin's pamphlet on imperialism, that he began to understand the imperialist character of the war.[10]

---

9   Pokrovskii 1924b, p. 253.
10   Pokrovskii 1924b, p. 256.

On the section of Slepkov's review dealing with 'peasant capitalism', Pokrovskii discerned the author's reluctance to view the peasants as property owners, and to present them in a quasi-socialist light. To counter this tendency, Pokrovskii quoted extensively from Lenin, who cautioned against attributing to the peasants a sympathy for communism, which they did not have. Pokrovskii concluded that, whereas in the first part of his review, which questioned the class character of the autocracy, Slepkov came close to Trotsky, in the second part, on the socialist character of the peasantry, he was sounding like a Narodnik.

Slepkov was unconvinced by Pokrovskii's reply and suspected him of not taking Lenin's idea on peasant cooperation seriously.[11] Soon after Slepkov, G. Maretskii, another follower of Bukharin, wrote a similar critique of Pokrovskii's conception of a merchant capitalist autocracy.[12] Maretskii, however, was unable to add anything substantial to what had been already said by Slepkov. After his rather lengthy reply to Slepkov, reaffirming the merchant capitalist nature of autocracy, Pokrovskii left Maretskii's article unanswered.

Since both Slepkov and Maretskii were associates of Bukharin, the question arises whether their objections to Pokrovskii's scheme of history had a political dimension. This is indeed strongly suggested by Slepkov's article entitled 'The Agrarian Peasant Problem in the Era of the Proletariat's Struggle for Power'. Here Slepkov attempts to show the revolutionary character of the peasant movement in modern times. His argument is that because in all countries the landowning class is closely associated with industrial capitalism, in opposing the landowners the peasantry thereby undermines the capitalist system. Having supported the Russian peasants in their aspirations to divide the landlord estates amongst themselves, the Bolsheviks achieved the overthrow of large-scale capitalism in the country.[13]

This objectively revolutionary, anti-capitalist, characterisation of the peasant movement presupposes that the economic nature of the Russian autocratic State is industrial and finance capitalist. If the autocracy is merely merchant capitalist, unconnected with, and even antagonistic to, industrial capitalism, then the argument does not apply. In Pokrovskii's scheme of Russian economic development, the peasantry does not play the kind of role assigned to it by Slepkov. It was probably for this reason that Slepkov found Pokrovskii's interpretation of Russian history unsatisfactory.

11   Slepkov 1925b, pp. 65–73.
12   Maretskii 1926, pp. 88–97.
13   Slepkov 1925a, p. 43.

The criticisms of Slepkov and Maretskii presented no great threat to Pok-rovskii's scheme, especially when compared with those of Trotsky in 1922. Mainly, this was because Slepkov and Maretskii accepted so much of the Pok-rovskii conception of Russian history in general, and of the State in particular. What is more, they had made no independent analysis of the autocracy, and had come to the debate unequipped with any new corpus of factual material. The best they could do was look for contradictions in Pokrovskii himself or con-front him with a barrage of quotations from Lenin, a ploy to which Pokrovskii reciprocated in kind.

On the other hand, Slepkov and Maretskii, in raising the question of the nature of the autocracy in the era of imperialism, had quite accurately indic-ated one of the difficulties of the Pokrovskii system. For this indeed was the key question: what was the autocracy which had been overthrown by the Russian revolution, which class did it represent? It was precisely this which defined the nature of the revolution itself. It was generally held that socialism could only be born out of the ruins of an imperialist state, one in which capitalism had reached its highest stage, completed its historical mission. Yet, in what sense was this true of Russia, which was still, as everyone recognised, a backward country, where capitalism was still in its infancy? Pokrovskii's scheme had to this date, more than anything else, served to evade the issue since, as Slepkov indicated, his definition of imperialism was sufficiently wide. But when this definition was shown to be at variance with Leninist orthodoxy, it left the prob-lem unanswered, and created a major difficulty for Soviet ideology.

It was also recognised that the answer to this question lay outside the sphere of purely Russian history – in Russia's position with regard to the system of world imperialism, since the revolution had to be looked at in a general-European perspective. Just at this time a doctrine on the subject had been formulated by Stalin in his series of lectures entitled 'On the Foundations of Leninism', which were published in *Pravda* in April and May 1924. It was in these lectures that Stalin introduced his theory of 'socialism in one country', a theory which he attributed to Lenin.

The other theory that Stalin attributed to Lenin in the lectures was that: 'The front of capital will be pierced where the chain of imperialism is weakest, for the proletarian revolution is the result of the breaking of the chain of the world imperialist front at its weakest link'.[14] In 1917 the chain of the imperial-ist world front proved to be weaker in Russia than in the other countries. It was there that the chain broke and provided an outlet for the proletarian revolution.

---

14   Stalin 1953, p. 37.

This was a remarkable assertion, because the doctrine of the chain of imperialism breaking at its weakest link belonged not to Lenin, but to Bukharin, and that when Lenin encountered it in Bukharin's book *Economics of the Transition Period*, he registered his disagreement with it.[15] The false attribution had to be made, however, because theories could carry no weight if they were not 'Leninist', even though, as in this case, no actual quotation from Lenin was possible.

Even with the cloak of 'Leninism', Stalin's lectures were not taken on board by Pokrovskii and his followers at IKP. For them, the perspectives for socialism in Russia tended to centre on the extent of the country's indigenous economic development. The prospects for socialism were much brighter if it could be shown that the country, by its own efforts, had reached the imperialist stage, that Russia was an imperialist country in its own right. If, on the other hand, Russia's capitalist development was an artificial growth, fostered by the investments of the European powers, then socialism in Russia was clearly impossible, and in such a case Trotsky's thesis would have been proved correct.[16]

It is this which explains the great preoccupation of Soviet historians in the 1920s with the figures for foreign and national investment in Russian industry before 1917. It was hoped that this kind of analysis would yield the desired results, a preponderance of indigenous over foreign investment, and no stone was left unturned to achieve this. Yet, in spite of these efforts, the opposite conclusion invariably emerged, creating a serious dilemma for Soviet scholarship.

2   Vanag

In 1925 the IKP graduate N.N. Vanag published his monograph *Finance Capital in Russia before the World War*. Vanag begins by asking the question: when did capitalism in Russia enter its monopoly stage? The material for answering this question has so far been lacking, since there have been no studies specially devoted to finance capital in Russia. This, according to Vanag, has led to some

---

15   Bukharin 1971, p. 221.
16   The Programme of the Communist International (Comintern) in 1928 divided countries into three groups: those with highly-developed capitalism, those with medium development, and colonial and semi-colonial countries. Only the former two categories were held to possess the prerequisites for a dictatorship of the proletariat and socialist construction. The last category included those countries '... whose most important branches of industry, trade, banking concerns, means of transport ... were concentrated in the hands of foreign imperialist groups'. In these countries a socialist revolution was thought possible only after a number of intermediate stages. Mif 1934, pp. 21–2.

mistaken opinions about the period and the character of the development of
Russian imperialism. Moreover:

> Among the erroneous opinions one must include that of such an author-
> itative historian as M.N. Pokrovskii, who has stated that 'Russian imper-
> ialism is rather older than we had hitherto been led to believe' and that
> the 'era of imperialism begins from the end of the 1880s'.[17]

Pokrovskii's justification for this statement was the definition of imperialism
given by Hilferding. Vanag, however, points out that the correct, Leninist, criterion for indicating the existence of imperialism is not the presence of high
tariff barriers, or the acquisition of new territories, but the presence of finance
capital, and the necessary degree of its concentration in the form of monopolies.

Having presented an analysis of the concentration of capital in Russia, Vanag
concludes that in the 1890s the degree of concentration had not yet reached a
stage that could be termed monopoly but had only formed the basis on which
such a concentration could take place at a much later date – after the revolution
of 1905.[18]

The age of imperialism in Russia provides a key to its character. The years
before the first revolution marked a serious recession in Russian heavy industry.
By that time the programme of extensive railway construction, which had
maintained it, was over, as it was then desperately short of credit, which the
Russian banks were unable to supply. The only way out of the crisis was to apply
for support from the foreign banks.

Consequently, Vanag states:

> ... we are confronted by the fact that foreign finance capital, principally
> French, played the greatest role in reorganising Russian industrial under-
> takings. The start of the development of Russian monopoly capitalism
> is closely linked with international banking capital, which by no means
> limited itself to this initial reorganisation, but began to sink its roots deep
> into Russian industry, until, before the war, it, in fact, monopolised the
> whole system of Russian industrial capital, or at least its commanding
> heights. Only the monopolisation of Russian industry by international
> banking capital was carried on in a refined form, which hid the essence

---

17   Vanag 1925, p. 5.
18   Vanag 1925, pp. 8–9.

of the process from the casual observer: international banking capital
subordinated Russian industry to itself through the Russian commercial
banks ....[19]

After giving a survey of the various branches of Russian industry, Vanag concludes that foreign capital controlled three quarters of the whole Russian banking system, and of this the biggest share was in the hands of the French banking
consortium – 53.2%. The Germans controlled 36.4%, and the British – 10.4%.
That is, the Entente powers controlled 63.6%, and the Germans – 36.4% of all
foreign investment in Russian industry.[20]

The influx of foreign capital, however, concerned mainly heavy industry,
since light industry in Russia was not so drastically affected by the recession,
and did not experience the necessity to attract foreign investment in order
to survive. The main reason for this was that light industry, in particular the
textile industry, found a ready market for its products in Persia, China and Afgh-
anistan. It was this sector of the economy which was the last refuge of ethnic
Russian capitalism.[21]

Soon after Vanag's book appeared, it was followed by that of S.L. Ronin,
Foreign Capital and Russian Banks (1926), which also emphasised the dominant part played by foreign banks in the Russian system of finance capitalism.
Ronin's book had a foreword written by the economist L.N. Kritsman, which
took a more extreme position than either Vanag or Ronin. Whereas Vanag and
Ronin had spoken in terms of the subordination of Russian industry to foreign
capital, Kritsman denied that there was any indigenous element at all in the
system of Russian monopoly capitalism. In his opinion:

> The merger of monopolies of banking capital and the monopolies of
> industrial capital was in Russia basically the merger of foreign capital with
> foreign capital, i.e. there took place not the creation of a system of Russian
> finance capital, but the expansion of the sphere of exploitation of foreign
> finance capital ... As a result – instead of a system of Russian finance cap-
> ital we had, on the territory of Russia, parts of three mighty systems of
> finance capital – the French, the German and the British, of which two,
> the French and British, became, as we know, at the time of the war, parts
> of the mighty coalition 'the Entente'.[22]

---

19   Vanag 1925, p. 25.
20   Vanag 1925, p. 54.
21   Vanag 1925, p. 170.
22   Tarnovskii 1964, p. 18.

In his book *Russian Imperialism*, published in 1927, M. Gol'man, a follower of Trotsky, put a rather different gloss on Vanag's findings. Unlike Kritsman, he conceded that there was indeed an indigenous accumulation of monopoly capitalism, but this was unable to emancipate itself from the hold that foreign capital had on the Russian banking system. Russian imperialism became a subsidiary of Western European countries. In Gol'man's view, Russia's status was that of a semi-colony in the system of Western-European imperialist powers.

In the second edition of *Studies in the History of the Russian Revolutionary Movement in the XIX and XX Centuries*, published in 1927, Pokrovskii incorporated the findings of Vanag and Ronin. He remarked:

> In the first edition of the present book I still regarded the policy of Nicholas in the Far East as something self-contained – and, as for a self-contained policy in the Far East, any motives other than imperialist ones it was impossible to propose, so there followed my characterisation of Russian imperialism at the end of the XIX century and the start of the XX. Since that time there have appeared works – especially those of Comrades Vanag and Ronin – which have explained, with all clarity, that one cannot speak of 'Russian imperialism' in this period without doing violence to the term 'imperialism', as it is employed in theoretical literature. Moreover, the work of Comrade Ronin has shown that even in 1914 to speak of 'Russian imperialism' can be done only conditionally – that Russia, even on the eve of the imperialist war, was the arena of action of very much more foreign capital than indigenous.[23]

The findings of the Vanag school of thought did not go uncontested. Other scholars, like I.F. Gindin, E.L. Granovskii, and A.L. Sidorov, while not denying the significant role played by foreign capital in Russian industry and banking, maintained that Russia was nevertheless an economically independent country, with its own system of monopoly capitalism. But as Pokrovskii recognised:

> It is comrade A. Sidorov's opinion that the dependence of Russian capitalism on that of the Entente, the economic captivity of the Russian banks, was not so great as comrades Vanag, Ronin and Kritsman would have us believe ... I think that the conclusions of Comrade A. Sidorov introduce only those 'correctives' which inevitably accompany any over-simplified

---

scheme. From this we can estimate the influence of foreign capital on Russian industry not at 75 but at 63%; but the basic premise – that Russia entered the war in 1914 as the vassal of the Entente – is very little shaken.[24]

The different points of view were represented in the discussion on Vanag's paper given at the First All-Russian Conference of Marxist Historians, which was held in Moscow at the end of 1928 and the beginning of 1929. Some of the contributions were amplified in articles published in a special issue of *Istorikmarksist* in 1929. At the Conference most participants agreed that the question of whether Russia was dominated by foreign capital was not to be decided by economic statistics alone, that the complex inter-relationship of foreign capital and indigenous accumulation had to be examined in detail. Gindin emphasised that it was wrong to think in terms of Russian finance capital being completely foreign or completely indigenous; it would be a combination of both elements.[25]

Any reservations which Pokrovskii may have had about Vanag's findings were dispelled by 1928 by the failure of Sidorov's attempt to refute them. At the All-Russian Conference of Marxist Historians Pokrovskii announced that he considered Vanag's point of view to a 'significant degree correct', but he still assigned an important part to merchant capitalism in Russia's war aims, in the struggle for the Straits. This, according to Pokrovskii, had no relation to the aspirations either of international finance capital, or of ethnic Russian imperialism, which was more concerned with annexations in Persia, Mongolia and the Far East in general. 'The struggle for the Straits was an old merchant capitalist aim and had nothing to do with imperialism'.[26]

In a paper entitled 'Leninism and Russian History', which he read at the Conference, Pokrovskii linked the question of imperialism in Russia with that of methodology, and once again stressed the dangers of 'economic materialism'. He confessed that he himself bore the traces of having passed through the school of 'Legal Marxism', which tended to exaggerate the economic element in the explanation of events. In this connection, Pokrovskii referred to Stalin's verdict on the debate between himself and Trotsky:

Recognising that Trotsky's scheme was quite un-Marxist, comrade Stalin noted the correctness of Pokrovskii's conception, remarking only that it

---

24   Pokrovskii 1927b, p. vi.
25   *Trudy pervoi vsesoiuznoi konferentsii istorikov-marksistov* 1930, pp. 339–45.
26   Pokrovskii 1929b, pp. 234–5.

suffered from some degree of simplification, in that it over-emphasised the role of the economic factor.[27]

The articles by Vanag and Gindin in *Istorik-marksist* provide scholarly surveys of the problem of the respective roles of foreign and native capital in Russia's economic development. Granovskii's contribution, on the other hand, is principally a tirade against Vanag, supported by a battery of quotations from Lenin, his chief concern apparently being orthodoxy.

For Vanag, finance capital does not exist at all until after 1905, the period of the great influx of foreign investment. Before that date, the autocracy is simply the instrument of agricultural interests. The railway construction of the nineties was designed to get Russian agriculture out of its state of crisis, while the tariff barriers were intended to protect, not Russian manufacturers, but agricultural production. It is only after 1905 that the autocracy begins to express the interests of finance capital, and foreign at that.[28]

Gindin in this respect considers Vanag one-sided. He sees a gradual coalescence taking place in the last years of the nineteenth century between the autocracy and finance capital. He thinks that nowhere else has industry been so well supported by government subsidies, for example, the sugar industry, and railway construction. The policy of Sergei Witte too expressed the interests of industrial capital.[29]

Although both writers pay chief attention to the influence of foreign capital in Russia, they do not fail to emphasise that ethnic industrial development did take place. Vanag in particular stresses the importance during 1916–1917 of the antagonism between the two rival groups of capitalists, between those connected with foreign companies in Petrograd, and the Russian national capitalists, like Guchkov, Konovalov and Riabushinskii, centred in Moscow.[30]

The political implications of the imperialism discussion were never far from the surface at the Conference. Those who emphasised the part played by indigenous Russian capitalism in the system of imperialism, upholders of the 'nationalisation' theory, were branded by Vanag as Mensheviks. The 'Mensheviks', for their part, were not slow to draw similar parallels. Gorin remarked: 'The views of Vanag on the role of foreign capital in Russia are close to those of Trotsky. The latter, in the preface to his book *1905*, also ignores the role of indigenous capital in Russia. The ideas of Vanag and Trotsky are exactly alike. Of course, I

---

27   Pokrovskii 1929b, p. 235.
28   Vanag 1929, pp. 37–8.
29   Gindin 1929, p. 77.
30   *Trudy pervoi vsesoiuznoi konferentsii istorikov-marksistov* 1930, p. 327.

am not saying that Vanag is a Trotskyist, but Trotsky's error of ignoring the role of indigenous accumulation should be taken into account by those who subscribe to the theory of "denationalisation"'.[31]

This meant that the results of all the investigations tended to fly in the face of the doctrine of socialism in one country, and to provide a clear vindication for Trotsky and his theory of permanent revolution – a fact of which everyone was keenly aware. Sidorov himself confirmed the deep political significance of the discussion. He recalls:

> My part in the discussion was modest. Besides the work in *Studies* [*in the History of the October Revolution*] I published an article in *Proletarskaia revoliutsiia* (1928) where I outlined my own attitude to the discussion. I was closer to Granovskii's point of view, but I did not like his extravagant concessions to Vanag, or his unfounded attacks on M.N. Pokrovskii. Besides this, I gave a radio talk from the lecture theatre of the Sverdlov University. In this talk the academic question of the character of imperialism in Russia was linked with the question of the Leninist theory of socialism in one country, and of the 'maturity' of Russian capitalism for such construction. Although I was then politically in agreement with Granovskii and Vanag, it is true that Vanag's views found many supporters among the oppositionists. Therefore, the problem of Russian imperialism took on a great political significance in the struggle against the Trotskyists. I do not say that it should have been directly connected with the struggle within the party; perhaps it would have been better to regard it purely academically and dispassionately. However, such was not the case.[32]

Pokrovskii, who had identified himself with Vanag's views, was also accused of Trotskyism. His last article, written in 1931, was a reply to these accusations, made by an 'anonymous author' (whom O.D. Sokolov later identified as A.L. Sidorov) in the third volume of the *History of the VKP(b)* edited by Iaroslavskii.[33] There it was claimed that: 'Denying the independent character of Russian imperialism, Pokrovskii, Vanag and Kritsman have regarded Russia as a colony of French and English imperialism, and the government of Nicholas II as a passive toy'. Pokrovskii rejected as baseless the assertion that he had regarded Russia as a colony, interjecting: 'Did anyone actually say this? When?' To the suggestion that he thought of Nicolas II's government as a passive toy,

---

31   Pokrovskii 1929b, p. 233.
32   Sidorov 1964, pp. 131–2.
33   Sokolov 1970, p. 203.

Pokrovskii protested: 'I devoted 15 years of my work to the question of Constantinople and the Straits, i.e. precisely to show the presence in tsarism of independent aims and objectives in the war!'[34]

Shortly before his death, probably at the end of 1929, Pokrovskii's attitude to Vanag's scheme underwent a final modification. In a note to Stalin he described his pupil's ideas as 'semi-Trotskyist', and disclaimed them completely.[35] By 1930 Pokrovskii made a poor target for the accusations of Trotskyism put forward by Iaroslavskii and Sidorov in the *History of the VKP(b)*. Having enlisted the aid of Stalin, Pokrovskii was one of the chief beneficiaries of the letter to *Proletarskaia revoliutsiia* in 1931. It was this which served to put Iaroslavskii and his other opponents to flight and ensured that it was they who suffered a campaign of slander and repression, and not he.[36] By some manoeuvres of his own, and Stalin's support, Pokrovskii was able to end his days having lost nothing of his former eminence and authority.

3   Soviet Anniversaries

The debate on imperialism could not but affect Pokrovskii's views on the perspectives for socialism in Russia and bring about some considerable reorientation. This is evident from two articles he wrote, one in 1924 and the other in 1926, that is, before and after Pokrovskii became acquainted with Vanag's research. The articles also reveal Pokrovskii's position on the Soviet political spectrum at that time.

The first of the two articles, 'The Soviet Chapter of Our History', was published in the journal *Bol'shevik* in 1924.[37] There Pokrovskii divides up the seven years from the Bolshevik revolution to the present time into five phases. His focus is on the economic development of the country, and on the extent to which the successive economic policies have helped, or hindered, the transition to socialism.

Pokrovskii's first phase comprises the period from the October revolution to the summer of 1918. It was in this period that the foundations of the socialist economy were laid. They consisted in the implementation of the policy Lenin

---

34   Pokrovskii 1932, p. 17.
35   Tarnovskii 1964, p. 51.
36   *Vsesoiuznoe soveshchanie o merakh uluchsheniia podgotovki nauchno-pedagogicheskikh kadrov po istoricheskim naukam* 1964, p. 362.
37   Pokrovskii 1924e, pp. 10–19.

had outlined in the autumn of 1917: 1) the amalgamation of all the banks in the country into a single bank, and its nationalisation; 2) nationalisation of the capitalist trusts and syndicates. These measures would be the first steps towards a planned socialist economy. In this period, before the Civil War, it was assumed that the transition to socialism would be peaceful, and would be effected on an all-European scale, when the international revolution triumphed. That Pokrovskii viewed the nationalisation of the banks as the key measure in the foundation of a planned economy indicates that he still thought of socialism in Hilferding's terms. Since, for Hilferding, the banks controlled industry, it was through control of the banks that a planned economic system could be created.[38]

The onset of the Civil War in the summer of 1918 brought an end to this first, peaceful, period of socialist construction. Pokrovskii referred to it as a period of 'pacifist illusions', no doubt influenced by his experience in Moscow during the October revolution, when the defeated Iunkers had been allowed to leave Moscow and join anti-Bolshevik forces in the south. The examples of 'pacifist illusions' Pokrovskii mentioned in his article included: 1) the failure to arrest the Moscow committee of the Kadet party; 2) allowing the SRs freedom to organise acts of sabotage on the railways; 3) doing nothing to prevent the SRs collaborating with White Guard officers to muster anti-Bolshevik forces in the Volga region. The Soviet government had been taken by surprise by the revolt of the Czecho-Slovaks in Siberia at the end of May 1918.[39]

In the summer of 1918 the Soviet regime suffered a series of reverses: the uprising by the Left SRs in Moscow, the uprising of the Right SRs in Samara, the rising organised by Savinkov in Iaroslavl', the murder of Volodarskii, the murder of Uritskii, and, finally, the attempt on Lenin's life on 30 August – all these episodes taken together acted to dispel completely the pacifism of the first period of Soviet history. In the autumn of 1918, the Bolsheviks launched the Red Terror, and concentrated their efforts on fighting the Civil War, which Pokrovskii considered to extend from August 1918 to the spring of 1920.

Pokrovskii calls the second period of Soviet history, which ran from 1918 to 1919, the period of 'spontaneous militarisation', when almost all aspects of Soviet life, including education, were militarised. The economy was the area most militarised in the period. There were formed 'labour armies', and the whole of the countryside was made subject to a semi-military regime.

---

38   Pokrovskii 1924e, p. 12.
39   Pokrovskii 1924e, p. 14.

There were two main factors, Pokrovskii believed, which inspired this militarisation. One was the delay of the workers' revolution in the West, ending hopes for the creation of an international socialist economy, whose existence had been assumed in the first, 'pacifist', period of socialist construction. It had now become clear that the Russians would have to rely on their own resources. The second factor was that, although the Civil War had been expected to drag on indefinitely, in fact the Red victory had come surprisingly quickly, after only two years. This success gave rise to the hope that success in the economic sphere could be attained just as quickly, that it was simply a matter of applying the same military methods. And certainly, 'War Communism' for a time enjoyed a limited success.[40]

Pokrovskii's third period is that of 'War Communism'. He emphasises that he refuses to consider 'War Communism' as any continuation of the socialist measures introduced in 1918. There was nothing military about the measures, the most important of which, the nationalisation of the banks, was implemented in the era of 'pacifist illusions'. The measures were carried out, not by orders from above, but under pressure from the worker masses. A planned economy was being brought into being by the needs of industry, which required the direction of the banks. In this first phase of development, it was economics which dictated the policies adopted, and not politics. With 'War Communism', in the period 1920 to the spring of 1921, the reverse was the case; it was politics that determined economic policy.

The beginning of the fourth period, extending from 1921 to 1923, was marked by the introduction of the New Economic Policy (NEP). In Pokrovskii's view, NEP brought an end to the illusions that had dominated agrarian policy during 'War Communism'. Now, plans for the future of agriculture would deal with the countryside, not as it was imagined to be, but as it really was. This new approach, Pokrovskii stressed, did not imply the abandonment of communism, but only the rejection of military methods of introducing communism into the countryside.

The first period of NEP was also characterised by illusions. The Soviet government's illusion was to over-estimate the contribution that private enterprise would make to developing the industry of the country. It had been assumed that both domestic and foreign capitalists would immediately take advantage of the business opportunities that had opened up in Russia. These hopes were not fulfilled, and it was realised that industry would have to be reconstructed

---

40   Pokrovskii 1924e, p. 15.

by the Soviet regime, unaided. European capital was loath to operate in Soviet conditions, when it could function in the bourgeois environment it was accustomed to.[41]

The period from 1923 to the present time, Pokrovskii designated as the fifth phase. This was the gradual return to a planned economy, as disillusion with the policies of NEP set in. 1923 was the year of the 'scissors crisis', when the prices of industrial goods outstripped those of agricultural produce, and acted as a turning-point within NEP. What Pokrovskii expected to follow would be the resumption of the attempts, begun in 1918, to build a planned socialist economy, free from the illusions that had dogged earlier phases of Soviet history.[42]

Pokrovskii's periodisation of Soviet history to 1924 shows that he judged events against the criterion of whether they contributed to the emergence of a socialist planned economy in Russia. On those grounds, he finds both 'War Communism' and NEP wanting. He looks forward to the abandonment of NEP and the resumption of policies aimed at instituting a system of economic planning. In this light, it is understandable why Pokrovskii should later support Stalin's 'great turn' of 1928, but there is no indication in Pokrovskii's article that he envisaged the pace of change that Stalin would impose.

In 1924 Pokrovskii did not raise the question of whether Russia's pre-war economy had reached the level that could support a socialist system. His assumption had always been that Russia had a well-developed system of imperialism, and, in this respect, was no different from the countries of Western Europe. He had no doubt that socialism was possible in Russia, and he believed that the country was on track for the creation of a planned economy.

Vanag's research, published in 1925, however, showed that the Russian economy was, in fact, backward in comparison with that of the Western-European powers. It confronted Pokrovskii with the problem of explaining how socialism could be possible in a country whose economy was poorly developed and was heavily dependent on foreign investment. In the article 'On the Ninth Anniversary', published in 1926,[43] Pokrovskii set out to re-interpret the history of the October revolution, considering the recent findings on Russia's pre-war economy.

How could it be, Pokrovskii inquired, that one of the most backward countries in the world should be faced with the task of constructing a socialist state? This was something never envisaged by Marx and Engels. The reason, he

---

41   Pokrovskii 1924e, p. 18.
42   Pokrovskii 1924e, p. 19.
43   Pokrovskii 1926a, pp. 3–22.

suggests, lay in the 'disproportion between the political structure of the country, and its economic development'. This disproportion was brought about as follows. Although essentially a backward country, economic development proceeded in Russia at an enormous pace. In no other country had the pace of development been so rapid. The political regime, on the other hand, remained extremely backward and unchanging. Nicholas II wanted to ensure that what he had inherited from his predecessors would be passed on to his son undiminished. Not only the political structure, but also the autocracy as such, changed very little. Pokrovskii confessed that he had been accused of non-Marxism for predicating the extreme political stagnation and rigidity of the old Russian State. But, as he pointed out, no historian could make up history. If the autocracy did not change, there was nothing one could do about it. One just had to accept it.[44]

It was the disproportion between the country's economic growth and its political structure that determined the revolution's proletarian character. The political structure continued to exist out of economic necessity, otherwise it would have disappeared, as in other countries. The government fostered the construction of railways for strategic considerations, the demand for rails stimulating the development of the metallurgy industry. In this way, Russian economic development was determined mainly by the autocracy, the apex of that system of primitive capitalist exploitation, which Pokrovskii called 'merchant capitalism'.[45]

This swift economic development, originated by the autocracy and financed by foreign capital – here Pokrovskii cites Vanag's research – led to the creation of a social order which quickly made the autocracy itself an anachronism, a state machine which had no relation to actual social requirements.[46] Yet from this situation there inescapably follows the proletarian nature of the revolution which swept away the autocratic state structure. For the Russian bourgeoisie itself, being a prisoner of foreign capital, was too feeble to carry out this task. It was:

> ... not in a condition to resolve this disproportion between the country's political structure and its economic development ... and to give the country the kind of government it required.[47]

---

44   Pokrovskii 1926a, p. 5.
45   Pokrovskii 1926a, p. 7.
46   Pokrovskii 1926a, p. 10.
47   Pokrovskii 1926a, p. 12.

The Russian proletariat, on the other hand, which had begun to organise itself politically long before the Russian bourgeoisie did, was in such a position.

This presentation of events brings Pokrovskii very close to Trotsky's viewpoint, and indeed Pokrovskii in practice admits this with a reference to Trotsky's alter ego, the Narodniks. He says:

> Perhaps some people will say that I am repeating Narodnik views – for the Narodniks also said that our industry was a hothouse growth, artificially created by the State. But I can only say that in this respect the Narodniks were right ... .[48]

For Pokrovskii, then, Russian capitalism is not an indigenous development, but created by the State as a foreign importation – on this Pokrovskii and Trotsky are now in agreement. The economic argument for socialism in one country no longer exists. But, since Pokrovskii will not follow Trotsky's reasoning to its logical conclusion – that socialism in one country is impossible – he is forced to have recourse to moral considerations. He therefore argues that the revolution must bear a national character, since it is carried out within the confines of a nation, and the proletariat of each nation must first of all deal with its own bourgeoisie. Once the proletariat has taken power into its hands, it also takes over the economy, and so constructs its own, proletarian, economy. Given these circumstances, it was difficult to understand why there should be debates about whether or not it was legitimate to construct socialism in the country. Pokrovskii's conclusion was that: 'History has determined that we have that right. History has presented us with this highly responsible task and we cannot and must not refuse it'.[49]

In 1931 Pokrovskii stated this position in more succinct terms: '... there is no longer any possibility of stressing the "objective causes." For now the objective causes are against us ... The objective logic of the old "economic materialism" is against us – and yet we are going forward ...'.[50]

---

48   Pokrovskii 1926a, p. 7.
49   Pokrovskii 1926a, p. 3.
50   Pokrovskii 1967d, p. 451.

4   People's Will

From its inception it was the policy of the Society of Marxist Historians to mark
the anniversaries of key revolutionary events in Russian history. The first of
these was the centenary of the Decembrist revolt in 1925. This provided Nechkina with the opportunity to publish a series of articles on the subject in *Istorik-
marksist*. The following year was the 50th anniversary of the death of Mikhail
Bakunin, and this was marked by articles in *Istorik-marksist* by Iu.M. Steklov
and V.P. Polonskii. 1928 was the centenary of the birth of Chernyshevskii, which
was marked by the publication of a collected edition of his works, and a number of articles in *Istorik-marksist*, one of them by Pokrovskii, entitled 'Chernyshevskii as a Historian'.[51]

Pokrovskii thought of Chernyshevskii as a Janus figure, someone who looked
both to the future and to the past. On the positive side, Chernyshevskii believed
that all peoples in the world had the potential to develop capitalist systems,
and that capitalism had already taken root in Russia. On the negative side, was
the fact that Chernyshevskii had an idealist view of historical development. He
believed in the power of ideas, and the ability of the State to bring about economic change. These kind of deficiencies Pokrovskii found in Chernyshevskii's
'Letters without Address', and his other writings on the 1861 peasant reform. To
Pokrovskii, it was mistaken to think of Chernyshevskii as some kind of proto-
Marxist.[52]

The proceedings surrounding anniversaries in the 1920s had been relatively
sedate, with discussions centred on finding the correct Leninist approach to the
given question. The fiftieth anniversary in 1929 of the founding of the People's
Will (*Narodnaia volia*) group was a much more frenetic affair, since it took place
against the background of the collectivisation drive, and the political campaign
against the 'Rightists'. The discussion on People's Will could not escape being
caught up in the politics of the day, and its scholarly value being diminished as
a result.

The most contentious of the articles on People's Will was that by I.A. Teodorovich entitled 'On the Historical Significance of the People's Will Party'.
Teodorovich had been a social democrat since the mid-1890s and had been
expelled from Moscow University at the time of the protests against Kliuchevskii organised by Skvortsov-Stepanov. When the Bolsheviks had taken
power, Teodorovich had become the Commissar for Supply in the new Sovn-

---

51   Alatortseva 1979, pp. 100–14.
52   Pokrovskii 1928c, pp. 3–26.

arkom. During the 1920s he had served in the Commissariat for Agriculture but had been removed from his post due to his opposition to collectivisation. He continued to be the chief editor of the journal of former political prisoners and exiles, *Katorga i ssylka*, in which his article on People's Will was published.[53]

Teodorovich's article had three distinct elements to it. In the first of these, Teodorovich contested Pokrovskii's contention in his *Brief History* that People's Will held that revolution was made by 'critically-thinking individuals, and that they were incapable of making a direct and open appeal to the masses'. Quoting extensively from the People's Will programme and its publications, Teodorovich showed that this was not true: that, on the contrary, People's Will envisaged that in any revolutionary action the masses would be involved. Also by quoting from People's Will publications, Teodorovich demonstrated the falsity of Pokrovskii's claim in his *History of Russia from the Earliest Times* that 'People's Will did not rebel against the bourgeoisie, and exploitation in general, but set itself the definite task of bringing about, by means of a conspiracy, a political revolution to overthrow the tsarist government, and convoking a constituent assembly'.[54]

Pokrovskii was vulnerable to this kind of criticism, because he had relied on secondary works to write the section on the Russian revolutionary movement in both of his books. Teodorovich, on the other hand, had studied the subject thoroughly, and had a good command of the literature.

The second element in Teodorovich's article was also well documented. This was a survey of the relationship of Marx and Engels to People's Will. Here Teodorovich could quote Marx and Engels's preface to the Russian translation of the *Communist Manifesto*, with its concluding passage allowing for the possibility of socialism in Russia being based on the peasant commune. *Narodnaia volia*, the journal of People's Will, had published this preface, and added the comment:

> We have pleasure in including the 'foreword' in view of the considerable scholarly and practical interest in the questions it raises. It is especially pleasant for us to note the concluding words: we see in them confirmation of one of the basic propositions of the theory of People's Will – confirmation based on the researches of such authoritative scholars as Marx and Engels. The long-awaited continuation of Marx's celebrated work

---

53   Mertsalov 1991, p. 257.
54   Teodorovich 1929, pp. 8–15.

(*Capital*) will of course develop, with the requisite fullness, among other things, the propositions which the 'foreword' could only touch upon.[55]

Further evidence of Marx's preference for People's Will, rather than Plekhanov's Black Repartition group, was contained in his letter to F.A. Sorge of 5 November 1880. In it Marx observed:

> In Russia *our* success is even greater ... the terrorist Central Committee, whose recent programme ... aroused considerable ire among the anarchist Russians in Switzerland, who bring out The *Black Repartition*. Unlike the terrorists, who risk life and limb, these men – most of whom (but not all) left Russia of their own accord – (In order to disseminate propaganda in Russia) – they remove to Geneva![56]

Teodorovich also reproduced a lengthy extract from Marx's letter to Nikolai Danielson of 1879 on the subject of Russian economic development, showing, that from the 1850s Marx had hopes for a peasant revolution in Russia.[57]

The third element in Teodorovich's article was the argument that key features of Bolshevik theory and practice had been anticipated by People's Will. Thus, for example, the idea of smashing the State machine, propagated in Lenin's *State and Revolution*, had been advocated by A.A. Kwiatkowski in *Narodnaia volia*. Lenin's conception in *What is to be Done?* of a conscious intelligentsia leading a movement of the masses could also be found in the literature of People's Will. The system of autonomous local communes, which People's Will proposed as the future form of government in Russia, was, in Teodorovich's view, an anticipation of the Soviets in Bolshevik Russia. Most important, a transition period from capitalism to socialism had been an idea of People's Will, and corresponded to the policy of NEP, to whose current fate Teodorovich did not refer. Although nowhere stated explicitly, an implication that could be drawn from Teodorovich's article was that the tradition to which the Bolshevik party belonged was one which dictated adherence to NEP and rejection of collectivisation.[58]

In mid-January 1930 the question of People's Will's heritage was discussed at special sessions of the Society of Marxist Historians. The participants were left in no doubt about the contemporary significance of the subject, as the

---

55   Teodorovich 1929, p. 23.
56   ibid.
57   Teodorovich 1929, pp. 32–4.
58   Teodorovich 1929, p. 44.

official doctrine was that 'the attempt to resurrect neo-Narodnik ideology by Teodorovich and his sympathisers is mistaken and politically harmful'.[59] Being at that time in Berlin for medical treatment, Pokrovskii was not present at the discussions, but his pupils I.L. Tatarov, Gorin, Fridliand and Genkina were, and Teodorovich could remark that this group of his opponents attempted to justify their teacher.[60]

By and large, this was a discussion on Lenin's views on People's Will, rather than a discussion of People's Will itself. Most of the contributions consisted of collections of quotations from Lenin's works, produced without any regard for the context in which they were written. There were, however, some exceptions. One of these was the contribution by S.I. Mitskevich, who gloried in Bolshevism's People's Will heritage. Whereas, he said, Plekhanov came from Black Repartition, Lenin came from People's Will, as did the whole of the first cohort of Social Democrats, to which Mitskevich himself was proud to belong. It also included such figures as Teodorovich, Meshcheriakov, Feliks Kon and Ol'minskii. Mitskevich thought that this group had taken from People's Will what was best, most progressive, and, with the help of Marx's doctrine, had transformed it into Bolshevism.[61]

The only participant to discuss the attitude of Marx and Engels to People's Will, and to refer to Marx and Engels's writings, was the IKP graduate A.F. Ryndich. Expressing his agreement with Mitskevich, Ryndich declared that he was unconvinced that any connection existed between Teodorovich's ideas and the Right-wing deviation. Unlike the majority of speakers, he did not quote Lenin, but the writings of Marx and Engels. These were, by and large, the ones mentioned by Teodorovich. The conclusion that Ryndich drew from these was that 'between the views of the Narodniks on the peasant commune, and the views of Marx on this same question, there is no difference'.[62] This view, which supported Teodorovich's case, was extremely unwelcome to the Soviet leadership, causing Ryndich to be singled out for severe criticism.[63]

Pokrovskii's student Tatarov summed up the discussion, and wrote the 'Theses on the 50th Anniversary of People's Will' for the Culture and Propaganda Department (Kultprop) of the party's Central Committee. The 'Theses', which was published in *Pravda* on 9 April 1930, reflected Pokrovskii's views.[64]

---

59   Nevskii 1930, pp. 1–2.
60   Nevskii 1930, p. 173.
61   Nevskii 1930, p. 86.
62   Nevskii 1930, pp. 86–8.
63   Nevskii 1930, p. 2.
64   Nevskii 1930, pp. 193–205; Artizov 1998b, p. 126.

Pokrovskii's own response to Teodorovich came in an article in *Istorik-marksist* entitled 'On the Anniversary of People's Will'. One would have expected a direct reply to Teodorovich to address the three areas that Teodorovich had covered in his article: the question of People's Will and conspiracy, the attitude of Marx and Engels to People's Will, and the question of continuity between People's Will and the Bolsheviks. In Pokrovskii's article the topic of the relationship of Marx and Engels was not touched upon at all. The questions of People's Will's revolutionary tactics, and its continuity with the Bolsheviks, were both dealt with by a collection of quotations from Plekhanov and Lenin, who, for polemical motives, had accused People's Will of conspiratorial methods. By comparing the characterisation of the Russian State in a People's Will publication with what Trotsky had said on the subject in his book *1905*, Pokrovskii equated Teodorovich's ideas with Trotskyism, and by extension, with the Rightist political position of Slepkov. Pokrovskii's article on People's Will was one of sophistry and evasion more than of historical scholarship.

As Teodorovich observed at the end of the discussion on People's Will, none of his opponents had analysed, or even mentioned, any documents emanating from People's Will. Neither had they referred to works by Marx and Engels, and they had quoted Lenin without giving the context in which he had written.[65] The discussion was indicative of the fact that, although there was ample evidence to establish the attitude of Marx and Engels to Russia's economic development, and how the founders of Marxism viewed the Russian revolutionary movement, this subject was off limits for Soviet historians. The possibility of writing a genuinely Marxist history of Russia, based on the writings of Marx and Engels, was rejected out of hand. It had become obligatory to evaluate the events and personalities of Russian history from the point of view of Lenin.

Iaroslavskii had not taken part in the People's Will discussion and had asked Pokrovskii not to go hard on Teodorovich, with whom he had been friendly for many years. In a letter dated 27 February 1930 Pokrovskii replied:

> If you think the evaluation of Teodorovich as a writer who is close, theoretically, to the Narodniks, is wrong ... you can take the matter up with the Central Committee. But if I take it upon myself to suppress criticism by my personal authority, then I can assure you ... nothing will come of it, beyond the loss of what authority I have.[66]

---

65   Nevskii 1930, pp. 167–9.
66   Sokolov 1970, p. 99.

In answer to Iaroslavskii's plea that Teodorovich should not be defamed, Pokrovskii reassured him that Teodorovich would not be given a rough passage. Only 'holes would be picked' in him, as had happened to Pokrovskii himself. He recalled:

> They 'picked holes' in me in *Bol'shevik* in 1924 ... they 'picked holes' in me from then on in IKP (the last time three days ago, at the first year seminar) ... they 'picked holes' in me in the Society of Marxist Historians ... And it is true that I willingly admitted my mistakes when they were pointed out. I have never set myself up as an infallible pope, nor have I tried to throw mud at my opponents, or make them a laughing stock in the lecture room.[67]

As it happened, what was in store for Teodorovich was more serious than merely being criticised by Pokrovskii's pupils. Perhaps unknown to Pokrovskii, the OGPU was then in the process of preparing a case against the so-called 'Labouring Peasants' Party', and Teodorovich's name had been mentioned in the evidence given by those arrested.

The exchanges between Pokrovskii and Iaroslavskii on the subject of Teodorovich were indicative of a rivalry that had grown up between the two men and their supporters. What was at stake was not any ideological issue, but competition for showing loyalty to the regime and its current economic policies. Against the background of show trials, scholarly disagreements became accusations of treachery and subversion. Pokrovskii seems to have realised the futility of the attitude, for, as he wrote to Gorin on 15 October 1930:

> Exposing heresies is a laudable thing, but the masses do not need this ... Yet we keep on rooting out heresies – and soon we shall fall into the position of the Deborinists. They also rooted out – and they thought they were doing great things. And then they were ousted. They will oust us out too, if we do not come to our senses in time and realise that serving the masses by following our party line is now the chief thing. I should like it very much if the comrades would make this clear to themselves.[68]

Nevertheless, the tone in which the anniversary of the 1905 revolution was marked in 1930 was one of rooting out heresies.

---

67   Sokolov 1970, p. 191.
68   Gorin 1933, p. 107.

The history of the 1905 revolution was an area where the pro-peasant Right wing of the party had made substantial inroads, following the campaign against Trotsky. Since Trotsky had allegedly 'underestimated the peasantry', it had become incumbent on Soviet historical science to make good this error. Pokrovskii noted early in 1931 that: 'There exists a number of mistakes connected with the participation of the peasantry in our bourgeois revolution ... one may hear even today that our revolution of 1905 ... was only a peasant revolution, that in this evaluation is believed to be the difference between Leninism and Trotskyism, which ignored the peasantry'.[69]

This was a point on which Pokrovskii showed astute judgement. While concluding that the peasantry had played a considerable part in 1905, he continued to emphasise the leadership of the proletariat in the revolution. What the respective roles of these two social forces had been formed the subject of Pokrovskii's writings on 1905 during the last years of his life. It was a subject too on which an impassioned debate was waged between Iaroslavskii on the one hand, and Pokrovskii and Gorin on the other. It was inflamed by Gorin's review of the second volume of the four-volume *History of the VKP(b)* that Iaroslavskii edited.

In his review Gorin insisted that one should not be indulgent towards the kind of errors that were found in Iaroslavskii's book, because the masses would be misled by them; it was essential that errors of this kind should be exposed. It was deeply mistaken, he believed, for the authors of the book to characterise 1905 as a peasant revolution. What he had in mind was the statement that:

> If the proletariat is the most reliable, the most consistent and most progressive revolutionary force in tsarist Russia, then the participation of the ... peasant masses, on the one hand, makes the Russian revolution a genuinely mass revolution, and, on the other hand, determines the social content of the revolution.[70]

This, in Gorin's opinion, was a Narodnik interpretation of the 1905 revolution, which, he pointed out, was not only inconsistent with what had been said on the subject, not only by Lenin, but also by Stalin, who was being increasingly cited as an authority in such matters.

Before going into hospital on 8 March 1931, Pokrovskii infuriated Iaroslavskii by postponing the publication of the latter's reply to Gorin in *Istorik-marksist*.

---

69   Pokrovskii 1967d, p. 217.
70   Gorin 1930, p. 167.

As a consequence, Iaroslavskii wrote a letter to Stalin complaining about Pokrovskii's behaviour. On Pokrovskii's advice, Gorin wrote a lengthy note to Stalin answering Iaroslavskii's complaints and mentioning that in the second volume of the *History of the VKP(b)* there were serious mistakes. Due to his illness, Pokrovskii himself was unable to take part in the polemic, but from the Crimea, where he and Liubov' moved to at the beginning of May, he gave encouragement to Gorin. On 29 May Pokrovskii wrote: 'Your polemic with Iaroslavskii begins to remind me of the battle at Preussisch Eylau, when Napoleon claimed victory for himself, and so did Bennigsen. His last article is quite a Napoleonic bulletin. But be a Bennigsen to him ...'.[71]

The article in question was a spirited rebuttal by Iaroslavskii of the criticisms that had been levelled against the book he had edited, by Gorin, Sidorov and, by implication, Pokrovskii. The core of the article consisted of quotations from Lenin's writings on the 1905 revolution. It highlighted several misapprehensions, misrepresentations and inaccuracies contained in Gorin's review. More telling, however, was when Iaroslavskii went over to the offensive and attacked Gorin's book on the Soviets in 1905. In parallel columns, Iaroslavskii reproduced passages from Gorin's book and Trotsky's *1905*, making it obvious that much of Gorin's work was plagiarised from Trotsky. In the political environment of the day, this was a devastating critique. According to Sidorov, since Gorin was found to have made too many borrowings from Trotsky's book on the 1905 revolution, he had to leave Moscow and return to Belorussia.[72] For the moment, Iaroslavskii had defeated his Bennigsen, but his Waterloo was not far off.

---

71   Gorin 1933, p. 107.
72   Sidorov 1964, p. 136.

CHAPTER 9

Merchant Capitalism in Retreat

1 Merchant Capitalism

In the early twenties the doctrine of merchant capitalism enjoyed wide accept-ance among Soviet historians. The only significant critic to appear at that time was Trotsky, who found that Pokrovskii's merchant capitalism came into con-flict with his own theory of 'permanent revolution'. His attack on it was the natural consequence of the use to which Pokrovskii put it. Whereas Pokrovskii required his merchant capitalism to tie the autocracy to society, Trotsky, for the purposes of his theory, required an independent state organisation, and as a result merchant capitalism for him was entirely superfluous.

From 1924 onwards critics began to appear more frequently. A.N. Slepkov, G.P. Maretskii and S.G. Tomsinskii all objected to Pokrovskii's insistence that the domination of merchant capital lasted until the February Revolution in 1917. It would be more reasonable, they supposed, to consider that in the imme-diate pre-war period the autocracy expressed the interests, not of merchant, but of industrial capital. According to Tomsinskii, Pokrovskii had erred because in his presentation of Russian history the role of merchant capital, and the social nature of Russian State power, did not undergo any changes from the XVI till the XX century. Although Pokrovskii mentioned the connection of Rus-sian trade with banking capital in the XX century, this did not prevent him from 'isolating trade completely from the relations of production'. Merchant capital for Pokrovskii was a self-contained factor, and he 'did not see any difference between the role and character of trade and colonial wars in the era of mer-chant and industrial capital'. In Tomsinskii's view, the contradictions between merchant and industrial capital were not very deep or were entirely absent.[1] In his lengthy reply, Pokrovskii did not relent on any of the issues Tomsinskii had raised. He explained that merchant capital did not remain the same over time, but played different roles in response to changed circumstances, in the same way that the adoption of NEP had not changed the social nature of Bolshev-ism.[2]

---

1   Tomsinskii 1926, p. 257.
2   Pokrovskii 1926b, pp. 294–5.

The first real attack on merchant capitalism as a distinct social formation was made in a paper given by V.N. Rakhmetov, at the IKP in May 1927. Rakhmetov objected to Pokrovskii's division of the history of capitalism into merchant, industrial and finance stages. In reply Pokrovskii argued that Marx's statements on merchant capital gave one the right to speak of merchant capital as an independent epoch in the development of capitalism, when merchant capital dominated.

Up to this point in time Pokrovskii had used the terms 'merchant capital' and 'merchant capitalism' interchangeably, but with the emergence of the concept of a 'socio-economic formation', the question arose whether merchant capitalism constituted such a socio-economic formation.[3] Pokrovskii denied that he had ever considered merchant capitalism to be such a formation. In the course of the discussion, he proceeded to make some modifications to his original scheme, on the grounds that he had not previously considered the internal market, and its significance. He then put forward the idea that there had existed two merchant capitalist groups – the greater merchants and the large landowners who engaged in foreign trade, and the local merchants and the smaller landowners who, until the end of the eighteenth century, were concerned with internal trade. Between these two groups a certain conflict took place. Pokrovskii now thought that as a result of the Oprichnina and the Time of Troubles, the large landowners had gained the upper hand. But in the second half of the seventeenth century and the first quarter of the eighteenth they were replaced by the second group, as the internal market developed.[4]

The question of merchant capitalism arose again on the occasion of the discussion on D.M. Petrushevskii's book *Studies in the Economic History of Medieval Europe*, held by the Society of Marxist Historians in the spring of 1928. Petrushevskii, a pupil of Vinogradov and author of a book on the Watt Tyler uprising, was at that time the director of RANION's Institute of History. His latest work on European history aroused controversy because of its ideological debt to Heinrich Rickert and Max Weber, and because it treated feudalism as a purely political institution, unconnected with any particular economic system. He also disagreed with his teacher Vinogradov that the ancient Germanic tribes were egalitarian and held the land in common. In Petrushevskii's view, the evidence pointed to the existence of private property and social inequality. Although E.A. Kosminskii thought Petrushevskii's book a valuable contribution to the study of Medieval history, and 'easily translatable into the language of

---

3 The question of socio-economic formations is discussed at length in Barber 1981, pp. 47–67.
4 Volkov 1965, p. 85.

Marxism',[5] the majority view of the participants in the discussion was that Petrushevskii had mounted an attack on Marxism, and that his book should be condemned.

In his own response to Petrushevskii's book, Pokrovskii recalled that in 1904 he had contributed an article on Rickert's ideas to a 'Marxist journal'. He took the opportunity to rehearse the arguments he had deployed against Rickert in his *Pravda* article, on this occasion with the benefit of almost a quarter of a century's reflection. He pointed out that Rickert had illegitimately equated the terms 'unique' and 'unrepeatable', and that it was impossible to characterise any historical phenomenon without recourse to general concepts.[6]

Pokrovskii continued to put up a stout defence of his favourite construct, and, to this end, in 1928 he published in the journal *Arkhivnoe delo* Lenin's letter to him commending his *Brief History of Russia*, and suggesting that it should be translated into several languages. Pokrovskii could thereafter claim that Lenin had 'found no objection in principle' to his conception of merchant capitalism. In the preface to the tenth edition of the *Brief History* this conception was bolstered up by a whole series of quotations from Lenin.

Nevertheless, the attacks continued. At the end of 1928 and the beginning of 1929 IKP conducted a series of discussions on the subject of merchant capitalism, and the criticisms put forward forced Pokrovskii to retract his long-held belief that the Russian autocracy was the dictatorship of merchant capital.[7]

In 1929 S.M. Dubrovskii published his monograph, *On the Question of the Nature of Feudalism, Serfdom, the 'Asiatic Mode of Production' and Merchant Capitalism*, where again Pokrovskii's ideas were severely challenged. Dubrovskii's book showed that the question of merchant capital had implications for the policy of the Communist International towards China. According to Dubrovskii:

> Very often in relation to pre-capitalist eras there is used the term 'the era of merchant capital'. Bogdanov, for example, writes about a special 'merchant-capitalist production' almost in the sense of a special means of production, about a special 'era of merchant capital', to which the absolute monarchy corresponds as a political organisation. For example, we

---

5   'Disput o knige D.M. Petrushevskogo' 1928, p. 95.
6   Pokrovskii 1928d, pp. 9–10.
7   Volkov 1965, p. 87.

hear very often, especially the Trotskyists, speaking of pre-revolutionary and contemporary China as a country dominated by merchant-usurer capital.[8]

What Dubrovskii had in mind here was the conflict between Stalin and Trotsky on the evaluation of the Chinese revolution. In Stalin's estimation, China as a colonial and agrarian country, was only ripe for a bourgeois-democratic revolution, and therefore communists in China should concentrate their efforts on creating an alliance with the progressive bourgeois groups. In particular, they should join the ranks of the Guomindang and submit themselves to its discipline. Trotsky, on the other hand, while admitting China's backwardness, laid greater stress on the development of capitalism in the country, the relative strength of the proletariat, and advanced the idea that the dictatorship of the proletariat and a socialist revolution were possible, if the correct tactics were applied by the Chinese communists. He argued that feudal relations in China had only developed in a rudimentary form, and the main burden of exploitation felt by the Chinese peasant was that of the kulak-usurer. The revolution in China would therefore be just as much anti-bourgeois as it would be anti-feudal in character. In his book Dubrovskii was defending the approach taken by Stalin against Trotsky.[9]

The objections Dubrovskii raised to Pokrovskii's conception of merchant capitalism were that merchant and usurer capitals did not organise production, and that merchant and industrial capitals were not antagonists, since the former was the precursor of the latter. The discussion which took place on the book at IKP in April 1929 produced more radical objections than Dubrovskii himself had raised. The most important of these was put forward by M.S. Zorkii, who thought it mistaken to attribute to merchant capital everything that had happened in the enigmatic era of merchant capitalism. Why, he enquired, was it that in the course of a thousand years, merchant capital (in particular the merchant capital of ancient Rome) had not given rise to capitalism? To this Pokrovskii could only reply that there was no merchant capital in ancient Rome. Zorkii repeated the contention, voiced by Dubrovskii, that merchant capital did not organise production.[10]

Most participants at the April meeting, however, continued to support Pokrovskii. Dubrovskii thought that the formulation that the autocracy was the

8   Dubrovskiĭ 1929, p. 105.
9   Trotsky 1970b, pp. 208–9; Shteppa 1962, pp. 72–3.
10   Volkov 1965, p. 87.

dictatorship of merchant capital was entirely acceptable, with the proviso that the Russian autocracy was also the dictatorship of the nobility, or the serf-owners.[11]

Pokrovskii received a great deal of support when Dubrovskii's book was discussed at a meeting of the Leningrad section of the Society of Marxist Historians. One of his defenders was Tomsinskii, who said that he appreciated the fact that it was possible to have an academic dispute with Pokrovskii without political rancour.[12] O.A. Lidak conceded that 'with Pokrovskii there are some exaggerations' but went on to say that 'of all the historians Pokrovskii ... was the pioneer of Marxist methodology in Russian history. He created a school of Marxist historians, and we, young Marxist historians, his pupils, can be proud of him'.[13] I.D. Shakhnazarov put Pokrovskii's conception of merchant capitalism into historiographical context when he argued:

> In this connection, some people think that Pokrovskii has overemphasised the role of merchant capital. I think that he was right to do so. If you take the whole of bourgeois historiography, even Soloviev in his 29 volumes, in essence, says nothing about the role of merchant capital. With Kliuchevskii we see a step forward in the matter of analysing socio-economic phenomena, in the matter of analysing serfdom and the serf economy.[14]

Shakhnazarov's implication was that Pokrovskii had continued a current of historical investigation that Kliuchevskii had initiated.

On 11 December 1929 P.S. Drozdov presented a sophisticated critique of merchant capitalism in a paper given at the Sverdlov University. Drozdov held that it was an elementary methodological mistake to speak of merchant capitalism as though it was some kind of system of production. With reference to Marx and Lenin, he argued that by its very nature merchant capital was incapable of subsuming production to itself, because the subsumption of production to merchant capital would mean the negation of merchant capital as such. In contrast to Pokrovskii, Drozdov argued that the autocracy in Russia was the dictatorship of the single class which was dominant in production – the class

11   Volkov 1965, pp. 87–8.
12   Zaidel', Lozinskii, Prigozhin, and Tomsinskii 1930, p. 155.
13   Zaidel', Lozinskii, Prigozhin, and Tomsinskii 1930, p. 144.
14   Zaidel', Lozinskii, Prigozhin, and Tomsinskii 1930, p. 153.

of landowning serf-owners. It was in their interests, in Drozdov's opinion, that there took place Russia's conquest of the Baltic and Black Seas.[15]

On the day of the discussion at the Sverdlov University Pokrovskii wrote to Gorin: '"The omens are multiplying", as Lenin once wrote, that the Right wing is preparing a massive attack on us. Have you read Drozdov's theses?! We shall have to see clearly what the opinion is in the Society'.[16]

Pokrovskii's prognosis about the attack was fully justified, for in January 1930 the subject of socio-economic formations was discussed at IKP, and again merchant capitalism came under severe criticism. The attack was led by Zorkii and Dubrovskii, the latter contending that:

> A rebellion should be raised against the mistaken conception of the role of merchant capitalism, because this gives ... a completely erroneous scheme of the whole historical development of pre-revolutionary Russia.[17]

The fact that Drozdov's paper was not published testifies to the strength of the pro-Pokrovskii forces. Apparently, at this date there was no systematic attempt to discredit merchant capitalism, and Pokrovskii in general; this element was only gradually beginning to insinuate itself into the discussions. It was still possible for the concept of merchant capitalism to be judged on its own merits.

Merchant capitalism came under fire again at three seminars which were held at IKP on 20 November and 24 December 1930, and on 16 February 1931.[18] On these occasions the criticism seems to have been completely unprincipled and politically motivated. Following these seminars, Pokrovskii published an article entitled 'On Russian Feudalism, the Origin and the Nature of Absolute Monarchy in Russia', in the journal *Borb'a klassov*, in which he set out the modifications he was prepared to make to his conception of merchant capitalism. Pokrovskii made it clear that the changes he was making were the result of his own reconsiderations, not ones dictated by his critics. As he observed:

> I owe no useful suggestions to my opponents. Instead of criticising my errors, using Marx and Lenin for their starting points, they tried to prove things that could not be proved, for instance, that merchant capitalism had no relation whatever to the rise of autocracy and of absolute mon-

---

15 Volkov 1965, p. 91.
16 Gorin 1933, p. 102.
17 Volkov 1965, pp. 92–3.
18 Pokrovskii 1967c, p. 559.

archy in Russia; or that what the autocracy represented was not merchant, but industrial capital; ... or that feudal methods of production exclude all possibility of commodity production; or that there was no feudalism in Russia, but a special formation of 'serfdom economy'.[19]

In a remark which summed up the contemporary state of history as a discipline in the Soviet Union, Pokrovskii observed: 'The dispute about how to interpret Russian history has become, by degrees, a dispute about how to interpret Leninism ...' And in fact, much of Pokrovskii's article consists exactly of quotations from Lenin. An ace card in Pokrovskii's defence against his critics was to remind them that his *Brief History of Russia* had received Lenin's approval, and that therefore the conception of Russian history contained in it could scarcely be considered un-Leninist.[20]

However, there were instances, Pokrovskii admitted, when he had expressed himself in an insufficiently Leninist way. Such an instance was the use of the phrase 'merchant *capitalism*'. This was because capitalism was a system of production, whereas merchant capital did not produce anything, but was only a means of exchange. Moreover, because merchant capital produced nothing, it could not determine the nature of the political superstructure of a given society. For this reason, the definition of tsarism as 'merchant capital in the cap of Monomakh' was entirely wrong.[21]

An examination of Pokrovskii's last word on the subject of merchant capitalism, his article 'On Russian Feudalism ...' leads one to the inescapable conclusion that it contains nothing new in comparison with his admissions at previous seminars during the period 1927–28. The mistakes and amendments which he noted in this article were all things which he had admitted following the earlier criticisms, and his modified version of the merchant capitalist scheme had not been abandoned. It would appear that Pokrovskii would go so far, and no further.

On 5 February 1931 he wrote two letters to the Central Committee in which he repeated his final conclusions and protested against the unhealthy atmosphere which obtained in academic circles, against the campaign of slander which was being waged against him and his pupils. He deplored the fact that for his opponents it was not enough that he should admit his individual errors; they wished to prove that: '... the Pokrovshchina in history was the same thing as Rubinshchina in economics and Deborinshchina in philosophy, that this was

---

19   Pokrovskii 1931b, p. 81.
20   Pokrovskii 1931b, pp. 79–80.
21   Pokrovskii 1931b, p. 80.

a pure distortion of the Leninist understanding of the historical process in general, and of the Russian historical process in particular'.[22]

What lay behind Pokrovskii's references to 'Rubinshchina' and 'Deborinshchina', was that on 9 December of the previous year Stalin had marshalled his allies at IKP P.F. Iudin and M.B. Mitin to open an attack on Riazanov and his Marx-Engels Institute. In 1929–30 the pair, in collusion with the party ideologues, conducted a smear campaign against two prominent members of IME – the economist I.I. Rubin and the philosopher A.M. Deborin. They were accused of formalism, the divorce of theory from practice, of Menshevism, idealism, and various other failings. In an article in *Pravda* on 15 January 1931 by B.I. Bazilevskii, Riazanov himself came under attack. Like many of his associates at IME, Riazanov refused to recognise a distinct Leninist stage in Marxism, as required by party doctrine.[23] On 16 February 1931 Riazanov was arrested and expelled from the party by the Presidium of the Central Control Commission. Pokrovskii, who was a member of the Commission, voted in favour of his expulsion.[24]

Pokrovskii took measures to shore up his own position by making manifest his loyalty to the party and its policies. To this end, he gave a new interpretation of the dictum 'history is politics projected into the past'.

> The struggle on the historical front is the struggle for the general line of the party. The statement that 'history is politics projected into the past' means that every historical scheme is a link in a chain of attack on the general line of the party. There exists a very close link between the struggle for the general line of the party and the struggle on the historical front. They cannot be separated. It is hard to imagine such a probability that a supporter of the general line of the party would be a revisionist in historical works. History is not a task in its own right, history is a great weapon in the political struggle; history has no other meaning.[25]

In the middle of January 1931, a letter of complaint against Pokrovskii's leadership of the Society of Marxist Historians, signed by the Academic Secretary of the Communist Academy O.P. Dzenis, the head of economic extra-mural studies K.V. Ostrovitianov, and the Vice Chairman of the Communist Academy E.B. Pashukanis, was sent to the party Central Committee. Pokrovskii was

---

22 Volkov 1965, p. 94; Ivanova 1968, p. 180.
23 Rokitianskii and Müller 1996, p. 103.
24 Artizov 1998b, p. 134.
25 Artizov 1998b, p. 132.

accused of failing to organise the work of the Society satisfactorily, and of suppressing criticism on the historical front. Practically simultaneously, a letter of similar content was sent by a group of former IKP students, including Drozdov, alleging that Pokrovskii's historical conceptions had contained Bogdanovist-Struvian errors, that although Pokrovskii claimed to have corrected his errors, in practice he did not do so, and that Pokrovskii's conceptions diverged widely from Lenin's.[26]

Pokrovskii, however, had become too close to the centres of power to fall victim to these attacks. At that time, he was heading the commission consisting of A.I. Stetskii and M.B. Mitin which drafted the decision on the journal *Pod znamenem marksizma*, incorporating the ideas of Stalin on the reorganization of the philosophical front. As co-reporter, he also presented the completed draft report to the session of the Politburo on 25 January. With the support of Stetskii and L.M. Kaganovich, he used his influence to quell the criticism directed against him. By the end of January Pokrovskii had received an abject apology from Dzenis, Ostrovitianov and Pashukanis, with the assurance that no harm had been intended.[27] A.L. Sidorov alludes to this episode in his memoirs. He writes:

> Some members of the Praesidium of the Communist Academy 'rebelled' against M.N. Pokrovskii, finding his position insufficiently self-critical. Pokrovskii defended himself cunningly. He said that his mistakes were talked about too much and too often, while his critics did not follow his good example. Pokrovskii appealed to the Central Committee of the party and Stalin supported him.[28]

Sidorov himself was one of the young scholars who tried to make Pokrovskii correct his errors and revise his writings in accordance with Lenin's works. He recalled that he and N.L. Rubinstein had had the temerity to suggest that Pokrovskii correct his four-volume history of Russia in this light. It was, he said, done with the best intentions, and with a clear conscience. The result was that Pokrovskii ensured that both he and Rubinstein were sent to do practical work in the provinces, Rubinstein to Ivanovo, and he to Nizhnii Novgorod.[29] Sidorov's revenge was to accuse Pokrovskii of Trotskyism in a chapter he contributed anonymously to the history of the VKP(b) edited by Iaroslavskii.

---

26   Artizov 1998b, p. 135.
27   ibid.
28   Sidorov 1964, p. 132.
29   ibid.

2   The Academy Case

On the invitation of the Society for the Study of Eastern Europe (*Deutsche Ges-
sellschaft zum Studium Osteuopas*) Pokrovskii led a delegation of Soviet historians to attend a historical week in Berlin between 7–14 July 1928. It was an opportunity to showcase Soviet scholarship abroad, and the members of the delegation were chosen to present this to the best advantage. Besides scholars who
considered themselves Marxist – I.I. Mints, V.V. Adoratskii, E.B. Pashukanis,
and S.M. Dubrovskii, and Pokrovskii himself, the delegation had a non-Marxist
component, which included V.I. Picheta, S.F. Platonov, M.K. Liubavskii and
D.N. Egorov. Different Soviet nationalities were also represented in the delegation in the persons of the Ukrainians M.I. Iavorskii and V.A. Iurinets, and the
Belorussian Picheta.

On the German side the event was a high-level affair, with an opening recep-
tion in the Prussian Academy of Sciences. Speeches were delivered by the
Prussian Minister of Education Becker and the vice-chairman of the Society
for the Study of Eastern Europe Otto Hoetsch, and by the Soviet Ambassador
to Germany N.N. Krestinskii. The lectures given by the Soviet delegation were
attended by some Reichstag deputies and several eminent German academics, including Karl Stählin, Hans Delbrück, and Engels's biographer Gustav
Mayer.[30]

When he gave an account of the Berlin event to the Society of Marxist Historians, Mints was able to indicate a number of ways in which the Soviet delegation had favourably impressed its German audience:

1)   By the inclusion of a number of non-Marxist scholars, the delegation had
      dispelled the impression that Marxism was the only approach that was
      allowed in the Soviet Union. It showed that non-Marxist historians were
      free to teach and to publish their works.

2)   The exhibition of Soviet historical publications and archival documents
      demonstrated that historical scholarship was thriving in the Soviet envir-
      onment.

3)   The fact that the Soviet delegation had a Ukrainian and a Belorussian
      component showed that Soviet scholarship was genuinely inclusive of the
      nationalities of the former Russian Empire.

4)   The range of subjects covered by the papers presented was evidence that
      the study of history in the Soviet Union was all-embracing, and not lim-

---

30   Pashukanis 1928, p. 240.

ited to particular periods or geographical areas. Besides Pokrovskii's paper on 'The Theories of the Origins of the Autocracy', other contributions were:

S.F. Platonov – The problem of the Russian North in recent historiography.

V.V. Adoratskii – The Soviet archives.

M.K. Liubavskii – The colonisation of the Great Russian centre.

S.M. Dubrovskii – The Stolypin agrarian reform.

D.N. Egorov – A critique of medieval works on the history of Western
Europe.

E.B. Pashukanis – The Councils of Soldiers' Deputies in Cromwell's army.

V.I. Picheta – The agrarian reform in the second half of the 16th and
beginning of the 17th century in the eastern districts of Lithuania.

M.I. Iavorskii – The West-European influence on the Ukrainian social
movement in the nineteenth century.

V.A. Iurinets – The social process as reflected in Ukrainian literature in
the twentieth century.

Mints himself did not give a paper, but he had obviously spent some time sounding out the opinions of the Germans he had met in Berlin and was able to share his impressions with his audience. According to Mints, the German *grande bourgeoisie* and the former Junkers dreamt of revenge and the military defeat of the Allies. For this group, despite the difference in economic systems, the Soviet Union seemed the most suitable ally. 'Together with the Soviet Union', Mints reports one professor at the banquet as saying, 'we could conquer the whole of Europe'.

For the middle and *petite bourgeoisie*, Mints had discovered, the idea of revenge had quite another incarnation. The Social Democrats, reflecting the illusions of the *petite bourgeoisie*, had a strategy of 'revolt on their knees'. By cunning, by stealth, they would gain one concession after another from the Entente, at the expense of their Soviet neighbour, and perhaps in that way get their revenge.[31]

Mints's impressions of German opinion in 1928 are significant, because they provide the international context for several things. They are the light in which one can understand Pokrovskii's dissatisfaction with Tarle's perceived pro-Entente bias in his book on the Great War. The Soviet distrust of the German Social Democrats provides the background to Stalin's letter to the editorial

---

31   Mints 1928, p. 85.

board of *Proletarskaia revoliutsiia* in 1931, and it may have been a factor leading to the conclusion of the Nazi-Soviet pact in 1939.

At the time of the Berlin Soviet Week Pokrovskii was in Germany for medical treatment. From there he and Liubov' proceeded directly to Oslo, where Soviet historians had been invited to take part in the Sixth International Congress of Historical Sciences, which took place from 14–19 August. Pokrovskii was ill when he reached Oslo, and Alexandra Kollontai, the Soviet ambassador to Norway, was able to arrange his admission to a local sanatorium.[32]

The invitation to the Congress had been extended by Halvdan Koht, Professor of History at the University of Oslo. Koht placed great importance on Soviet participation at the Congress, which he intended to promote international understanding and reconciliation after the war. Scholars from Germany and Austria, countries which were held responsible for the war, had been excluded from the Fifth Congress, held in Brussels in 1923. The boycott was also applied to Bolshevik Russia. For the Oslo Congress Koht was adamant that delegations from all countries, irrespective of their previous military alignments, should be invited.[33]

There were about 950 participants at the Sixth Congress from some 38 countries, the largest contingents being from Norway (273), France (132) and Germany (121). With a delegation of 15, the Soviet historians felt themselves at a considerable disadvantage. Despite the mission of the Congress to promote reconciliation, old antagonisms persisted. Mints noticed that the French and the Poles formed a united front against the Germans.

As at the Berlin Week, the Soviet contingent included Marxist and non-Marxist historians, with representation from national minorities. But at Oslo, Pokrovskii, to his intense chagrin, discovered that there was one crucial social category that he had overlooked – women. Although the Soviet State claimed to embody equal rights for women, the Soviet delegation did not include one. And it was not as though there were no suitably qualified women available. On the contrary, among Pokrovskii's best students were Pankratova, Nechkina and Genkina. Of the Polish delegation, on the other hand, about a quarter were women.[34] The range of subjects covered in papers given by the Soviet historians was, if anything, more varied than that in Berlin. They were as follows:

---

32 Pokrovskii 1928e, p. 232.

33 Myhre Jan Eivind, '6th International Congress of Historical Sciences Oslo 1928', available at: https://ichs2020poznan.pl/en/the-4th-congress-in-london-2-2.

34 Pokrovskii 1928e, p. 236.

B.P. Bogaevskii – The gods of pottery art in Minoan Crete.

P.F. Preobrazhenskii – The realist features of the ancient religious beliefs.

E.A. Kosminskii – The English village in the thirteenth century.

V.P. Volgin – Socialism and egalitarianism in the history of socialist theories.

V.V. Adoratskii – Archival studies in the RSFSR.

M.I. Iavorskii – Western European influences in the ideology of the Ukrainian social movement.

S.M. Dubrovskii – The peasant movement in Russia in the XX century.

V.A. Iurinets – The main currents in the contemporary Ukrainian literature.

Pokrovskii again gave his paper on the origins of the Russian autocracy. Mints was pleased to note that, with the exceptions of France and the USA, countries which were hosts to émigré Russian scholars had not included these scholars in their delegations. On the second day of the Congress, the émigré Russian medievalist M.I. Rostovtsev, who was a member of the American delegation, gave an interview to the newspaper *Aftenposten*, in which he objected to Pokrovskii's election to the Praesidium of the Congress. Rostovtsev conceded that, while it may have been politically justified to invite the Soviet delegation on grounds of international cooperation, there could be no cooperation in the sphere of scholarship. For, whereas to most participants in the Congress, the study of history meant the search for truth, which they knew to be elusive, Soviet-Russian historians believed that they were already in possession of the truth. This was Marxism; for them, historical materialism was not science, but theology. Their research was not scholarship, but merely an attempt to fit the facts to a preconceived theological dogma.[35]

In giving a report to the Communist Academy on the Oslo Congress, Pokrovskii said that he was grateful for Rostovtsev's interview. With only 15 members, the Soviet delegation was in danger of being overlooked, but Rostovtsev had performed the useful service of drawing attention to it. Koht, who considered himself to be a Marxist, had dissociated himself and the Congress in general, from Rostovtsev's remarks in a newspaper article. And the non-Marxist members of the Soviet delegation had declared that they were living proof of the freedom of historical scholarship in Soviet Russia. Pokrovskii himself gave

---

35   Mints 1928, p. 92.

a newspaper interview in which he rebutted Rostovtsev's contentions. Overall, the episode had done the reputation of Soviet scholarship more good than
harm.[36]

An important lesson Pokrovskii took from the Oslo Congress concerned the
Russian Academy of Sciences.[37] Prior to the Congress, the Soviet representation on the committee which organised the congresses, had been the Academy
of Sciences in the person of its permanent chairman Academician S.F. Ol'den-
burg. This, however, had been an informal arrangement since the Soviet Union
did not have an official representative on the committee. Pokrovskii had taken
steps to remedy this situation by becoming the official Soviet representative on the International Committee of Historical Sciences (ICHS), and nam-
ing the Communist Academy as the body it should deal with in the Soviet
Union.[38]

Pokrovskii had also noticed at the Congress, that the Academy of Sciences
did not enjoy a high standing abroad. Indicative of this was what had happened
with the academician Tarle. It had been intended to include him in the Soviet
delegation, but when the Congress was due to open, he had sent a telegram
from Paris saying that he was unwell and could not attend.[39] Pokrovskii had
anticipated that the absence of a representative of the Academy of Sciences
would create a great sensation, but in the event, nobody had remarked on it. In
retrospect one can see Pokrovskii's reflections on the international standing of
the Academy of Sciences as a prelude to the offensive against it he was about
to make in the coming months.

Because of its prestige and its willingness to cooperate, although reluctantly, with the Bolshevik government, the Academy of Sciences had been left in
peace by the Soviet authorities. Early schemes to subordinate it to Narkompros,
and reform it, had been resolutely quashed by Lenin.[40] The situation changed,
however, with the 'great turn'. The serious miscalculations in economic and
social policy caused food shortages, necessitating the introduction of ration-
ing, and resulting in the growth of popular discontent. Rather than admit his
mistakes, Stalin blamed the disruption on 'wreckers', who were, in the main,
intellectuals who had contributed their expertise to the Soviet experiment.
'Bourgeois specialists' who had been widely employed in many fields of activ-

---

36 Pokrovskii 1928e, p. 234.
37 The Academy of Sciences was established by Peter the Great in 1725 under the name of
    the St Petersburg Academy.
38 ibid.
39 Mints 1928, p. 96.
40 Fitzpatrick 1970, p. 72.

ity, were now looked upon with suspicion. The distrust of non-communists was soon extended into the academic sphere, a chief target being the Academy of Sciences.

The first in the series of show trials involving 'bourgeois specialists' was the so-called 'Shakhty case' which opened in Moscow on 18 May 1928. It involved a group of mining engineers from the Donbass, who were charged with sabotage in the coal industry, allegedly acting on the orders of French, Polish and British capitalists. In 1930 the trial of the 'Labour Peasant Party', in which Teodorovich was implicated, took place. Among the accused were the economists N.D. Kondratiev and L.N. Iurovskii, whose 'wrecking' included warnings that the programme of rapid industrialisation would create a shortage of consumer goods, and a rift between the proletariat and the peasantry.[41] The end of 1930 saw the trial of the so-called 'Industrial Party', a group of engineers, allegedly carrying out the orders of their French masters to undermine the economic power of the Soviet state.

In accordance with Stalin's offensive against 'bourgeois specialists', Pokrovskii conducted a campaign to dissolve RANION and establish a new Institute of History, which would be attached to the Communist Academy. This was accomplished in October 1929, and indicated the end of the cooperation between Marxist and non-Marxist historians. It was a landmark too in the increasingly intolerant climate, in which all historians operated.[42]

The 'Academy case' show trial had its origins in the attempts of the Soviet authorities to exert control over the Academy of Sciences. The first step in this direction was the bid to increase the Communist presence in the Academy's membership. Accordingly, the candidates were: Bukharin, I.M. Gubkin, G.M. Krzyzhanovskii, Pokrovskii, Riazanov, Deborin, N.M. Lukin and Friche.

At the general meeting of the Academy held on 12 January 1929 only five members from the list were elected. Five days later, the Academy was forced to convene a new meeting in order to elect the three remaining candidates. The token resistance that the Academy had shown to the Soviet authorities was to cost it dear.[43]

The pretext for the offensive against the Academy was the discovery in its library of important historical documents. These included the original of the acts of abdication of Nicholas II and the Grand Duke Michael, documents of the SR party, the SR Central Committee, and several other items, which should have long ago been handed over to the keeping of the Soviet archives. S.F. Platonov,

---

41   Kin 1931, p. 22.

42   Artizov 1998a, p. 89; Enteen 1980, pp. 102–3.

43   Tolz 1997, pp. 44–5.

the permanent secretary of the Academy, was removed. Between November 1929 and January 1930 mass arrests took place, including the academicians N.P. Likhachev, M.K. Liubavskii, Platonov, Tarle and Got'e. They were charged with creating a secret subversive organisation, the 'National Council for the Struggle for the Revival of a Free Russia'. Altogether about 130 people were taken into custody by the OGPU.[44]

Some of those arrested consented to cooperate with the investigation, and gave the required testimonies, confirming the existence of the secret counter-revolutionary organisation, and their membership of it. Platonov gave this kind of confession, as did Tarle, whose testimony ran to hundreds of pages.[45] The leaders of the 'plot' were sentenced in August 1931 to 'exile in remote places in the USSR for a term of five years', a penalty remarkably lenient for the ostensible seriousness of the crime. Platonov was exiled to Samara, Tarle to Alma-Ata, Liubavskii to Ufa and Picheta to Viatka. But ordinary members of the 'National Council' fared worse. Six members of its military organisation were shot and others served 5–10 years in labour camps.

From their place of exile the historians wrote to Pokrovskii, protesting their innocence of the crimes for which they had been convicted, complaining of the hardships they endured in the remote locations, and imploring Pokrovskii's help to alleviate their situation. The reply from Pokrovskii, if it came at all, was unsympathetic, and written with an eye to his own standing with the security services. The letter he sent to Tarle in mid-September 1931 read as follows:

> When you were writing your letter, Evgenii Viktorovich, you obviously did not know that I had read your deposition in the original and that just as a historian I am confronted with something of a dilemma: either you are mentally disturbed (but then what kind of academic work is there to speak of?), or your stay in Alma-Ata is evidence only of the extraordinary leniency of the Soviet government: if you had been a French citizen and did what you said you did in relation to France, you would be on Devil's Island. So, the question remains only about using you as a scholar, irrespective of your political past. Since the prisoners in Solovki are engaged in scholarly research, and their research is printed, I do not think there is any reason why this would be impossible for a person interned in Alma-Ata. But I am very much afraid that the appearance of works bearing your name, due to the notoriety that name has acquired in the USSR, will meet

---

44   Tolz 1997, pp. 54–5.
45   Tolz 1997, p. 60.

with very great difficulties. Moreover, as you may surmise, I cannot give any definite answer without having consulted the people in charge: and this is complicated by the fact that I am at present ill, lying in bed and dictating this letter, because I can't write by myself. At the first opportunity I shall try to have a word with those in charge and inform you of the outcome.[46]

Perhaps Pokrovskii was as good as his word, because Tarle was allowed to return from exile after only two years. Pokrovskii was right that it was possible to do academic work in Alma-Ata, for it was there that Tarle began to write his biography of Napoleon, which won the praise of Stalin.[47]

However, the evidence is that Pokrovskii's actions were not calculated to improve the situation of his correspondents. What he did was to collect their letters into a bundle and send them to the OGPU with the accompanying note dated 29 September 1932:

> From time to time I receive letters from historians who are interned in various regions of the Soviet Union. Since these letters can be of interest to the OGPU, I am forwarding them to you, because they are of no use to me whatever. Please accept my apologies for the delay in forwarding them. It is to be explained, firstly, by the fact that I have been ill for the past few months, and secondly, I wanted to collect together several such letters – they arrived at different times.[48]

One could explain these letters by the fact that Pokrovskii was near death and probably in great pain, so that his judgement was impaired. But they represent the culmination of a direction in his thinking that had been present for the previous five years. They represent the authentic Pokrovskii, and show him not as a victim of Stalin's oppression, but as one complicit in its emergence.

3   Trotsky's *History of the Russian Revolution*

Following the defeat of the Left Opposition in 1927, Trotsky was deported from the Soviet Union in 1929. He settled on the Turkish island of Prinkipo, and there wrote two of his main works: his autobiography *My Life* and *The History of the*

---

46   Esina 1996, p. 109.
47   Black 1956, pp. 268–76.
48   Esina 1996, p. 111.

Russian Revolution. My Life, which appeared in 1930, is a work of considerable literary merit, and has served as the main source for subsequent scholarly biographies of Trotsky. But it is also a highly political work. The impression Trotsky wanted to convey in it was already foreshadowed in 'Lessons of October'. It was that only Lenin and he, Trotsky, among all the Bolsheviks, had the kind of leadership qualities and insight that the situation required. This emerges with utmost clarity in *My Life*, in the chapter entitled 'Trotskyism in 1917'. There Trotsky states:

> In New York, at the beginning of March 1917, I wrote a series of articles dealing with the class forces and perspectives of the Russian revolution. At that very time, Lenin, in Geneva, was sending to Petrograd his 'Letters from Afar'. And both of us, though we were separated by an ocean, gave the same analysis and the same forecast. On the peasantry, toward the bourgeoisie, the Provisional Government, the war, and the world revolution, our views were completely identical.[49]

It was not sufficient, however, to show that he and Lenin had formulated the same ideas; it also had to be demonstrated that Trotsky alone, and no one else, had come up with the same conclusions as Lenin. This allowed Trotsky to make the desired point that only he and Lenin had been able to orientate themselves in the new situation created by the February revolution. Thus, Trotsky argues:

> I realize, of course, that at various times in their lives they have repeated Lenin's words and gestures after him. But the beginning of 1917 found them left to their own resources. The political situation was difficult. Here was their chance to show what they had learned in Lenin's school, and what they could do without Lenin. Let them name one of their number who arrived independently at the position achieved identically by Lenin in Geneva and by me in New York. They cannot name a single one. The Petrograd *Pravda*, which was edited by Stalin and Kamenev until Lenin's arrival, will always remain a document of limited understanding, blindness, and opportunism.[50]

Why this argument is effective is because by 1930 the criterion of political probity was conformity with Lenin's ideas. There was no other; it was the be all and

---

49 Trotsky 1970a, p. 329.
50 Trotsky 1970a, p. 330.

end all. If Trotsky could show that he was a genuine Leninist, and Stalin was not, he would have delivered a massive blow to his rival by undermining the legitimacy of his power.

Before leaving for the Crimea to recuperate in the spring of 1930, Pokrovskii was given the assignment of writing a review of Trotsky's *My Life* for *Bol'shevik*. He did what was expected of him, and the review is predictably negative. Pokrovskii begins by comparing Trotsky to Kerenskii. What the two men have in common is boastfulness and their talent for oratory. Trotsky looks on the masses from his speaker's platform. The most vivid pages of *My life* are those when Trotsky recalls addressing crowds at the Cirque Moderne in Petrograd.

The most interesting part of Pokrovskii's review is that concerned with the negotiations at Brest-Litovsk, as it is, to a great extent, a continuation of the notes he made in 1918. Pokrovskii was infuriated by Trotsky's behaviour. He did not conduct any serious diplomacy, but gambled on there being a revolution in Germany that would sweep away the existing government and make the negotiations unnecessary. He engaged only in rhetoric. It was as though, Pokrovskii thought, Trotsky had transferred the Cirque Moderne to Brest-Litovsk.

A more recent source of grievance for Pokrovskii against Trotsky was the upheaval among students caused by Trotsky's 'New Course' in 1923. At that time thousands of party cells in the FONs had voted for resolutions against the party Central Committee. While the controversy was raging, Trotsky was elsewhere, and avoiding any responsibility for what was taking place. It was an episode that Trotsky omitted from his memoirs.

Pokrovskii mentioned that the leitmotiv of Trotsky's book was that Lenin was Trotsky's friend and teacher, but he did not reveal the argument Trotsky had advanced in the chapter 'Trotskyism in 1917'. He does not challenge Trotsky's account of the behaviour of Stalin and Kamenev prior to Lenin's return to Petrograd in April 1917. Pokrovskii's tactic was to attack Trotsky's credibility, rather than to disprove episodes in the book.

In 1931 the first volume of Trotsky's *History of the Russian Revolution* was published in Berlin, to be followed by a further two volumes in 1933. Pokrovskii's review of *My Life* suggests why Trotsky would be motivated to embark on writing a history of 1917. It was easy to dismiss what Trotsky said in his autobiography as the subjective assertions of a biased individual. In his *History* Trotsky counters this objection by stressing that what he is writing is not subjective reminiscences, as in *My Life*, but an objective historical account. He undertakes not to rely on his own memory, but, in the manner of a historian, to base his exposition upon 'strictly verified documents'. To signal that he is writing history rather than autobiography Trotsky refers to himself throughout in the third person. What are these strictly verified documents? According to Trotsky:

The sources of this book are innumerable periodical publications, newspapers and journals, memoirs, reports, and other material, partly in manuscript, but the greater part published by the Institute of the History of the Revolution in Moscow and Leningrad ... Among the books which have the character of collective historical works we have particularly used the two-volume *Studies in the History of the October Revolution* (Moscow-Leningrad, 1927). Written by different authors, the various parts of this book are unequal in value, but they contain at any rate abundant factual material.[51]

In other words, what Trotsky is using as source material is mainly the publications of Istpart, in particular the two-volume collection of essays compiled by the participants in Pokrovskii's seminar on the October revolution at IKP. That Trotsky had been following the debates occasioned by Vanag's research is evident from the re-statement of his theory of 'permanent revolution' in the introductory chapter of his *History*. It incorporates the findings that:

> Foreigners owned in general about 40 per cent of all the stock capital of Russia, but in the leading branches of industry that percentage was still higher. We can say without exaggeration that the controlling shares of stock in the Russian banks, plants and factories were to be found abroad, the amount held in England, France and Belgium being almost double that in Germany.[52]

The real passion which drives Trotsky's *History* emerges from the pages of the work itself. It is the desire to pursue the campaign against the Soviet leadership, and especially against Stalin, that was begun in 'Lessons of October' and continued in *My Life*. Trotsky sets out to show that he, along with Lenin, should take the credit for the success of the October revolution; that he, Trotsky, is the best Leninist; and that Stalin and the rest of the Soviet leadership have no claim whatsoever to Leninist credentials. It is this aspect of Trotsky's *History* that had the greatest impact on the Soviet historiography of 1917.

In the first volume of the *History* Trotsky deals with the February revolution and Lenin's return to Petrograd in April 1917. In Trotsky's *History* the chapter corresponding to 'Trotskyism in 1917' in *My Life* is called 'The Re-Arming of the Party'. 'Re-arming' (*perevooruzhenie*) was the term which Trotsky used in

---

51   Trotsky 1937a, p. xxii.
52   Trotsky 1937a, p. 10.

his *History* to denote the change of direction in Bolshevik policy occasioned by Lenin's return to Petrograd and the promulgation of his 'April Theses'. But whereas in *My Life* Trotsky was able to express himself in his own words, in the *History* he was obliged to support his political assertions with documentary evidence.

This evidence was to hand. In the second volume of his memoirs, *The Year 1917*, published in 1925, Alexander Shliapnikov had described how, on returning from exile on 12 March, Stalin, Muranov and Kamenev had taken over the editorship of *Pravda* and changed its stance on its attitudes to the Provisional Government and the war. The editorial written by Kamenev in *Pravda* for 15 March 1917 contained the following passage:

> When an army faces an army, it would be the most absurd policy to propose to one of them to lay down arms and go home. This would not be a policy of peace; it would be a policy of slavery, which a free people would repudiate with scorn. No, we will firmly hold our posts; we will answer a bullet with a bullet and a shell with a shell.[53]

Besides advocating the continuation of a 'defencist' war, the new editors gave conditional support to the Provisional Government. Shliapnikov recalls:

> The day that the first number of the 'transformed' *Pravda* came out, 15 March, was one of jubilation for the defencists. The whole Tauride Palace from the members of the Duma Committee to the very heart of revolutionary democracy – the Executive Committee – were completely absorbed by a single item of news, the victory of the moderate, sensible Bolsheviks over the extremists. This was the first and only time that *Pravda* evoked the approval of even the inveterate defencists of the liberal school.[54]

Trotsky quotes this passage in his *History*,[55] without, however, revealing to his readers what the policies of *Pravda* were prior to its 'transformation', or mentioning that Shliapnikov goes on to say that on these policies he and his associates were fully in accord with Lenin, and, by implication, he with them. Trotsky's use of Shliapnikov's memoirs is selective. He does not wish to give the Bolshevik organisations any credit for the part they played in the February days.

---

53   Shliapnikov 1925, pp. 183–4.
54   Shliapnikov 1925, p. 185.
55   Trotsky 1937a, p. 291.

To this end, when posing the question: who led the February insurrection? he resorts to Iakovlev's formula: 'Conscious and tempered workers educated for the most part by the party of Lenin'.[56]

In Trotsky's opinion, the events surrounding Lenin's return to Petrograd were not treated adequately in *Studies in the History of the October Revolution*. This was a section written by Baevskii, who emphasised the overall agreement within Bolshevik ranks which followed the acceptance of Lenin's 'April Theses'. According to Trotsky:

> There have been plenty of attempts of late years to prove that the April party crisis was a passing and almost accidental confusion. They all go to pieces at first contact with the facts ... In the large collected volume issued under the editorship of Professor Pokrovskii, *Studies in the History of the October Revolution*, an apologetic work is devoted to the 'April Confusion' by a certain Baevskii, which for its unceremonious treatment of facts and documents might be called cynical, were it not childishly impotent.[57]

Trotsky does not engage with Baevskii's arguments, nor do we learn how exactly Baevskii has misrepresented the facts and documents in question.

Trotsky's *History* appeared at a time when Stalin was particularly vulnerable. The rapid pace of industrialisation and forced collectivisation had led to dislocation of the economy, with mass unemployment, hunger and overcrowding in the towns, as peasants fled the countryside. Abroad, in the face of an increasing danger of war, Stalin's leadership of the Communist International had left it weakened and ineffective. Internal opposition to Stalin and his methods was growing within the party itself, and 1932 would see the emergence of the Riutin and Syrtsov-Lominadze groups.[58] In this situation, Stalin had to take the charge of ideological failings contained in Trotsky's book against him seriously.

Nor was this any ordinary book; it was a substantial work of high literary merit, documented, in great part, by materials approved by a department of the Central Committee. Moreover, Trotsky's contention that Stalin and the other returnees from Siberia had been out of step with Lenin simply repeated what had been said in the fourth volume of the *History of the VKP(b)* edited by Iaroslavskii that had come out in 1929. The section of the volume in question had been written by a young IKP graduate D.Ia. Kin, using Shliapnikov's

---

56 Trotsky 1937a, p. 152.
57 Trotsky 1937a, p. 301.
58 Medvedev 1989, pp. 295–7.

memoirs as his main source. On the subject of the change in party policy when Kamenev, Stalin and Muranov had returned from exile to Petrograd Kin wrote:

> But beginning from the ninth issue, *Pravda* departed from this line. In this was reflected the influence of the comrades who had returned from Siberia, in particular L.B. Kamenev, whose stance was furthest to the Right among the returned comrades, and shaped and reinforced the semi-Menshevik tendencies observable among some sections of the Bolsheviks. Comrades Muranov and Stalin also took an erroneous stance on basic questions.[59]

Presumably, Trotsky's book would have been reviewed by Pokrovskii, in the same way as he had reviewed *My Life*. But Pokrovskii was by now seriously ill and no longer capable of writing. In this situation, the response to Trotsky's *History*, though an inexplicit one, was Stalin's letter to *Proletarskaia revoliutsiia* in October 1931.

4   Stalin's Letter to *Proletarskaia revoliutsiia*

The occasion for Stalin's letter to the editorial board of *Proletarskaia revoliutsiia* was to protest against its publication of the article by A.G. Slutskii on 'The Bolsheviks on German Social Democracy in the Period of its Pre-War Crisis'. The heroine of Slutskii's article was Rosa Luxemburg, who belonged to the radical wing of the German Social-Democrat Party. Although she had been the ally of Kautsky in the campaign against Bernstein's revisionism, she perceived that, despite his leftist rhetoric, Kautsky was a centrist and inclined towards opportunism. The antagonism between the radicals and the centrists created a split in the German party. Kautsky's defencist stance on the outbreak of the war in 1914 vindicated Luxemburg's position.

In Slutskii's view, Lenin was slow to give his support to Luxemburg and the German Left, because of fractional considerations; the Mensheviks were antipathetic to Kautsky, so that Lenin's reaction was to take his part. Moreover, Lenin had reservations about Luxemburg, because she disagreed with him fundamentally on the national question, and she could see no point in the Bolshevik-Menshevik split. These factors, in Slutskii's opinion, led to some underestimation by Lenin of the danger posed by centrism in the German party

---

59   Iaroslavskii 1929, p. 77.

before the war. Lenin's attitude was shared by Zinoviev and other members of the Bolshevik party who expressed views on the subject.[60]

Slutskii's is an informative and well researched article, well worthy of publication. But in the context of the times, it is not difficult to see why it should be met with such vituperation by Stalin.

1) There was the suggestion of Lenin's fallibility: he had 'underestimated the danger of centrism'.

2) In recognising the danger of centrism Luxemburg had shown herself to be more perceptive than Lenin.

3) Slutskii had been presumptuous enough to pass judgement on Lenin.

4) The most fundamental objection to Slutskii's article, however, was its approach to Lenin. In the article Lenin was treated as a subject to be researched, not as the ultimate criterion of the truth.

In effect, Slutskii's article challenged the basis on which Soviet scholarship was based. If Lenin's pronouncements were to be considered as the criterion of truth, it would be contradictory to inquire: were they right or were they wrong? It would also undermine the universal validity of Lenin's statements if one looked into the question of the context in which they were made, as it might emerge that they were not applicable in all circumstances. Stalin could not let Slutskii's article stand.

In his letter to the journal, Stalin held the editorial board of *Proletarskaia revoliutsiia* culpable on two counts: they had published Slutskii's article, and they were preparing to open a discussion on it. This meant that they were turning the 'axiom' of Lenin's Bolshevism into a question requiring 'further analysis'. Here Stalin was stating what the existing situation was. Since Lenin's word was the ultimate criterion for the accuracy of any given statement, it was impossible that this should be a matter for discussion. Lenin's pronouncements were indeed 'axioms'.

Despite the contempt Stalin shows for Slutskii, putting his designation 'historian' in quotation marks, most of Stalin's letter is devoted to answering points that Slutskii made in his article. He rejected completely Slutskii's claim that Lenin had underestimated the danger posed by centrism in the German party before the war. He points out that the Bolsheviks were quite right to be sceptical of Luxemburg and the German Left, and that Lenin had good cause to reject Luxemburg's ideas on the national question. He denied Slutskii's suggestion that fractional considerations had influenced Lenin's attitude towards the German Left and condemned it as despicable.

---

60   Slutskii 1930, pp. 38–73.

On Slutskii's preliminary remarks that not all the material on the subject had been made available, Stalin considered reliance on written documents to be the characteristic of hopeless bureaucrats and archive rats. For Stalin, a party and its leaders should be judged by their deeds, not by rummaging among fortuitously selected papers.

Stalin went on to inquire why *Proletarskaia revoliutsiia* had published Slutskii's article at all. His answer was that the journal had been induced to do so by its 'rotten liberalism'. And, he insisted, this was a dangerously mistaken attitude, because some Bolsheviks were under the impression that Trotskyism was a variety of communism – albeit one which made mistakes, which did foolish things, and was sometimes anti-Soviet, but which nevertheless was a current within communism. In fact, Stalin declared, Trotskyism had long ceased to be a variety of communism; it was now the vanguard of the counter-revolutionary bourgeoisie. For that reason, any toleration of Trotskyism was stupidity bordering on crime, and on treason to the working class.

According to Stalin, there were two lines of approach used by so-called writers and historians to infiltrate their Trotskyist contraband. One was to imply that in under-estimating the danger of centrism Lenin was not yet a real revolutionary, and to become one required to be 're-armed' with the help of Trotsky. The other line of approach was to imply that before the war Lenin did not realise the necessity of the bourgeois-democratic revolution's passing into a socialist revolution. Here too the implication was that Lenin was not yet a real Bolshevik, and here too needed to be 're-armed' with Trotsky's help. The references to 're-arming' came from the chapter in Trotsky's *History* entitled 'Re-Arming the Party'. They indicate the real stimulus for Stalin's letter to *Proletarskaia revoliutsiia*.

In Stalin's view, the function of the *Proletarskaia revoliutsiia* editorial board was to put the study of party history on a scientific, Bolshevik, footing, and to unmask Trotskyists and other of its falsifiers. This was especially necessary, Stalin observed, because some genuine party historians were not free from the kind of mistakes which gave encouragement to the likes of Slutskii. 'Here, unfortunately', Stalin continued, 'comrade Iaroslavskii is no exception; his books on the history of the Russian Communist Party, despite their merits, contain a number of errors of principle and history'.[61]

The problem that the letter to *Proletarskaia revoliutsiia* was meant to tackle was that Trotsky's charge of non-Leninism against Stalin was very well documented. It was supported by Iaroslavskii's book, and by Shliapnikov's mem-

---

61   Stalin 1937, p. 17.

oirs (and ultimately by the issues of *Pravda* published prior to Lenin's return). The method Stalin employed was to present matters in such a way that it appeared that it was not Trotsky who was repeating statements by Iaroslavskii and Shliapnikov, but that it was Iaroslavskii and Shliapnikov who were repeating statements by Trotsky. Besides performing this inversion of sequence, it was necessary to put Trotsky beyond the pale, to deny him any claim to be a socialist, and to equate him with the counter-revolutionary bourgeoisie. It then followed that any utterance made by Trotsky had a nefarious and counter-revolutionary intent. Thus, when Trotsky claimed that in April 1917 Stalin was out of step with Lenin, it should be taken as an example of Trotskyist slander. If any Soviet historian should make the same or similar claims, and in this way give support to Trotsky's falsifications, it would count as 'Trotskyist contraband', and could not be tolerated.

Stalin's letter had a devastating effect on the historians' community. According to Piontkovskii, 'dozens of university lecturers were removed and expelled from the party, people for some mistakes made five years ago were thrown out, excluded, driven almost to suicide and to distraction'.[62] Prominent among the victims were those mentioned in the letter. Slutskii was expelled from the Society of Marxist Historians and dismissed from his post at the Sverdlov Communist University. V.O. Volosevich, who got a passing mention in Stalin's letter, was dismissed from his post at the Institute of History of the Communist Academy's Leningrad section. M.A. Savel'ev was replaced as editor of *Proletarskaia revoliutsiia*. Party meetings of the various historical institutions were held to discuss Stalin's letter, the most imposing being those of the communist fraction of the Society of Marxist Historians, which took place over three evenings on 11, 14 and 18 November, with several hundred people in attendance. Iaroslavskii and the scholars who had contributed to his *History of the VKP(b)*, such as Baevskii, El'vov, Kin, Vanag and Mints, were severely criticised. Meetings to discuss the letter were held all over the country, and *Pravda* and *Bol'shevik* were inundated with resolutions on the letter from provincial towns, and even from communist parties abroad.[63]

The impact of the letter was enhanced by its enigmatic character. Almost none of its readers would have known of the existence of Trotsky's *History*, let alone read it. They would not know why the problem of 'Trotskyist contraband' had suddenly become acute, and what exactly should be done about it. One participant in a Society of Marxist Historians meeting inquired what was new

---

62   Piontkovskii, Litvin, Brandenberger, and Dubrovskii 2009, pp. 450–1; Artizov 1998b, p. 139.
63   Mertsalov 1991, pp. 268–9.

about the injunction to be vigilant against manifestations of Trotskyism.[64] This was an apt question, because in his article in *Istorik-marksist* in 1931 entitled 'The Tasks of Historical Science in the Reconstruction Period', Pokrovskii had written precisely on the subject of the need to unmask opportunists and deviationists, who masqueraded under a Leninist disguise. Pokrovskii mentioned Trotskyism in this connection. The article also emphasised that history as a discipline should be at the service of the party, that there was no such thing as apolitical scholarship, and that history was 'the most political of all the sciences'.[65] Pokrovskii's article, in some respects, was an anticipation of Stalin's letter. The impact of the letter was felt keenly by Iaroslavskii. Piontkovskii recalls that:

> When I visited him, he was sitting by himself in the office of the Central Control Commission, with his head in his hands, distractedly looking out of the window. What struck me more than anything else was that he was not able to come up with any theoretical basis for the severe criticism he had received. His only explanation for it was that in the 4-volume history Stalin had not been made to appear the most important person, that the motivations were personal in nature, not ones of principle.[66]

Iaroslavskii's discomfort that Piontkovskii describes was brought about by a profound change in the character of Soviet historical writing. The significance of Stalin's letter was precisely that it brought an end to scholarship that had a 'theoretical basis'. Henceforward, it would be personal, rather than principled considerations that would apply.

At the meeting of the communist fraction of the Society of Marxist Historians on 18 November it was noted that the main source from which the authors of Iaroslavskii's four volumes derived the material for the 'slanderous, falsifying interpretation of the history of the party' was the counter-revolutionary works of Shliapnikov, 'which could have been written only by an enemy of the party'.[67] At this meeting the chairman V. Knorin made it clear that Stalin's letter applied not only to *Proletarskaia revoliutsiia*, but to all fields of history. Henceforth the main attention of all historians was to be directed towards putting the history of Bolshevism on a 'scientific footing'. This was a directive that elimin-

---

64   Mertsalov 1991, p. 272.

65   Pokrovskii 1931c, p. 5.

66   Piontkovskii, Litvin, Brandenberger, and Dubrovskii 2009, p. 451.

67   Khronika. Rezoliutsiia fraktsii obshchestva istorikov-marksistov po dokladu t. Knorina 'O politicheskikh urokakh t. Stalina i zadachakh istoricheskogo fronta.' 1932, p. 214.

ated the distinction that had formerly existed between Istpart and IKP. Now all historical fields would be under the same strict party control. Knorin also took the opportunity to point out that the theory that the October revolution was socialist because it was anti-imperialist was a Trotskyist theory and should not have appeared in Iaroslavskii's *History*. Mints, a contributor to the *History*, was rebuked for his 'confession' that: 'We approached matters not from the point of political expediency ... but from the point of view of that objectivity, which is absolutely uncharacteristic of our political history, and is a vestige of bourgeois liberalism'. Mints was given to understand that *partiinost'* was the very essence of objectivity.[68]

Pokrovskii was in the Crimea when Stalin's letter was published and was informed of it by a letter from Pankratova of 1 November. 'The biggest event of our historical front' she wrote, 'is Stalin's article in *Proletarskaia revoliutsiia* ... This article is in connection with the mistakes in the works of Slutskii and Volosevich, and partly in the *History of the VKP* edited by Iaroslavskii. It is, or ought to be, for historians a political and historical milestone, especially in relation to realising the main slogan – *partiinost'* in historical science'. She went on to say that Stalin's article 'had made the whole community of historians sit up'. Pankratova declined to go into further detail, because Iaroslavskii was on his way to the Crimea and would tell Pokrovskii everything he needed to know.[69] In the middle of November Pokrovskii returned to Moscow and was admitted to the Kremlin hospital, where he spent the last months of his life. (He died on 10 April 1932). On 1 December, accompanied by doctors, he attended the ceremony at the Bolshoi Theatre to mark the tenth anniversary of the founding of IKP.

This was to be the last speech that Pokrovskii gave, and it was one of the most carefully crafted. Ostensibly he gave his support to Stalin's letter, but in fact he comprehensively subverted it. It was a speech that reaffirmed the value of historical studies that Stalin had reviled.

Pokrovskii recalled for his audience how IKP had come about. It was descended from the study groups that had met before the 1905 revolution. A step in the direction was the organisation of party schools on Capri and in Bologna. These, however, had fallen into the hands of oppositionists, and it was only the party school that Lenin established in Longjumeau that functioned satisfactorily, and produced such outstanding communists as Orjonikidze.[70]

---

68   Knorin 1932, p. 30.
69   Mertsalov 1991, p. 274.
70   Pokrovskii 1933c, p. 400.

(There was no suggestion in his speech that Pokrovskii himself had been a participant in the 'oppositionist' party schools and had refused to lecture in Lenin's.)

On the founding of IKP in 1921, Pokrovskii recalled that they had begun with 80 students, a large proportion with higher education; now there were 2,400, a large proportion of whom were workers. Pokrovskii put a positive gloss on this transformation, but the increase in numbers, and change in social composition, signified that IKP was no longer the elite graduate school it had originally been. It was now a party institution for the training of Soviet functionaries. This was borne out by statistics Pokrovskii produced: of the 96 IKP graduates then working in Moscow, only 43 were in education; the remaining 53 were employed in various party institutions.[71]

The change in the character of IKP that Pokrovskii alluded to had been brought about by widespread purges of the student body, the most recent being of Bukharin supporters. Increasing the proletarian element in IKP had been the favoured method of lessening its oppositionist inclinations. The measure seemed to have worked, because the audience applauded when Pokrovskii claimed that the students of IKP took it as a mark of pride when Trotsky referred to them as 'Stalin's formations'.[72]

Pokrovskii cautioned his audience not to become too specialised in their studies. Specialisation had produced deviationists like Rubin and Deborin. They were so specialised that no one knew what they were doing; and what they were doing was subversion. The role models, Pokrovskii insisted, were Lenin and Stalin, who could always explain things in a way that everyone could understand; these were the examples the students should follow. Workers, after all, were free from all academic prejudices, and went straight to the essence of things.

A novel element that Pokrovskii introduced into his speech was an argument to explain the superiority of the proletarian over the bourgeois viewpoint. This was that: 'All bourgeois theoreticians are distinguished by the fact that they never talk things through. If they did, they would have to talk about socialism, and this is something they cannot do, so they stop a decent number of kilometres from it'.[73] Pokrovskii continued the thought in the form of advice to his audience:

---

71   Pokrovskii 1933c, p. 410.
72   Pokrovskii 1933c, p. 401.
73   Pokrovskii 1933c, p. 405.

And my behest to you: do not go the 'academic' route that we went, because 'academism' contains within itself, as a necessary condition, the recognition of this same objective science, that does not exist.

Bolshevik science must be Bolshevik. Science is also class-based – bourgeois science differs from ours by the fact that bourgeois scholars do not take things to the logical conclusion. But we draw all the conclusions, and must do, because we go boldly towards our final goal – the socialist revolution throughout the whole world.[74]

In Pokrovskii's opinion 'academism' and 'rotten liberalism' were closely related. Referring to Stalin's remarks about Trotskyist contraband in the historical field, Pokrovskii cautioned that smugglers of this kind were not easy to uncover. They might conceal their contraband behind quotations from Lenin. That is why it was essential to know Lenin's works, as well as the writings of Marx and Engels, thoroughly, to recognise contraband wherever it appeared. With Slutskii's article in mind, Pokrovskii gave as an example a smuggler who wrote some nonsense about Lenin's attitude to centrism in the II International. The antidote to this, in Pokrovskii's view, was to know the history of the II International and the developments within it.

The other piece of advice Pokrovskii offered the members of his audience was to master thoroughly the discipline that they had chosen. They should not content themselves with knowing one area of history; they ought to know it all. He gave three examples of this. One was from his experience working on the *Great Soviet Encyclopaedia*. It had been necessary to commission a non-communist to write about the 1861 peasant reform in Russia, because none of the communists had sufficient knowledge of the subject. The second was from a recent seminar at the Sverdlov Communist University on modern Britain, at which there had arisen the question of when the English parliament had originated. The organiser said he would find out. But, to Pokrovskii's mind, this was not satisfactory; the answer should have been known. Pokrovskii's third example came from his stay at the Kremlin hospital. He had been asked by a young boy when the Kremlin had been built and had been able to satisfy the boy's curiosity.[75]

Pokrovskii had set ambitious targets for his audience. To acquire a thorough knowledge of Marxist theory and history was no easy matter. IKP graduates who succeeded in doing so would be well on the way to being scholars in their own

---

74   Pokrovskii 1933c, p. 406.
75   Pokrovskii 1933c, p. 409.

right. They would not be likely to accept uncritically Stalin's 'axioms'. By interpreting Stalin's letter in his particular way, Pokrovskii had changed its meaning completely. He had made it a call for the assiduous study of theory and history. He encouraged in the students not passive acceptance, but 'thinking things through'. The speech was a worthy end to Pokrovskii's career as a historian.

L.M. Kaganovich also spoke at the ceremony, using the opportunity to enlarge on what Stalin had said in his letter to the editors of *Proletarskaia revoliutsiia*. Like Pokrovskii, Kaganovich referred to the party schools on Capri and at Longjumeau – in Kaganovich's case – to illustrate the principle of mobilising scholarship for practical purposes. His point was that:

> The theoretical training of our cadres was always imbued with real political content. Take the case of the old Bolshevik school organised by Lenin in Longjumeau, and compare the experience of this school with that of another school, organised on the island of Capri by Bogdanov, the Otzovist. Two schools, two programmes, two different approaches to the question of training cadres. In Bogdanov's school on the island of Capri, the history of social philosophy, the history of art, the history of Russian literature, the study of the Church and State in Russia, were the principal subjects taught. In Lenin's school, however, the main subjects were: the agrarian question, the theory and practice of socialism, and labour legislation. In one school, the history of art, in the other, the theory and practice of socialism; in one school, the history of Russian literature, in the other, the history of the RSDRP; in one school, the Church and State in Russia, in the other, labour legislation.[76]

Kaganovich did not mention the teaching of history at the Capri school, and the courses Pokrovskii had given, but he said nothing that would exempt Pokrovskii from the implied criticism. It is noteworthy that in a ceremony to mark the success of IKP, Kaganovich did not give any recognition to Pokrovskii's role in its founding.

Regarding Stalin's letter, Kaganovich made it clear that what Stalin objected to was not Slutskii's article as such, but the fact that the editors of *Proletarskaia revoliutsiia* had given Slutskii the opportunity to publish it, and by doing so had demonstrated their 'rotten liberalism'. Kaganovich wanted his audience to appreciate what the true focus of Stalin's letter was. He stated:

76 Kaganovich 1932, p. 14.

It would be paying a compliment to Slutskii to take his libellous nonsense seriously. It is enough that Stalin, in passing, smashed it to pieces. The question here is not so much that Slutskii wrote this libellous nonsense. More important is the fact that a Bolshevik journal offered its columns to Slutskii's nonsense. It is the rotten liberalism displayed by some of our Communists towards writers with a Trotskyist outlook that matters.[77]

Kaganovich made more explicit Stalin's somewhat cryptic reference to Iaroslavskii in his letter. It was regrettable, he said, that *Proletarskaia revoliutsiia* was not the only weak spot; Iaroslavskii's *History of the VKP(b)* was another. As the editor of the four-volume work, Iaroslavskii had committed a grave error by giving a free hand to the young historians he gathered around him. Not only had Iaroslavskii not prevented attempts to pervert party history, but he had endorsed these attempts by putting his name to them. About what the errors in Iaroslavskii's *History* were, Kaganovich was not specific, but he was confident that, in due course, they would be fully criticised.[78]

Kaganovich must have been informed of Mints's caricatured self-criticism at the meeting of the Society of Marxist Historians, when he confessed that in his contribution to Iaroslavskii's *History*, he had written 'not from the point of view of political expediency, but from the point of view of that objectivity which is ... a reflection of liberalism'. For this sally Mints was severely taken to task by Kaganovich, who reminded him that 'history, including the history of the VKP(b), must be scientific, objective, and absolutely truthful, that otherwise history became mythology'.[79]

How Stalin's letter was being interpreted on the ground was revealed in a speech made by P.P. Postyshev on 11 January 1932. This was that communists were being indiscriminately expelled from the party. No attempts were made to help those who had erred, in a comradely way, so that they might correct their errors. The treatment they received either broke them completely, or at best, left them cowed. This, Postyshev said, was incorrect; Stalin had written the letter as a warning that one needed to have vigilance on the ideological front to be able to recognise manifestations of rotten liberalism and excessive trustfulness. The letter was written to encourage the study of Leninism, and, most of all, to recognise in time manifestations of Trotskyism and other types of contraband.[80]

---

77   Kaganovich 1932, p. 24.
78   Kaganovich 1932, p. 25.
79   Kaganovich 1932, p. 28.
80   Kaganovich 1932, p. 36.

Iaroslavskii had understood in what respect Stalin had found his history of
the Bolshevik party wanting. He had wasted no time in writing to Stalin on
28 October apologising for Kin's chapter, and its use of Shliapnikov's memoirs,
in extenuation pointing out that *The Year 1917* had been approved by Istpart,
and so was a legitimate source for Kin to use.[81] But Iaroslavskii realised that
Stalin's concern was not simply to defend himself against Trotsky's accusations
against him of non-Leninism in his *History of the Russian Revolution*, but to
appear in the history of the Bolshevik party as its most important figure. This
aspect of the letter to *Proletarskaia revoliutsiia* was noted by the oppositionist
M.N. Riutin, when he stated:

> Finally, Stalin's 'historical' article in *Proletarskaia revoliutsiia* completely
> and with supreme cynicism showed his true intentions: to present history
> in the way that Stalin should occupy in it a 'fitting' place as a great man
> – such is the subtext of Stalin's article. Now, after 15 years of proletarian
> dictatorship, all the textbooks on party history are no good, containing as
> they do 'Trotskyist contraband'. From now on party history will be written,
> or more precisely, fabricated, anew. At the Moscow district party confer-
> ence Iaroslavskii in his repentance speech openly and cynically blurted
> out the 'secret'. He said: 'I must emphasize that in some textbooks on party
> history, and here I have in mind principally my own, the role of Comrade
> Stalin in the development of Bolshevism, especially in the pre-war years,
> is not sufficiently examined'. There is where the roots of all the cries about
> 'Trotskyist contraband' are, the slander on the party, the rotten liberalism
> etc.[82]

---

81   Pikhoia and Zelenov 2006, p. 138.
82   Riutin 1990, p. 202.

CHAPTER 10

Epilogue

1 Stalin and History

In October 1932 the Soviet government resolved to attach Pokrovskii's name to Moscow University. In April of the following year the Praesidium of the Communist Academy decided to petition that the History Institute of the IKP should be named in honour of Pokrovskii.[1]

Although Pokrovskii was held in high esteem after his death, his reputation began to undergo a subtle evolution. Some elements in his writings were emphasised, while others were down-played. One of the effects was to eradicate any suggestion of his former association with Vanag's ideas, and to emphasise his activities in the first half of the twenties, when he fought against Trotskyism. The process started with his obituaries in 1932 which recalled Pokrovskii's debate with Trotsky a decade earlier on the subject of the Russian State.[2] This tendency to depict Pokrovskii as an anti-Trotskyist hero was reflected in the collection of his articles published in 1933, under the general title *Historical Science and the Class Struggle*.[3]

The items in this two-volume collection are tendentiously chosen. All Pokrovskii's articles in the debate with Trotsky are reproduced in full, leading to a considerable amount of repetition. Those written towards the end of his life, in the same spirit, are also included, but all the works concerned with the Vanag discussion have been omitted. The impression is given of unswerving adherence to the same doctrine between 1922 and 1930. With Pokrovskii's death, one important chapter of his career had already been consigned to oblivion.

In this period, it had become universally accepted that ideas on 'denationalisation' – the dependence of Russian capitalism on foreign powers – were to be considered as a Trotskyist heresy. Vanag admitted this himself in a letter to *Istorik-marksist* in 1932, in which he stated that: 'The Trotskyist conception of the backwardness of tsarist Russia is but the corollary of the counter-revolutionary thesis of the impossibility of the construction and victory of

---

1 Alatortseva and Alekseeva 1971, pp. 170–8.
2 Pankratova 1932, p. 28.
3 Pokrovskii 1933b.

socialism in our country'.[4] Vanag thereafter set about what Sidorov describes as 'popularising the works of Stalin in historical science', in an attempt to redeem himself for his past heresies.[5] Vanag's efforts seem to have been successful, because in 1934 he was charged with producing a textbook on the history of the USSR.

The process by which Pokrovskii was discredited between 1936 and 1938 is a complex one and cannot be attributed to Stalin's initiative alone. The first in the sequence of events leading up to Pokrovskii's fall from grace was the publication in May 1934 of the resolution on school textbooks. This did not come out of the blue. The question of history textbooks for schools had come up at the First Conference of Marxist Historians in 1928. Some participants doubted whether there should be textbooks at all, since they were necessarily dogmatic, and did not allow the pupils to make up their own minds about events. To cater for this need 'workbooks' of documents had been published. Other participants objected that the interpretation of history should not be left to the pupils, because their minds were not *tabula rasa*; they were saturated with petty-bourgeois and peasant ideology. It was also pointed out that 95% of schoolteachers were non-Marxists, and they were liable to interpret collections of documents in a non-Marxist way. Some educational institutions did not teach history, but 'social studies', resulting in the reduction of historical events to 'sociological schematism'. As for Russian history, there was no suitable general textbook. Pokrovskii himself had warned that his *Brief History* and his four-volume *History of Russia from the Earliest Times* were not textbooks.[6]

A.I. Gukovskii recalls how he was the author of a workbook on history and of a reader on the history of the age of feudalism, written in collaboration with O.V. Trakhtenberg. Gukovskii discussed these works with A.S. Bubnov, who had taken over from Lunacharskii at Narkompros in 1929. Being himself a historian, Bubnov set in motion measures designed to improve the way history was taught in schools. It was, Bubnov believed, important to have standardised textbooks for the purpose. It was on Bubnov's initiative that a special session of the Politburo was held in May 1934 to set in motion the drive to produce new textbooks for the teaching of history in secondary schools.[7]

4 Vanag 1932, p. 357.
5 *Vsesoiuznoe soveshchanie o merakh uluchsheniia podgotovki nauchno-pedagogicheskikh kadrov po istoricheskim naukam* 1964, p. 334.
6 *Trudy pervoi vsesoiuznoi konferentsii istorikov-marksistov* 1930, pp. 470–577.
7 Gukovskii 1965, p. 96.

This was a matter in which Stalin intervened personally, despite the seeming incongruity of a head of state concerning himself with the content of school history textbooks. Gukovskii describes what happened at the Politburo meeting:

> Then Stalin got up. He walked leisurely to the table with the materials on it and came back with a book of some kind in his hand (Trakhtenberg quietly nudged me with his elbow, but I didn't understand what he meant; being short-sighted I did not see that it was our textbook) and, standing in the central passage by his seat, began to speak, while glancing in our direction. Not surprisingly, we just stood and gaped ... . Then he stepped a little forward and addressed the hall. 'My son asked me to explain what is written in this book. I looked at it but I didn't understand it either'. That is how Stalin began. Then he said that the book should be written differently, that there should not be general schemes, but precise historical facts. He did not speak long, five or ten minutes, not more. Someone asked us whether we wanted to say anything, but it was obvious that we were expected to say 'no'.[8]

It must be said that Stalin had picked a very suitable target for his accusation of schematism. Even the most cursory examination of Gukovskii and Trakhtenberg's book shows it to be indigestible and tedious.[9] A resolution 'On the Teaching of Civil History in the Schools of the USSR' was duly passed by the Soviet government on 16 May 1934. It stated that:

> Instead of teaching civil history in a lively and attractive way, with the exposition of the most important events and facts in their chronological sequence, with the description of historical figures, the pupils are presented with abstract definitions of socio-economic formations, in this way replacing the cogent exposition of civil history with abstract sociological schemes.[10]

It recommended that school textbooks should be produced which presented their factual material in a chronological sequence, avoiding 'abstract sociological schemes'; only courses taught in this way could lead the pupils to a Marxist

---

8   Gukovskii 1965, p. 97.
9   Gukovskii and Trakhtenberg 1934.
10   Stalin 1937, p. 19.

understanding of history.[11] A number of groups of historians were established to draw up outlines for the proposed textbooks, Vanag being put in charge of the group concerned with the history of the USSR. In August of 1934 the outlines were read, and commented upon, by a panel consisting of Stalin, Zhdanov and Kirov. The panel found that Vanag's outline was unsatisfactory in a number of ways:

1) It was an outline of the history of Russia rather than of the USSR; it neglected the nationalities who formed the USSR, such as the peoples of Ukraine, Belorussia, Finland and other Baltic territories, the Caucasus, Central Asia, and the North.

2) It did not emphasise the annexationist-colonial role of Russian tsarism, together with the Russian bourgeoisie and the landowners (tsarism – as 'the prison of nations').

3) It did not emphasise the counter-revolutionary role of Russian tsarism in foreign policy, from the time of Catherine II until the 1850s, and beyond (tsarism as the 'international gendarme').

4) It lumped together feudalism and the pre-feudal period, when the peasants were still not enserfed; the autocratic structure of the state, and the feudal structure, when Russia was fragmented into a number of independent petty states.

5) It lumped together the concepts of reaction and counter-revolution, revolution 'in general', the bourgeois revolution, and the bourgeois-democratic revolution.

6) The conditions and origins of the national-liberation movement of peoples of Russia, subject to tsarism, are not given, and thus, the October revolution as a revolution freeing these peoples from the national yoke, remains unexplained, as does the creation of the Soviet Union.

7) It is loaded with trite and hackneyed expressions, such as 'the police terrorism of Nicholas I', 'Razinshchina' (the Razin uprising), 'Pugachevshchina' (the Pugachev uprising) and so on. The authors blindly copy the trite and completely unscientific definitions of all kinds of bourgeois historians, forgetting that they are obliged to teach our young people Marxist definitions based on science.

8) It does not reflect the influence of Western-European bourgeois-revolutionary and socialist movements on the formation of the bourgeois revolutionary movement and the proletarian-socialist movement in Russia.

---

11   Stalin 1937, p. 18.

The authors of the outline forget that the Russian revolutionaries thought of themselves as followers of the leading lights of Marxist thought in the West.

9) It does not take into account the origins of the first imperialist war and the role of tsarism in this war, as a reserve for the Western-European imperialist powers. Nor is account taken of the dependent role, both of Russian tsarism and Russian capitalism, on that of Western Europe, in view of which the significance of the October revolution as the liberator of Russia from its semi-colonial situation remains unexplained.

10) It does not take into account the presence of a general-European political crisis before the world war, expressing itself, among other things, in the decline of bourgeois democracy and parliamentarianism, in view of which the significance of the Soviets, from the viewpoint of world history, as the bearers of proletarian democracy and the organs of the liberation of the workers and peasants from capitalism, remains unexplained.

11) No account is taken of the struggle of tendencies within the ruling Soviet Communist Party, and the struggle against Trotskyism, and against manifestations of petty-bourgeois counter-revolution.[12]

As the comments are on an outline for a book rather than on the book itself, it is impossible to say how readable Vanag's textbook would have been. But since there are no criticisms of how the outline is structured, one must assume that in it historical events were arranged in chronological order, and that, in this respect at least, Vanag had adhered to the specification he had been given. Nor do the comments signify any radical departure from Pokrovskii's approach to history. Pokrovskii too had believed that it was wrong to write the history of Russia, ignoring those of the peoples who made up the Russian Empire. In an article written in 1930, he explained that he had given his book the title *Brief History of Russia* because, in 1920, when he had given the lectures on which it was based, only Soviet Russia existed. However, with the formation of the Soviet Union, the term 'Russian history' had become obsolete, and it was now appropriate to speak of the 'history of the peoples of the USSR'.[13] Pokrovskii had already put this principle into practice by editing a volume with the title *Reader in the History of the Peoples of the USSR*.[14] Moreover, Pokrovskii's articles in *History of Russia in the XIX Century* were pioneer works on the history of the peoples of the Caucasus and Central Asia. The expansionist policies of Catherine II were well covered in several of Pokrovskii's writings. Taken as a

---

12   Stalin 1937, pp. 22–4.
13   Pokrovskii 1930a, p. 18.
14   Pokrovskii, Viktorov, and Presniakov 1930.

whole, the comments on Vanag's outline do not represent any new synthesis of Russian history to replace Pokrovskii's interpretation.

As a former Commissar for Nationalities, and the author of a book on the national question, it is natural that Stalin should emphasise the national dimension in Russian history. There is some inconsistency, however, in the list of nationalities he mentions. Finland and the Baltic states were no longer in the Soviet Union, but they had been part of the Russian Empire, and ought to be included. But to be consistent, Poland too should be included on the list.

The ninth point is the one that is the most surprising, and must have come as a shock to Vanag. He had been severely criticised for suggesting that Russian capitalism was dependent on that of Western Europe, and that Russia was a semi-colony. He had recognised this as a serious error, because it placed in doubt the possibility of socialism in Russia. Now he was being criticised by Stalin for *not* expressing these views. What had formerly been heretical was now the orthodoxy.

On 1 December 1934 Kirov was assassinated. This event changed the political climate of the country, beginning a new series of show trials and purges, which reached their peak in 1937–1938. It was against this background that the campaign against Pokrovskii took place.

On 26 January 1936 a directive was issued, over the signatures of Stalin and Molotov, for the establishment of a commission to oversee, improve, and, if necessary, to re-write textbooks on history. It was to be chaired by A.A. Zhdanov, and had as its members K.B. Radek, A.S. Svanidze, Gorin, N.M. Lukin, Iakovlev, V.A. Bystrianskii, V.P. Zatonskii, F.U. Khojaev, K.Ia. Bauman, Bubnov and Bukharin. The commission was empowered to organise groups for the overseeing of individual textbooks, and to announce a competition for textbooks to replace those which were considered to require radical revision. The main priority had to be the oversight of textbooks for the elementary course of the history of the USSR, and modern history.[15]

The directive was published the following day in *Pravda*, along with other documents, under the general heading of 'On the Historical Front'. The key document was a bulletin headed 'In the Council of People's Commissars and the Central Committee of the Russian Communist Party', which reproduced the resolution of 16 May 1934 on school textbooks, and recounted how the subject groups had been set up, and the outlines commented upon. The comments on the groups concerned with the History of the USSR and Modern History were

---

15   Molotov and Stalin 1936.

reproduced in full. None of this had anything to do with Pokrovskii. However, in accounting for the lack of success to date in producing suitable textbooks, Pokrovskii's influence was held responsible.

> The circumstance that the authors of the textbooks mentioned continue to persist in the definitions and positions that have as their basis the well-known errors of Pokrovskii, cannot but lead Sovnarkom and the Central Committee to believe that among sections of our historians, especially historians of the USSR, there are rooted anti-Marxist, anti-Leninist, in essence liquidationist, anti-scientific attitudes to historical science. Sovnarkom and the CC emphasise that these harmful tendencies and attempts to liquidate history as a science are connected first and foremost with the dissemination among some of our historians of erroneous historical views, characteristic of the so-called 'Pokrovskii historical school'. Sovnarkom and the CC indicate that the task of overcoming these harmful views is the essential pre-condition for compiling textbooks on history, and also for the development of a Marxist-Leninist historical science and raising the standard of historical education in the USSR ... .[16]

This was the first shot in the campaign against Pokrovskii. But what were the 'well-known errors' that Pokrovskii had committed? The implication was that the documents accompanying the bulletin referred to these. But the resolution of 16 May had been a response to textbooks such as the one produced by Gukovskii and Trakhtenberg. The comments by Stalin, Kirov and Zhdanov had been on the draft written by Vanag and his group. According to Nechkina, who had examined the manuscript of the bulletin, the references to Pokrovskii in it were handwritten interpolations in Zhdanov's typescript, made by Stalin.[17]

Evidence of Pokrovskii's errors was supplied, in an obviously orchestrated way, by an article in *Pravda* by Radek, and one in *Izvestiia* by Bukharin, both on

---

16   'V Sovnarkome Soiuza SSR i TsK VKP(b)' 1936.
17   The passage from the document in question is reproduced in Brandenberger 1998, p. 70. In Brandenberger's view the idea to discredit Pokrovskii came from Bukharin, who wanted to ingratiate himself with Stalin. This seems unlikely, because: 1. the effect of Stalin's letter to *Proletarskaia revoliutsiia* was to make Stalin the sole – and unpredictable – arbiter of developments in the field of history. Such a major enterprise as discrediting Pokrovskii could only be set in motion at Stalin's initiative. 2. The anti-Pokrovskii campaign showed that the criticisms levelled at Pokrovskii were carefully vetted to align them with the historical doctrines that Stalin wished to project – something that only Stalin himself was in a position to ensure.

that same 27 January. Anna Larina, Bukharin's wife, recalls that Stalin ordered her husband and Karl Radek to write 'devastating' (*razgromnye*) articles against Pokrovskii.[18]

Bukharin's article 'Do we need a Marxist historical science?' began by paying tribute to Pokrovskii as a great scholar and Marxist historian, noting his service in refuting the bourgeois conceptions of such historians as Karamzin, Chicherin, Kliuchevskii, Miliukov, Plekhanov and Rozhkov. Pokrovskii's limitation, in Bukharin's view, was the lack of a truly dialectical approach to basic methodological problems. His dictum that 'history was politics projected into the past' indicated that he believed all science was subjective, including that of the proletariat. He did not understand that, although the proletariat had a class position, this did not prevent its being objective, because it could look both to the future and the past without fear. The class position of the bourgeoisie, on the other hand, limited its horizons, and made it see the world in a distorted light.[19]

Although Bukharin's article was written to order, it nevertheless identified a real weakness in Pokrovskii's methodology. Pokrovskii could show that previous historians had approached their subject in their class interests, and the proletariat did so too. But why should the proletarian viewpoint be any more objective than that of their class enemies? This is a question Pokrovskii did not pose until very late in his career. In his last speech he had argued that bourgeois scholars did not take their research to its logical conclusion, because then they would be forced to talk about socialism, a consideration that did not exist for proletarian science. This is very like the idea that Bukharin puts forward in his article, which is thereby at the same time a critique and a veiled endorsement of Pokrovskii.

Radek's article in *Pravda*, 'The Significance of History for the Revolutionary Proletariat', was hardly 'devastating' to Pokrovskii, since it did not mention him directly. The nearest it came was the observation that:

> Our historians have not yet managed to assimilate the great historical heritage of Marx, Engels and Lenin: this is very clear from the very fact of the domination of Pokrovkii's school in the field of Russian history, a school which has not overcome the influence of Luxemburgism and Trotskyism in the interpretation of general modern history ....[20]

---

18   Larina 1989, p. 32.
19   Bukharin 1936.
20   Radek 1936.

What Radek did find to criticise was Pokrovskii's theory of merchant capital-ism, to which, Radek admitted, he himself had formerly subscribed. Though it might appear that the role of merchant capital was a question that belonged to ancient Russian history, in the light of the revolutionary events in China, it had turned out to be an urgent question of the present day. Errors in the way the role of merchant capital in China had been interpreted had given rise to mistakes in political struggles of the present time. In general, Radek declared, abstract schemes which replaced historical reality inevitably caused simplific-ation of reality, and this led to political miscalculations.

At the beginning of 1936 P.S. Drozdov, who had criticised Pokrovskii in 1929, published an article in *Istorik-marksist* entitled 'The Decision of the Party and Government on History Textbooks and The Tasks of Historians'. Like the articles of Bukharin and Radek, it was likely to have been written on orders from above, but in this case, some at least of the criticisms of Pokrovskii were genuine.

Drozdov's article began by summarizing what had been done so far to pro-duce suitable textbooks for schools, from Stalin's condemnation of existing textbooks in May 1934, to the decision to establish a commission on text-books in January 1936. Like Bukharin, Drozdov paid tribute to Pokrovskii for his contribution to the discipline of history in the USSR, and for his cam-paign against bourgeois and landowner historiography, as represented by the works of Pogodin, Chicherin and Kliuchevskii. Also praiseworthy had been Pokrovskii's polemics against the Menshevik historiography of Plekhanov and Trotsky, who had been prisoners of bourgeois and landowner historical con-ceptions.[21]

Pokrovskii's flaw, to Drozdov's mind, was that, whilst struggling against the bourgeois-landowner and petty-bourgeois historians, he had opposed to their schemes not the views of Marx, Engels, Lenin and Stalin on historical devel-opment, but his own historical scheme. The scheme he constructed was anti-Marxist, and therefore unscientific. Having got wide dissemination, thanks to Pokrovskii's influence on young historians, this scheme did enormous damage to historical science in the USSR and impeded its development. This, in Droz-dov's estimation, was why it had been so difficult to produce school textbooks that were free from the errors Stalin had identified.[22]

In this part of his article Drozdov reveals what most likely was Stalin's real objection to Pokrovskii's scheme of history. It had nothing to do with any sup-posed 'errors' in Pokrovskii's methods, his alleged 'schematism' or 'abstraction'.

---

21   Drozdov 1936, p. 13.
22   Drozdov 1936, p. 14.

It was because Pokrovskii's historical scheme was his own scheme; it owed nothing to Stalin. By 1936 Stalin could not tolerate the existence of an independent intellectual current which he did not control. He took steps to eliminate it at the same time as he was eliminating its adherents physically.

There is nothing in Drozdov's article that suggests that in it he used any of the arguments he deployed against Pokrovskii in his paper given in 1929. That level of sophistication was presumably ruled out by the instructions Drozdov had been given, so that the objections he could raise to his former teacher's historical conceptions were only approved ones. On the whole, however, Drozdov's article has the marks of being written by someone who knew Pokrovskii's work well, and had, in better times, been able to criticise it for the limitations he actually perceived in it.

2   Shestakov's Textbook

The report of the jury for the history textbook competition was published in *Pravda* on 22 August 1937. It was recognised that the authors had, in the main, complied with the guidelines, and avoided abstract sociological schemes. But among the shortcomings which remained a prominent defect was that: 'The Stalin thesis that Russia was beaten "because of its military backwardness, because of its cultural backwardness, because of its governmental backwardness, because of its industrial backwardness, because of its agricultural backwardness", which provides one of the most important keys to Russian history in the last centuries, has not been understood by several authors of textbooks'. The report went on to say that if Russia's backwardness was not understood, the part played by Soviet power in transforming it from a poor and weak country into a rich and powerful one would not be appreciated.[23] Now, apparently, the theme of Russian backwardness, which had been associated with Trotsky until 1930, was to be attributed to Stalin.

In the same year as the jury reported, Stalin drew up an outline for the projected textbook on the history of the Russian Communist Party, the book which was to be his 'Encyclopedia of Marxism'. Symptomatically, he was especially anxious that the authors of the textbook should mention the 'petty-bourgeois' nature of the country, in order to explain the great variety of currents and fractions within the party, and in the working class as a whole, against which it was necessary to wage an unrelenting struggle. The published version of the *History*

---

23   Stalin 1937, p. 33.

of the Russian Communist Party (bolsheviks): A Short Course, which appeared in
1938, duly stressed Russia's backwardness with the assertion:

> That Russia entered the imperialist war on the side of the Entente ...
> was not accidental. It should be borne in mind that before 1914 the most
> important branches of Russian industry were in the hands of foreign cap-
> italists, chiefly those of France, Great Britain and Belgium, that is, of the
> Entente countries ... All these circumstances, in addition to the thousands
> of millions borrowed by the tsar from France and Britain in loans, chained
> tsardom to British and French imperialism, and converted Russia into a
> tributary, a semi-colony of those countries.[24]

The insistence on Russia's historical backwardness was important to Stalin,
because he used it to justify his refusal to slow down the pace of collectivisation
and industrialisation, his own brand of 'revolution from above'. In February 1931
he made the argument to a meeting of industrial executives. 'I am sometimes
asked', he said:

> whether it would be possible to slow down the tempo somewhat, to put a
> check on the movement. No, comrades, it is not possible! The tempo must
> not be reduced! On the contrary, we must increase it as much as is within
> our powers and possibilities. This is dictated to us by our obligations to
> the workers and peasants of the USSR. This is dictated to us by our obliga-
> tions to the working class of the whole world. To slacken the tempo would
> mean falling behind. And those who fall behind get beaten. But we do not
> want to be beaten. No, we refuse to be beaten! One feature of the history of
> old Russia was the continual beatings she suffered because of her back-
> wardness. She was beaten by the Mongol khans. She was beaten by the
> Turkish beys. She was beaten by the Swedish feudal lords. She was beaten
> by the Polish and Lithuanian gentry. She was beaten by the British and
> French capitalists. She was beaten by the Japanese barons. All beat her
> – because of her backwardness, because of her military backwardness,
> cultural backwardness, political backwardness, industrial backwardness,
> agricultural backwardness. They beat her because it was profitable, and
> could be done with impunity.[25]

---

24   *Istoriia vsesoiuznoi kommunisticheskoi partii (bol'shevikov): Kratkii kurs* 1938, p. 156.
25   Stalin 1954a, pp. 40–1.

If this argument sounded oddly familiar to the industrial executives, it was because they had read it in Trotsky's book *1905*, where the case is made that the pressure for Russia to reform in the eighteenth century 'came from Lithuania, Poland, and Sweden. In order to stand up to a better-armed enemy, the Russian State was compelled to create industry and technology at home'.[26] Stalin was using the same logic: the country had to be industrialised at a rapid pace to overcome the weaknesses that would leave the Soviet Union at the mercy of more economically advanced foreign powers.

The now official doctrine of Russia's backwardness and its semi-colonial status with regard to the Western powers was in keeping with Stalin's 1924 essay 'The Foundations of Leninism'. There Stalin had maintained that the proletarian revolution occurred first in Russia, because it was there that the chain of imperialism broke at its weakest link. However, the doctrine of Russia's backwardness stood in stark contradiction to the series of articles that Pokrovskii had written against Trotsky's conception of Russian history in 1922, and which appeared prominently in the collection of Pokrovskii's writings that had been published in 1933. For that reason, in the many denunciations of Pokrovskii that appeared in the 1930s, scant mention was made of his polemic against Trotsky.

It would, of course, have been unthinkable to launch a campaign against Pokrovskii on the grounds that he had attempted to refute Trotsky's theory of 'permanent revolution', as the logic of the situation demanded. Instead a whole series of assorted accusations were trumped up against him, with a varying amount of justice. Some had a certain basis of truth, while others were completely without foundation. Some of the criticisms made were points put forward by Trotsky in 1922; others were of a later vintage, often from the seminars on merchant capitalism, at the end of the twenties.

The winner of the competition for school textbooks was A.V. Shestakov's *Short Course of the History of the USSR*.[27] Although the work duly took account of other nationalities of the USSR, the Ukrainians, Belorussians, the peoples of the Caucasus and Central Asia, as instructed, its main focus was on the history of Russia. It was a chronological account of Russia's historical development from the earliest times until the promulgation of the Soviet Constitution in 1936. It was written in clear and comprehensible language, and all specialised terminology was explained.

Some of the chapter headings of Shestakov's book would have annoyed Pokrovskii, because they implied that the driving force of Russian history was the

---

26   Trotsky 1922a, p. 18.
27   Shestakov 1937.

State. Among them were: 'The Kievan State', 'The Formation of the Russian National State', and 'The Expansion of the Russian State'. Homage was paid to the Marxist approach to history, with chapters entitled 'Russia in the Eighteenth Century – an Empire of Landowners and Merchants' and 'The Development of Capitalism in Tsarist Russia'. The class struggle and national movements were acknowledged in the chapter 'Peasant Wars and the Uprisings of Subject Peoples'. In deference to Stalin's comment on textbooks, the first half of the nineteenth century was designated as 'Tsarist Russia – the Gendarme of Europe'.

Shestakov's book was illustrated with pictures and maps. There were also full-page photographs of Marx, Engels, Lenin and Stalin. The author had contrived to mention Stalin 61 times. Some of the mentions of Stalin were in sections on the Caucasus and Transcaucasus, so that, being a history of the USSR rather than of Russia implied more mentions of Stalin and his native Georgia. Shestakov's book left its readers in no doubt of Stalin's world-historical significance, which must have counted in its favour in the competition.

Shestakov had been a pupil of Pokrovskii's and had even written an article in his honour on the occasion of Pokrovskii's sixtieth birthday.[28] He is someone who would be familiar with Pokrovskii's ideas. This in fact is evident in his textbook, where one finds many examples of Pokrovskii's interpretation of the events of Russian history. That, for example, the wealth of Kievan Rus' was based on foreign trade; that the Kievan prince could not go to war without the consent of the *veche*; that Ivan the Terrible's campaign against the boiars was occasioned by their perceived treachery in the war against Livonia; that the Crimean War was the result of Nicholas I's attempt to acquire Constantinople; that Alexander I's conflict with Napoleon was caused by the Russian aristocracy's discontent with the prohibition of British imports; that in the World War Russia tried to take Constantinople from Turkey. Although the overall structure of Shestakov's textbook and its mode of exposition are in accordance with Stalin's prescriptions, the content owes a great deal to Pokrovskii's interpretations. Pokrovskii himself never had the patience or the inclination to provide his readers with the basic facts of Russian history; he expected them to have familiarised themselves with them from a textbook. Ironically, Shestakov's would have been the perfect textbook for the purpose.

A significant innovation in Shestakov's book is that it no longer adheres to the scheme of the 1917 revolutions, established by Iakovlev in 1922, of a spontaneous February revolution, and an October revolution, organised and led by the

---

28   Shestakov 1928; Dushchenko 2010.

Bolsheviks. With Shestakov, the armed uprising in October is well organised, with Stalin playing a significant part in its success. But the February revolution is no longer held to be spontaneous, since: 'The Bolsheviks directed the workers' struggle'.[29] The new interpretation was probably in response to Trotsky's *History of the Russian Revolution*, which had used the spontaneity of the February revolution to great effect against the members of the Soviet leadership. From the early 1930s Bolshevik direction of the February revolution became the accepted doctrine and was incorporated in Stalin's *History of the Russian Communist Party (bolsheviks): A Short Course*, in 1938.[30] Shestakov does not name the Bolsheviks who had directed the workers' struggle in February 1917, and could not do so, because people like Shliapnikov and Kaiurov had been placed in the category of 'enemies of the people' and could no longer be mentioned.

3   Against the Historical Conceptions of M.N. Pokrovskii

It is a tribute to Pokrovskii's influence on Soviet historical writing even after his death that two volumes of essays were published in order to combat it, one volume in 1939, entitled *Against the Historical Conceptions of M.N. Pokrovskii*, and one in 1940, with the more tendentious title of *Against the Anti-Marxist Conceptions of M.N. Pokrovskii*. The first of the two volumes is the more substantial in terms of scholarly content. Among its contributors are the senior academics B.D. Grekov, S.V. Bakhrushin. K.B. Bazilevich, E.A. Morokhovets, A.S. Erusalimskii, and Picheta, as well as Pokrovskii's former students Pankratova, Nechkina, Baevskii and Sidorov. Although the essays have been written to order, with the intention of refuting Pokrovskii's interpretations, and discrediting Pokrovskii as a scholar, they are nevertheless informative, and in some cases, well researched. They were written by people under severe duress, who had little choice but to comply with the orders handed down. It would be wrong, however, to write off the essays as worthless. The disagreements they express with Pokrovskii's conceptions are often genuine, and the information about Pokrovskii's works is generally accurate.

The volume was introduced by Pankratova's lengthy essay 'The Development of M.N. Pokrovskii's Historical Views'. On Pokrovskii's death, Pankratova had published an article in *Bor'ba klassov*, extolling her teacher and his intellectual

---

29   Shestakov 1937, p. 153.
30   *Istoriia vsesoiuznoi kommunisticheskoi partii (bol'shevikov): Kratkii kurs* 1938, p. 169.

legacy.[31] Now she deployed her considerable talent as a writer in the cause of denouncing him as the purveyor of views which gave comfort to 'Trotskyist-Bukharinist hirelings of fascism, wreckers, spies and terrorists'.[32] Pankratova's essay is a curious amalgam of improbable accusations of nefarious plots, and a detailed knowledge of Pokrovskii's life, writings and ideas.

Given the political environment of the times, Pankratova's assignment to discredit Pokrovskii was not difficult. He had been, at different times, an associate of both Bogdanov and Trotsky, now pariahs of the Stalin regime. Moreover, for a great part of his career, Pokrovskii had taken no account of Lenin's writings, and so was an easy target for the charge of anti-Leninism. These were aspects of Pokrovskii's biography that she utilised to the full.

Pokrovskii's association with Bogdanov was particularly useful to Pankratova, because she could attribute to Bogdanov the origin of Pokrovskii's conception of merchant capital, and also the dictum that 'history is politics projected into the past'. Pokrovskii's denial of the objectivity of historical science, she argued, came from his adoption of the Bogdanovist rejection of objective truth.[33]

Pankratova enlarged on Pokrovskii's membership of the anti-Leninist 'Vpered' group, and his participation in the Capri and Bologna party schools. Here she could refer to Kaganovich's speech on the tenth anniversary of IKP in 1931, contrasting the Bogdanovist Capri and Bologna schools with Lenin's school at Longjumeau, implying that Kaganovich had Pokrovskii in mind.[34]

With Trotsky things were more problematic. Obviously damaging to Pokrovskii was his cooperation with Trotsky in contributing to *Bor'ba*, and his co-authorship with Trotsky in the book marking 300 years of the Romanov dynasty. But Pokrovskii had also polemicised against Trotsky in 1922 on the subject of Russia's historical development. As Stalin had now adopted a stance on the subject very like Trotsky's, this episode in Pokrovskii's career was passed over with the briefest of mentions. Also, Pokrovskii had been accused of Trotskyism through his support for Vanag's findings on foreign investment in Russian industry. Pankratova, however, was unable to take advantage of this accusation, because it would now have applied to Stalin.

Unlike Bukharin, Radek and Drozdov, who paid tribute to Pokrovskii for his campaign against landowner and bourgeois historiography, Pankratova could not bring herself to say anything positive about Pokrovskii, in any of his endeav-

---

31   Pankratova 1932.
32   Pankratova 1939, p. 5.
33   Pankratova 1939, p. 30.
34   Pankratova 1939, pp. 40–1.

ours. She concurred with earlier critics in condemning Pokrovskii's approach to history as abstract and schematic. It was, she argued, inspired not by Marxism, but by 'economic materialism'.[35]

The essays that followed Pankratova's were aimed at demolishing the elements which composed Pokrovskii's interpretation of Russian history. Grekov made the case that Kliuchevskii and Pokrovskii had both erred in their interpretation of the evidence in concluding that the wealth of Kievan Russia was based on foreign trade rather than on agriculture. In Grekov's view, Kievan Rus' was essentially an agrarian society.

The task which both Picheta and Erusalimskii tried to accomplish in their essays, Picheta on the war of 1812, and Erusalimskii on the 1914–1918 war, consisted in refuting Pokrovskii's depiction of Russia as the aggressor. It had been a characteristic feature of Pokrovskii's conception of Russia's history to show Russia as an active agent in its relations with other countries. This conception was not in keeping with Stalin's perception of Russia, because of its weakness, as the victim of foreign powers.

In his essay on Pokrovskii's conception of the 1861 peasant reform, Morokhovets divulged that the task given to him was 'to show the confusion reigning in Pokrovskii's conceptions of the political consequences of the reform'.[36] There was ample scope to do this because Pokrovskii had written on the subject repeatedly over the years, and his approach had not remained the same. Morokhovets made, but did not develop, the point that: 'Russia's defeat in the Crimean War showed clearly to the ruling group the technological backwardness in exactly those areas of industry which directly served the army'.[37] It was a case where military defeat stimulated economic reform – the kind of scenario that Stalin wished to promote. More important to Morokhovets was to show that Pokrovskii's conception of the role of *barshchina* labour on the eve of 1861 came from Struve, and not from Lenin. It was evident to Morokhovets that when Pokrovskii wrote about the 1861 reform, he had not consulted Lenin's writings.

By and large, the contributions to the two volumes adhere to the simple formula of comparing what Pokrovskii wrote with what Lenin said on the same subject, showing that Pokrovskii had said something different from Lenin, and concluding that Pokrovskii's views were un-Leninist. This was perverse reasoning. Of course, Pokrovskii's writings differed from Lenin's; it was he who had written them, not Lenin. That this was not pointed out is an indication of the

---

35   Pankratova 1939, p. 13.
36   Morokhovets 1939, p. 418.
37   Morokhovets 1939, p. 403.

degree to which Soviet society was forced to conform in the Stalin era. It was unjust to Pokrovskii, certainly, but one can hardly be sympathetic towards him, considering that he too had used Leninism as a criterion of the truth, and was himself a builder of the Stalin system.

The second volume of essays against Pokrovskii, *Against the Anti-Marxist Conceptions of M.N. Pokrovskii*, completes the work of refuting Pokrovskii's historical interpretations, even of some minor episodes. The main contribution to the collection is by Iaroslavskii, entitled 'The Anti-Marxist Distortions and Vulgarisations of the So-Called Pokrovskii "School."' As the title implies, it is even more tendentious than Pankratova's essay in the first volume. It is denunciation without the biographical detail that Pankratova supplied. In this way it is more effective in establishing the image of Pokrovskii that was to be maintained for the next three decades. It was that Pokrovskii's writings were vulgar schematic sociological abstractions, that he was an 'economic materialist', and that he denied the objectivity of historical science, teaching that 'history is politics projected into the past'. It is an image that 'rehabilitation' and time have not fully eradicated.

Conclusion

Viewed as a whole, Pokrovskii's academic career is a journey of discovery, beginning with the articles in Vinogradov's *Readings in Medieval History*, and ending with the articles on Russia's foreign policy in the Great War. Throughout his writings, Pokrovskii is searching for the materialist factors that will explain the phenomena of Russian history. His initial inspiration to do this comes not from Marx, but from the succession of Russian historians, ending in his teacher Kliuchevskii. Before Pokrovskii, Kliuchevskii revealed the tsar as the 'the chief Merchant in all the Empire', and showed 'class interests', including that of merchant capital, as motivating forces in Russian history.

In his lectures on Russian historiography, it is clear that Pokrovskii saw himself as the inheritor of a rich tradition of Russian historical thought. Vinogradov was not a historian of Russia, and so was not included in these lectures. But his influence on Pokrovskii was strong. Vinogradov's Positivism assumed patterns in history – the belief that all countries pass through the same stages of social development, and that there is a progression towards freedom and democracy. Associated with this belief was the premiss that what drove history forward was not the 'political superstructure' – the State, but the evolution of social and economic forms of organisation.

Already in Pokrovskii's chapters for Vinogradov's *Readings in Medieval History* special attention is paid to the economic dimension of events, and this focus is continued in the chapters he contributed to *Russian History in the XIX Century*. In terms of historical method, there is a smooth transition from Pokrovskii's liberal to his Marxist phase. The challenge of *Russian History from the Earliest Times* was to find an economic explanation that would account for historical phenomena over an extended period of time. For this he uses trade, and, in the modern period – the alteration in grain prices.

In *Study in the History of Russian Culture*, written during his last years of exile and his first months after his return to Russia in 1917, Pokrovskii elaborated his final, and most flexible, economic explanation of historical events – the concept of 'merchant capitalism', and its competition with 'industrial capitalism'. The struggle between the two types of capitalism provides a dynamic that can account for both continuity and change throughout Russian history.

The advantage of the concept of merchant capitalism is that it ties together the different periods in Russian history, so that Pokrovskii's various writings illuminate each other. The *Brief History*, for example, provides the background to the articles on foreign policy, while at the same time echoing many themes from *History of Russia from the Earliest Times*. They are not disparate works, but integral elements of a historical system. In this respect, Pokrovskii can be compared not only with his teacher Kliuchevskii, but also with his erstwhile friend Alexander Bogdanov, who elaborated a materialist system based on the principle of universal organisation.

In his role of Deputy Commissar of Narkompros Pokrovskii contributed greatly to the establishment of early Soviet academic institutions. He inspired the founding of the Socialist (later Communist) Academy, the Institute of Red Professors and the Society of Marxist Historians. He was also involved in the setting up of Istpart, though he subsequently took little part in its activities. These institutions had a profound influence on how history was studied, and written, in the Soviet Union during the 1920s. Because Pokrovskii avoided the more politicised Istpart, and centred his teaching and research in IKP, neither he nor his students produced a substantial history of the 1917 revolution that included an account of the accession of the Bolsheviks to power.

The most significant phenomenon in the development of Soviet historiography, and Soviet ideology in general, was the emergence of 'Leninism' after 1924. One can see from the article that Preobrazhenskii wrote in 1922, describing the status of the Socialist Academy, that he regarded Marxism as 'the official ideology of the victorious proletariat'.[1] Two years later this could no longer be said, as Leninism came to dominate the intellectual life of the country. For whereas Marx's ideas were still in the process of being discovered and disseminated, Lenin's writings were readily available, and easily understood. The adoption of Leninism made it possible for the Soviet regime to have a stable and predictable ideology, which, termed 'Marxism-Leninism', could claim to be a form of Marxism.

Leninism had a deadening effect on Soviet historical writing, discouraging originality and compelling scholars to make their works conform to Lenin's utterances, irrespective of the context in which they were made. Historians' findings had to be justified by quotations from Lenin. Pokrovskii did nothing to oppose this development, but, on the contrary, encouraged it, quoting extensively from Lenin in his own writings, and defending his works with claims that they were Leninist in spirit.

It is unlikely that when Bukharin first launched Lenin as a theoretician in 1924 he had any inkling of the quotation mania he had created. He envisaged that there would emerge a systematiser, who would be able to abstract from the many individual pronouncements that Lenin had made, and come up with a

---

1   Preobrazhenskii 1922, p. 7.

generalisation that could serve as a guide for particular applications. This process of systematisation never took place, and Leninism never got beyond being a collection of quotations.

The most dispiriting aspect of Pokrovskii's biography is his accommodation with Stalinism. He can hardly be viewed as a victim of the Stalinist system, when he did so much to create it. The purging of the Academy of Sciences and the persecution of non-communist scholars place him among the perpetrators of Stalin's crimes. But what was the alternative? He might have resisted the trend, as Riazanov did, but he would then have shared Riazanov's fate, first exile and then death. It is probable that, had Pokrovskii lived a few years more, he too would have become a victim of the purges.[2]

It cannot have been easy for Pokrovskii to witness the dismantling of the institutions he had put in place to ensure that Soviet scholarship would be in no way inferior to the pre-revolutionary system it replaced. He had to serve a regime which had no regard for academic achievement, and even treated Marxist theory, the doctrine it purported to follow, in a cavalier way, altering it to suit Stalin's personal preferences. Stalin's method of rising as an outstanding theoretician was by driving down the intellectual level of the country. In these circumstances, the most Pokrovskii could hope for was the physical survival of himself and his family.

In evaluating Pokrovskii as a historian it is important to realise how little his main historical works were subject to political pressures. His chapters for *Readings in Medieval History*, his *History of Russia in the XIX Century*, his *History of Russia from the Earliest Times*, and the first part of *Study in the History of Russian Culture*, were all written in pre-Soviet times. The constraints upon them were those of tsarist censorship, but this was less stringent after 1905, when these works were written. *Tsarism and Revolution*, and the *Brief History* were published in the relatively free conditions of the early days of the Soviet regime, and they developed themes discussed in earlier works. *Studies in the History of the Revolutionary Movement in the XIX and XX Centuries* was Pokrovskii's attempt to supplement the corresponding section in *History of Russia from the Earliest Times*, and also was written in a period relatively free from political interference. Even Pokrovskii's excursions into diplomatic history in Soviet times build on the article 'Those Responsible for the War', which was

---

2 Many of the historians who were associated with Pokrovskii, both his supporters and his critics, perished in the purges of 1937–38. They included Fridliand, Gorin, Lukin, Piontkovskii, Tatarov, Vanag, Drozdov, Kin, Lomakin, Slepkov, Nevskii, Teodorovich. See Artizov 1994. Among the survivors were Mints, Pankratova, Nechkina, Genkina Baevskii, A.L. Sidorov, Slutskii, Dubrovskii.

written in 1915. Although in the Soviet period Pokrovskii wrote a great many articles, reviews and newspaper items, which do reflect current politics and Soviet ideology, the centre of gravity of Pokrovskii's scholarly output is in tsarist times. His critics were right when they complained that, although Pokrovskii promised to alter his writings to make them conform to Lenin's pronouncements, he never actually did so. Sokolov lists the changes that Pokrovskii made to his *Brief History*, and they are, for the most part, minor. The main body of Pokrovskii's scholarly output represents, therefore, his own scheme of Russian history, independently arrived at, and relatively free from the ideological imperatives that would be characteristic of the Stalin era.

Stalin's letter to *Proletarskaia revoliutsiia* was a watershed in Soviet historiography, ending the structures and relationships of the 1920s, and paving the way for the emergence of his *Short Course* that would become the programmatic text par excellence. It also had far reaching consequences for how the 1917 revolution was perceived, both in the Soviet Union and in the West. By effectively ending Soviet scholarship on 1917, Stalin had ensured that Trotsky's *History of the Russian Revolution* would be challenged by no Soviet competitor. Yet the basic contours of the spontaneous February revolution, the well organised October revolution, the preponderance of Lenin – all have their origins in Soviet historiography. The credibility Trotsky's version achieved, and the impression that it provided an alternative to the Soviet interpretation, contributed to obscuring its early Soviet roots.

News of Pokrovskii's death came to Trotsky when he was in the process of writing his *History of the Russian Revolution*, and the book contains an epitaph on the deceased historian. It reads: 'Having joined the Marxists from the liberal camp when he was already an accomplished scholar, Pokrovskii enriched the most recent historical literature with valuable works and initiatives, though he never completely mastered the dialectical materialist method. It is a matter of simple justice to add that Pokrovskii was a person not only of exceptional erudition and high gifts, but also of profound loyalty to the cause he served'.[3]

---

3 Trotsky 1937b, v.

The Debate between Pokrovskii and Trotsky on the Special Features of Russia's Historical Development

M.N. Pokrovskii, 'Is it true that absolutism "existed in Russia regardless of social development"'? (*Krasnaia nov'* No. 3, May–June 1922)

Comrade Trotsky has done a very good thing in republishing his studies on the history of the first workers' revolution in Russia. Apart from the fact that for the period 1905–07 we have as yet no *handbook* (there are two published by the Mensheviks, but for us they can serve only as collections of materials) of our own, and the main chapters of Comrade Trotsky's book to some extent fill this lacuna – the book is excellent as a work in itself. It was written freshly after the events (some things as early as 1905, and the latest in 1908–09), and it captures all the *atmosphere* of our revolutionary spring. Now you will not be able to write that way, whatever sources you have to hand. The latest handbooks will be fuller from the factual side, being able to impart details that Comrade Trotsky in his time could not have known, tracing the ups and downs of the struggle only from one side of the barricades, but such a poem in prose about 1905 will be beyond them.

If one was to add that here and there in the book there are scattered invaluable details of purely memoir character (such as the priceless picture of the salon revolution in the drawing room of the Baroness Uexküll sketched on page 169–70 of the book), we shall understand that not only for those who are using it for study until such time as a handbook appears, but also for those who will be writing such handbooks, Trotsky's *1905* is indispensable.

The intellectual content of the book is so significant that it will of course be the subject of lengthy debates in the party press. Without depriving oneself of the pleasure of taking part in these debates, the present writer would like to touch upon a question, which from the point of view of the main task of the book might be secondary, yet not lacking in practical pedagogical significance. I repeat, at the risk of boring the reader: the book is a handbook so long as there is nothing to replace it. *It will be studied.* And since we are dealing with an author whose *every* word carries extraordinary weight, every pronouncement of the book will be imprinted on thousands of young minds. And due to the lapidary-artistic style in which the book is written, that impression will be so lasting that it will not be erased by the dozens of books that are written with less artistic talent and by authors who carry less authority.

And here one must say directly: it is good that Comrade Trotsky has republished his studies, but it is not good that he has published them without any excisions. What was useful and even necessary in 1908–1909 for the public abroad, with its boundless ignorance of the Russian past is entirely unnecessary for present-day youth, who have already learnt a thing or two. And there is a danger that they will begin to re-educate themselves: certainly, it would be a simple matter – *Trotsky* said so!

This applies mainly to the introductory chapters, and to the first chapter in particular: 'The social development of Russia and tsarism'. These chapters – and especially the first one – have the aim of imparting the scheme of Russian historical development up to the beginning of the revolution. Like every scheme which is clear and precise, Trotsky's scheme is easily memorised and assimilated. And this is a great pity. Because, firstly, it is not *our* scheme; and secondly, it is *objectively wrong*.

We shall try to prove both of these things.

'The Russian state, having arisen on a primitive economic foundation, collided with state organisations, which had formed on a higher economic basis. Here there opened up two possibilities: the Russian state would fall in the struggle with them, as the Golden Horde had fallen in the struggle with Muscovite tsardom, or it had to *outpace the development of its own economic relations*, swallowing up under external pressure an incomparably greater portion of its vital juices ... In order to stand up to better armed enemies the Russian state was compelled to create industry and technology, to hire military specialists, state money forgers and gunpowder-makers, obtain textbooks on fortifications, establish naval schools, factories privy and real councillors ... As a result of this pressure from Western Europe *the autocratic state* absorbed a disproportionately large share of the surplus product, i.e. it *lived at the expense of the developing privileged classes* and by so doing restricted their development, which was in any case a slow one ... In its aspiration to create a centralised state apparatus, tsarism was obliged not so much to oppose the claims of the privileged estates as to struggle against the barbarity, poverty and disunity of the country, separate parts of which lived completely independent economic lives. *It was not the equilibrium of the economically dominant classes, as was the case in the West, but their social weakness and political impotence which created the bureaucratic autocracy as a self-contained organisation* ... The more centralised the state and the more independent it is of the ruling classes, the more rapidly it is transformed into a self-contained organisation standing above society ...'.[1]

---

1   *1905*, pp. 16–21, *passim*. Our emphasis.

What is this, if not the theory of the *supra-class state*, which Miliukov elaborated without the help of Marxist terminology and Struve with it? Let Trotsky dissociate himself from Miliukov on page 19 (it is symptomatic that he felt the need to do so!): nevertheless, taking up his position he cannot say more about the Kadet historian than that his scheme is 'terrible exaggeration'. An exaggeration of what? Of a mistake or of a basically correct understanding of the Russian historical process? Obviously it is of the latter ...

In fact, what *class* or *classes* did the autocracy represent in Russian history? Not the 'privileged' ones – this is clear from the above quotation: the autocracy stood *above* them. Then, perhaps: the *non*-privileged? But this question is a purely rhetorical one: Trotsky could not adopt the viewpoint of a 'social monarchy'. It means that the autocracy did not represent any class, it stood *above* classes, which is said word for word on page 21 ('the autocratic organisation, standing *above* society').

It is understandable why Kadet historians found it necessary to support the illusion of the *supra-class* Russian autocracy. The supra-class pinnacle of the Russian state presupposed the possibility of a non-class reconstruction of this pinnacle. The autocracy had to be replaced by a constitutional monarchy: but where did classes come in? Where did the proletariat and the peasantry come in? One could dispense with them by making concessions in the 'social' sphere (the 8-hour working day 'where possible', and giving the peasants land for redemption payments). And political power would remain 'supra-class' – that is *bourgeois*.

I repeat, all this integrates splendidly with Kadet policy. But how does this fit in with our calls to the proletariat – to struggle with the bourgeoisie *for power*? How can you take something from the bourgeoisie, when the bourgeoisie doesn't have it? One has to struggle with the bureaucracy, the army, the police, but what is the point of getting tangled with the bourgeoisie? The autocracy certainly lived at its expense ('lived at the expense of the emerging privileged classes and in doing so retarded their development', page 18). This is what the Kadets said against the Bolsheviks: they complicate the struggle, they direct their energy in the wrong direction, they waste it, in short – indirectly, by misunderstanding, they help the absolutism. This is exactly what the Kadets said, completely consistently applying to current politics their historical theory – the supra-class autocracy.

No, this is not our theory. In the past it had one proponent – Plekhanov by name, who followed the same path (and subsequently went much further): at first, in 1905–1907, he began to apply the Kadet theory in practice, and then, in 1913–1914 he used it to interpret Russian history (for readers of the introduction to the *History of Russian Social Thought* the introductory chapters of Trotsky's book will of course sound familiar). We have to struggle against this theory in the most decisive way, no less energetically than we now struggle against religious prejudices. I say more: it is less important to prove that historically Jesus Christ did not exist than to prove that in Russia a supra class state never existed.

In relation to *modern* times the matter is much more favourable than it might appear to the reader of *1905*. Nobody now, not even Kadet historians, would contest the class character of the bourgeois reforms of Alexander II, the anti-bourgeois, i.e. also the class character of the counter-reforms of Alexander III, the class content of the law of 9 November 1906, or the property qualification system of elections to the State Duma. In any case, the great Narodnik authority in the sphere of Russian history, the late V.I. Semevskii, as long as he lived deplored any attempt to attribute a class character to the Decembrists, willingly agreed that the chapters on the peasant reform in the *History of Russia in the XIX Century* (published by Granat)[2] were 'the best concise account' of this subject that existed in Russian literature: and these chapters are written from the most definite class point of view. Now even Miliukov in the latest phase of his development, agrees to recognise as the mainspring of the whole revolutionary movement in Russia the *peasants' struggle for land*: that is, a purely class factor (see the introduction to the second edition of his *History of the Russian Revolution*). And to the class pressure from below corresponded the class pressure from above: if the essence of the revolution was the attempts of the peasants to seize the gentry's land, then the essence of the reaction was obviously expressed in the aspirations to defend the gentry's property. And the organ of reaction, the autocracy, was, consequently, the nobility's class government.

We fear to go on with these truisms – we fear to hear the disapproving voice of Comrade Trotsky declaring that he knows all this perfectly well. Of course he knows it: one cannot imagine a single Marxist agitator, let alone Comrade Trotsky, who would not know it. But what Comrade Trotsky has written is the exact opposite: and there are serious grounds to fear that having read the 'new' theory, rank-and-file agitators will begin to be converted to it ...

But if with the passage of time matters have become favourable with modern history, things are not so simple with the *origins of the Russian autocracy*. This question of the origins of Russian absolutism, is the hook on which the bourgeois historians have caught two remarkably great Marxist fish. They have caught them so easily that the Marxists here, in this question, were completely

2   Written by Pokrovskii [JW].

defenceless before them: because the existing bourgeois books do not of course give a *materialist* explanation for the fact. And they do not give it not even because they deliberately close their eyes to it, conceal the truth, but simply because they themselves look the other way; not evincing the slightest doubt with regard to the dogma of the supra-class state. Nor of course do the bourgeois historians look for an economic basis for the autocracy. They need a political explanation; and they find an entirely satisfactory one, from their point of view, *in the interests of military defence from an external enemy*. Why did Rus' rally round Moscow? It was necessary to defend oneself from the Tatars. Clear and simple.

To the credit of Trotsky's historical taste, he is not satisfied with this banal explanation. 'The struggle against the Crimean and Nogai Tatars called for a great concentration of forces. But, it was of course, no greater than that involved in the Hundred Years' War between France and England. It was not the Tatars which forced Rus' to introduce firearms and form regular regiments of sharpshooters. It was not the Tatars who later forced the creation of cavalry and infantry' (page 16). It seems, one might say here: it was not *military*, i.e. not the *political* interests which lay at the basis, but economic ones; the Muscovite autocracy reflected someone's class interests. But since not a single fact, leading in this direction is adduced by Trotsky in 1909 (Plekhanov in 1913 did have facts – but then his Kadet spurs were so firmly attached to him that he didn't want to see them), that he was completely helpless before Miliukov – his undoubted source in the given question. He only tried to find among the facts which he could find in Kadet historiography those which were most decent from the viewpoint of a Marxist. And he tried to refine somewhat the 'military' hypothesis: not the primitive demands of the struggle with Tatar raiders, but the struggle with *Western* countries forged the military dictatorship of the Muscovite tsar. 'The pressure came from Lithuania, Poland and Sweden'.

But a chain is only as strong as its weakest link. The explanation 'blaming Tatars' was of course very feeble and banal – but *final*. Because the Tatars came to *plunder* Rus' – and only that; here the question of *self-preservation* really arose: it remained only to the bourgeois historians to inflate to infinity this, in itself undoubted, only not very significant fact. But over what did the fight with 'Lithuania, Poland and Sweden begin'? These after all were no steppe raiders? Had they some kind of economic motivation to attack Rus' (let us suppose for a minute that it was they who were the attackers: presently we shall see that it was the other way round)? What motivations? Were they trying to acquire valuable Russian raw materials – coal, oil, iron ore? But excuse me, this was two hundred years before the invention of machines, and nobody was thinking of using coal and oil; equally, nobody suspected that within the borders of Russia there was good iron ore – it was discovered in the Urals much later. So, what were they after?

As far as possible let us make contemporaries speak. Here is one of the foes of Muscovite Russia in the XVI century – Poland. The Polish king Sigismund *explains* to the English queen Elizabeth why Poland has to blockade Narva (the event happened in the midst of the Livonian war between the Moscow tsardom and the Polish-Lithuanian state in 1568):

> ... As we wrote formerly, so we write now to your Highness, that we know and are reliably informed that the enemy of all freedom under heaven, the Muscovite, is becoming stronger by the day by bringing in through Narva various articles, because from there he receives not only goods, but also weapons, which were unknown to him previously, and craftsmen and artists, due to which he grows strong for victory over all other states. It is impossible to put a stop to this as long as there is shipping to Narva.[3]

So, what was the cause of the war between Poland and Russia? For the seaport of Narva. Or more generally speaking, for trading routes. King Sigismund was trying to persuade Elizabeth that were this trading route opened to the Muscovites, this would cause irreparable harm to the 'whole of Christendom' (in those days whatever evil deeds diplomats were plotting, they always referred to the interests of 'all Christendom': just as now they speak about the 'interests of mankind and civilisation'). Tsar Ivan saw things from the opposite point of view (and Elizabeth took his part). Why then did he take up a fight for trading routes?

Let us hear from another contemporary. Some fifty years before the Livonian War Baron Herberstein served as the ambassador of the German Emperor in Russia. He was very interested in this country, which was then as new for Western Europeans, as in the nineteenth century China and Japan were for them, and he left a very balanced description of all that he saw. Since events took place around 1530 it would seem that Herberstein would find among the Muscovites such a 'natural' economy as the orang utans would have at the time: Miliukov assured his readers that as late as the XVIII century the Russian manor was a completely self-contained economic unit. But three hundred years before this the German baron had the chance to experience at first hand the entire

---

3   *The First Forty Years of Relations between Russia and England, 1553–1593. Papers collected and published by Iu. Tolstoi*, pp. 32–3.

bankruptcy of Kadet historiography. 'Usury', he complained, 'is extremely wide-spread: and although they (the Muscovites) call it a great sin, nevertheless nobody refrains from committing it. It reaches unbearable proportions: often one in five, i.e. 20%. The churches, it seems, are not so cruel: they, it is said, charge ten percent'.

Not only is there present a developed money circulation, but already there are felt the obvious advantages of *large-scale* capital: 'churches' – i.e. monas-teries – which operate with much larger sums, take half of what small usurers take. It is just like in Russia at the end of the XIX century: the landowner in the bank received money on the security of his estate at 6–7% while the peasant was given credit by a minor village kulak at 40%.

But, excuse me, the reader will say: usury does not figure in the development of a commodity economy. After all, interest is considered to be a sin, the norm being precisely the natural economy. Let us cite another extract from the same source.

> I asked one boiar (*consiliarium Principis*) to assist me in the purchase of furs, so that I would not be cheated: he at once promised me his help, and then began to drag things out. He wanted to foist his own furs on me; and at the same time traders began to approach him, promising him a reward (!) if he would supply me with their wares at a good price.[4]

Thus, it was not a matter of minor village usury, on which the large-scale cap-ital of the monasteries could develop; there was a market, there were large commercial operations, in which took part the most prominent people of the country, the members of the Boiar duma.

The breadth of these commercial operations, – i.e. their territorial extent: by the sums, the market at that time was of course a hundred times narrower than the one we have now, after the war – we are dumbfounded by the railway network and the new economic geography it has created, which is enough to take your breath away. Who would have thought that Dmitrov (in the Moscow Province) and Viazma could be the centres of *international* exchange? And yet, listen to Herberstein. 'Dmitrov is a town with a fortress, around 12 miles (Her-berstein everywhere counts a German mile as 7 versts) North-West of Moscow. Through flows the river Iakhroma, which flows into the Sestra, and the Sestra flows into the Dubna, which flows into the Volga. Due to such a convenient disposition of the rivers there are many traders who bring their goods from the

---

4 *Rerum Moscoviticarum auctores varii*, pp. 43–4.

Caspian Sea along the Volga and distribute them, without great difficulty, in different directions as far as Moscow'. 'Beside the town of Viazma the river of the same name nearby at a distance of about three versts flows into the Dnieper: whence ships loaded with goods sail down the Dnieper and sail up it to Viazma'. By such a route there went to Lithuania goods from Moscow, and from the fair to Kholop'e, a small town (at the mouth of the Mologa). Herberstein himself travelled along this route, from Orsha through Smolensk, with the baggage of the embassy on vessels to Viazma.[5]

With such a disposition of trading routes it is no wonder that the wooden dishes, which the Kaluga craftsmen made, went abroad, to that very Lithuania. As for the social weighting of Muscovites of the XVI century interested in commerce, there is the anecdote, 40 years later, it happened to the English, who had then opened the route into Russia through the White Sea. 'Before the arrival of Bowes (Elizabeth's ambassador) in Moscow the Dutch Company were concerned to end the commercial advantages given to the English by the Muscovite government, and acquired friends in Moscow – Nikita Romanov (N.B. the ancestor of the Romanov dynasty M P), Bogdan Belskii and Andrei Shchelkalov, because, besides the daily gifts to these tsarist councillors, the Dutch borrowed from them so much money at 25 % interest that they paid each of them 5,000 roubles yearly; but the English merchants did not have a single supporter at court.'[6]

Thus the shareholders in the Dutch Company trading in Russia in the reign of Ivan the Terrible, were the tsar's brother in law, the current favourite of the tsar and minister of foreign affairs. The company – would do credit to a modern 'cultured' state! But the English soon found their feet, and a few years later the shareholders in their company were Boris Godunov – the de facto tsar – and Fedor Ivanovich – the nominal tsar; after this they had nothing to fear from the competition of the Dutch.

When we, in the midst of all this, learn from the most authoritative ecclesiastical preacher of the times that his contemporaries scorned agriculture and thought only of trade, when we hear that another more renowned cleric,

---

5   Ibid, pp. 57 and 52–3.
6   Kliuchevskii, *Foreigners' Tales of the Muscovite State*, 1918 ed. p. 276. The Russian rouble in those days was worth the equivalent of 25 present-day gold roubles. For those interested in the Russian economy of the Muscovite era it is extremely useful to read the chapter on the subject ('Trade') in Kliuchevskii's compilation. It is exactly the reports of foreigners, who came into contact with this economy who are best placed to dispel the myth of the 'primitive economic base', on which it is alleged the Muscovite autocracy emerged. In fact the 'base' was no more 'primitive' than that on which in France there arose the autocratic last direct Capetians (XIII–XIV centuries).

the archpriest Silvester, the tsar's confessor, a kind of Rasputin – only of a less decadent type than our contemporary – regularly organised commercial education, and many of his pupils 'traded in different countries with various commodities' this should not surprise us. It only remains for us to give a few examples, showing how close governmental power was to the commercial world – and how closely the bearers of governmental power followed the affairs of this world.

In 1572 Ivan the Terrible received Elizabeth's ambassador Jenkinson in the Alexandrov Quarter. Complaining about Jenkinson's predecessor Randolph, the tsar said: 'All his talk was about commercial matters and said nothing about our matters. *We know that we have to listen to speeches about trading matters, because they are the support of our state exchequer*; but first it is necessary to see to the affairs of rulers and only then of the merchants'.

For Ivan at this moment a *political* alliance with England was extremely important, and Elizabeth stubbornly kept to the line of 'trading relations'. What he needed was *de jure*, while what she proposed was *de facto*. But Ivan well understood the importance of this 'de facto', as can be seen from his words just quoted and even more from what he said four years later to the next English agent Daniel Silvester. 'We well remember, how profitable for England were the commodities of our country; especially our permission for the English to build houses for the manufacture of ropes (which was forbidden to all other peoples), not only profitable for the merchants, but also advantageous for the whole English State. If we do not meet in the future in our Sister more preparedness than now then all this, and also the other advantages will be taken away, and we shall give this trade to the Venetians and the Germans, from whom the English receive a greater part of those goods which they supply to us'.

If those close to the tsar were shareholders, then the tsar himself was the director of the share-holding company. And when this cunning Moscow kulak, the worthy descendant of Ivan the Moneybags, seized upon the first pretext to attack the disintegrating Livonian Order – and seized a port for himself, and a port on the Baltic Sea at that, this should surprise us even less. The tsar of a trading country – and such was the Moscow State of the XVI century – could not act otherwise.

And in order to carve out trading routes, it was necessary to have an army with firearms, and later infantry and cavalry regiments, in this Trotsky is entirely correct. But he is wrong in tracing all this from the slow economic development and the backwardness of the Moscow State. The matter is not in the backwardness, but in the fact that this was a new country, seized with the development of merchant capitalism, and that it had to carve out for itself a place in the sun, among older, well-established competitors. For this, Russian merchant capital had to forge the country with iron discipline and construct a real dictatorship. The incarnation of this dictatorship of merchant capital was the Muscovite autocracy.

∴

L. Trotsky, 'On the Peculiarities of Russia's Historical Development. (A Reply to M.N. Pokrovskii)', *Pravda* 1–2 July 1922.

I

In No. 3 of *Krasnaia nov'* (May–June 1922) Comrade Pokrovskii published an article devoted to my book *1905*. This article demonstrates – negatively, alas! – what a complicated business it is trying to apply the methods of historical materialism to living human history, to what clichés even extremely well-informed people like Comrade Pokrovskii are sometimes liable to reduce history. The doubts aroused by Comrade Pokrovskii's article start with the title: 'Is it True That Absolutism "Existed in Russia Regardless of Social Development"?' The words 'existed regardless of social development' appear in quotation marks, and in this way it is made to appear that I assert that absolutism *in general* 'existed regardless of social development' and that there falls to Comrade Pokrovskii the rewarding and not very difficult task of restoring common sense on the matter. But in reality, my idea, which gave occasion for this distorted quotation, was that tsarism, having come into complete contradiction with the demands of Russia's social development, continued to exist thanks to the power of its organization, the political insignificance of the Russian bourgeoisie and its increasing fear of the proletariat. In the spirit and sense of the same historical dialectic, we can rightly say, – as was said in the Manifesto of the Communist International – that capitalism now exists regardless not only of the demands of historical development, but also of basic needs of human existence.

Further on, while admitting the usefulness of the publication of my book as a whole, Comrade Pokrovskii energetically objects to the re-issue of its introductory chapter 'Russia's Social Development and Tsarism'. 'What was useful and even necessary – he says – in 1908–1909 for the public abroad, with its boundless ignorance of the Russian past, – is entirely unnecessary for present-day youth, who have already learnt a thing or two'. Comrade Pokrovskii goes on to say that in this introductory chapter I put forward liberal, 'Miliukovist' (literally) views on tsarism as an absolutely self-contained state organization not connected with the exploiting classes. 'This scheme (Trotsky's) firstly, is not our scheme; and secondly, it is objectively wrong. 'And we have to struggle against this erroneous and alien theory no less energetically than we now struggle against religious prejudices'. (!!!). Neat, isn't it? But if I really expounded such monstrous anti-Marxist views in my German book – unnoticed, one might add, by any of the German Marxist reviewers of the book at the time – how could these views have been 'useful' and even 'indispensable' for a foreign public in 1908–09, although one with 'boundless ignorance'? Why could the liberal banalities, so kindly attributed to me by Comrade Pokrovskii, be useful to the German workers 12 years ago – is completely incomprehensible, unless we subscribe to the formula of national peculiarity: 'what is good for a Russian is death to a German'. But even my humble self, who recognises the great peculiarity of our historical development, cannot accept this latter formula. Still less should Comrade Pokrovskii, who, as emerges from his article, believes that the Russian has no such historical peculiarities in comparison with the German.

Comrade Pokrovskii sinks deeper into confusion when he presents matters as if my erroneous theory 'In the past had one proponent – Plekhanov by name, who followed the same path (and subsequently went much further) ...'. Isn't that neat? Here it is not spelt out where exactly I went, but because 'Plekhanov went much further' (on the way to liberalism), the reader is sufficiently prepared for the conclusion already indicated, that it is necessary to struggle against my views on Russian history 'no less energetically than we now struggle against religious prejudices'. What a terrible dream! But it is only a dream, because here we have entered the realm of theoretical and even chronological fantasy. The story seems to be that, first of all, Plekhanov adopted the liberal theory of historical development (for a common bloc with the Kadets), that I then, following him, developed this liberal theory in 1908–1909 for the Germans; that this was not actually harmful, but was even useful (just what the German needed!); but that, since I have now taken to presenting Plekhanov's views to our young workers, for whom Comrade Pokrovskii is the special guardian, he now practically equates me with the Patriarch Tikhon and proposes to wage a 'no less' energetic struggle against me.

All this is confusion, principally chronological. My introductory chapter on the peculiarities of historical development was written, not for the Germans, but first appeared in Russian in my book *Our Revolution* published in Petersburg in 1907 (p. 224). I did the preparatory work for this chapter in 1905 and, later, in 1906 (in prison). It was occasioned by the desire to provide a historical basis and a theoretical justification for the slogan of the seizure of power by the proletariat as opposed both to the slogan of a bourgeois-democratic republic and to that of democratic government of the proletariat and the peasantry. As we see, Plekhanov's Kadetophilia is neither here nor there. In my preface

to Marx's *The Paris Commune* (1906) I formulated the view that the experience of the Commune had a direct significance for the Russian working class,
because the whole preceding development had placed before it the task of seiz-
ing power.[7]

This line of thought evoked great theoretical indignation on the part of a
large number of comrades, more exactly, the vast majority of them. Those
who expressed this indignation were not only Mensheviks, but also Comrades
Kamenev and Rozhkov (then a Bolshevik). Their point of view, in broad outlines, was as follows: The political rule of the bourgeoisie must precede the
political rule of the proletariat: the bourgeois democratic republic must be a
prolonged historic schooling for the proletariat; the attempt to jump over this
stage is adventurism; if the working class in the West has not yet conquered the
power, how can the Russian proletariat set itself this task? etc., etc. From the
point of view of this spurious Marxism, which feeds itself on historical clichés,
formal analogies, converting historic epochs into a logical succession of inflex-
ible social categories (feudalism, capitalism, socialism, autocracy, bourgeois
republic, dictatorship of the proletariat) – from this point of view the slogan
of the conquest of power by the working class in Russia must have seemed a
monstrous departure from Marxism. However, a serious empirical evaluation
of the social forces as they appeared in 1903–05 powerfully suggested the entire
viability of a struggle for the conquest of power by the working class. Is this a
peculiarity or is it not? Does it assume profound peculiarities in the whole historical development or does it not? How did it come about that such a task
arose before the proletariat of Russia – that is, the most backward (with Pokrovskii's permission) country in Europe? And in what consists the backwardness of Russia? Merely in the fact that Russia is belatedly repeating the history
of the western European countries? But in that case would it be possible to talk

---

7 'Social democracy', the 'Preface' states, 'must be, and wishes to be, the conscious expression
   of an objective development. But since, at a certain moment of the revolution, the objective development of the class struggle confronts the (Russian) proletariat with the alternative
   between assuming the rights and obligations of state power and surrendering its class position, the social-democratic party regards the seizure of state power as its next immediate task.
   In doing so it by no means ignores the objective processes of development of a deeper nature,
   processes of growth and concentration of production; but it says that, since the logic of the
   class struggle, which in the last analysis is based on the progress of economic development,
   impels the proletariat towards the dictatorship of the proletariat before the bourgeoisie has
   'exhausted' its economic mission (it has hardly begun its historical mission), this means only
   that history is placing colossally difficult tasks on the proletariat. It may be that the proletariat will be worn out by the struggle and will fall under the weight of its tasks; it may be. But
   it cannot refuse those tasks for fear of class disintegration or of the whole country falling into
   barbarism' (Marx: *The Paris Commune*. 1906 Edition. Preface, pp. X–XI).

of a conquest of power by the Russian proletariat? This conquest, however (we permit ourselves to remember), was actually made. What does the essence of this consist in? In the fact that the indubitable and incontestable belatedness of Russia's development under the influence and pressure of the higher culture from the West, results not in a simple repetition of the West European historic process, but in the creation of profound peculiarities demanding independent study. This is how the question was posed. And it is *our* way of posing it, despite the fact that Comrade Pokrovskii calls it '*not our*' way.

It is perfectly true that a few years later (in 1914) Plekhanov formulated a view of the peculiarities of Russia's historical development which came very close to the one put forward in the above-mentioned chapter of the book *Our Revolution*. In this connection Plekhanov quite rightly dismisses both the doctrinaire Westerner-Slovophile and the Narodnik-Slavophile schematic divisions, and, instead, reduces Russia's 'special character' to the actual, materially determined peculiarities of its historical development. It is fundamentally wrong to claim that from this Plekhanov made, or could make with any semblance of logic, any compromising conclusions (in the sense of forming a bloc with the Kadets, etc.). The weakness of the Russian bourgeoisie, and the bourgeois democracy that the Russian bourgeoisie has abandoned its claim to, represents an undoubted and very important peculiarity of Russian historical development. But it was exactly from this – given the other historical conditions – that there followed the possibility and the necessity for the proletariat's conquest of power. It is true that Plekhanov did not draw this conclusion. But then neither did he draw the conclusion from another of his unquestionably correct propositions, that: 'The Russian revolutionary movement will triumph as a workers' movement, or it will not triumph at all'. If we connect everything that Plekhanov said against the Narodniks and the vulgarisers of Marxism with his Kadetophilia and his patriotism, then nothing of Plekhanov remains. In fact, much remains of Plekhanov, and it does no harm to learn some things from him ....

That production lies at the basis of the historical life of every society; that from this production classes and their groups emerge; that on the foundations of the class struggle the State is formed; that the State is the organ of class oppression – these ideas were no mystery to me in 1905, or to my opponents. Within these limits Russian history is subordinated to the same laws as the history of France, England and any other country. In this regard the peculiarities of Russia's historical development do not figure. If tsarism is the weapon of the propertied, exploiting, classes, and does not differ in this sense from all the other State organisations, it does not at all mean that the correlation of forces between the autocratic power (monarchy, bureaucracy, army and the other organs of compulsion), on the one hand, and the nobility and bourgeoisie, on the other, was the same in Russia as in France, Germany or England. This profound uniqueness of our political situation, which led to the victorious October revolution before the beginning of the proletarian revolution in Europe, had its roots in the peculiar correlation of forces between the different classes and the State power. When Comrades Pokrovskii and Rozhkov argued with the Narodniks or liberals, saying that the organisation and policies of tsarism were determined by the economic development and the interests of the possessing classes, they were basically right. But when Pokrovskii tries to repeat this against me, he is simply wide of the mark.

Comrade Pokrovskii's thought is gripped in a vice of rigid social categories which he puts in place of live historical forces. He substitutes for the relative, i.e., historically conditioned and socially limited independence of the autocracy from the ruling classes, some kind of absolute independence, thus transforming tsarism into a mere form without content. And then, having ascribed to me this kind of depiction of tsarism, he writes: 'But how does this fit in with our calls to the proletariat – to struggle with the bourgeoisie for power? How can you take something from the bourgeoisie when the bourgeoisie doesn't have it?' etc. Comrade Pokrovskii poses the question thus: either the bourgeoisie had *all* the power, or it had no power *at all*. If it had no power, then how could we 'take away' power from the bourgeoisie? And if we took power from the bourgeoisie, then how can we say that it did not have power? Such a posing of the question is neither historical, materialist, or dialectical. It does not even pass the test of formal logic. Even if you accept that the bourgeoisie in Russia had no power, the proletariat could struggle for power exactly in order that it should not be gained by the bourgeoisie. But of course, there was no such formalist alternative. The bourgeoisie did not possess the entirety of power, but was only just becoming familiar with it. This familiarisation was not complete. The course of events, i.e. first of all the military defeat and the pressure from below caused the gap between the autocracy and the bourgeoisie to widen. The monarchy fell into this gap. The bourgeoisie tried to come to power wholly and directly (March 1917). But power was seized by the working class, with the support of the peasant army (October 1917). In this way the result of our *belated* historical development in the conditions of full-blooded imperialism in Europe was that our bourgeoisie did not manage to push out tsarism before the proletariat had become an independent revolutionary force.

But for Comrade Pokrovskii the question which is at the centre of our investigations does not even exist. In his review of a book by Vipper (in the same issue of *Krasnaia nov'*) Comrade Pokrovskii writes: 'To portray the Moscow Rus' of the sixteenth century on a background of general European relations of that time is an extremely alluring enterprise. There is no better way to refute the prejudices prevailing until now, even in Marxist circles, about the alleged "primitiveness" of those economic foundations upon which the Russian autocracy arose'. And further: 'To present this autocracy in its real historic connections, as one of the aspects of commercial-capitalist Europe ... that is an undertaking not only of extraordinary interest to the historian, but also of extraordinary educational importance for the reading public: there is no more radical way of putting an end to the legend of "peculiarities" of the Russian historic process'. This is all a dig at us! As we see, Comrade Pokrovskii flatly denies the primitiveness and backwardness of our economic development and in doing so, relegates the peculiarities of the Russian historic process to the sphere of legend. The trouble is that Comrade Pokrovskii is completely hypnotized by the relatively wide development of Russian trade in the sixteenth century, a fact which both he and Rozhkov noticed. It is difficult to understand how Comrade Pokrovskii could have fallen into such an error. Anyone might think that trade is the foundation and the infallible criterion of economic life. About twenty years ago the German economist Karl Bücher tried to find in trade (the path between producer and the consumer) the criterion of all economic development. Struve, naturally, hastened to transfer this 'discovery' to Russian economic 'science'. Bücher's theory was, quite naturally, energetically refuted by Marxists at the time. We seek the criteria of economic development in production – in technology and the social organization of labour – and we regard the path travelled by the product from the producer to the consumer as a secondary phenomenon whose roots are to be found in the self-same production.

However paradoxical it may sound from the viewpoint of the Bücher-Struve criterion, the great (at least in the spatial sense) expansion of Russian trade in the XVI century is to be explained precisely by the extraordinary primitiveness and backwardness of the Russian economy. The West-European town was dominated by artisanal corporations and trade guilds. Our towns, on the other hand, were primarily administrative-military centres, and were thereby centres of consumption rather than of production. The artisanal guild life of the West was formed at a relatively high level of economic development, when all the basic processing industries had separated themselves from agriculture, transformed themselves into independent trades, created their own organizations, their centres (the towns) and their own, initially limited (local, regional), but nevertheless a stable market. Thus the medieval European town was based on a relatively advanced differentiation of the economy which gave rise to regular relations between the centre – the town – and its agricultural periphery. Our economic backwardness, however, found its expression first and foremost in the circumstance that handicraft, which did not separate from agriculture, retained the form of cottage industry. In this respect we are closer to India than to Europe, just as in the Middle Ages our towns were closer to Asiatic than to European ones, and our autocracy stood between European absolutism and Asiatic despotism, being closer in many respects to the latter.

Given the boundless expanse of our territory and the sparseness of the population (surely another quite objective indication of backwardness?) the exchange of products presupposed the intermediate role of merchant capital on the widest scale. Such a scale was possible precisely because the West was far more developed than ourselves, had a wide variety of complex needs, sent us its merchants and its goods and by so doing advanced the exchange of goods in Russia itself on the basis of Russia's extremely primitive and in many respects barbarian economic relations. Not to see this, the greatest peculiarity of our historical development, means not to see our whole history.

My Siberian boss (I spent two months entering poods and arshines in his ledger), IakovAndreevich Chernykh – this was not in the XVI century, but at the very beginning of the XXth – had practically unlimited dominion within the limits of Kirensk district, through his trading operations. He bought up furs from the Tungus, bought in the parish contributions in kind from the priests of more remote districts, imported calico from the Irbitsk and Nizhnii-Novgorod market, and above all supplied vodka (at that time the vodka monopoly had not yet been introduced in Irkutsk province). Iakov Andreevich was illiterate, but a millionaire (in the way 'zeros' were counted in those days, but not now). His dictatorship, as a representative of merchant capital, was indisputable: he never said anything other than 'my little Tunguzes'. The town of Kirensk, like Verkholensk and Nizhne-Ilimsk, was a residence of sheriffs and magistrates, kulaks in hierarchical dependence one upon another, all kinds of officials, and a few wretched artisans.

I never found any organised artisanal activity there as a basis of urban economic life – no corporation holidays, no guilds, although Iakov Andreevich was officially listed as a 'merchant of the second guild'. Really, this living piece of Siberian reality leads us to a much better understanding of the historical peculiarities of Russian development than what Pokrovskii says on the subject. It really does. The trading operations of Iakov Andreevich extended from the mid-reaches of the Lena to its eastern tributaries, to Nizhnii-Novgorod and even Moscow. Few Western European trading firms can register such distances on their business maps. Yet this merchant dictator, this 'king of clubs' in the language of the Siberian farmers, was the most perfect and convincing incarnation of our economic backwardness, our barbarity and primitiveness, the sparseness of our population, the dispersion of our peasant villages, and our dirt roads which form impassable marshy blockades for two months every spring and autumn in our counties, districts and villages, our universal illiteracy, etc. And Chernykh had risen to his trading prominence on the basis of this Siberian (mid-Lena) barbarism because the West – 'Rasseia', 'Moscow' – was taking Siberia on tow, creating an amalgam of a primitive nomadic economy with an alarm clock made in Warsaw.

II

Craft corporations formed the foundation of medieval urban culture which also radiated into the countryside. Medieval science, scholasticism, the Reformation all grew out of artisanal trade. This was not the case in Russia. Certainly, one can find the shoots, the symptoms, the signs, but in the West these were not just indications, but powerful economic-cultural formations with an artisan-corporation base. It was on this foundation that the medieval European town came into being, grew, and entered into conflict with the church and the feudal lords, deploying against the latter the hand of the monarchy. This same city created the technical premises for standing armies in the shape of firearms. Can one say – though perhaps it contradicts the class theory of the state? – that the monarchy in Western Europe became increasingly independent of the first estate as the towns grew and their antagonism with the feudal lords increased? In the last analysis, of course, the kingly power continued to remain an organisation of force over the toiling masses, first of all over the enserfed peasants. But surely there is a difference between state power, which amalgamates with the landowner, and power which separated from it, which creates its own bureaucratic apparatus, gathers a great force into its hands, i.e., protects the interests of exploiters against the exploited, becomes itself (as the kingly power, the bureaucracy, the standing army) an independent force – not absolutely independent of course, but relatively independent, being the primary one among other dominant forces.

But where were our craft-corporation towns which even remotely resembled those of Western Europe? Where was their struggle against the feudal lords? And did any struggle of the industrial and commercial town with the feudal lords form the basis for the Russian autocracy? The very nature of our towns precluded any such struggle taking place, just as it precluded a Reformation. Is this a peculiarity or is it not? Our crafts remained at the stage of cottage industries, i.e. they did not separate themselves from peasant agriculture. The Reformation remained at the stage of a peasant sect, because it did not find leadership on the part of the towns. Primitiveness and backwardness here cry out to the high heavens, but Comrade Pokrovskii doesn't want to hear them. And tsarism too arose as an independent (again relative, within the confines of the struggle of living historical forces on an economic base) state organisation not thanks to the struggle of mighty towns with mighty feudal lords, but despite the complete industrial anaemia of our towns, thanks to the anaemia of our feudal lords.

Poland by its social structure stood between Russia and the West, just as Russia stood between Asia and Europe. The Polish towns knew corporate artisan trades to a far greater extent than Russian ones did. But they didn't manage to raise themselves enough to help the royal power to break the hold of the feudal lords. State power remained directly in the hands of the nobility. The result was the total impotence of the state and its collapse. If there are no 'peculiarities' there is no history, but only a pseudo-materialist geometry. Instead of studying the living and changing material of economic development, it is sufficient to notice particular signs and fit them to ready-made stereotypes. Such a primitive way of study is sufficient in the struggle with Narodnik or liberal prejudices, not to mention Slavophilism ('in everything it has a different character') but completely inadequate for explaining the actual paths of Russia's historical development.

What has been said of tsarism applies to capital and the proletariat: it is incomprehensible why Comrade Pokrovskii should direct his ire only at my first chapter, which talks about tsarism. Russian capitalism did not develop from handicraft through manufacture to the factory, because European capital, first in the form of merchant, and then in the form of finance and industrial capital, inundated us at a time when most Russian artisanal trade had not yet separated itself from agriculture. Hence the appearance in Russia of the most modern capitalist industry in a primitive economic environment: a Belgian or American factory, and around it dirt roads and villages built of straw and wood, which burn down every year, and so on. The most primitive beginnings and the most modern European endings. Hence the enormous part played by Western European capital in Russia's economy. Hence the political weakness of the Russian bourgeoisie. Hence the ease with which we were able to settle accounts with the Russian bourgeoisie. Hence the difficulties which followed when the European bourgeoisie intervened in the affair, when the former owners of mills and factories talked to us at Genoa and The Hague through Lloyd George and Barthou and others.

And our proletariat? Did it pass through the school of medieval apprentice fraternities? Does it have the age-old tradition of the guilds? It has nothing of the kind. It was thrown right into the factory boiler, taken straight from the plough. I remember, an old friend of mine, Korotkov, a joiner from Nikolaev, wrote (in 1897) 'The Proletarians' March', which began with the words: 'We are the alpha and the omega, the beginning and the end ...' That's it exactly! The first and the last letter, with the middle ones missing. Hence the absence of conservative traditions, the absence of caste in the proletariat itself, revolutionary freshness, hence, taken together with other reasons, October, the first workers' government in the world. But hence too – the illiteracy, the backwardness, the lack of habits of organisation, system in work, cultural and technical upbringing. We feel all these minuses at every step in our economic and cultural construction.

European communism has to overcome an incomparably more conservative environment – both external, in the state, and internal, within the proletariat itself; but when it succeeds, it will command incomparably more powerful objective and subjective resources for its work of construction. Is this a peculiarity or is it not? The very necessity of posing such a question in the summer of 1922 seems to us to be ... a 'peculiarity' too far, but it too, no doubt, stems from our historical development: we took power first, the tasks facing us were colossal, cultured forces were few, people had to fragment themselves into a thousand pieces, there was no time to think. And that is why Comrade Pokrovskii, in talking about new and very complex problems, puts forward old arguments, which were of value in other connections and at another logical level, but which become the very opposite of Marxism, in so far as they are given the character of an absolute stereotype.

I have pointed out how much our development has been influenced by the circumstance that on our western frontiers we constantly came into contact with states that were more developed, better organized and technically better armed than ourselves. A backward society more directly and more strongly experiences the influence of stronger neighbouring enemies through the mediacy of military organisation and military technique. Under this pressure the autocracy reformed itself, establishing sharpshooting regiments, and then a cavalry and an infantry. In this regard, Comrade Pokrovskii remarks: 'It seems, one might say here: it was not military, i.e. not the political interests which lay at the basis, but economic ones; the Muscovite autocracy reflected someone's class interests'. It is hard to understand here what he means by contrasting military and political interests to economic ones. When economic interests are defended by the state they always acquire the character of political aims and tasks. And when they have to be defended, not by diplomatic means, but by force of arms, they become military tasks.

Comrade Pokrovskii tries to prove that the interests which were dominant in the politics of the autocracy in the XVI century were those of merchant capital. The way Comrade Pokrovskii presents this question has, in my opinion, something in the nature of a caricature. But to this narrower and more specialised question we hope to return on another occasion. For the present we shall say only that in constructing a merchant capitalist Russia in the XVI century, Comrade Pokrovskii falls into the error committed by the German professor Eduard Meyer, who discovered capitalism in ancient society. Meyer, no doubt, correctly noted the schematic simplification of the previously dominant view (of Rodbertus and others) on the economic structure of Greece and Rome, which saw it as a series of self-contained natural-economic cells (*oikos*). Meyer showed that these basic cells were connected in a rather developed commodity circulation, both with each other, and with foreign countries. At the same time there was also observed in some areas and sectors the phenomenon of mass production. Applying the economic relationships and concepts of the present day, Meyer constructed retrospectively a Graeco-Roman capitalism. His error consisted in the fact that he did not appreciate the quantitative and thereby also the qualitative relationships of the different elements in the economy: the *oikos*-type, a simple commodity economy and the capitalist system. Such, I repeat, is basically the same error that Comrade Pokrovskii made. But for the moment this is not the essence of the question for us. Let us suppose that the interests of merchant capital really were the dominant ones in the policy of the autocracy in the XVI century, and that the autocracy was the 'dictatorship of merchant capital'. But for trading objectives, which, of course, corresponded to the economic interests of particular classes, the autocracy struggled in Persia, in Turkey, in the Baltic area, in Poland, and in relations with more distant Western countries. This struggle acquired the character of military conflicts. It is completely beside the point who was the attacker and who was the defender (a question raised needlessly by Comrade Pokrovskii, who falsely ascribes to me the idea that the autocracy only 'defended' Russia from external attack). It was in these military confrontations, which of course implied the implementation of political aims, arising from economic interests, that the Russian state came into conflict with the military organisations of Western nations, standing on a much higher economic, political and cultural level.

Thus, Russian capital at its first steps collided with the much more developed and powerful capital of the West and fell under its domination. Thus too the Russian working class in its first steps found a ready-made weapon, forged by the experience of the Western European proletariat: Marxist theory, the trade-union, the political party. Anyone who explains the nature and politics of the autocracy only by the interests of the *Russian* possessing classes forgets that besides the more backward, poorer, more ignorant exploiters of Russia, there were the richer, more powerful exploiters of Europe. The possessing classes of Russia had to encounter the hostile or semi-hostile possessing classes of Europe. These encounters took place through the mediacy of the state organisation. The autocracy was such an organisation. The whole structure and the whole history of the autocracy would have been different if there had been no European towns, European gunpowder (because it wasn't us who invented it), if there had been no European stock exchange. In the final period of its existence the autocracy was not only the organ of the possessing classes of Russia, but also the organisation of the European stock exchange for the exploitation of Russia. This dual role again endowed it with very significant independence. A vivid illustration of this independence was the fact that the French stock exchange, in order to support the Russian autocracy, granted it a loan in 1905 against the will of the parties of the Russian bourgeoisie.

In essence, there is one small fact which demolishes Comrade Pokrovskii's historical conception without trace. This fact is the recent imperialist war and the part played in it by tsarism.

From Comrade Pokrovskii's point of view the matter is very simple: tsarism was the state form of the dominant bourgeoisie, which had entered the imperialist stage of development. In this sense, tsarism did not differ from the republican-parliamentary regime in France, from the imperialist-parliamentary monarchy in England, etc. etc. And this is true. But it is true within the bounds of the broadest approach to the question – within the bounds of struggle with the social-patriotic and pacifist prejudices, with the criteria of defence and attack, and so on. But it is completely insufficient (and therefore *untrue*) for evaluating the role in the war of Russia, England, Germany, of each country taken separately, of those internal changes, which each of them was subject to, of those revolutionary perspectives which opened up before each of them, all of which determines the approach that we should take to every country involved.

Despite the fact that as far back as 1904–1905, tsarism in the war with Japan, showed itself to be unsustainable, the bourgeoisie was reconciled to it, fearing the proletariat. The self-sufficiency of tsarism, in the crudest forms of the self-sufficiency, in the Rasputin era, by no means contradicts the class theory of the state, and is in fact explained by it. Only, however, this theory should be applied not mechanically, but dialectically. But things do not end there: tsarism was smashed by the imperialist war. Why? Because the level of its productive bases was too low to support it (its 'primitiveness'). As regards military technology, tsarism tried to develop according to the most advanced models. In this it was helped in every way by its richer and more enlightened allies. Thanks to this tsarism had at its disposal the most highly perfected weapons of war. But it did not have and could not have the means of reproducing these weapons and transporting them (and also personnel) on railway lines and waterways with sufficient speed. In other words, tsarism was defending the Russian possessing classes in the international struggle, supported by a more primitive economic base than its enemies and allies.

During the war tsarism exploited this base ruthlessly, that is, it consumed a much greater percentage of the national product and national income than its powerful enemies and allies. This fact was confirmed, on the one hand, in the system of war debts, and, on the other, by the complete ruination of Russia. Or does Comrade Pokrovskii doubt this?

All these circumstances, which directly set the scene for the October revolution, the victory of the proletariat and its subsequent difficulties, cannot at all be explained by Comrade Pokrovskii's platitudes about a supra-class state never having existed, and that it is through the mediacy of state power that the exploiting classes expressed and still express their will. That is hardly Marxism – it is only its first letter. And that is where Comrade Pokrovskii would have us stop.

From the peculiarities of our historical development, whose existence Comrade Pokrovskii denies, came for the proletariat not the denial (in retrospect?) of the class struggle, but the seizure of state power and the struggle to keep it in its hands. But from these same peculiarities have emerged the enormous international and internal economic difficulties following the accession to power. The understanding of these peculiarities is the best insurance for the new generation of the proletariat against passivity in face of difficulties, against pessimism and scepticism. Presenting historical development in terms of platitudes cannot teach anybody anything.

28 June 1922

∵

M.N. Pokrovskii, 'The Peculiarity of the Russian Historical Process and the First Letter of Marxism: Something in the Nature of a Reply to Comrade Trotsky', *Pravda*, 5 July 1922

In reply to a short journal article about 1905 (*Krasnaia nov'*, 1922, issue 3, May–June) Trotsky placed in *Pravda* two enormous essays, taking up one and a half times the space of my article ('On the Peculiarities of Russia's Historical Development', issues for 1 and 2 July).

The size of the reply alone testifies that not all is well with it. 'When they want to give you a lashing they don't hang about.' For such a master of style as Comrade Trotsky two hundred lines would have been sufficient to give a lashing to such a luckless opponent. If he needed to write two thousand lines, that means that things are bad – bad for the theory whose defence Comrade Trotsky was careless enough to undertake in 1907, and from which, we hasten to add, he has obviously already distanced himself at the present moment.

At the present moment – as I shall try to prove it in my text below – Comrade Trotsky stands almost entirely on our, i.e. the general Marxist position on this question. If not entirely, then it would seem only because in the short span of time between reading my article and writing his essays he didn't manage to familiarise himself with the factual side of the matter. When he finds the leisure to do this our positions will come even closer together, and we will acquire one more defender of the materialist interpretation of the Russian historical process, and a brilliant defender at that.

I am physically unable to reply to Comrade Trotsky in such detail as he replied to me. To wait until such an opportunity arises would take at least three weeks, yet the accusations made against me by the respected author of *1905* are too grave to ignore. I must therefore try, for now, albeit in brief, to parry at least the most important of them. Comrade Trotsky intends to continue the polemic – I hope on the pages of the same *Krasnaia nov'* in which it began, and from which, perhaps, it should never have strayed. Then I too will find the time to answer in detail and 'point by point'. For now, I repeat, – I am only dealing with the main issues.

What the chief accusation was the reader will of course have already guessed, because it is assumed by the guiding principle of the polemic. And Trotsky 'has given a salute to classicism': I – am not a Marxist. It is true that the non-Marxist company chosen for me is not just any one: in the first essay I appear between Bücher and Struve, in the second one I am held to be in the orbit of Eduard Meyer. It is true too that in another place I am dubbed a 'vulgariser' of Marxism, and in the third place it is declared that in my 'platitudes' I fall short of Marxism – they were only its 'first letter'. Struve – is, as it were, not the first, but the last letter in the Marxist alphabet, something in the nature of a superfluous one. One must add that nobody has fought more against Struvism in Russian historiography than I have. All the corresponding chapters of *Russian History from the Earliest Times* and *Study in the History of Russian Culture* are substantial refutations of Struve's approach to the question of the ending of feudalism in Russia – an approach which, alas! is quite close to what is said on page 25 of *1905*.

But I do not intend to hide either behind my past services, or the contradictions of Trotsky's article. I suggest Trotsky open *Capital* volume I at Chapter XXIV ('So-Called Primary Accumulation') and would be so good as to read the following passages (whether they are 'platitudes' or not is a matter of taste):

'But the Middle Ages had handed down two distinct forms of capital, which mature in the most different economic social formations, and which, before the era of the capitalist mode of production, are considered as capital quand même – usurer's capital and merchant's capital (page 774)'.

'The discovery of gold and silver in America, the extirpation, enslavement and entombment in mines of the aboriginal population, the beginning of the conquest and looting of the East Indies, the turning of Africa into a warren for the commercial hunting of blackskins, signalised the rosy dawn of the era of capitalist production. These idyllic proceedings are the chief moments of primitive accumulation. On their heels treads the commercial war of the European nations, with the globe for a theatre. It begins with the revolt of the Netherlands from Spain, assumes giant dimension in England's Anti-Jacobin War, and is still going on in the opium wars against China, etc. The different moments of primitive accumulation distribute themselves now, more or less in chronological order, particularly over Spain, Portugal, Holland, France, and England. In England at the end of the 17th century, they arrive at a systematical combination, embracing the colonies, the national debt, the modern mode of taxation, and the protectionist system. These methods depend in part on brute force, e.g., the colonial system. *But they all employ the power of the State, the concentrated and organised force of society*, to hasten, hothouse fashion, the process of transformation of the feudal mode of production into the capitalist mode, and to shorten the transition. Force is the midwife of every old society pregnant with a new one. It is itself an economic power (page 775)'.

'Today industrial supremacy implies commercial supremacy. In the period of manufacture properly so called, it is, on the other hand, the commercial supremacy that gives industrial predominance. Hence the preponderant rôle that the colonial system plays at that time. It was 'the strange God' who perched himself on the altar cheek by jowl with the old Gods of Europe, and one fine day with a shove and a kick chucked them all of a heap. It proclaimed surplus value making as the sole end and aim of humanity. Here originated the system of state loans and credit (page 778)'.

So then did those phenomena which Marx treats on these pages of *Capital*, occur only in 'Spain, Portugal, Holland, France and England', or did they take place in Russia too? Was the 'colonial system' applied only in countries with a hot climate and a coloured population, or can one envisage it in the conditions of the Siberian Taiga or the North Russian marshes? Was it necessary for this system that ostriches should roam the steppes, rhinoceroses should wander in the forests, or was it sufficient that there should be foxes, sables and ermines?

Trotsky himself gives an exhaustive answer to this in his example from his Siberian reminiscences of Iakov Andreevich Chernykh. This Siberian merchant, who 'bought up furs from the Tungus, bought in the parish contributions in kind from the priests of more remote districts, imported calico from the Irbitsk and Nizhnii-Novgorod market, and, above all, supplied vodka' gives us as vivid an illustration of Russian 'primitive accumulation', of the Russian 'colonial system' in its early stages, as one could wish for.

Siberia, which lagged behind central Russia for centuries, preserved, as it were, on purpose for the historian, Muscovite, and even pre-Muscovite Rus'. With the help of a Siberian 'sketch' N.A. Rozhkov at one time explained the mysterious 'boundary oak tree' of *Russkaia Pravda*. Chernykh makes an appearance now, as if on cue, to convince the most sceptically inclined that merchant capital of Moscow Rus' of the xvi–xvii centuries is no fantasy. 'Iakov Andreevich was illiterate, but a millionaire (in the way "zeros" were counted in those days, but not now)'. In what way was he inferior to the Stroganovs, his distant social predecessors? Trotsky is right when he says that 'this living piece of Siberian reality leads us to a much better understanding of the historical peculiarities of Russian development than what Pokrovskii says on the subject'. It goes without saying that one historical fact is far more convincing than dozens of arguments by historians. These historical facts help us escape from the captivity of the Miliukovs and Co., as they, in their time, helped Marx escape from the captivity of bourgeois political economy.

Nevertheless, historians are not helpless, in so far as they can connect some facts with others, and reflect upon them. In this case Chernykh did not remind Trotsky of the Stroganovs, but he did remind me. Trotsky saw around this 'king of clubs' 'police constables and police inspectors', not recalling Marx's words about how the methods of primitive accumulation 'employ the power of the State, the concentrated and organised force of society, to hasten, hothouse fashion, the process of transformation of the feudal mode of production into the capitalist mode,' and did not notice that for the existence of dozens and hundreds of Chernykhs with their means of making gains it was necessary to have 'the administrative, military and financial power of absolutism', which 'power' finds here a full and exhaustive explanation of its class significance. There is no need to go further. Trotsky saw one thing: Chernykh was illiterate, the 'little Tunguz' were dirty – hence these are all the signs of 'backwardness'. Backwardness compared with what? With the modern Chernykhs of European life or with the previous incarnations of the Chernykh life represented by the 'little Tunguzes'? Was the concentration of capital in millions of units a step forward for Siberia?

Trotsky is wrong in thinking that I disagree with him when he convincingly concludes his first article: 'And Chernykh had risen to his trading prominence on the basis of this Siberian (mid-Lena) barbarism because the West – 'Rasseia', 'Moscow' – was taking Siberia on tow'. He hadn't read my article well enough –

it contains enough convincing examples of how the West, in the XVI century, in the shape of Dutch and English capital, took contemporary Russia 'on tow'. Of course, it was only necessary to tow it – a tugboat tows a barge, and not an empty space. Contact with Western Europe in the most powerful way stimulated, encouraged the development of our merchant capitalism: but if this contact had not been preceded by indigenous accumulation, Russia would have been a mere colonial country, similar not even to India (which also had its own accumulation), but to Central Africa. That Russia's development, in type, is that of a colonial country is exactly one of my heresies, and now I shall produce documentary proof – but I must protest against exaggeration in this direction. The phenomenon of a colonial Russia did not exist. Yet if one believes what Trotsky relates about the 'extreme primitiveness and backwardness of the Russian economy', then it would be a complete historical conundrum why it was that Russia was not turned into a colony? Why was it that the Europeans did not simply, with their bare hands, take over these economically naked people, but had to subordinate them with the help of the complicated apparatus of state credit (an apparatus, being part of the 'colonial system' according to Marx), thereby taking the risk of that unpleasantness which overtook them in October 1917, and with the consequences that they have not resolved until the present time? Here Chernykh, having created the indigenous apparatus of 'organised social force', played a 'national' role – and not for nothing, depicted by the sculptor as Minin, he to the present day stands in front of the Kremlin, pointing imperiously at his construction.

But the question of 'more' or 'less' – is nevertheless one of degree. Having recognised that the West's pressure on Russia was, in the first instance, an economic pressure, Trotsky has made a big step in the direction of the materialist explanation of Russian history, going far in advance of Plekhanov (in whose *History of Russian Social Thought* there is not a hint of this economic pressure for the ancient period), and even in advance of what he wrote in *1905*. There, on page 20, it is clearly stated: 'In the pre-capitalist era, the influence of Europe on the Russian economy was, of necessity, limited. The natural, consequently the self-contained, character of the Russian national economy (!) protected it from the influence of higher forms of production'. And for Trotsky, the 'pre-capitalist' era lasted to the reign of Nicholas I, consequently, neither in the reign of Ivan the Terrible, nor even of Peter the Great, can there be any suggestion of the economic influence of the West on Russia. To avoid any unnecessary argument, I now make a reservation: I did not quote these words of Trotsky in my first article because I thought them a slip of the pen. But the author of such cruel articles against me does not make slips of the pen – his whole conception is completely alien.

We find this conception in a more condensed form in the second article.

'Russian capitalism did not develop from handicraft through manufacture to the factory, because European capital, first in the form of merchant, and then in the form of finance and industrial capital, inundated us at a time when most Russian artisanal trade had not yet separated itself from agriculture. Hence the appearance in Russia of the most modern capitalist industry in a primitive economic environment: a Belgian or American factory, and around it dirt roads and villages, built of straw and wood, which burn down every year, and so on. The most primitive beginnings and the most modern European endings. Hence the enormous part played by Western European capital in Russia's economy. Hence the political weakness of the Russian bourgeoisie. Hence the ease with which we were able to settle accounts with the Russian bourgeoisie'.

These are lines that I subscribe to whole-heartedly. I do so for the simple reason that a year and a half ago I wrote practically the same thing, but drawing from them a conclusion that I don't know if Trotsky would agree with.

'In fact, Russia is an exceptionally valuable example in methodological terms of the swift growth of a capitalist society on an extraordinarily primitive social-economic base. Prejudices about the slowness of Russia's historical development are based on a one-sided observation of the pre-capitalist period of this development. It is completely true that, influenced by mainly geographical factors, the growth of the surplus product in connection with this growth of the primitive accumulation took place in Russia with great slowness. But once it got going, Russian capitalism, supported by all the successes in technology and organisation that Western capitalism had achieved by this time, took enormous strides, with amazing speed creating new forms of economic life, and forming new ideologies, while by the start of the xx century Russia had not finally "caught up with" Europe in this respect'.

'In the political sphere the distinctness of the basic lines of progress is partly blurred by the co-existence within the bounds of a single territory and the intertwining of two stages of capitalist development – merchant and industrial ... In the purely cultural sphere that same distinctness of the basic lines is disturbed by another co-existence – that of the primitive base of Russian capitalism, which has been mentioned previously, and the developed forms of the latter. The hen-house of the peasant stands directly alongside the magnificent example of European architecture in the shape of the landowner's dwelling. The crudest methods of handicraft work, only able to find parallels in Central Africa or New Guinea – side by side with the factory, all the lathes of which are driven by electricity. This existence of the "primitive" and the "last word in science and technology" strongly reinforced the prejudice about the "backwardness" and "slow development" of Russia, compared with Western countries. The function of the teacher is, using examples from the lives of colonial countries, to show the pupils that this, on the contrary, is one of the signs of a catastrophically swift development of capitalist Russia, which did not know those gradual transitions, that are characteristic of the old, cultured countries of the West, England or France for example'.[8]

The last sentence might surprise a reader by its conversion – I hasten to add that the quotation is taken from the explanatory note to *A Model Programme on History for the Second Grade*. In unexpected places one sometimes has to express one's theoretical views ... The content of my sentence leads us to the central question of the whole discussion: how a proletarian revolution was possible in Russia.

But this question is so great and important that to debate it at the end of a newspaper article would not be appropriate. Here we really have the 'common ground' of Marxism in its application to Russian history, but our historical literature is so contaminated by the anti-Marxist Kadet nonsense that one will have to go on about this common ground for a long time, just as in his day Chernyshevskii had to go on about his ABC. These of course are the first letters of Marxism, but what can you do if the public at large have still not taken them in?

∴

L. Trotsky, 'A Steamer is not a Steamer but a Barge', *Pravda*, 7 July, 1922.

Comrade Pokrovskii termed the article which he wrote against me yesterday 'something in the nature of a reply to comrade Trotsky'. In truth, it was 'something in the nature' ... It was no reply.

1) Comrade Pokrovskii explained at great length that had I been right, I should have expressed myself more briefly: my article was one and a half times longer than his. I confess, Mikhail Nikolaevich, that I did not measure it. However, my literary observations have convinced me that it is much easier to go astray in a short article than to come at the truth in a long one.

2) Comrade Pokrovskii declared the idea of Russia's primitive economic nature to be a myth, and repeated this sharply, definitely, after the fashion of a schoolmaster, without any reservations. What he wrote in his last article is completely contradictory. Why does comrade Pokrovskii ask me whether the development of merchant capitalism was a step forward or a step backwards

---

8   *A Model Programme on History for the Second Grade*. 1920, pp. 39–41.

in comparison with what went before? I do not understand. This, moreover, is obviously something from the old repertoire, from the times of the struggle against Narodism. So, what is the conclusion? Comrade Pokrovskii's conclusion is that Russia was backward – but (!) it was backwardness compared with 'European conditions', and not with the conditions in Russia before the existence of merchant capital. Well, there you are! It is the first time I knew that one could speak of the backwardness of the XVI century as compared ... with the XV. Of course, we are referring to the comparison between Russia of the XVI and other centuries with its contemporary Western Europe. In his review of my book comrade Pokrovskii (*Krasnaia nov'* No. 3, p. 150, note) refutes the idea of Russian backwardness by the fact (or, to be more accurate, with his contention, since it is not really a fact), that the Russian economy in the XVI century was no more primitive than the French economy of the XII–XIV centuries. How then is one to define backwardness?! In the last analysis all peoples are descended from the apes. Russian economic development in the XVI century was at no lower a level of development than the European economy in the XIII. Agreed. But this, after all, is a backwardness of three centuries. Tsarist power in the XVI was, one must suppose, forced to reckon, not with state organisations of the XIII century, but incomparably higher developed ones. What followed from this? An enormous intensification of the forces of the Russian economy, the absorption by tsarism of the greater share of the national income than took place in the West. Hence there was a different relationship of forces between the state organisation and the ruling classes – in favour of the state organisation. Without an understanding of this 'different' alignment of forces it is impossible even now to comprehend the October revolution, just as it would have been more impossible *to foresee it in its internal social mechanism almost two decades ago*.

3) The rhythm of our economic development was slower as a result of natural causes, but the presence of Europe forced development to accelerate, this pressure being most decisively felt through the military apparatus (the Petrine era, the reforms of Alexander II, 1905, 1914–1917). Did we catch up with Europe? No, we were far from doing that. As a result of this, economic development acquired a sharply contradictory character: throughout there was an accumulation of monstrous extremes, the very great antagonism between the town and the country, etc. In this lies our 'peculiarity'.

4) And in recent times? Comrade Pokrovskii said in his last article (quoting himself): 'The existence of both the elementary and the last words of science had led to the strengthening of the prejudice about the backwardness and the slow development of Russia as compared with Western countries'. Again 'prejudices'. But for backwardness there exist some objective criteria: *the productivity*

of labour. If Comrade Pokrovskii agrees to regard Russia as a national-economic whole, then, it appears, that here, on the eve of the war, it was several times lower than in the leading capitalist countries. Therefore, Russia continued to remain an economically backward country. But on the basic background of this backwardness, under the stimulus of the West, there were created, as I have shown in my book, highly qualified economic formations of enormous significance for the total development of our country. And on the basis of a high type of capitalist development the proletariat developed, and its ideology was formed – a fact of decisive political importance for the destiny of Russia.

5) But here there is something unexpected: 'That Russia's type of development is that of a colonial country is precisely one of my heresies ...' So that in his 'heresies' comrade Pokrovskii affirms exactly the opposite of what he says in his 'orthodoxy'. *A colonial development is the development of backward countries.* How can one call Russia's backwardness a legend and a prejudice and at the same time recognise Russia's type of development to be colonial?!

6) But the point is that Comrade Pokrovskii, having admitted the colonial type, thereupon protests against 'exaggeration in this direction'. He even admits that Europe had us on tow. So: now you see, it has come out: there was no backwardness, but we had to be towed. However, Comrade Pokrovskii consoles us and himself with the thought: if we were on tow, that means that there was a 'barge and not just an empty space'. But why should *backwardness* have to mean an *empty space*? And if Russian development was so primitive, continues Comrade Pokrovskii, 'why then was Russia not formally turned into a colony?' This question is of a purely rhetorical nature, and, in any case, it is misdirected. I have answered this in sufficient detail. To be precise, in the first chapter of the book *1905* I pose the question in a different form: either the Russian state had to fall in the struggle with states of a higher organisation or she had to concentrate drastically the economic forces of the nation. My answer is this: 'For the first eventuality Russian national economy was already *not sufficiently primitive.* The state did not crumble, but began to grow in face of the great concentration of the people's economic resources (page 16)'. Therefore, I did not at all exaggerate. I did not only not deny the existence of a 'barge', but in every way took it into account. I denied only the *identification of a barge with a steamer.*

7) All the remainder of what Comrade Pokrovskii said in his article is, unfortunately, only 'something in the nature'. It is incomprehensible what the quotations from Marx are supposed to demonstrate, or the confused references to authors, the distortion of my exact indications of the inaccuracy of economic development in general, the formless discussions on Struvism, and the not quite felicitous aphorisms about the Kadets. Comrade Pokrovskii began by calling the conception of Russia's retarded and unique economic development

a *legend*. But he ends thus: a steamer – is not a steamer, but nevertheless we had a barge. One could well stop here: the combination of a steamer and a barge made it possible to get us through October; perhaps this picture will enable us to get to historical truth as well.

L. Trotsky

∵

M.N. Pokrovskii, 'I conclude …' *Pravda*, 13 July 1922.

As punishment for my failure to give an exhaustive reply to his article, Trotsky decided not to answer me at all. In fact, in his last remark ('A Steamer is not a Steamer, but a Barge', *Pravda* for 7 July) there is not a word about my article, unless you count the couple of contemptuous lines at the end saying, 'It is incomprehensible what the quotations from Marx are supposed to demonstrate'. (! It would be clear to any reasonable person that the essence of my reply to Trotsky is in these quotations. Or does he want to imply by this that he is completely familiar with these quotations without my mentioning them? In this I have not the slightest doubt, but he did not have the right to suppose that all the readers of *Pravda* know Marx by heart.)

To show that I am a courteous and decent person, I am prepared to follow Trotsky's example – and also say nothing about his new article. So much the more so since there is nothing to say. When Trotsky with extraordinary thoroughness proves that Russia was not at the head, but at the tail of the economic development of Europe, I do not know with whom he is arguing; it is certainly not with me. When he assures us that his 'supra-class' scheme led him not only to the understanding, but also to the prediction of the October revolution, this is also his personal affair. In itself there is nothing improbable, that, starting from false premisses, people accidentally arrive at objectively valuable results: starting from false calculations of Toscanelli, Columbus set out to find a route to India – and discovered America. But, I think, Columbus did not get angry with the people who pointed out that Toscanelli was a poor mathematician. At least I haven't read anywhere that he did.

In any case, Trotsky ends with a categorical assertion that he did not deny the existence of 'the barge' (that is, merchant capital of Muscovite Russia?), he 'did not only not deny the existence of "the barge", but in every way took it into account. I denied only *the identification of a barge with a steamer*' (Comrade Trotsky's emphasis).

That is, Trotsky denied that the Muscovite 'primitive accumulation' went ahead of the Western European! But this is again a complete waste of energy.

It never occurred to anybody to doubt that in Moscow there were no Medicis, no Fuggers, and that all the 'profiteers' in the time of Peter the Great could not hold a candle to a single Colbert. What is important is that in Moscow comparable phenomena, although in a more primitive form, also existed, – and that precisely by them, and not by 'natural, hence the self-contained character of the Russian economy' it is necessary to explain such facts as the 'emergence of the Russian state' (more exactly – 'the Muscovite autocracy', because of course we are not interested in Riurik and his brothers).

But in the question of 'primitiveness' Comrade Trotsky is prepared, as it were, to make his scheme more precise, and now stresses that in his old characterisation of the Muscovite state he had presented it as 'not sufficiently primitive'.

If all this means that we are on the way to 'getting to historical truth' – good luck! I am completely prepared 'to end on this', as far as our newspaper polemic is concerned at least. But I reserve the right at some time, not in the form of a newspaper article, but in a more substantial format, to explain to those interested how the 'supra-class' scheme came about, the scheme which played in Trotsky's historical disquisition the same role as did the calculations of Toscanelli. This is exactly the obligation of a Russian Marxist historian. In a very elementary form this obligation has already been discharged, and even twice (in one of my essays which appeared in Trotsky's old paper *Bor'ba* in 1914,[9] and in the supplementary chapter of part II of *Brief History of Russia*). But it will do no harm to examine such a subject in more detail.

---

9   See Pokrovskii 1914a.

Bibliography

Alatortseva, A.I. 1979, *Zhurnal "Istorik-marksist", 1926–1941 gg*, Moscow: Nauka.

Alatortseva, A.I. and G.D. Alekseeva 1971, *50 let sovetskoi istoricheskoi nauki: Khronika nauchnoi zhizni, 1917–1967*, Moscow: Nauka.

Aleksandrov, M.S. 1919, *Gosudarstvo, biurokratiia i absoliutizm v istorii Rossii*, Moscow: Kommunist.

Artizov, A.N. 1992, 'Nikolai Nikolaevich Vanag (1899–1937 gg.)', *Otechestvennaia istoriia*, 6: 95–109.

Artizov, A.N. 1994, 'Sud'by istorikov shkoly M.N. Pokrovskogo (seredina 1930-kh godov)', *Voprosy istorii*, 7: 34–48.

Artizov, A.N. 1998a, 'M.N. Pokrovskii: final kar'ery – uspekh ili porazhenie?', *Otechestvennaia istoriia*, 1: 77–96.

Artizov, A.N. 1998b, 'M.N. Pokrovskii: final kar'ery – uspekh ili porazhenie?', *Otechestvennaia istoriia*, 2: 124–143.

Barber, John 1981, *Soviet Historians in Crisis, 1928–1932*, London: Macmillan Press in association with Centre for Russian and East European Studies University of Birmingham.

Bazarov, V.A. 2019, *Productive Labor and Labor that Generates Value: Translated and Introduced by David G. Rowley*, Alden, Michigan: Independently Published.

Berkman, Alexander 1989, *The Bolshevik myth: (Diary 1920–1922)*, London: Pluto.

Black, Cyril E. (ed.) 1956, *Rewriting Russian History: Soviet Interpretations of Russia's Past*, New York, F.A. Praeger.

Bogdanov, A. 1990, *Voprosy sotsializma: Raboty raznykh let*, Moscow: Izd-vo politicheskoi lit-ry.

Bogdanov, A. 2020, *Empiriomonism: Essays in philosophy*, Leiden, Boston: Brill.

Brandenberger, David 1998, 'Who killed Pokrovskii? (the second time): The prelude to the denunciation of the father of Soviet Marxist historiography, January 1936', *Revolutionary Russia*, 11, 1: 67–73.

Brandenberger, David and M.V. Zelenov (eds.) 2019, *Stalin's master narrative: A critical edition of the History of the Communist Party of the Soviet Union (Bolsheviks): short course*, New Haven, London: Yale University Press.

Bukharin, N.I. 1924, 'Lenin kak marksist', *Vestnik Kommunisticheskoi akademii*, 7: 22–68.

Bukharin, N.I. 1936, 'Nuzhna li nam marksistskaia istoricheskaia nauka?: (O nekotorykh sushchestvenno vazhnykh, no nesostoiatel'nykh vzgliadakh M.N. Pokrovskogo)', *Izvestiia*, 27 January.

Bukharin, N.I. 1971, *Economics of the Transformation Period: With Lenin's Critical Remarks*, New York: Bergman.

Buryshkin, P.A. 1954, *Moskva kupecheskaia*, New York: Izd-vo im. Chekhova.

Byrnes, Robert F. 1995, *V.O. Kliuchevskii, Historian of Russia*, Bloomington: Indiana University Press.

Byvshii student 1896, 'Besporiadki 1894–95 v moskovskom universitete', *Materialy dlia istorii russkogo sotsial'no-revoliutsionnogo dvizheniia*.

Chagin, B.A. and V.I. Klushin 1975, *Bor'ba za istoricheskii-materializm v SSSR v 20-e gody*, Leningrad: Nauka Leningr. otd-nie.

Chernobaev, A.A. 1992, *"Professor s pikoi", ili tri zhizni istorika M.N. Pokrovskogo*, Moscow: Lit.

Corney, Frederick C. 2004, *Telling October: Memory and the Making of the Bolshevik Revolution*, Ithaca, N.Y., London: Cornell University Press.

Corney, Frederick C. (ed.) 2016, *Trotsky's Challenge: The "Literary Discussion" of 1924 and the Fight for the Bolshevik Revolution*, Leiden, Boston: Brill.

David-Fox, Michael 1997, *Revolution of the Mind: Higher Learning among the Bolsheviks, 1918–1929*, Ithaca N.Y.: Cornell University Press.

Dekrety sovetskoi vlasti: vol. 13 1989, Moscow: Politizdat.

Desnitskii, V. 1940, *M. Gorky: Ocherki zhizni i tvorchestva*, Leningrad: Goslitizdat.

'Disput o knige D.M. Petrushevskogo', 1928, *Istorik-marksist*, 8: 79–128.

Dolgorukov, P.D. and I.I. Petrunkevich 1905, *Politicheskii stroi sovremennykh gosudarstv: Sbornik statei*, St Petersburg: Tip. Slovo.

Drozdov, P. 1936, 'Reshenie partii i pravitel'stva ob uchebnikakh po istorii i zadachi sovetskikh istorikov', *Istorik-marksist*, 1: 9–22.

Druzhinin, N.M. 1967, *Vospominaniia i mysli istorika*, Moscow: Nauka.

Dubrovskii, S.M. 1929, *K voprosu o sushchnosti "aziatskogo" sposoba proizvodstva, feodalizma, krepostnichestva i torgovogo kapitala*, Moscow: Izd. Nauchn. assotsiatsii vostokovedeniia.

Dushchenko, E.S. 2010, 'A.V. Shestakov i stanovlenie istoricheskogo obrazovaniia v vuzakh SSSR', *Vestnik voronezhskogo gosudarstvennogo universiteta*, Seriia istoriia politologiia sotsiologiia, 2: 92–96.

Elizarova, A.I. 1930, 'Retrospektivnyi vzgliad na Istpart i na zhurnal "Proletarskaia revoliutsiia"', *Proletarskaia revoliutsiia*, 5: 156–158.

Emmons, Terence 1973, 'The Beseda Circle, 1899–1905', *Slavic Review*, 32, 3: 461–490.

Enteen, George M. 1980, *The Soviet Scholar-Bureaucrat: M.N. Pokrovskii and the Society of Marxist Historians*, University Park, PA: Penn State University Press.

Enteen, George M., Tatiana Gorn, and Cheryl Kern 1979, *Soviet historians and the study of Russian imperialism*, University Park, London: Pennsylvania State University Press.

Esina, A.V. 1993, 'Pervye shagi bol'shevistskoi diplomatii', *Vestnik rossiiskoi akademii nauk*, 2: 152–163.

Esina, A.V. 1996, 'Mne zhe oni sovershenno ne nuzhny': Sem' pisem iz lichnogo arkhiva M.N. Pokrovskogo', *Vestnik rossiiskoi akademii nauk*, 2: 103–114.

Fisher, H.A.L. 1927, *Paul Vinogradoff: A Memoir*, Oxford: The Clarendon press.

Fitzpatrick, Sheila 1970, *The Commissariat of the Enlightenment: Soviet Organization of Education and the Arts under Lunacharsky October 1917–1921*, Cambridge: Cambridge University Press.

Genkina, E.B. 1984, 'Vospominaniia ob IKP', *Istoriia i istoriki*: 258–273.

Getzler, Israel. 1967, *Martov: A Political Biography of a Russian Social Democrat*, Melbourne: Melbourne U.P.

Gindin, I.F. 1929, 'K spornym voprosam istorii finansovogo kapitala v Rossii', *Istorik-marksist*, 12: 47–90.

González, John 2017, *An Intellectual Biography of N.A. Rozhkov: Life in a Bell Jar*, Leiden, Boston: Brill.

Gorelov, I.E. 1990, *Bol'sheviki: Dokumenty po istorii bol'shevizma s 1903 po 1916 god byvshego Moskovskogo Okhrannogo Otdeleniia*, Moscow: Izd-vo polit. lit-ry.

Gorin, P.O. 1926, 'Chronicle', *Istorik-marksist*, 1: 317–319.

Gorin, P.O. 1930, 'K voprosu o kharaktere revoliutsii 1905 g.', *Istorik-marksist*, 20: 164–173.

Gorin, P.O. 1933, *M.N. Pokrovskii – bol'shevik-istorik: Sbornik statei o M.N. Pokrovskom*, Minsk: Tip. Belorusskoi Akademii nauk.

Got'e, Iurii Vladimirovich 1988, *Time of Troubles: The Diary of Iurii Vladimirovich Got'e, Moscow, July 8, 1917 to July 23, 1922, translated, edited, and introduced by Terence Emmons*, London: Tauris.

Govorkov, A.A. 1976, *M.N. Pokrovskii o predmete istoricheskoi nauki*, Tomsk: Izdatel'stvo Tomskogo universiteta.

Govorkov. A.A. and A.A. Chernobaev (eds.) 1993. *Bibliografiia proizvedenii akademika M.N. Pokrovskogo*, Moscow, AIA.

Gukovskii, A.I. 1965, 'Kak ia stal istorikom', *Istoriia SSSR*, 6: 76–99.

Gukovskii, A.I. 1968a, 'Kak sozdavalas' "Russkaia istoriia s drevneishikh vremen" M.N. Pokrovskogo', *Voprosy istorii*, 8: 120–132.

Gukovskii, A.I. 1968b, 'Kak sozdavalas' "Russkaia istoriia s drevneishikh vremen" M.N. Pokrovskogo', *Voprosy istorii*, 9: 130–142.

Gukovskii, A.I. and O.V. Trakhtenberg 1934, *Istoriia epokhi feodalizma: Uchebnik dlia srednei shkoly: 6–7 gody obucheniia*, Moscow: Gos. uchebno-pedagog. izd-vo.

Holmes, Larry E. 2021, *Revising the Revolution: The Unmaking of Russia's Official History of 1917*, Bloomington: Indiana University Press.

Iakovlev, Ia.A. 1922, *Ob istoricheskom smysle Oktiabria*, Moscow: Krasnaia nov'.

Iakovlev, Ia.A. 1927, 'Fevral'skie dni 1917 g.', *Izvestiia*, 10 March.

Iakushevskii, A.S. 1976, *Propagandistskaia rabota bol'shevikov sredi voisk interventov v 1918–1920 gg.*, Moscow: Nauka.

Iaroslavskii, E.M. (ed.) 1929, *Istoriia VKP(b): Vol. 4*, Moscow-Leningrad: Giz.

Iaroslavskii, E.M. (ed.) 1935, *Piatyi s"ezd RSDRP: Mai-iiun' 1907 goda*, Moscow: Partizdat.

Institut marksizma-leninizma pri TsK KPSS 1983, *KPSS v rezoliutsiiakh i resheniiakh s"ezdov, konferentsii i plenumov TsK (1898–1986)*, Moscow: Politizdat.

Istoriia vsesoiuznoi kommunisticheskoi partii (bol'shevikov): Kratkii kurs, 1938, Moscow: Gos. Izd-vo.

Ivanova, L.V. 1968, *U istokov sovetskoi istoricheskoi nauki. (Podgotovka kadrov istorikov-marksistov v 1917–1929 gg.)*, Moscow: Mysl'.

Kaganovich, L.M. 1932, *Questions Concerning the History of Bolshevism: A Symposium*, Moscow: Co-operative publishing society of foreign workers in the USSR.

Kaiurov, V.N. 1923, 'Shest' dnei fevral'skoi revoliutsii', *Proletarskaia revoliutsiia*, 1(13): 157–170.

Kheraskov, Ivan 1952, 'Reminiscences of the Moscow Students' Movement', *Russian Review*, 11, 4: 223–232.

'Khronika. Rezoliutsiia fraktsii obshchestva istorikov-marksistov po dokladu t. Knorina "O politicheskikh urokakh t. Stalina i zadachakh istoricheskogo fronta"' 1932, *Istorik-marksist*, 1: 213–214.

Kin, D.Ia. 1927, 'Semnadtsatyi god v izobrazhenii t. A. Shliapnikova', *Istorik-marksist*, 3: 40–55.

Kin, D.Ia. 1929, 'Vpered' in *Bol'shaia sovetskaia entsiklopediia*, Moscow: Sovetskaia entsiklopediia.

Kin, D.Ia. 1931, 'O proletarskoi revoliutsii, burzhuaznykh restoratorakh, i melkoburzhuaznom likvidatorstve', *Istorik-marksist*, 21: 19–37.

Kizevetter, A.A. 1974, *Na rubezhe dvukh stoletii: Vospominaniia, 1881–1914*, Cambridge: Oriental Research Partners.

Kliuchevskii, V.O. 1866, *Skazaniia inostrantsev o moskovskom gosudarstve*, Moscow: Universitetskaia tipografiia.

Kliuchevskii, V.O. 1867, *Khoziaistvennaia deiatel'nost' Solovetskogo monastyria v Belomorskom krae*, Moscow: Universitetskaia tipografiia; (Katkov i Ko).

Kliuchevskii, V.O. 1871, *Drevnerusskie zhitiia sviatykh kak istoricheskii istochnik*, Moscow: Soldatenkov.

Kliuchevskii, V.O. 1902, *Boiarskaia duma drevnei Rusi*, Moscow: Sinodal'naia tipografiia.

Kliuchevskii, V.O. 1990, *Sochineniia v deviati tomakh: Stat'i*, Moscow: Mysl'.

Knorin, V. 1932, 'Za bol'shevistskuiu partiinost' v istoricheskoi nauke', *Bor'ba klassov*, 1: 22–31.

Koenker, Diane 1981, *Moscow Workers and the 1917 Revolution*, Princeton, N.J.: Princeton University Press.

Komarov, N.S. 1958, 'Sozdanie i deiatel'nost' Istparta: (1920–1928 gg.)', *Voprosy istorii KPSS*, 5: 153–165.

Koniushaia, R.P. (ed.) 1952, *Arkhiv Marksa i Engel'sa: XII*, Moscow: Gospolitizdat.

Kosarev, V.M. 1922, 'Partiinaia shkola na ostrove Kapri', *Sibirskie ogni*, 2: 63–75.

Kuznetsov, I.V. and A.V. Shumakov 1968, *Bol'shevistskaia pechat' Moskvy*, Moscow: Moskovskii Rabochii.

Lapina, I.A. 2010, 'Zhmu serdechno ruku. Predannyi Vam, Trotskii', *Terra Humana*, 4, 17: 47–59.

Lagno, A.P. 2009, 'Fakul'tet obshchestvennykh nauk Moskovskogo universiteta kak shkola podgotovki spetsialistov dlia sovetskogo gosudarstvennogo apparata', *Uchenye trudy fakul'teta gosudarstvennogo upravleniia*, 7: 297–311.

Larina, A.M. 1989, *Nezabyvaemoe*, Moscow: APN.

Lebedev-Polianskii, P.I. (ed.) 1918, *Protokoly pervoi vserossiiskoi konferentsii proletarskikh kul'turno-prosvetitel'nykh organizatsii: 15–20 sentiabria 1918 g.*, Moscow: Proletarskaia kul'tura.

Lemke, M.K. 1923, 'Review of L.B. Kamenev, *Mezhdu dvumia revoliutsiiami* (Moscow, 1923)', *Krasnaia letopis'*, 7: 435.

Lenin, V.I. 1921, 'Pis'ma V.I. Lenina 1917 g.', *Proletarskaia revoliutsiia* 10: 94–114.

Lenin, V.I. 1958a-65, *Polnoe sobranie sochinenii*: vol. 16, Moscow: Gospolitizdat.

Lenin, V.I. 1958b-65, *Polnoe sobranie sochinenii*: vol. 34, Moscow: Gospolitizdat.

Lenin, V.I. 1958c-65, *Polnoe sobranie sochinenii*: vol. 41, Moscow: Gospolitizdat.

Lenin, V.I. 1958d-65, *Polnoe sobranie sochinenii*: vol. 47, Moscow: Gospolitizdat.

Lenin, V.I. 1958e-65, *Polnoe sobranie sochinenii*: vol. 48, Moscow: Gospolitizdat.

Lenin, V.I. 1958f-65, 'Primechanie k stat'e M.N. Pokrovskogo' in *Polnoe sobranie sochinenii*: vol. 11, p. 177, Moscow: Gospolitizdat.

Levin, Kirik 1906a, 'Politicheskie i sotsial'nye vozzreniia Dekabristov' in *Tekushchii moment: Sbornik*, Moscow: Tip. A.P. Poplavskago.

Levin, Kirik 1906b, 'Vooruzhennoe vosstanie v Moskve: Dni 7–19 dekabria 1905 g.' in *Tekushchii moment: Sbornik*, Moscow: Tip. A.P. Poplavskago.

Levshin, B.V. 1974, 'U istokov zhurnala *Istorik-marksist*', *Voprosy istorii*, 6: 97–107.

Livshits, S.I. 1924, 'Kapriiskaia partiinaia shkola (1909 g.)', *Proletarskaia revoliutsiia*, 6(29): 33–73.

Lukashev, A.V. 1973, *Letopis' geroicheskikh dnei, 1917: Khronika vazhneishikh istoricheskopartiinykh i revoliutsionnykh sobytii v Moskve i Moskovskoi gubernii*, Moscow: Moskovskii rabochii.

Lutskii, E.A. 1965, 'Razvitie istoricheskoi kontseptsii M.N. Pokrovskogo' in *Istoriia i istoriki: Istoriografiia istorii SSSR: Sbornik statei*, edited by M.V. Nechkina, Moscow: Nauka.

Maretskii, G. 1926, 'K voprosu ob evoliutsii samoderzhaviia', *Bol'shevik*, 5: 86–97.

Maurer, Georg Ludwig von 1854, *Einleitung zur Geschichte der Mark-, Hof-, Dorf- und Stadtverfassung und der öffentlichen Gewalt*, Munich: Kaiser.

McMeekin, Sean 2011, *The Russian Origins of the First World War*, Cambridge, Mass.: Belknap Press of Harvard University Press.

Medem, Vladimir Davidovich and Samuel A. Portnoy 1979, *Vladimir Medem: The life and soul of a legendary Jewish socialist*. Ed. & Tr. By Samuel A. Portnoy, N.Y.: Ktav Pub. House.

Medvedev, Roy 1989, *Let History Judge: The Origins and Consequences of Stalinism*, Oxford: Oxford University Press.

Mehring, Franz 1966, *Gesammelte Schriften*: vol. 15, Berlin: Dietz.

Mertsalov, A.N. (ed.) 1991, *Istoriia i stalinizm*, Moscow: Politizdat.

Mif, P. (ed.) 1934, *Strategiia i taktika Kominterna v natsional'no-kolonial'noi revoliutsii*, Moscow: Izd. In-ta MKh i MP.

Miliukov, P.N. 1955, *Vospominaniia (1859–1917)*, New-York: Izd. im. Chekhova.

Mints, I.I. 1928, 'Marksisty na istoricheskoi nedele v Berline i VI mezhdunarodnom kongresse istorikov v Norvegii', *Istorik-marksist*, 9: 85–96.

Molotov, V.M. and I.V. Stalin 1936, 'Postanovlenie TsK VKP(b) i SNK Soiuza SSR', *Pravda*, 27 January: 2.

Morokhovets, E. 1939, 'Krest'ianskaia reforma 1861 g. v osveshchenii M.N. Pokrovskogo' in *Protiv istoricheskoi kontseptsii M.N. Pokrovskogo: Sbornik Statei*, Akademiia Nauk SSSR Institut istorii, Moscow-Leningrad: Izdatel'stvo Akademii Nauk SSSR.

Morozova, A.Iu. 2020, *'Neleninskii bol'shevizm' A A. Bogdanova i 'Vperedovtsev': Idei, al'ternativy, praktika*, Moscow-St Petersburg: Nestor Istoriia.

Myhre, Jan Eivind, '6th International Congress of Historical Sciences Oslo 1928', available at: https://ichs2020poznan.pl/en/the-4th-congress-in-london-2-2.

Na boevom postu marksizma: Stenogramma torzhestvennogo zasedaniia, posviashchennogo 60-letiiu so dnia rozhdeniia i 35-letiiu nauchnoi deiatel'nosti M.N. Pokrovskogo 1929, Moscow: Izd-vo Kommunisticheskoi akademii.

Nechkina, M.V. 1922, *Russkaia istoriia v osveshchenii ekonomicheskogo materializma: Istoriograficheskii ocherk*, Kazan: Gos. izd-vo.

Nechkina, M.V. 1974, *Vasilii Osipovich Kliuchevskii: Istoriia zhizni i tvorchestva*, Moscow: Nauka.

Nechkina, M.V. 1990, 'Vopros o M.N. Pokrovskom v postanovleniiakh partii i pravitel'stva 1934–1938 gg. o prepodavanii istorii i istoricheskoi nauke: (k istochnikovedcheskoi storone temy)', *Istoricheskie zapiski*, 118: 232–246.

Nevskii, V.I. 1925, *Ocherki po istorii Rossiiskoi Kommunisticheskoi Partii*, Leningrad: Priboi.

Nevskii, V.I. (ed.) 1930, *Diskussiia o 'Narodnoi vole': Stenogrammy dokladov V.I. Nevskogo, I.A. Teodorovicha, I.L. Tatarova i prenii po dokladam, s prilozheniem tezisov Kul'tpropa TsK VKP(b) o piatidesiatiletii 'Narodnoi voli'*, Moscow: Izd-vo Kommunisticheskoi akademii.

Nikulenkova, E.V. 2015, 'Struktura i rukovodstvo Instituta krasnoi professury v 1920-e gody', *Vestnik Leningradskogo gosudarstvennogo universiteta imeni A.S. Pushkina*, 4, 3: 158–164.

Ol'minskii, M.S. 1906, '"Gruppa narodovol'tsev" (1891–1894 g.)', *Byloe*, 11: 1–27.

Ol'minskii, M.S. (ed.) 1921, *Ot gruppy Blagoeva k 'Soiuzu bor'by' (1886–1894)*, Rostov on Don: Gosizdat.

Ol'minskii, M.S. 1923, 'Ot Istparta', *Proletarskaia revoliutsiia*, 10: 267.

Ol'minskii, M.S. 1930, 'Vozniknovenie Istparta i zhurnala *Proletarskaia revoliutsiia*', *Proletarskaia revoliutsiia*, 5: 154–155.

Ostroukhova, K.A. 1967, 'O rabote v Istparte', *Voprosy istorii KPSS*, 6: 92–99.

Pankratova, A.M. 1932, 'M.N. Pokrovskii – bol'shevistskii istorik', *Bor'ba klassov*, 4: 20–35.

Pankratova, A.M. 1939, 'Razvitie istoricheskikh vzgliadov M.N. Pokrovskogo' in *Protiv istoricheskoi kontseptsii M.N. Pokrovskogo: Sbornik Statei*, Akademiia nauk SSSR Institut istorii, Moscow-Leningrad: Izdatel'stvo Akademii nauk SSSR.

Pashukanis, E.B. 1928, 'Nedelia sovetskikh istorikov v Berline: (Doklad E.B. Pashukanisa na zasedanii Biuro Prezidiuma Kom. akademii 22/XI-28 goda)'., *Vestnik Kommunisticheskoi akademii*, 30: 238–246.

Pikhoia, R.G. and M.V. Zelenov 2006, *I.V. Stalin: Istoricheskaia ideologiia v SSSR v 1920–1950-e gody: perepiska s istorikami, stat'i i zametki po istorii, stenogrammy vystuplenii: sbornik dokumentov i materialov*, St Petersburg: Nauka-Piter.

Piontkovskii, S.A. 1924, *Oktiabr'skaia revoliutsiia v Rossii: Ee predposylki i khod*, Moscow: Gosizdat.

Piontkovskii, S.A. 2009, *Dnevnik istorika S.A. Piontkovskogo (1927–1934)*, Kazan: Kazanskii gosudarstvennyi universitet.

Pipes, Richard 1970, *Struve: Liberal on the Left, 1870–1905*, Cambridge, Mass., London: Harvard University Press; Distributed by Oxford University Press.

Pistrak, M. 1932, *M.N. Pokrovskii kak rabotnik narodnogo prosveshcheniia i pedagog*, Rostov on Don: Severnyi Kavkaz.

Pokrovskii, M.N. 1899, 'Khoziaistvennaia zhizn' Zapadnoi Evropy v kontse srednikh vekov' in *Kniga dlia chteniia po istorii srednikh vekov: Sostavlennaia krugom prepodavatelei*, edited by P.G. Vinogradov, Moscow: Kushnerev.

Pokrovskii, M.N. 1903, 'Mestnoe samoupravlenie v drevnei Rusi' in *Melkaia zemskaia edinitsa: Sbornik statei*, edited by K.K. Arsen'ev, V.G. Bazhaev, and P.G. Vinogradov, St Petersburg: Izd. P.D. Dolgorukova i D.I. Shakhovskago.

Pokrovskii, M.N. 1905a, 'Professional'naia intelligentsiia i sotsial-demokraty: Pis'mo v redaktsiiu', *Proletarii*, 9 (22) August.

Pokrovskii, M.N. 1905b, 'Zemskii sobor i parlament' in *Konstitutsionnoe gosudarstvo: Sbornik statei*, edited by I.V. Gessen and L.I. Kaminka, St Peterburg: Obshchestvennaia pol'za.

Pokrovskii, M.N. 1906a, 'Pobediteli' in *Voprosy dnia*, Moscow: I.N. Kholchev i Ko.

Pokrovskii, M.N. 1906b, 'Voennaia tekhnika i vopros o militsii' in *Tekushchii moment*, edited by N.A. Rozhkov, Moscow.

Pokrovskii, M.N. 1907a, 'Aleksandr I' in *Istoriia Rossii v XIX veke*: vol. 1, St Petersburg: Granat: 31–66.

Pokrovskii, M.N. 1907b, 'Dekabristy' in *Istoriia Rossii v XIX veke*: vol. 1, St Petersburg: Granat: 69–179.

Pokrovskii, M.N. 1907c, 'Pavel Petrovich' in *Istoriia Rossii v XIX veke*: vol. 1, St Petersburg: Granat: 21–30.

Pokrovskii, M.N. 1907d, 'Rossiia v kontse XVIII veka. Khoziaistvo. Obshchestvo. Gosudarstvennaia vlast'.' in *Istoriia Rossii v XIX veke*: vol. 1, St Petersburg: Granat: 1–20.

Pokrovskii, M.N. 1908, 'Krest'ianskaia reforma' in *Istoriia Rossii v XIX veke*: Vol. 3, St Petersburg: Granat: 69–179.

Pokrovskii, M.N. 1910, 'Finliandskii vopros', *Vpered*, July: 10–15.

Pokrovskii, M.N. 1911, 'Krest'ianskaia reforma 19 fevralia 1861 goda: K piatidesiatiletiiu', *Vpered*, 2: 6–15.

Pokrovskii, M.N. 1912, 'Trista let Romanovykh i Lzhe-Romanovykh' in *Iubilei pozora nashego (1613–1913)*, edited by M.N. Pokrovskii and L.D. Trotsky, Vienna: Pravda.

Pokrovskii, M.N. 1914a 'Iz istorii obshchestvennykh klassov v Rossii: Ocherki', *Bor'ba*: 1: 13–18; 2: 8–12; 4: 14–18; 5: 10–13; 7–8: 10–17.

Pokrovskii, M.N. 1914b, *Ocherk istorii russkoi kul'tury*, Part 1, Moscow: Mīr.

Pokrovskii, M.N. 1918a, *Ocherk istorii russkoi kul'tury*, Part 2, Moscow: Mir .

Pokrovskii, M.N. 1918b, *Tsarizm i revoliutsiia*, Moscow: Izdatel'stvo Vserossiiskogo Tsentral'nogo Ispolnitel'nogo Komiteta Sovetov.

Pokrovskii, M.N. 1918c, *Vneshniaia politika: Sbornik statei (1914–1917)*, Moscow: Dennitsa.

Pokrovskii, M.N. 1920, *Ekonomicheskii materializm*, Peterburg: Gosizdat.

Pokrovskii, M.N. 1922a, 'Institut krasnoi professury: K pervoi godovshchine', *Pravda*, 2 December.

Pokrovskii, M.N. 1922b, 'Prof. R. Vipper i krizis istoricheskoi nauki', *Pod znamenem marksizma*, 3: 33–36.

Pokrovskii, M.N. 1923, *Diplomatiia i voiny tsarskoi Rossii v XIX stoletii: Sbornik statei*, Moscow: Krasnaia nov'.

Pokrovskii, M.N. 1924a, *Marksizm v programme shkoly I i II stupeni: Doklad na s"ezde tsentral'nykh i mestnykh opytno-pokazatel'nykh uchrezhdenii i predstavitelei biuro gubono 28 maia 1924 g.*, Moscow.

Pokrovskii, M.N. 1924b, 'O pol'ze kritiki, ob absoliutizme, imperializme, muzhitskom kapitalizme, i o prochem: (Nechto vrode khrestomatii)', *Pod znamenem marksizma*, 12: 250–259.

Pokrovskii, M.N. 1924c, *Ocherki po istorii russkogo revoliutsionnogo dvizheniia XIX–XX vv.*, Moscow: Krasnaia nov'.

Pokrovskii, M.N. 1924d, 'Po povodu stat'i tov. Rubinshteina', *Pod znamenem marksizma*, 10–11: 210–212.

Pokrovskii, M.N. 1924e, 'Sovetskaia glava nashei istorii', *Bol'shevik*, 14: 10–19.

Pokrovskii, M.N. 1925a, *Bor'ba klassov i russkaia istoricheskaia literatura*, Leningrad: Priboi.

Pokrovskii, M.N. 1925b, 'Literatorskaia gruppa MK v 1905 g.', *Izvestiia*, 25 December: 4.

Pokrovskii, M.N. 1925c, *Marksizm i osobennosti istoricheskogo razvitiia Rossii: Sbornik statei 1922–1925 gg.*, Leningrad: Priboi.

Pokrovskii, M.N. 1925d, *Znachenie revoliutsii 1905 goda*, Leningrad: Gosizdat.

Pokrovskii, M.N. 1926a, 'K deviatoi godovshchine: Doklad na sobranii nauchnykh rabotnikov Moskvy 6 noiabria 1926 g.', *Nauchnyi rabotnik*, 11: 3–22.

Pokrovskii, M.N. 1926b, 'Otvet tov. Tomsinskomu', *Vestnik Kommunisticheskoi akademii*, 15: 284–299.

Pokrovskii, M.N. 1926c, 'P.G. Vinogradov (1854–1925)', *Izvestiia*, 29 April.

Pokrovskii, M.N. 1926d, 'Zadachi Obshchestva istorikov-marksistov: Rech' proiznesennaia na otkrytii Obshchestva 1 iiunia 1925 g.', *Istorik-marksist*, 1: 3–10.

Pokrovskii, M.N. 1927a, 'Burzhuaznaia revoliutsiia protiv burzhuazii', *Izvestiia*, 12 March.

Pokrovskii, M.N. 1927b, *Ocherki po istorii Oktiabr'skoi revoliutsii: Rabota istoricheskoi seminarii instituta krasnoi professury*, Moscow: Gosizdat.

Pokrovskii, M.N. 1927c, *Ocherki po istorii russkogo revoliutsionnogo dvizheniia XIX–XX vv.*, Moscow: Krasnaia nov'.

Pokrovskii, M.N. 1928a, 'A.A. Bogdanov [Malinovskii]: Skonchalsia 7 aprelia 1928 g.', *Vestnik Kommunisticheskoi akademii*, 25: 5–10.

Pokrovskii, M.N. 1928b, *Imperialistskaia voina: Sbornik statei 1915–1927*, Moscow: Izd-vo Kommunisticheskoi akademii.

Pokrovskii, M.N. 1928c, 'N.G. Chernyshevskii kak istorik', *Istorik-marksist*, 8: 3–26.

Pokrovskii, M.N. 1928d, '"Novye" techeniia v russkoi istoricheskoi literature', *Istorik-marksist*, 7: 3–17.

Pokrovskii, M.N. 1928e, 'O poezdke v Oslo: (Doklad M.N. Pokrovskogo na zasedanii Prezidiuma Komm. Akademii 15/XII-1928 g.)', *Vestnik Kommunisticheskoi akademii*, 30: 231–237.

Pokrovskii, M.N. 1928f, 'Ot redaktsii', *Istorik-marksist*, 9: 108–109.

Pokrovskii, M.N. 1929a, *Oktiabr'skaia revoliutsiia: Sbornik statei 1917–1927*, Moscow: Izdatel'stvo kommunisticheskoi akademii.

Pokrovskii, M.N. 1929b, 'Vystuplenie po dokladu N.N. Vanaga "O kharaktere finansovogo kapitala v Rossii" na Pervoi konferentsii istorikov-marksistov', 11: 233–235.

Pokrovskii, M.N. 1930a, 'K istorii SSSR: (Predislovie k cheshskomu perevodu "Russkoi istorii v samom szhatom ocherke")', *Istorik-marksist*, 17: 17–20.

Pokrovskii, M.N. 1930b, 'O vozniknovenii Istparta', *Proletarskaia revoliutsiia*, 7–8: 138–139.

Pokrovskii, M.N. 1931a, *Imperialistskaia voina: Sbornik statei 1915–1927*, Moscow: Izd-vo Kommunisticheskoi akademii.

Pokrovskii, M.N. 1931b, 'O russkom feodalizme, proiskhozhdenii i kharaktere absoliutizma v Rossii', *Bor'ba klassov*, 2: 78–89.

Pokrovskii, M.N. 1931c, 'O zadachakh marksistskoi istoricheskoi nauki v rekonstruktivnyi period', *Istorik-marksist*, 12: 3–7.

Pokrovskii, M.N. 1932, 'Po povodu nekotoroi putanitsy', *Istorik-marksist*, 1–2: 13–25.

Pokrovskii, M.N. 1933a, *Brief history of Russia*, London: M. Lawrence.

Pokrovskii, M.N. 1933b, *Istoricheskaia nauka i bor'ba klassov*: vol. 1, Moscow-Leningrad: Gosudarstvennoe sotsial'no-ekonomicheskoe izdatel'stvo.

Pokrovskii, M.N. 1933c, *Istoricheskaia nauka i bor'ba klassov*: vol. 2, Moscow-Leningrad: Gosudarstvennoe sotsial'no-ekonomicheskoe izdatel'stvo.

Pokrovskii, M.N. 1967a, *Izbrannye proizvedeniia*: vol. 1, Moscow: Mysl'.

Pokrovskii, M.N. 1967b, *Izbrannye proizvedeniia*: vol. 2, Moscow: Mysl'.

Pokrovskii, M.N. 1967c, *Izbrannye proizvedeniia*: vol. 3, Moscow: Mysl'.

Pokrovskii, M.N. 1967d, *Izbrannye proizvedeniia*: vol. 4, Moscow: Mysl'.

Pokrovskii, M.N. 1979, 'Kak rozhdalsia "Imperializm"' in *Vospominaniia o Vladimire Il'iche Lenine*: vol. 2, (ed.) G.N. Golikov, Moscow: Izdatel'stvo politicheskoi literatury.

Pokrovskii, M.N. 1995, '"Vremia prokhodit nelepeishim obrazom": Pis'mo M.N. Pokrovskogo L.N. Pokrovskoi. Dekabr' 1917 g.', *Istoricheskii arkhiv*, 4: 220–221.

Pokrovskii, M.N., V. Viktorov, and A. Presniakov (eds.) 1930, *Kniga dlia chteniia po istorii narodov SSSR*, Kharkov: Proletarii.

Poole, Randall Allen 2003, *Problems of idealism: Essays in Russian social philosophy*, New Haven, London: Yale University Press.

'Pozitsiia Ts.K. partii v oktiabr'skie dni 1917 g.', 1922, *Proletarskaia revoliutsiia* 10: 459–65.

Preobrazhenskii, E.A. 1922, 'Blizhaishie zadachi sotsialisticheskoi akademii', *Vestnik sotsialisticheskoi akademii*, 1: 5–12.

Radek, Karl 1936, 'Znachenie istorii dlia revoliutsionnogo proletariata', *Pravda*, 27 January: 3.

Redaktsiia 1932, 'Neskol'ko dokumentov iz tsarskikh arkhivov o M.N. Pokrovskom', *Krasnyi arkhiv*, 52, 3: 5–36.

Reed, John 1919, *Ten Days that Shook the World*, New York: International Publishers.

Riazanov, D.B. 1923, 'Novye dannye o literaturnom nasledstve K. Marksa i F. Engel'sa', *Vestnik sotsialisticheskoi akademii*, 6: 351–376.

Riazanov, David Borisovich 2018, *Vchityvaias' v Marksa: Izbrannye raboty po marksovedeniiu: k 200-letiiu Karla Marksa, pamiati D.B. Riazanova*, Moscow: ROSSPEN.

Ribot, Théodule Armand 1899, *The Evolution of General Ideas*, Chicago: Open Court Publishing Co.

Rickert, Heinrich 1902, *Die Grenzen der naturwissenschaftlichen Begriffsbildung*, Tübingen and Leipzig: Verlag von J.C.B. Mohr.

Rickert, Heinrich 1986, *The limits of concept formation in natural science: A logical introduction to the historical sciences*, Cambridge: Cambridge University Press.

Riutin, M.N. 1990, 'Platforma "soiuza marksistov-lenintsev" ("gruppa Riutina")', *Izvestiia TsK KPSS*, 8: 200–207.

Rokitianskii, Iakov and Reinhard Müller 1996, *Krasnyi dissident: Akademik Riazanov –*

opponent Lenina, zhertva Stalina: biograficheskii ocherk, dokumenty, Moscow: Izd-vo Academia.

Rozhkov, N.A. 1903, 'Znachenie i sud'by noveishego idealizma v Rossii: (po povodu knigi "Problemy idealizma")', *Voprosy filosofii i psikhologii,* 11 (67): 324–332.

Rozhkov, N.A. 1906, 'Tekushchii moment' in *Tekushchii moment,* edited by N.A. Rozhkov, Moscow.

Rozhkov, N.A. 1918 [1904], *Gorod i derevnia v russkoi istorii: Kratkii ocherk ekonomicheskoi istorii Rossii,* Petrograd: V.S. Klestov.

Rozhkov, N.A. 1923, 'K metodologii istorii revoliutsionnogo dvizheniia', *Krasnaia letopis',* 71–74.

Rozhkov, N.A. and A.O. Sokolov 1925, *O 1905 gode: Vospominaniia,* Moscow: Moskovskii rabochii.

Ruckman, Jo Ann 1984, *The Moscow Business Elite: A social and cultural portrait of two generations, 1840–1905,* DeKalb, Ill.: Northern Illinois University Press.

Serebriakova, Z.L. 1977, *Oblastnye ob'edineniia Sovetov Rossii, mart 1917-dekabr' 1918,* Moscow: Nauka.

Shcheglova, Tatiana and Dmitrii Drozhetskii 2014, 'Ustnaia istoriia (Oral History) v rossiiskoi istoricheskoi praktike 1920–1930 gg.: k diskusii o poniatii i vremeni vozniknoveniia ustnoi istorii', *Izvestiia Altaiskogo gosudarstvennogo universiteta,* 4–2, 84: 254–260.

Shestakov, A.V. 1928, 'M.N. Pokrovskii – istorik-marksist', *Istorik-marksist,* 9: 3–17.

Shestakov, A.V. 1937, *Kratkii kurs istorii SSSR,* Moscow: Gos. uchebnoe-pedagogicheskoe izdatel'stvo.

Shliapnikov, A.G. 1923, 'O knigakh N. Sukhanova', *Pechat' i revoliutsiia,* 4: 46–50.

Shliapnikov, A.G. 1925, *Semnadtsatyi god,* vol. 2, Moscow-Leningrad: Gos. izd-vo.

Shliapnikov, A.G. 1927, 'Otvet kritikam', *Bol'shevik,* 11–12: 99–104.

Shteppa, Konstantin 1962, *Russian Historians and the Soviet State,* New Brunswick, N.J.: Rutgers University Press.

Sidorov, A.L. 1964, 'Nekotorye razmyshleniia o trude i opyte istorika', *Istoriia SSSR,* 3: 118–138.

Sivolapova, G.F. 1976, 'Issledovanie Ia.A. Iakovleva po istorii Oktiabr'skoi revoliutsii' in *Istoriia i istoriki: 1974,* edited by M.V. Nechkina, Moscow: Nauka.

Skvortsov-Stepanov, I.I. 1925, *Ot revoliutsii k revoliutsii: Sbornik statei 1905–1915 gg.,* Moscow: Gos. izd-vo.

Skvortsov-Stepanov, I.I. 1930, *Izbrannye proizvedeniia,* Leningrad: Gosizdat.

Slepkov, A.N. 1924, Review of M.N. Pokrovskii, *Ocherki po istorii revoliutsionnogo dvizheniia v Rossii XIX i XX vv., Bol'shevik,* 14: 113–122.

Slepkov, A.N. 1925a, 'Agrarno-krest'ianskaia problema v epokhu bor'by proletariata za vlast'', *Bol'shevik,* 7: 30–43.

Slepkov, A.N. 1925b, '"Ne soglasny!": (Otvet t. Pokrovskomu)', *Bol'shevik,* 6–7: 65–72.

Slutskii, A.G. 1930, 'Bol'sheviki o germanskoi sotsial-demokratii v period ee predvoennogo krizisa', *Proletarskaia revoliutsiia*, 6: 38–73.

Sokolov, O.D. 1963, 'V.I. Lenin i formirovanie bol'shevistskikh vzgliadov M.N. Pokrovskogo', *Voprosy istorii*, 8: 30–41.

Sokolov, O.D. 1966, 'Razvitie istoricheskikh vzgliadov M.N. Pokrovskogo' in *M.N. Pokrovskii: Izbrannye proizvedeniia*, edited by M.N. Tikhomirov, Moscow: Mysl'.

Sokolov, O.D. 1969, 'M.N. Pokrovskii – vydaiushchiisia organizator nauchno-issledovatel'skoi raboty v SSSR', *Voprosy istorii*, 6: 30–45.

Sokolov, O.D. 1970, *M.N. Pokrovskii i sovetskaia istoricheskaia nauka*, Moscow: Mysl'.

Solovei, V.D. 1990, 'Institut krasnoi professury: podgotovka kadrov istorikov partii v 20–30 gody', *Voprosy istorii KPSS*, 12: 87–98.

Sovnarkom 1920, 'Postanovlenie Soveta Narodnykh Komissarov ob uchrezhdenii kommissii dlia sobraniia i izucheniia materialov po istorii oktiabr'skoi revoliutsii i istorii Rossiiskoi Kommunisticheskoi partii', *Izvestiia VTsIK*, 25 September: 3.

Stalin, I.V. 1918, 'Oktiabr'skii perevorot', *Pravda*, 6 November: 2.

Stalin, I.V. 1937, *K izucheniiu istorii: Sbornik*, Moscow: Partizdat.

Stalin, Joseph 1953, *Problems of Leninism*, Moscow: Foreign Languages Pub. House.

Stalin, Joseph 1954a, *Works*, vol. 13, Moscow: Foreign Languages Publishing House.

Stalin, Joseph 1954b, *Works*, vol. 9, Moscow: Foreign Languages Publishing House.

Struve, P.B. 1894, *Kriticheskie zametki k voprosu ob ekonomicheskom razvitii Rossii*, St Petersburg: Skorokhodov.

Struve, P.B. 1952, *Sotsial'naia i ekonomicheskaia istoriia Rossii s drevneishikh vremen do nashego, v sviazi s razvitiem russkoi kul'tury i rostom rossiiskoi gosudarstvennosti*, Paris.

Sverdlova, K.T. 1960, *Iakov Mikhailovich Sverdlov*, Moscow: Molodaia gvardiia.

Szporluk, Roman (ed.) 1970, *Russia in world history: Selected essays by M.N. Pokrovskii*, Ann Arbor: University of Michigan Press.

Tarle, E.V. 1928, 'K voprosu o nachale voiny: (Otvet M.N. Pokrovskomu)', *Istorik-marksist*, 9: 101–107.

Tarle, E.V. 1958, *Sochineniia: v dvenadtsati tomakh*, Moscow: Izd-vo Akademii nauk SSSR.

Tarnovskii, K.N. 1964, *Sovetskaia istoriografiia russkogo imperializma*, Moscow: Nauka.

Temkin, Ia.G. 1968, *Lenin i mezhdunarodnaia sotsial-demokratiia: 1914–1917*, Moscow: Nauka.

Teodorovich, I.A. 1929, 'Istoricheskoe znachenie partii "Narodnoi voli"', *Katorga i ssylka*, 8–9: 7–53.

Thatcher, Ian D. 1994, 'Trotsky and *Bor'ba*', *The Historical Journal*, 37, 1: 113–125.

Thatcher, Ian D. 2021, 'The 1905–07 Russian Revolution as a "Moment of Truth": An Overlooked Contribution from Menshevism', *Revolutionary Russia*, 2: 1–21.

Tikhomirov, M.N. (ed.) 1966, *M.N. Pokrovskii: Izbrannye proizvedeniia*, Moscow: Mysl'.

Tolz, Vera 1997, *Russian Academicians and the Revolution: Combining Professionalism and Politics*, Basingstoke: Macmillan in association with Centre for Russian and East European Studies.

Tomsinskii, S. 1926, 'K voprosu o sotsial'noi prirode russkogo samoderzhaviia', *Vestnik Kommunisticheskoi akademii*, 15: 255–283.

'Tribuna' 1914, *Bor'ba*, 5, 16 May.

Trotsky, L.D. 1922a, *1905*, Moscow: Gos. izdat.

Trotsky, L.D. 1922b, 'Vospominaniia ob Oktiabr'skom perevorote', *Proletarskaia revoliutsiia*, 10: 43–93.

Trotsky, L.D. 1924–1927, 'Vol. 3: 1917 Ot fevralia do oktiabria' in *Sochineniia*, Moscow: Gosizdat.

Trotsky, Leon 1919, *From October to Brest-Litovsk*, New York: The Socialist Publication Society.

Trotsky, Leon 1937a, *The History of the Russian Revolution*, vol. 1, New York: Simon and Schuster.

Trotsky, Leon 1937b, *The History of the Russian Revolution*, vol. 2, New York: Simon and Schuster.

Trotsky, Leon 1962, *The Stalin School of Falsification*, New York: Pioneer Publishers.

Trotsky, Leon 1970a, *My Life*, New York: Pathfinder Press.

Trotsky, Leon 1970b, *The Third International after Lenin*, New York: Pathfinder Press.

Trudy pervoi vsesoiuznoi konferentsii istorikov-marksistov: 28.XII-1928–4.I-1929, 1930, Moscow: Izd-vo Kommunisticheskoi akademii.

Tugan-Baranovskii, M.I. 1898, *Russkaia fabrika v proshlom i nastoiashchem: Istoriko-ekonomicheskoe issledovanie*, St Petersburg: Panteleev.

'V Sovnarkome Soiuza SSR i TsK VKP(b)', 1936, *Pravda*, 27 January: 2.

Udal'tsov, A.D. 1922, 'Ocherk istorii sotsialisticheskoi akademii: 1918–1922 gg.', *Vestnik sotsialisticheskoi akademii*, 1: 13–37.

Vanag, N. 1925, *Finansovyi kapital v Rossii nakanune mirovoi voiny*, Moscow: Kommun. u-t im. Sverdlova.

Vanag, N. 1929, 'K metodologii izucheniia finansovogo kapitala v Rossii', *Istorik-marksist*, 12: 5–46.

Vanag, N. 1932, 'Pis'mo v redaktsiiu', *Istorik-marksist*, 4–5: 355–358.

Varlamov, K.I. and N.A. Slamikhin 1964, *Razoblachenie V.I. Leninym teorii i taktiki 'levykh kommunistov', noiabr' 1917 g.–1918 g.*, Moscow: Mysl'.

Vinogradoff, Paul 19 July 1884, 'A Note Book of Bracton', *Athenaeum*: 81–82.

Vinogradoff, Paul 1888, 'Brackton's Note Book', *Law Quarterly Review*, 4, 4: 436–441.

Vinogradoff, Paul 1904, *The Teaching of Sir Henry Maine: An inaugural lecture delivered in Corpus Christi College Hall on March 1, 1904*, London: Henry Frowde.

Vinogradov, P.G. 1880, *Proiskhozhdenie feodal'nykh otnoshenii v Langobardskoi Italii*, St Petersburg, Tip. V.S. Balasheva.

Vinogradov, P.G. 1887, *Issledovaniia po sotsial'noi istorii Anglii v srednie veka*, St Petersburg: Tip. V.S. Balasheva.

Vinogradov, P.G. (ed.) 1896, *Kniga dlia chteniia po istorii srednikh vekov: Sostavlennaia krugom prepodavatelei*, Moscow: Kushnerev.

Vinogradov, P.G. 1914, *Uchebnik vseobshchei istorii: Chast' 1*, Moscow: Kartsev.

Volkov, L.V. 1965, 'Vopros o roli torgovogo kapitala v istorii Rossii v sovetskoi istoricheskoi nauke kontsa 20-kh – nachala 30-kh godov', *Trudy Moskovskogo gosudarstvennogo istoriko-arkhivnogo instituta*, 21: 81–96.

Vsesoiuznoe soveshchanie o merakh uluchsheniia podgotovki nauchno-pedagogicheskikh kadrov po istoricheskim naukam: 18–21 dekabria 1962 g., 1964, Moscow: Nauka.

Waldenberg, Marek 1972, *Wzlot i upadek Karola Kautsky'ego: Studium z historii myśli społecznej i politycznej*, Krakow: Wydawn. Literackie.

White, James D. 1974, 'The First *Pravda* and the Russian Marxist Tradition', *Soviet Studies*, 26, 2: 181–204.

White, James D. 1979, 'The Sormovo-Nikolaev Zemlyachestvo in the February Revolution', *Soviet Studies*, 31, 4: 475–504.

White, James D. 1985, 'Early Soviet Historical Interpretations of the Russian Revolution 1918–24', *Soviet Studies*, 37, 3: 330–352.

White, James D. 1996, *Karl Marx and the intellectual orgins of dialectical materialism*, Basingstoke: Macmillan.

White, James D. 2019, *Red Hamlet: The life and ideas of Alexander Bogdanov*, Leiden, Boston: Brill.

White, James D. 2021, 'Leon Trotsky and Soviet Historiography of the Russian Revolution (1918–1921)', *Revolutionary Russia*, 2: 276–295.

Windelband, Wilhelm 1980, 'Rectorial Address, Strasbourg, 1894', *History and Theory*, 19, 2: 169–185.

Zaidel', G., Z. Lozinskii, A. Prigozhin and S. Tomsinskii (eds.) 1930, *Spornye voprosy metodologii istorii*, Kharkov: Proletarii.

Zelnik, Reginald E. 2005, *Perils of Pankratova: Some Stories From the Annals of Soviet Historiography*, Seattle: Published by the Herbert J. Ellison Center for Russian, Eastern European, and Central Asian Studies, University of Washington.

Index